mylabschool™
Where the classroom comes to life!

From watching actual classroom video footage of teachers and students interacting to building standards-based lessons and web-based portfolios . . . from a robust resource library of the "What Every Teacher Should Know About" series to complete instruction on writing an effective research paper . . . **MyLabSchool** brings together an amazing collection of resources for future teachers. This website gives you a wealth of videos, print and simulated cases, career advice, and much more.

Use **MyLabSchool** with this Allyn and Bacon Education text, and you will have everything you need to succeed in your course. Assignment IDs have also been incorporated into many Allyn and Bacon Education texts to link to the online material in **MyLabSchool** . . . connecting the teachers of tomorrow to the information they need today.

PEARSON **VISIT www.mylabschool.com to learn more about this invaluable resource and Take a Tour!**

Here's what you'll find in mylabschool™
Where the classroom comes to life!

VideoLab ►
Access hundreds of video clips of actual classroom situations from a variety of grade levels and school settings. These 3- to 5-minute closed-captioned video clips illustrate real teacher–student interaction, and are organized both topically *and* by discipline. Students can test their knowledge of classroom concepts with integrated observation questions.

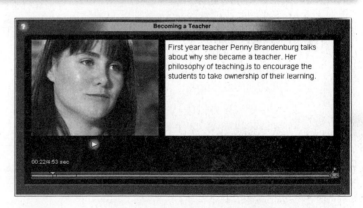

Becoming a Teacher

First year teacher Penny Brandenburg talks about why she became a teacher. Her philosophy of teaching is to encourage the students to take ownership of their learning.

00:22/4:53 sec

Lesson & Portfolio Builder

| New Lesson Plan | New Portfolio | | Copy | Open | Print | Delete |

Type ▼ Name	modified ▼
New Lesson Plan	11/20/06
social s	
MCC	
UNM L	
The leg	
reading	
New Le	
The Ca	
Countin	

Lesson & Portfolio Builder

New Lesson Plan (Basic Info)

- Basic Info
- Objective
- Academic Standards
- Rationale Statement
- Materials and Resources
- Procedures
- Assessment
- Style and Export
- Export Instructions

Lesson Title: What do you call this lesson?
New Lesson Plan

Area of study: What is the subject area? (e.g. Social Studies, English, Math)

Teacher Name: Enter your professional name here

Grade Level: For what grade levels is this lesson plan designed (e.g. 6th)

Duration of Instruction: How long will it take to conduct this lesson?

◄ Lesson & Portfolio Builder
This feature enables students to create, maintain, update, and share online portfolios and standards-based lesson plans. The Lesson Planner walks students, step-by-step, through the process of creating a complete lesson plan, including verifiable objectives, assessments, and related state standards. Upon completion, the lesson plan can be printed, saved, e-mailed, or uploaded to a website.

Here's what you'll find in mylabschool™

Where the classroom comes to life!

Simulations ▶

This area of MyLabSchool contains interactive tools designed to better prepare future teachers to provide an appropriate education to students with special needs. To achieve this goal, the IRIS (IDEA and Research for Inclusive Settings) Center at Vanderbilt University has created course enhancement materials. These resources include online interactive modules, case study units, information briefs, student activities, an online dictionary, and a searchable directory of disability-related web sites.

◀ Resource Library

MyLabSchool includes a collection of PDF files on crucial and timely topics within education. Each topic is applicable to any education class, and these documents are ideal resources to prepare students for the challenges they will face in the classroom. This resource can be used to reinforce a central topic of the course, or to enhance coverage of a topic you need to explore in more depth.

Research Navigator ▶

This comprehensive research tool gives users access to four exclusive databases of authoritative and reliable source material. It offers a comprehensive, step-by-step walk-through of the research process. In addition, students can view sample research papers and consult guidelines on how to prepare endnotes and bibliographies. The latest release also features a new bibliography-maker program—AutoCite.

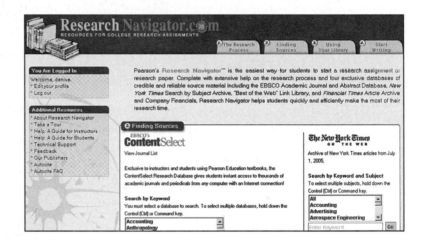

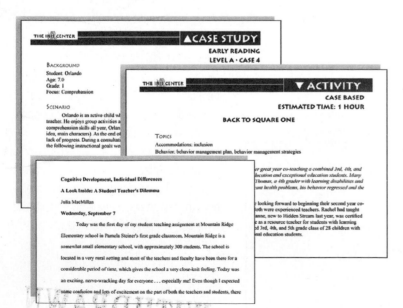

◀ Case Archive

This collection of print and simulated cases can be easily accessed by topic and subject area, and can be integrated into your course. The cases are drawn from Allyn & Bacon's best-selling books, and represent the complete range of disciplines and student ages. It's an ideal way to consider and react to real classroom scenarios. The possibilities for using these high-quality cases within the course are endless.

Helping Young Children Learn Language and Literacy:
Birth through Kindergarten

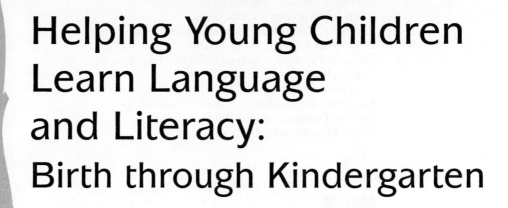

Helping Young Children Learn Language and Literacy:
Birth through Kindergarten

Second Edition

Carol Vukelich
University of Delaware

James Christie
Arizona State University

Billie Enz
Arizona State University

PEARSON

Boston   New York   San Francisco
Mexico City   Montreal   Toronto   London   Madrid   Munich   Paris
Hong Kong   Singapore   Tokyo   Cape Town   Sydney

KH

Executive Editor: *Aurora Martínez Ramos*
Editorial Assistant: *Lynda Giles*
Executive Marketing Manager: *Krista Clark*
Production Editor: *Gregory Erb*
Editorial Production Service: *Nesbitt Graphics, Inc.*
Composition Buyer: *Linda Cox*
Manufacturing Buyer: *Linda Morris*
Electronic Composition: *Nesbitt Graphics, Inc.*
Interior Design: *Nesbitt Graphics, Inc.*
Cover Administrator: *Joel Gendron*

For related titles and support materials, visit our online catalog at www.ablongman.com.

Between the time website information is gathered and then published, it is not unusual for some sites to have closed. Also, the transcription of URLs can result in typographical errors. The publisher would appreciate notification where these errors occur so that they may be corrected in subsequent editions.

ISBN 13: 978-0-205-53267-4   ISBN 10: 0-205-53267-5

Library of Congress Cataloging-in-Publication Data

Vukelich, Carol.
    Helping young children learn language and literacy: birth-kindergarten / Carol Vukelich, James Christie, Billie Enz. -- 2nd ed.
        p. cm.
    Includes bibliographical references and index.
    ISBN 0-205-53267-5
    1. Language arts (Preschool)   2. Children--Language.   I. Christie, James F.   II. Enz, Billie.   III. Title.
LB1140.5.L3V85 2008
372.6--dc22

                                                                2006039314

Photo credits: p. 31, courtesy of Grace and Dan Bass; p. 58, Elizabeth Crews/Stock, Boston; p. 80, Jeffry Myers/Stock, Boston; p. 219, Bob Daemmrich/Bob Daemmrich Photography.

Printed in the United States of America

10   9   8   7   6   5   4   3   2   1   CIN   11   10   09   08   07

7/29/08

Carol Vukelich is the Director of the Delaware Center for Teacher Education and the Hammonds Professor in Teacher Education at the University of Delaware where she teaches courses in early literacy and teaching writing. Her research interests include early literacy development and children's writing development. Dr. Vukelich is co-author of *Teaching Language and Literacy: Preschool through the Elementary Grades* (Allyn & Bacon, 2007). She is co-director of the *Delaware Early Reading First* project.

James Christie is a Professor of Curriculum and Instruction at Arizona State University where he teaches courses in language, literacy, and early childhood education. His research interests include early literacy development and children's play. Dr. Christie has co-authored *Play, Development, and Early Education* (Allyn & Bacon, 2005). He is co-director of the *Arizona Centers of Excellence in Early Education* Early Reading First project.

Billie Enz is the Associate Director of the Division of Curriculum and Instruction in the Fulton College of Education at Arizona State University. She is a member of the Early Childhood faculty and teaches language and literacy courses. Her research interests include early language and literacy development and parent involvement. Dr. Enz is the co-author of *Teaching Language and Literacy: Preschool through the Elementary Grades* (Allyn & Bacon, 2007). She is also the president of New Direction Institute, a nonprofit organization for infant development and parent education.

CONTENTS

chapter **9** **Assessment and Adapting Instruction to Meet the Needs of Diverse Learners   181**

PREFACE

This book is about teaching the language arts—about facilitating reading, writing, speaking, and listening development for children, ages birth through kindergarten. The language arts are essential to everyday life and central to all learning. Through reading, listening, writing, and talking, children come to understand the world. This book explains how young children's language and literacy develop and how early childhood teachers can help children become fluent, flexible, effective users of oral and written language.

Themes

Children are at the center of all good language and literacy teaching. This principle underlies the three themes that run throughout this book: blending emergent literacy and scientifically-based reading research into a high quality program, respect for diversity, and instruction-based assessment.

Our first theme acknowledges the two very different views on how to teach language and literacy to young children: emergent literacy and scientifically-based reading research. We believe that both approaches to early literacy instruction have their advantages. Emergent literacy programs provide opportunities for children to learn about literacy on their own and with help from the teacher and peers. Learning can occur at the appropriate pace for each child and build on what he or she already knows. This approach provides children with rich opportunities to acquire oral language and to move through the developmental progressions in emergent reading and writing. The downside to this approach is that not all children are ready or able to take full advantage of these learning opportunities. These children have a tendency to "fall through the cracks" in emergent literacy programs and make very little progress. Such children need to be explicitly taught vocabulary, phonological awareness, alphabet, and concepts of print before they can fully profit from the learning experiences in an emergent literacy program. The book describes how children acquire language and literacy knowledge in many different contexts, how teachers can design authentic classroom reasons for using oral and written language, and how teachers can design developmentally appropriate ways to explicitly teach the core skills that have been found to be predictive of later reading achievement.

Our second theme is respect for diversity. Children's personal experiences, both at home and at school, are important factors in learning. In our diverse society, children come to school with vastly different backgrounds, both in terms of life experiences and language. This diversity needs to be taken into account when designing instructional activities for children and in evaluating children's responses to these activities. Illustrations of how teachers can work effectively with diverse learners can be found throughout this book. Special emphasis is given to linguistic diversity. In a series of Special Features, several colleagues describe how teachers can help English-language learners become bilingual and biliterate.

Every child comes to school with a wealth of information about how written and spoken language works in the real world. Teachers must discover what each student already knows in order to build on that student's knowledge through appropriate classroom activities. Because we recognize that assessment cannot be separated from good teaching, instructionally linked assessment is our third major theme. We introduce the principles of instruction-based assessment in Chapter 1. Many subsequent chapters contain information on strategies that teachers can use to understand children's language and literacy knowledge in the context of specific learning and teaching events.

New Features and Content

The second edition contains many new features and content. Chapter 1 has a new section on National Early Literacy Policies and Initiatives that overviews the significant national educational events that are currently impacting literacy education, including the standards movement, No Child Left Behind legislation, and the use of scientifically-based reading research to make curricular and instructional decisions. This chapter also contains a section on the Continuum of Instructional Approaches that advocates blending scientifically-based reading research with the emergent literacy perspective to create a value-added approach to language and literacy teaching and learning.

Chapter 2 describes the phenomenal growth of oral language that occurs between birth and age five and discusses the major theories that help us understand language acquisition. Special emphasis is placed on the biological view of development, which is an outcome of advances in brain research. New features explain the research techniques that cognitive and linguistic scientists have used to learn about young children's language preferences and abilities.

Chapter 3 presents strategies for facilitating oral language learning both at home and at school. It contains new features about direct instruction of vocabulary to preschool children and expanded information about how teachers can use electronic media to build vocabulary and comprehension.

Chapter 4 discusses sharing books with young children. It identifies many new resources for teachers' use in selecting high quality books for young children and contains a new special feature on matching books with children's ages and stages. Emphasis is placed on the physical characteristics needed to make libraries attractive to children. The chapter also contains expanded information about reading to young children, including new vignettes of storybook reading lessons, new research on how adults should read to young children, and a new Special Feature on a five-day set of procedures for shared big-book reading. It also contains a new checklist for assessing young children's book-related understandings based on state early literacy standards.

Chapter 5 presents the emergent literacy perspective. It describes what children learn about print during the early years and the home experiences that promote this learning. Chapter 6 describes the instructional strategies supported by the emergent literacy perspective for promoting early literacy and learning: functional literacy, linking literacy and play, and language experience/shared writing. New vignettes illustrate how these strategies can be used in scientifically-based programs such as Early Reading First.

Chapter 7 contains completely new content focusing on the scientifically-based reading research (SBRR) approach. It overviews research supporting the "core" knowledge and skills that young children must have to become successful readers. Coverage of phonological awareness and alphabet knowledge is updated and greatly expanded. Vignettes demonstrate how these skills are taught in Early Reading First Projects. A new Special Feature by Dr. Tanis Bryan has been added to explain how curriculum-based measurement can be used to continuously monitor children's learning of early literacy skills. A Special Feature by Dr. Karen Burstein discusses why standardized tests, such as Dynamic Indicators of Basic Early Literacy Skills (DIBELS), are becoming widely used at the preschool and kindergarten level. The feature contains an example of how standardized assessment data are being used in an Early Reading First program.

Chapter 8 focuses on the strategies for teaching writing in early childhood classrooms. New content includes research on using computers and word processing programs with young children, the importance of providing children with writing tools in all classroom centers (e.g., science, math, dramatic play), and examples of the explicit teaching of writing in the writing workshop.

Chapter 9 focuses on ongoing, instructionally linked assessment and explains how to use portfolios to demonstrate growth over time in children's language and literacy learning. Increased attention is given to standardized tests that have an important role in scientifically-based reading research programs. In addition, this chapter contains suggestions on how to adapt instruction to meet the needs of bilingual and second-language learners and children with developmental variations and disabilities. The chapter contains a new feature by Myae Han that provides information about how teachers can adjust instruction to meet the needs of second-language and bilingual learners.

Chapter 10 is aimed at helping teachers pull it all together and organize an effective language arts program. This chapter contains suggestions for integrating the curriculum, designing an effective classroom environment, and organizing the daily schedule. A new section, Make Literacy Materials a Part of the Fabric of Each Center, describes a tool that can be used to judge the quality of the integration of literacy materials in the classroom.

Finally, Chapter 11 describes how teachers can establish effective home–school links and help parents become effective "first teachers" of language and literacy. Suggestions are given for home visits, workshops, phone calls, and written communication. In addition, examples are given of how teachers and schools can supply resources to promote home language and literacy learning. The chapter contains a new vignette about a teacher conducting a family workshop.

Acknowledgments

Many outstanding educators helped us write this book. Our very special thanks to Sarah Hudelson, Irene Serna, and Myae Han for their Special Features on second-language and bilingual learners. Like us, they sat before their computers for many days. From them, we learned how our ideas about teaching the language arts are appropriate for use with children whose primary language is a language other than English. We are also greatly indebted to Karen Burstein and Tanis Bryan for their features on children with special needs and assessment.

Many classroom teachers shared their secrets, showing how theory and research link with quality classroom practice. We are grateful to Doreen Bardsley, Grace and Dan Bass, Chris Boyd, Virginia Emerson, Nancy Edwards, Kathy Eustace, Colleen R. Fierro, Dawn Foley, Debhra Handley, Phoebe Bell Ingraham, Maureen Jobe, Donna Manz, Tere Pelaez, Cyndy Schmidt, and Bernadette Watson. We are also grateful to the many pre-kindergarten teachers in our Early Reading First projects. From these teachers and others like them, we have seen how exciting language and literacy learning can be when teachers and children are engaged in purposeful language arts activities. From them and their students, we have learned much.

Several of our colleagues played a role in the construction of this book through their willingness to engage us in many conversations about children's language and literacy learning. Never unwilling to hear our ideas and to share their own, colleagues like Kathy Roskos, John Carroll University; Susan B. Neuman, University of Michigan; Mary Roe, Washington State University; Chari Woodward, Arizona State University; Sandy Stone, Northern Arizona University; and Bonnie Albertson, Julia Park, Gaysha Beard, Martha Buell, Christine Evans, Martha Ford, Myae Han, and Megan Runk, University of Delaware, have greatly helped us frame our arguments. We would also like to thank the reviewers of this edition who provided valuable feedback: Marcia Edson, Boston University; Jennifer Geringer, University of Northern Colorado; Diane S. Maletta, Purdue University North Central; Mary Medo, University of Wisconsin–Milwaukee; and Cheri Williams, University of Cincinnati.

The students we have nurtured and taught, both young children and college students, also have influenced the development of our ideas. Their questions, their talk, their play, their responses, their enthusiasm—each one of them has taught us about the importance of the language arts in our lives. Their positive response to our ideas fueled our eagerness to share those ideas more broadly.

Finally, our families have helped us write this book. Our grandchildren and grand nieces and nephews are providing wonderful examples of their use and enjoyment of oral and written language. The stories of their journeys to being competent language users brings life to the research and theory discussed in our book. Mary Christie, Don (Skip) Enz, and Ron Vukelich gave us time to write but also pulled us from our computers to experience antique shows, museums, trips, home repairs, life. And then, of course, there is our extended family—our parents, David and Dorothy Palm, Art and Emma Larson, Bill and Jeannine Fullerton, John and Florence Christie—who provided our early reading, writing, speaking, and listening experiences and helped us know first-hand the joys of learning and teaching the language arts.

Early Literacy Policy Initiatives

In recent years, the field of literacy has been thrust into the spotlight. A flurry of new studies, consensus reports, and national literacy policies have had a significant impact on literacy instruction in America. Additional financial resources have been funneled into the literacy field. The resulting research has increased our knowledge about literacy and the teaching of reading. This research, detailed in chapters throughout this book, has identified the (a) key language and early literacy skills preschool children need to know and be able to do if they are to become successful readers, and (b) effective instructional strategies that teachers of young children need to use to support their young learners' language and literacy development. Funded initiatives, in the form of national policies and programs described later in this chapter, provided incentives for educators to begin to use the new research-based strategies to teach young children the key skills.

This book draws on current research and best practices, blending the previously held theory and research-based instructional practices that have proved successful in supporting children's reading, writing, and speaking development with the new scientifically based reading research. Our goal is to provide teachers with the foundations—the core content and the best-practice teaching strategies—needed to provide high-quality reading, writing, and speaking programs for young children. While the field wants to divide reading instruction into "camps"—emergent literacy versus scientifically based reading research instruction, our position is that the two views need to be merged in order to provide an effective reading, writing, and speaking program for young children.

We begin this book with a brief overview of the recent key national policies and initiatives that have impacted the teaching of reading at the preschool level. We begin with this description of the national landscape because of the significant impact these policies and initiatives have had on the literacy field. Then we describe the beliefs and the research base of the diverging views on the teaching of reading. We end with a set of principles that guide our view of the effective teaching of literacy in preschool classrooms.

BEFORE READING THIS CHAPTER, THINK ABOUT. . .

- Your beliefs about how young children first learn to read and write. At what age do children begin to learn about literacy? Is knowledge about reading and writing transmitted from adults to young children, or do children construct this knowledge on their own?
- Your beliefs about effective language and literacy instruction. How can teachers best help young children become skilled speakers, listeners, readers, and writers?
- Your memories about how you learned to talk, read, and write. Do you recall, for example, reading cereal labels at an early age? Do you recall writing messages to loved ones?

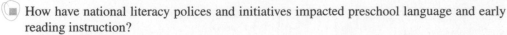

■ How have national literacy polices and initiatives impacted preschool language and early reading instruction?

■ How did the standards movement change literacy instructional practices and the assessment of children?

■ How is the emergent literacy perspective different from the scientifically based reading research perspective on young children's early literacy learning?

■ What principles should guide teachers' teaching of language and literacy?

Language and Literacy: Definitions and Interrelationships

The terms *language* and *literacy* can be defined in many ways. Language can be defined very broadly as any system of symbols that is used to transmit meaning (Bromley, 1988). These symbols can consist of sounds, finger movements, print, and so on. Literacy also has several different meanings. It can refer to the ability to create meaning through different media (e.g., *visual literacy*), knowledge of key concepts and ideas (e.g., *cultural literacy*), and the ability to deal effectively with different subject areas and technologies (e.g., *mathematical literacy, computer literacy*).

Because the topic of this book is early childhood language arts—the part of the preschool curriculum that deals with helping children learn to speak, listen, read, and write—we use school-based definitions of these terms. Language refers to oral language (communicating via speaking and listening), and literacy refers to reading and writing (communicating through print). However, as we describe how children grow in both these areas, it will become obvious that language and literacy acquisition are closely tied to the total development of the child—learning to think, to make sense of the world, to get along with others, and so on.

While we have organized this book into separate chapters on oral language and literacy, it is important to note that the two types of language are integrally connected and related to each other. Oral language provides the base and foundation for literacy. Oral language involves first-order symbolism, with spoken words representing meaning. Written language, on the other hand, involves second-order symbolism that builds on the first-order symbolism of oral language. Printed symbols represent spoken words that, in turn, represent meaning. Do you see the connections between language and literacy?

One obvious connection between oral and written language is vocabulary. In order for a reader to recognize and get meaning from text, most of the words represented by the text must already be in the reader's oral vocabulary. If the reader can recognize most of the words in the text, context cues might be used to figure out the meaning of a few totally unfamiliar words. Similarly, a writer's choice of words is restricted by his or her oral vocabulary.

Catherine Snow and her colleagues (1991) point out a less obvious, but equally important, link between oral language and literacy. She points out that oral language is actually an array of skills related to different functions. One set of skills is relevant to the negotiation of interpersonal relationships and involves the child's ability to engage in face-to-face conversations (contextualized language). Another involves the ability to use language to convey information to audiences who are not physically present (decontextualized language). Decontextualized language has a vital role in literacy because it is the type of language that is typically used in written texts.

Children gain experience in these different aspects of language through different activities. They become skilled at contextualized language by engaging in conversations with others, whereas they gain skill at decontextualized language by listening to stories and by engaging in explanations and personal narratives and by creating fantasy worlds (Snow, 1991). It not surprising, therefore, that research has shown that children with rich oral language experiences at home tend to become early readers (Dickinson & Tabors, 2000) and have high levels of reading achievement during the elementary grades (Wells, 1986).

The relationship between literacy and oral language becomes reciprocal once children become proficient readers. Extensive reading begins to build children's oral language capabilities,

BOX 1.1	**benchmark:** expected or anticipated skill or understanding at various developmental levels (e.g., by the end of the preschool years, children will know and be able to . . .)

BOX 1.1

Definition of Terms

benchmark: expected or anticipated skill or understanding at various developmental levels (e.g., by the end of the preschool years, children will know and be able to . . .)

content standards: define the knowledge and skills that students must attain in each content area (e.g., English language arts, mathematics, science)

decontextualized language: removed from the everyday and tangible experiences; listener must build ideas from the words alone

emergent literacy perspective: the view that children begin learning about reading and writing at a very early age by observing and interacting with adults and other children as they use literacy in everyday life activities

phonemic awareness: phonemes are the smallest units of sound in a language. English consists of about forty-one phonemes. Phonemic awareness refers to the ability to focus on and manipulate these phonemes in spoken words (official definition from www.nationalreadingpanel.org/FAQ/faq.htm#1).

particularly their vocabulary knowledge. Cunningham and Stanovich (1998) present evidence that people are much more likely to encounter "rare" unfamiliar words in printed texts than in adult speech, and Swanborn and de Glopper's (1999) meta-analysis of studies on incidental word learning revealed that during normal reading, students learn about 15 percent of the unknown words they encounter. The more children read, the larger their vocabularies become.

Because this book deals with the early stages of literacy development, the relationship between oral language and literacy is primarily one-way. Anything teachers can do to build children's oral language skills, particularly their vocabulary knowledge and ability to deal with decontextualized language, will also benefit children's literacy development. So even if a school's primary mission is to boost young children's literacy skills, attention also needs to be given to building children's oral language abilities.

National Early Literacy Policies and Initiatives

National literacy policies changed dramatically at the beginning of the twenty-first century, placing literacy, including early literacy, directly on center stage. The growing body of research indicating that early exposure to oral language and literacy skills (skills like phonological awareness and alphabet knowledge) put children at an advantage for later reading achievement pushed policy makers toward instituting new initiatives that changed instructional practices in early childhood programs. These new pre-K policies grew out of movements begun at the K–12 level in the 1980s. In this section, we provide a brief history of the genesis of several significant national literacy policies. Figure 1.1 summarizes some significant national educational events affecting literacy.

The Standards Movement

In 1983, the National Commission on Excellence in Education prepared the report titled *A Nation at Risk*. The commissioners warned that a "rising tide of mediocrity" in our schools threatened our future as a nation. Action was needed. The commissioners recommended creating standards as a solution. High and rigorous standards, the commissioners believed, would restore the nation's place in the world.

Standards? What are they? Standards define the knowledge and skills that students, all students, must attain. They clarify and raise expectations. Because they identify what all students must know and be able to do, they define what is to be taught and what kind of student performance is expected.

By the mid- to late 1990s, the K–12 standards were developed. State departments of education held meetings to introduce the public and educators to the standards and the grade-level benchmarks. Groups of educators began the work of aligning their curricula to their state's

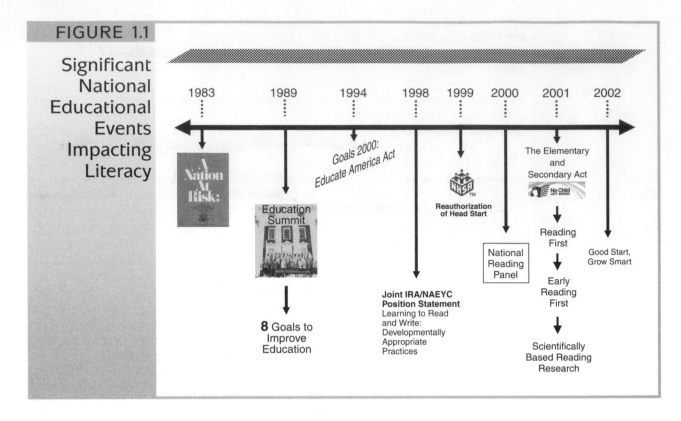

FIGURE 1.1

Significant National Educational Events Impacting Literacy

standards. Did the chosen reading series provide the district's students with the opportunity to learn the content by the designated time? If not, new series would need to be ordered or adjustments made to when the content would be delivered. Finally, state departments of education began selecting or designing standardized assessments (tests) linked to their standards. Were students achieving the standards? By 2004, all but one state (Iowa) had adopted K–12 standards. As 2006 began, states were beginning to make revisions to their earlier-developed K–12 standards, revisions aimed at ensuring consistency with the new knowledge about each of the content areas.

No Child Left Behind Act

The passage of the No Child Left Behind Act (NCLB) in 2001 dramatically increased the importance of the standards-based reform efforts. Before, to obtain some federal education funds (like Title I funds to improve the quality of education in high-poverty schools and/or give extra help to struggling students), the federal government required states to have standards. With the passage of NCLB, the federal government began requiring states to hold schools and students, *all* students, accountable for meeting the state's content standards. NCLB requires states to assess grades 3–8 students' success annually in meeting state standards in reading, mathematics, and science. It also requires states to design and then implement an accountability system that holds students and the education system (schools and districts) responsible for all students' achievement in the specified content areas. Further, every state's accountability system must ensure that all groups of students reach proficiency. That is, the assessment results must be broken out by poverty (family socioeconomic status), race, ethnicity, disability, and limited English proficiency. Student performance within each group must show improvement; no group can be left behind. The law requires that no later than twelve years after the end of the 2001–2002 school year, all students in each group must meet or exceed the state's proficiency level of academic achievement on the state assessments.

Good Start, Grow Smart

No Child Left Behind also drew attention to the need to prepare children before they start school. Supported by the burgeoning body of research on the importance of the early years

in young children's later achievement, some of which you will read about in this book, and the findings that some children enter school with deficits that put them at risk for long-term academic achievement, the George W. Bush administration developed a plan to strengthen early learning in order to equip young children with the skills they need to start school ready to learn. The initiative, known as Good Start, Grow Smart (2002), addressed three major areas:

■ **Strengthening Head Start.** Congress's 1999 reauthorization of Head Start mandated a set of learning goals for children enrolled in Head Start, goals like "develop phonemic, print, and numeracy awareness, recognize a word as a unit of print, and identify at least 10 letters of the alphabet" (Good Start, Grow Smart, 2002, p. 8). From the administration's perspective, the goals had not been fully or effectively implemented by 2002. Hence, the administration directed the Department of Health and Human Services (HHS) to develop an accountability system for Head Start to ensure that every Head Start center assesses every child's early literacy, language, and numeracy skills and that each center analyzes the data to judge the progress of its children toward the stated learning goals.

■ **Partnering with states to improve early childhood education.** The administration asked states to engage in three activities aimed at defining quality criteria for early childhood education: (1) Develop voluntary guidelines (standards) in prereading and language that aligned with their K–12 standards for children ages three to five. By the beginning of 2004, thirty-four states had developed early reading standards. (See Figure 1.2 for one state's language and early reading standards.) (2) Develop a plan for offering education and training activities to child care and preschool teachers and administrators. (3) Design a plan for coordinating at least four early childhood programs funded with federal and/or state dollars. Ultimately the administration's goal was for states to take steps that would help prepare children before they entered kindergarten to be ready to learn.

■ **Providing information to teachers, caregivers, and parents.** To assist states in writing their voluntary guidelines and to close the gap between research and current practices in early childhood education, the administration provided (a) Early Childhood Academies across the country where recent prereading and language research and research-based teaching techniques were overviewed; (b) a national training program to show Head Start teachers early literacy teaching techniques; (c) funding to identify effective prereading and language curricula and teaching strategies; and (d) several publications (called "guidebooks") for parents, families, and early childhood educators and caregivers (*A Child Becomes a Reader: Birth through Preschool* and *A Child Becomes a Reader: Kindergarten through Grade 3*), which summarized the scientific research and described activities that parents can do with their children to "start them down the road to becoming readers from the day they are born" (Armbruster, Lehr, & Osborn, 2003, p. 2).

Early Reading First

Funded in the No Child Left Behind Act and as a part of the administration's Good Start, Grow Smart initiative, Early Reading First is a competitive grant program. It provides funding to organizations serving low-income preschool children. The program was created to address the growing concern that many of the nation's children begin kindergarten without the necessary foundation to fully benefit from formal school instruction. The program's goals include (1) to enhance preschool children's language, cognitive, and early reading development, particularly low-income children's, by using scientifically based teaching strategies; (2) to demonstrate language and literacy activities based on scientifically based reading research that support young children's oral language, phonological awareness, print awareness, and alphabet knowledge; (3) to use screening assessments to effectively identify preschool-age children who may be at risk for reading failure; and (4) to create high-quality language and print-rich environments. To achieve these goals, funded programs must provide teachers with high-quality professional development experiences to build their knowledge of scientifically based language and early reading research and instructional teaching practices.

FIGURE 1.2

Virginia's Literacy Foundation

Source: Virginia Department of Education

ORAL EXPRESSION

The child will develop listening and speaking skills by communicating experiences and ideas through oral expression.

- Listen with increasing attention to spoken language, conversations, and stories read aloud.
- Correctly identify characters, objects, and actions in a picture book as well as stories read aloud, and begin to comment about each.
- Make predictions about what might happen in a story.
- Use two words to ask and answer questions to include actions.
- Use appropriate language for a variety of purposes (e.g., ask questions, express needs, get information).
- Engage in turn-taking exchanges and rules of polite conversation with adults and peers.
- Listen attentively to stories in a whole-class setting.

VOCABULARY

The child will develop an understanding of words and word meanings through the use of appropriate vocabulary.

- Use single words to label objects.
- Listen with increasing understanding to conversations and directions.
- Follow simple, one-step oral directions.
- Engage in turn-taking exchanges with adults and peers.
- Use new vocabulary with increasing frequency to express and describe feelings and ideas.

PHONOLOGICAL AWARENESS

The child will manipulate the various units of sounds in words.

- Successfully detect beginning sounds in words.
- Listen to two one-syllable words and blend the words together to form the compound word (e.g., *rain, bow* is *rainbow*).
- Identify words that rhyme; generate simple rhymes.
- Listen to a sequence of separate sounds in words with three phonemes and correctly blend the sounds to form the whole word (e.g., cat = /k/ /a/ /t/).

Using Scientifically Based Reading Research to Make Curricular and Instructional Decisions

Intertwined with the standards-based educational reform agenda described above is the recent requirement that federally funded programs, like Early Reading First, use curricula, programs, and instructional methods that have been "proven" to be effective. The official definition of what is acceptable as proof of effectiveness first appeared in federal legislation in 1999 in the Reading Excellence Act (see www.ed.gov/inits/FY99/REAguidance/sectionB.html). This statute defined acceptable research as "scientifically-based reading research." As defined, this research applies "rigorous, systematic, and objective procedures to obtain valid knowledge relevant to reading development, reading instruction, and reading difficulties."

This new policy has generated considerable debate. Some researchers are pleased with the focus on the kind of research supported by NCLB. Other researchers have expressed concern

FIGURE 1.2

(continued)

LETTER KNOWLEDGE AND EARLY WORD RECOGNITION

The child will demonstrate basic knowledge of the alphabetic principle.

- Correctly identify ten to eighteen alphabet (uppercase) letters by name in random order.
- Select a letter to represent a sound (eight to ten letters).
- Correctly provide the most common sound for five to eight letters.
- Read simple or familiar high-frequency words, including his or her name.
- Notice letters around him or her in familiar, everyday life, and ask how to spell words, names, or titles.

PRINT AND BOOK AWARENESS

The child will demonstrate knowledge of print concepts.

- Identify the front of a book.
- Identify the location of the title of a book.
- Identify where reading begins on a page (first word or group of words).
- Demonstrate directionality of reading left to right on page.
- Identify part of the book that "tells the story" (print as opposed to pictures).
- Turn pages one at a time from the front to the back of a book.

WRITTEN EXPRESSION

The child will write using a variety of materials.

- Copy letters using various materials.
- Print first name independently.
- Print five to eight letters with a pencil using appropriate grip.
- Copy simple words (three to five letters).
- Use inventive spellings to convey messages or tell stories.

about the implications of the legislation on research in education. Will only one kind of research (experiments, meta-analyses, and randomized trials) be judged as acceptable educational research?

A Continuum of Instructional Approaches

what did they do before they started it

Emergent Literacy Approach

The field of pre-kindergarten language and early literacy instruction has witnessed a debate between the proponents of two very different views of how to teach reading. On one side are the supporters of the *emergent literacy approach*. During the 1990s, pre-K reading had largely escaped the bitter debate that was raging at the elementary level. Emergent literacy was the predominant view of early reading and writing, and most conceptions of best practice stemmed from this meaning-centered perspective. According to this view, children begin learning about reading and writing at a very early age by observing and interacting with adults and other children as they use literacy in everyday life activities. For example, young children observe the print on cereal boxes to select their favorite brands, watch as their parents write notes and read the newspaper, and participate in special literacy-focused routines such as storybook reading with a parent or older sibling. On the basis of these observations and activities, children construct their own concepts about the functions and structure of print and then try these out by engaging in emergent forms of reading and writing, which often are far removed from the conventional forms adults use. Based on how others respond to their early attempts, children make modifications and construct more sophisticated systems of reading and writing. For example, early attempts at writing often shift from scribbles to random streams of letters (SKPVSSPK) and to increasingly elaborate systems of invented spelling such as *JLE* for *jelly* (Sulzby, 1990). Eventually, with lots of opportunities to engage in meaningful literacy activities, large amounts of interaction with adults and peers, and some incidental instruction, children become conventional readers and writers.

Proponents of emergent literacy believed that if provided the right kind of environments, experiences, and social interactions, most children require very little formal instruction to learn to read and write. Early childhood language arts programs based on the emergent literacy perspective feature the following components:

- print-rich classroom settings that contain large numbers of good children's books, displays of conventional print (e.g., alphabet friezes, charts written by teachers); functional print (e.g., helper charts, daily schedules, labels); student writing; play-related print (e.g., empty cereal boxes in the housekeeping dramatic play center); etc.
- frequent storybook reading by the teacher with lots of student interaction
- shared reading of big books coupled with embedded instruction on concepts about print (e.g., book concepts such as *author* and *title* and the left-to-right sequence of written language)
- shared writing experiences in which the teacher writes down oral stories dictated by children
- projects and/or thematic units that link language, reading, and writing activities together
- opportunities for children to engage in meaningful reading and writing during "center time" activities, and a family literacy component

Emergent literacy proponents contend that these types of emergent literacy experiences build on what children have already learned about written language, provide a smooth transition between home and school, and help to ensure initial success with learning to read and write. The teacher's role is to provide the materials, experiences, and interactions that enable children to learn to read and write. Direct instruction on skills such alphabet recognition and letter-sound relationships is only used with children who fail to learn these skills through meaningful interactions with print.

Scientifically Based Reading Research Approach

During the late 1990s, the standards movement and other national literacy policies and initiatives described at the beginning of this chapter began to have an impact on the field of early literacy. By 2002, initiatives such as Good Start, Grow Smart and the Early Reading First grant program pushed a skills-based approach to early literacy instruction, often referred to as scientifically based reading research (SBRR), into prominence. Perhaps the most valuable contribution of the SBRR movement has been identifying the "core" knowledge and skills that young children must have to become successful readers (Snow, Burns, & Griffin, 1998). Longitudinal studies have shown that preschool-age children's oral language (expressive and receptive language, including vocabulary development), phonological awareness, and alphabet knowledge are predictive of reading achievement in the elementary grades. Print awareness, which includes concepts of print (e.g., left-to-right, top-to-bottom sequence), book concepts (author, title), and sight word recognition has also been found to be positively correlated with reading ability in the primary grades.

SBRR investigators have also focused on identifying effective strategies for teaching this core literacy content to young children. One of the most consistent research findings is that core early literacy skills can be increased via **explicit, systematic instruction.** This instruction can often take the form of games and other engaging activities, but it also contains the elements of direct instruction: explanations, teacher modeling, guided practice, and independent practice.

SBRR instruction occurs in large and small group settings. Large-group instruction occurs during "circle time," when the entire class sits on the floor near the teacher, and may include:

- songs, such as "Down by the Bay," coupled with instruction on rhyme production ("Did you ever see a whale with a polka-dot . . . (tail), down by the bay.") [SBRR skill—phonological awareness]
- storybook reading, coupled with instruction on vocabulary (after reading "Did you see llamas eating their pajamas, down by the bay," the teacher asks, "Does anyone know what a llama is?") [SBRR skill—oral language] *Ask Question*
- alphabet charts with a poem for each letter that contains many examples of the "target letter." For example, after reading a poem for the letter *p* (Patty Panda likes to draw, holds a pencil in her paw . . ."), the teacher asks children to come up and point to the words that contain *p* and say the letter name [SBRR skill—alphabet knowledge]
- every-pupil response activities in which all children have a chance to respond at the same time. For example, the teacher might say a series of words, some of which begin with the /p/ sound and some that do not. Children hold their thumbs up if a word starts with sound of /p/ [SBRR skill—phonological awareness]

Instruction can also be conducted in small groups. The advantage is that if an activity requires that one child respond at a time, all children get multiple opportunities to participate. For example, using a pocket chart, a teacher can give a small group of children each a high-frequency-word flash card (my, the, is, big, fast) or a rebus picture card (truck, cat, girl, house). After reviewing the words on the cards, the teacher can help the children build sentences by saying words and placing cards in the chart ("My cat is big" "The truck is fast" "My house is big"). The SBRR skill being worked on here is print awareness.

Children also need opportunities to practice and consolidate what has been taught in large and small group settings. This practice usually occurs during an "activity" time when children work individually or in small groups in learning centers. This requires that the teacher link the center activities to the skills taught in the curriculum.

link activities

Blended Instruction: A "Value-Added" Approach

Both the emergent literacy and SBRR approaches to early literacy instruction have their advantages. Emergent literacy programs provide opportunities for children to learn about literacy on their own and with help from the teacher and peers. Learning can occur at the appropriate pace for each child and build on what he or she already knows. This approach provides children with rich opportunities to acquire oral language and to move through the developmental progressions in emergent reading and writing. The downside to this approach is that not all children are ready or able to take full advantage of these learning opportunities. These children have a tendency to "fall through the cracks" in emergent literacy programs and make very little progress. Such children need to be directly taught vocabulary, phonological awareness, alphabet, and concepts of print before they can fully profit from the learning experiences in an emergent literacy program.

We advocate instruction that blends together the key components of both approaches (see Figure 1.3). This approach features the print-rich classroom, storybook reading, shared writing, projects/units, and meaningful center-based literacy activities advocated by proponents of emergent literacy, coupled with direct instruction and practice on core language and literacy skills featured in the SBRR approach. So blended instruction is a "value-added" approach to early literacy instruction, combining the best aspects of the emergent literacy and SBRR perspectives.

Fortunately, we are not alone in this view. Most, if not all, of the comprehensive pre-K early literacy curricula developed since 2002 are blended programs. All have been strongly influenced by the SBRR perspective and use the term "science-based" in their promotional literature. These new instructional programs place heavy emphasis on the "big four" science-based skills: oral language, phonological awareness, alphabet knowledge, and print awareness. Direct instruction on these skills in large and small group settings is also now a standard feature, though the nature and intensity of this instruction varies from program to program. These programs also include the main components recommended by emergent literacy: frequent story-

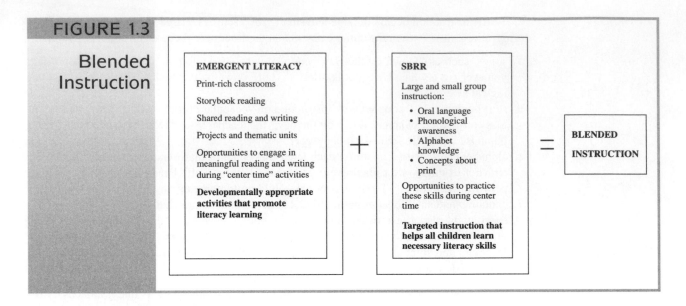

FIGURE 1.3

Blended Instruction

EMERGENT LITERACY

Print-rich classrooms

Storybook reading

Shared reading and writing

Projects and thematic units

Opportunities to engage in meaningful reading and writing during "center time" activities

Developmentally appropriate activities that promote literacy learning

+

SBRR

Large and small group instruction:

- Oral language
- Phonological awareness
- Alphabet knowledge
- Concepts about print

Opportunities to practice these skills during center time

Targeted instruction that helps all children learn necessary literacy skills

=

BLENDED INSTRUCTION

book reading, print-rich classroom environments, and center activities that involve reading and writing. Special Feature 1.1 describes the blended program that is being used in an Early Reading First project in Arizona.

Of course, how teachers implement a curriculum has a big influence on how appropriate and effective the curriculum will be for specific groups of children. Susan Neuman and Kathy Roskos (2005) give an observation that they made in a preschool using a commercially published early literacy curriculum that fits our definition of a "blended" program. The classroom did have a print-rich environment. However, the instruction that Neuman and Roskos observed was not developmentally appropriate for the three-and-a-half- and four-year-old children who were participating in the lesson. Here is a vignette that describes the lesson (Neuman & Roskos, 2005, p. 22).

The local school administrator recommends an exemplary school for us to visit. We watch a day unfold in a room filled with print. The walls are adorned with words; pocket charts, alphabet letters, numbers, signs, and environmental print claim every available space. A Big Book stands ready in the circle area, accompanied by a pointer for tracking print. The children sit "station style," with "quiet hands and feet," in their designated space in the circle and sing "Stop, Look, and Listen" along with their teacher. The day is about to begin.

Taking flash cards in hand, the teacher begins, "Good morning, Charley. Do you know the first two letters of your name?" Charley moves tentatively to the board and slowly writes *C* and *H*. Moving to the next child, then the next, the teacher follows a similar routine. Some 14 children later, she reviews many of the letters, asking children to spell the names of the helpers of the week. The days of the week are next, and children repeat them in chorus. They compare the letters in Monday to the letters in Tuesday, then Tuesday to Wednesday, and Tuesday to Thursday. What follows is the Counting Calendar and "My, oh my, it's the 30th of the month," and so the children count each day up to 30. And finally with an "I like how you're listening" some 45 minutes later, circle time is about to end. Even so, the transition allows for one last teachable moment focusing on the *t-t-t* in teacher, the *m-m-m* in *Ms.*, and the */j/* in *j-j-jingle*.

This vignette shows that it is possible to take a blended curriculum and skew it one way or the other—resulting in too little or too much instruction. There is nothing inherently wrong with the activities themselves: writing the letters in children's names, spelling the names of classroom helpers, reciting the days of the week, comparing the letters in the days of the week, counting, and sounding out the initial sounds in words. In fact, with a few modifications, each of these activities could have been a very effective lesson. The problem is that the lesson contained all of these activities, making the lesson much too long for three- and four-year-olds. These instructional activities could have been shortened (e.g., writing the beginning letters in several children's names, but not all fourteen!) and spread across several days.

SPECIAL FEATURE 1.1

The Arizona Centers for Excellence in Early Education Project

The Arizona Centers for Excellence in Early Education (ACE[3]) is an Early Reading First project that serves children in twenty Head Start and state-funded preschools in San Luis and Somerton, Arizona. The vast majority of these children are learning English as a second language. Like all Early Reading First projects, the primary goal of ACE[3] is to promote preschoolers' readiness for kindergarten by teaching them "science-based" early reading skills: oral language, phonological awareness, alphabet knowledge, and concepts of print.

The program uses a commercially published curriculum, *Doors to Discovery* (Wright Group/McGraw-Hill, 2002), which is a good example of a blended early literacy program. The Doors program is organized into one-month "explorations" or units that focus on topics that appeal to young children, such as transportation, nature, food, and school. The Doors curriculum consists of three interrelated components:

- **Large Group Time.** Song and rhyme posters are used as a "warm-up" and to teach phonological awareness (e.g., rhyme recognition). This is followed by shared reading of big books in which the teacher encourages children to read along and engage in book-related talk. Three shared-reading books are used in each unit: a narrative storybook, an informational book, and a concept book. When stories are initially introduced, the teacher does a "picture walk" to introduce key concepts and vocabulary. Instruction on concepts of print, phonological awareness, and alphabet knowledge are incorporated into the shared-reading sessions.

- **Discovery Center Time.** During a sixty-minute period, children engage in self-selected activities in a variety of learning centers, including dramatic play, art, blocks, writing, mathematics, and science. Many of these activities are linked to the theme and to the stories that are read during shared reading. The teacher manual contains lists of theme-related Wonderful Words to be used with the children while they are engaging in center activities. These centers are stocked with theme-related literacy props and materials, providing children with a print-rich environment. For example, during the unit on transportation, the dramatic play center is turned into a gas station. Props include a gas station sign (e.g., *Chevron*) and a cardboard gas pump with a label (*gas*) and numerals to represent the gallons and cost of gas that is pumped.

- **Small Group Time.** During the second ten-minute segment of Discovery Center Time, the teacher meets with small groups of students and

conducts a vocabulary lesson using an Interactive Book: a wordless big book that contains a number of illustrations related to the unit theme. For example, *Our Big Book of Driving*, which is used in the unit on transportation, contains pictures of different types of vehicles (bus, ambulance, motorcycle), parts of a car (door, tire, speedometer), and a scene of a busy intersection. Children are encouraged to discuss the pictures (initially in Spanish and then in English).

Once a week, during the third ten-minute segment of Discovery Center Time, the teacher also teaches a small group lesson using Our Big Scrapbook, a blank big book. In a variation of the language experience approach or shared writing, the teacher writes down children's oral language while they watch. The subject of the children's dictation is usually photographs of children's play activities or the children's artwork. For example, children may draw pictures of the type of vehicle that their parents drive. Each child then dictates a sentence ("My mom drives a blue van"), which the teacher writes below the picture. The children's contributions are then pasted or taped to the blank pages of the scrapbook. Completed scrapbooks are placed in the classroom library center for children to read during the center time.

A positive feature of this program is the way the different components and activities are linked to the current theme. The following vignette occurred during a unit on building and construction.

During large group circle time, the teacher and children sang a song that had to do with building a tree house. The teacher paused to point out the words that rhymed in the song and then encouraged the children to come up with other words that ended with the same rhyming sound. She also focused on several tool-related vocabulary terms: *hammer* and *nail*. Next, the teacher did a shared reading lesson with a big book about building a doghouse. Before reading the book with the children, she did a "picture walk," engaging the children in a discussion about objects in the photos in this informational book. The teacher focused children's attention on several tool vocabulary terms: *hammer, nail, saw, measuring tape,* and *safety goggles*. Then the teacher read the book and encouraged the children to read along. Some were able to do so because of the simple text and picture clues. During center time, several children chose to play in a dramatic play center that was set up as a house construction site. There was a "house" made out of large cardboard boxes. In addition, there were toy tools (hammers, saw, measuring tape, level), safety goggles, hard hats, some golf tees that were used as make-believe nails, and several

(continued on next page)

signs ("Hard Hat Area," "Danger," "Construction Site"). Two girls and a boy spent thirty minutes in the center, using the toy tools to measure, plan, and build the house. During this play, they used the target vocabulary repeatedly and also explored the uses of the tools. For example, when the boy attempted to use the toy saw without first putting on his safety goggles, one of the girls reminded him to put on the goggles. The dramatic play center was used as a means to provide children with an opportunity to practice and consolidate the vocabulary and concepts that were being taught in the instructional part of the curriculum.

The challenge, then, for early childhood educators is to carefully plan and teach the key elements through meaningful experiences. Our goal is to provide teachers with research-based information on how to combine the emergent literacy and the scientifically based reading research perspectives to create a balanced, effective early literacy program—one with meaningful experiences and with direct, developmentally appropriate instruction in the key early literacy areas.

A Blended Literacy Instructional Program

We believe that the two perspectives need to be interwoven to provide preschool children with a high-quality, effective reading, writing, and speaking program. We believe that both views make significant contributions to such a program. Children need meaningful interactions with print in print-rich environments and in books. They need social interactions with their peers and their teachers in literacy events. They need many opportunities to engage in meaningful reading, writing, and speaking events. In addition, they need explicit instruction in reading, writing, and speaking skills.

By combining the two perspectives, we have created a set of basic principles of effective literacy instruction. We believe these principles should guide how children are taught spoken and written language in preschool.

Effective Early Childhood Teachers Provide Children with a Print-Rich Classroom Environment

High-quality literacy programs require a literacy-rich environment with many materials to support children's learning. As Susan Neuman and Kathy Roskos (1993, pp. 20–21) explain, a print-rich classroom can help children to learn about language and literacy.

> The quality of the physical environment is a powerful factor in language learning. The objects and opportunities it provides are the stuff out of which basic concepts are spun. What is available to label and to talk about, how accessible it is to touch and explore, and how it is organized influence both spoken and written language development.

> Rich physical environments do not just happen; the creation of a classroom environment that supports children's learning, teachers' teaching, and the curriculum requires forethought. This type of environment offers children opportunities to talk, listen, read, and write to one another for real-life purposes.

Effective Teachers Demonstrate and Model Literacy Events

Children will try to do what others do. Therefore, demonstrating and modeling literacy events will lead to children imitating these events. When a teacher reads books to young children,

children independently pick up the books and say words in ways that would lead a listener to think they are reading. The children sound as though they are reading words, yet their eyes are focused on the illustrations. When children see parents and teachers using print for various purposes—writing shopping lists, looking up information in a book, and writing notes—they begin to learn about the practical uses of language and to understand why reading and writing are activities worth doing.

Effective Teachers Explicitly Teach Children Skills that Research Supports as Key Elements of Reading, Writing, and Speaking

Scientifically based reading research has identified key skills of early and later reading. This literature tells us that early language and literacy instruction should focus on the core content—the knowledge, skills, and dispositions that are predictive of later reading success (i.e., oral language, phonological awareness, alphabet knowledge, and concepts of print). There is a rich body of language development research to help teachers understand the key features of language (e.g., phonology, syntax, semantics, pragmatics). In each area, a rich literature identifies research-based instructional strategies for teaching children these skills, elements, and features. Many of these instructional strategies call for teachers to explicitly teach children—large groups of children, small groups of children, and individuals. In all instances, the strategies used should be appropriate for the age of the children.

Effective Early Childhood Teachers Provide Opportunities for Children to Work and Play Together in Literacy-Enriched Environments

Of course, teachers are not the only people in the classroom environment who offer demonstrations of literacy. Creating a "community of literacy learners" is often suggested in the professional literature. Children select books to "read" because their peers have selected the book. Children talk to each other about books they are reading or have had read to them. Children turn to each other for information and help in decoding or spelling words. "How do you spell *morning*?" "What's this word say?"

Several researchers have documented what happens when teachers create an environment where children can demonstrate for, or coach, each other. For example, Carol Vukelich (1993, p. 390) studied how children teach each other about the functions, features, and meaning of print in play. The following peer-to-peer interaction illustrates how one child coaches another child about how to spell his name.

> Jessie is the forest ranger. She is seated at the entrance to the campsite, directing potential campers to get a sticker from her before entering the campground, and then she'll tell them which tent they can use.
>
> ***Jessie:*** Ronald, how do you spell your name?
> ***Ronald:*** R. (*Jessie writes r.*) No, it's the big kind. (*Ronald forms the letter with his finger on the table. Jessie writes R.*) Good!
> ***Jessie:*** What else?

When teachers value children's contributions and celebrate what they know, children see the strengths in each other. Within such a supportive climate, children practice what they know and take the risks necessary for learning to occur. This kind of environment encourages young children to learn from themselves, from each other, and from the teacher.

Effective Early Childhood Teachers Link Literacy and Play

The previous example of children's teaching each other how to spell occurred in literacy-enriched play settings in Karen Valentine's kindergarten classroom. The play setting was a park. Valentine and the children generated ideas for the dramatic play setting. There needed to be a place to fish, so the water table became the fishing pond labeled "Lum's Pond" after the nearby pond. Fish and fishing poles were made in the art center. Paper clips were attached to the fish and magnets to the end of the string attached to the fishing pole. Soon children were reeling in fish. But to fish, you need a fishing license. A form was created and placed in the writing center. Park rangers ensured that no one fished who did not have a license. Soon the children needed clipboards with paper; tickets had to be issued to children caught fishing without a license.

And so the setting developed. Because the tools of literacy were available to the children, they began to incorporate print into the dramatic play theme in very natural and real-world ways. They wrote for many purposes (e.g., to control others' behavior, to share stories of vacation experiences, to reserve a tent). They read books and each other's writing. They talked "park" talk, negotiating their various "camping/park" schema to create a new shared schema. Within this play setting, they had the opportunity to practice the literacy events they had witnessed in the world outside the classroom and to add to their knowledge about literacy. Enriching play settings with appropriate literacy materials provides young children with important opportunities for literacy learning and for practicing literacy. As the National Association for the Education of Young Children reaffirms in its recent accreditation standards (NAEYC, 2004) and Lesley Morrow and Judy Schickedanz (2006) assert, it is critical that "play is integrated into our developing understanding of school readiness" (p. 269).

Effective Early Childhood Teachers Encourage Children to Experiment with Emergent Forms of Reading and Writing

As we blend the two perspectives it is important for teachers to allow children a "risk-free" environment where they practice and integrate new skills they are learning with what they already know. Years ago, young children were not considered to be writing until they were writing conventionally; that is, correctly forming the letters and spelling the words. They were not considered to be reading until they could correctly recognize numerous printed words. In the 1970s, Marie Clay (1975) and Charles Read (1971) helped us understand emergent forms of writing and reading. We learned that children construct, test, and perfect hypotheses about written language. Their research lead to Elizabeth Sulzby and her colleagues' (Sulzby, 1985a, 1985b; Sulzby, Barnhart, & Hieshima, 1989) creation of developmental sequences that children pass through on their way to becoming conventional readers and writers.

Today outstanding early childhood teachers do not expect young children's notions of writing and reading to conform to adult models of correctness. They expect children to experiment with print: to scribble, to make marks that look something like letters, to write strings of letters, and so forth. They expect children to look at pictures and "read" a story with an oral telling voice, to look at pictures and "read" a story with a written story voice, to attend to print and "read" in a written story voice, and so forth. Through such explorations, children create meaning and communicate. Their teachers support their explorations with materials and with comments. Their teachers confirm when their hypotheses about print are correct.

Effective Early Childhood Teachers Provide Opportunities for Children to Use Language and Literacy for Real Purposes and Audiences

Most research on learning supports the proposition that knowing the reason for a learning situation and seeing a purpose in a task helps children learn. By the time children come to school or the child care center, many have experienced a wide variety of purposes for writing to various audiences. If children are allowed to experiment with paper and pencils, these purposes will begin to show up in their early attempts at writing. They will write letters and messages to others, jot down lists of things they need to do, and make signs for their doors warning intruders to stay out.

Similarly, by the time children come to school or to the child care center, many have experienced many opportunities to read for real purposes. They have shopped in grocery stores—and sometimes screamed when their mothers refused to purchase the cereal box they "read" and wanted. They have told the car driver who slowed but didn't come to a full stop at the stop sign that "dat means stop!" They have enjoyed their personal "reading" of a book read and reread many times to them by an adult. They have pointed to the sign written in linear scribble and hung, just like their teenage sibling's sign, on their door and shouted, "Can't you read? It "says, 'Keep out!'" They have "read" the address on an envelope collected at the mailbox and said, "You won't like this one. It's a bill!"

Notice how many of these reading and writing opportunities are literacy events woven into the events of daily life. The event defines the purpose of the literacy activity.

Effective Early Childhood Teachers Make Use of Everyday Activities to Demonstrate the Many Purposes of Reading and Writing

Are they cooking tomorrow? The teacher reads the recipe today with the children, and together they make a list to help them remember the food items that need to be purchased at the grocery store. Did a parent or community person volunteer in the classroom? Together they write a thank-you note. The teacher might add special paper to the writing center so that individual children might write individual thank-you notes or letters. Effective teachers can provide young children with numerous opportunities to engage in purposeful reading and writing activities.

Effective Early Childhood Teachers Read to Children Daily and Encourage Them to Read Familiar Books on Their Own

Living in a print-rich world provides children with many opportunities to read *contextualized* print. That is, children form hypotheses about what words say because of the context in which the words are embedded. As described in other sections of the chapter, children learn to read cereal boxes, stop signs, and the McDonald's sign early in life. While making such connections with print is important, young children also need multiple experiences with decontextualized print. Susan Neuman and Kathy Roskos (1993, p. 36) explain the meaning of decontextualized print.

> Essentially, this means that unlike contextualized print experiences, written language has meaning apart from the particular situation or context of its use. The meaning of decontextualized print is derived from the language itself and from the conventions of the literary genre . . . . Over time, [children] develop a frame, or sense of story, . . . a mental model of basic elements of a story.

Reading stories to children is one of the best ways to familiarize them with decontextualized print. In fact, it has been the "cornerstone of literacy development and classroom practice for over a century" (Brabham & Lynch-Brown, 2002, p. 465). Effective early childhood teachers plan numerous opportunities for storybook reading experiences. These teachers read aloud daily to individual children, small groups of children, and the whole class. Sometimes the books are regular-size books, like the ones obtained from the public or school library. Other times, the books are big books, enlarged (about 24- to 26-inch) versions of regular-size books.

But hearing stories read aloud is not enough. Case studies of children who read early tell us of the importance of talk about the books read (Heath, 1983; Yaden, Smolken, & Conlon,

1989). Therefore, knowing teachers often begin their read-alouds by engaging children in a discussion related to the story about to be read. A teacher might read the title and ask the children what they think the story might be about, or the teacher might ask a question related to the book's content. While reading, the teacher might invite the children to make comments, to share reactions, or to ask questions. After reading, the teacher likely will engage the children in a discussion aimed at extending their understanding of the story. In this way, teachers help children learn how to process the decontextualized text found in books both in terms of the story's structure and by making connections between the context and the children's experiences.

It is also important to provide opportunities for children to independently read books by themselves and to one another. Through such occasions, children have the opportunity to practice what they have learned during the interactive storybook readings. That is, they can engage in "emergent storybook reading" behaviors (Sulzby, 1985a). Children who have heard the same book read to them a number of times (called repeated readings) will attempt to read the book to themselves and to others. They act as if they are readers. As noted above, opportunities to engage in emergent reading behaviors are important to children's development as conventional readers.

Effective Early Childhood Teachers Use Multiple Forms of Assessment to Find Out What Children Know and Can Do

Is the child's development following the expected stages? Is the child acquiring the core-content early literacy skills? Today teachers use standardized measures and ongoing progress monitoring tools to assess children's progress in acquiring the crucial elements or core content skills.

Not so very long ago, the literacy field recommended against the use of standardized tests, particularly with young children and particularly paper and pencil group-administered tests. For example, the 1998 International Reading Association and National Association for the Education of Young Children joint statement had the following to say about testing young children.

> **Accurate assessment** of children's knowledge, skills, and dispositions in reading and writing will help teachers better match instruction with how and what children are learning. However, early reading and writing cannot simply be measured as a set of narrowly-defined skills on standardized tests. These measures often are not reliable or valid indicators of what children can do in typical practice, nor are they sensitive to language variations, culture, or experiences of young children. Rather, a sound assessment should be anchored in real-life writing and reading tasks and continuously chronicle a wide range of children's literacy activities in different situations. Good assessment is essential to help teachers tailor appropriate instruction to young children and to know when and how much intensive instruction on any particular skill or strategy might be needed (p. 38).

This joint statement advised teachers of young children to use multiple indicators to assess and monitor children's development and learning. We concur.

However, the field now also acknowledges that standardized assessments, assessments like the Peabody Picture Vocabulary Test (Dunn & Dunn, 1997), the Individual Growth and Developmental Indicator (IGDI) (Early Childhood Research Institute on Measuring Growth and Development, 2000), or the Phonological Awareness Literacy Screening (PALS) (Invernizzi, Meier, Swank, & Juel, 1999), can provide teachers with valuable information. Repeated use of the same instruments allows teachers to chronicle children's development over time. However, neither standardized nor informal, ongoing assessment should be used alone. When multiple sources of data are used, then the likelihood of an accurate understanding of children's literacy knowledge and learning is increased (IRA/NCTE, 1994).

Effective Early Childhood Teachers Respect and Make Accommodations for Children's Developmental, Cultural, and Linguistic Diversity

Children arrive in the classroom with different individual language and literacy needs. Our challenge is to offer good fits between each child's strengths and needs and what we try to give the child. The instruction we provide needs to dovetail with where children are developmentally and with their language and culture.

Some children will come to school having learned how to talk in ways that are consistent with their teachers' expectations; other children will not. "We come to every situation with stories: patterns and sequences of events which are built into us. Our learning happens within the experience of what important others did" (Bateson, 1979, p. 13). In other words, the ways in which we make meaning and use words are dependent on the practices shared by the members of our community—the words chosen; the sentence structures used; the decision to talk after, or over, another's comment; and so on. As Allan Luke and Joan Kale (1997, p. 13) point out, "different cultures make meaning in different ways, with different patterns of exchange and interaction, text conventions and beliefs about reading and writing."

Given our increasingly diverse communities composed of many different cultures, teachers are more challenged than ever before to understand what this diversity means for their teaching and for their children's learning. Children cannot be asked to leave their family and cultural backgrounds at the classroom door and enter into a "hybrid culture" (Au & Kawakami, 1991). Teachers must teach in ways that allow their children to work to their strengths—and these strengths are going to be related to children's cultural backgrounds.

It is only since the 1980s that researchers have investigated early literacy learning in nonmainstream homes and communities. In a pioneering study, Shirley Brice Heath (1983) described how children growing up in one working-class community learn that reading is sitting still and sounding out words—following the rules—whereas children in another working-class community learn that being able to tell a story well orally is more important than being able to read written texts. These conceptions of literacy were quite different from those found in children from middle-class families. The important question is, should these types of cultural differences be viewed as deficits that must be "fixed" in order for children to succeed in school, or should these differences be viewed as positive characteristics that teachers can take advantage of when helping children learn language and literacy? Throughout this book, we give pointers on providing culturally sensitive language and literacy instruction.

A significant and growing group of diverse learners are second-language learners. The population of children who speak English as a second language was estimated at 3.5 million in the year 2000 and is projected to grow to six million by 2020 (Faltis, 2001). Of this group, those children who speak little or no English are referred to as limited English proficient (LEP). Other children are bilingual and can speak both English and their native language with varying degrees of proficiency. These children's native language might be Spanish, Portuguese, Japanese, or some other world language. When they come to school, young second-language learners are typically competent users of their native language. Their native language competence is a strength to be exploited by sensitive teachers.

We have included several Special Feature sections in subsequent chapters of this book that focus on second-language and bilingual learners' literacy development. From these features, readers will learn which strategies presented in this book are appropriate for use with children whose primary language is a language other than mainstream English and which strategies need to be adapted to meet the needs of these children.

Effective Early Childhood Teachers Recognize the Importance of Reflecting on Their Instructional Decisions

The importance of "learning by doing," standing back from each teaching/learning event to learn from one's teaching, is not new. John Dewey (1938) is usually credited with proposing the importance of this activity, and Donald Schon (1983) with reintroducing the idea into the educational literature. To reflect is to take an active role in studying one's own instructional decisions in order to enhance one's knowledge and make informed decisions. Not all of such reflections will be on past actions (retrospective); some might be on the potential outcomes of future actions (anticipatory), while others will be "in action" while teaching (contemporaneous) (van Manen, 1995). To reflect is to problematize teaching: to consider and reconsider the procedures for technical accuracy (e.g., the procedural steps to follow while conducting a guided reading lesson), the reasons for instructional actions and outcomes, and the underlying assumptions of actions that ensure that all children learn (e.g., curriculum mandates that affect teacher decision making or inequities that inhibit student learning).

Summary

In this chapter, we briefly explained the significant impact of recent national literacy policies on the early literacy field and compared the constructivist approaches to literacy learning (emergent literacy) with the new scientifically based reading research approach to literacy learning. We believe that the best literacy practices use strategies from both approaches. We firmly believe that teachers must use evidence (from research and from their students' performance) to guide their teaching.

In subsequent chapters, we provide many explanations of how to implement teaching strategies aimed at promoting different aspects of language and literacy development. In addition, the themes of respect for student diversity and instruction linked to assessment appear throughout the book. When appropriate, Special Features about the special needs of second-language learners are included. Further, a section titled "Assessment: Discovering What Children Know and Can Do" is included in several of the chapters.

To summarize the key points from this chapter, we return to the focus questions at the beginning of this chapter.

■ *How have national literacy polices and initiatives impacted preschool language and early literacy instruction?*

Beginning with the 1983 (*A Nation at Risk*) suggestion that students be held to high and rigorous standards to the passage of the No Child Left Behind Act in 2001 requiring schools and school districts to hold *all* students responsible for demonstrating that they know the content of the standards, recent national policies have had a significant impact on literacy instruction in America. Early Reading First, the program that aims to transform existing preschool programs into centers of excellence that prepare young children to enter kindergarten ready to learn and serve as models for other preschool programs to emulate, is an important early literacy program funded by the No Child Left Behind Act. To obtain these funds, agencies must demonstrate that they will use reading programs and instructional strategies that are consistent with scientifically based reading research and that they will provide teachers with extensive professional development on these programs and strategies.

Recent national initiatives and legislation have drawn attention to the need to prepare children before they start school. From the reauthorization of Head Start, to the writing of pre-kindergarten literacy standards, to funded research and preschool teacher professional development programs, to President George W. Bush's Good Start, Grow Smart initiative, the nation now realizes the importance of children's early years to their later academic success, particularly their reading achievement.

■ *How did the standards movement change early literacy instructional practices and the assessment of children?*

The No Child Left Behind Act requires states and school districts to hold all students, grades 3 through 8, responsible for demonstrating that they know the content of their state's English language arts standards. In addition, it invited states to voluntarily develop early learning guidelines or standards to define what young children should know and be able to do at the end of their preschool years. Clearly, if young children are to "know" and be able to demonstrate that they can "do" the standards, then the curriculum and instructional practices must be aligned with the standards. Teachers must ensure that their young students have the opportunity to learn the content specified by the standards. These standards, then, also should drive teachers' monitoring of children's progress.

■ *How is the emergent literacy perspective different from the scientifically based reading research perspective on young children's early literacy learning?*

The emergent literacy perspective suggests that children learn about language and literacy by observing, exploring, and interacting with others. Children assume the role of apprentice—mimicking, absorbing, and adapting the words and literacy activities used by more knowledgeable others. As they engage in social interactions, children integrate new experiences with prior knowledge, constructing and testing hypotheses to make meaning. They store this newly constructed knowledge in mental structures called schemas.

The scientifically based reading research perspective argues that children need to be explicitly taught those skills that the research literature has identified as predictive of later reading success. To date, eleven variables have been identified as predictive of later reading success. These eleven variables include *alphabet knowledge*, print knowledge, *oral language/vocabulary*, environmental print, invented spelling, listening comprehension, phonemic awareness, *phonological short-term memory*, rapid naming, *phonemic awareness*, visual memory, and *visual-perceptual* skills. Those skills in italics are those evidencing the highest correlation with school-age decoding.

A key difference between the two perspectives, then, is the early literacy practices recommended as appropriate—explicit instruction versus allowing the children to acquire the skills of literacy through multiple interactions with print and more knowledgeable others. Unfortunately, to date there are few research-based suggestions on early literacy instructional strategies and programs. What do appropriate instructional strategies look and sound like? Teachers of young children must ensure that inappropriate strategies do not creep into their teaching practices as they shift to teaching the skills identified as central to children's success as readers.

■ *What principles should guide early childhood teachers' teaching of language and literacy?*

Effective early childhood teachers:

- provide children with a print-rich classroom environment
- demonstrate and model literacy events
- link literacy and play
- encourage children to experiment with emergent forms of reading and writing
- provide opportunities for children to use language and literacy for real purposes and audience
- read to children daily and encourage them to read books on their own
- use multiple forms of assessment to find out what children know and can do
- respect and make accommodations for children's developmental, cultural, and linguistic diversity
- recognize the importance of reflecting on their instructional decisions

LINKING KNOWLEDGE TO PRACTICE

1. Access your state's department of education Web site to bookmark your state's early literacy guidelines. Compare what your state expects preschool children to know with what a neighboring state expects preschoolers to know.
2. Access information about the Early Reading First program on the U.S. Department of Education Web site. List three things you learned about Early Reading First that surprised you. Are there any Early Reading First–funded programs in your area? Arrange to visit the nearest program.
3. Observe an early childhood teacher in a nearby classroom. How does this teacher's language and literacy instruction match up with the teaching principles described in this chapter?
4. Investigate the National Early Literacy Panel. Has this panel reported any additional findings?

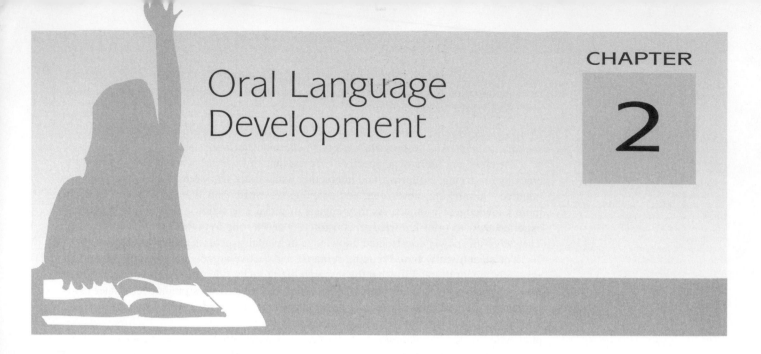

Oral Language Development

Perched in the shopping cart, nine-month-old Dawn babbles away to her mother. As they approach the checkout register, the clerk greets her mother. Dawn smiles, loudly says "Hi!" and waves her hand. The startled clerk smiles at Dawn and begins to talk to her. Dawn, obviously pleased with this attention, now babbles back to the clerk.

As this scenario reveals, the power of language is evident to even its youngest users. Dawn demonstrates that she knows how to use language to express—and realize—her desire to become a significant, communicating member in her world. By age eighteen months, Dawn will have a vocabulary of dozens of words, and she will begin speaking in rule-governed, two-word sentences. By age thirty-six months, her vocabulary will number in the hundreds of words, and she will be using fully formed, five- and six-word sentences.

Children's oral language development is remarkable. Lindfors (1987, p. 90) outlines the typical accomplishments of young language learners.

> Virtually every child, without special training, exposed to surface structures of language in many interaction contexts, builds for himself—in a short period of time and at an early stage in his cognitive development—a deep-level, abstract, and highly complex system of linguistic structure.

How does Dawn—and every other human child, for that matter—learn to communicate? How does this development occur so rapidly and without any seeming effort on the part of children or their parents? This question has fascinated scholars and parents for hundreds of years and is the subject of this chapter.

BEFORE READING THIS CHAPTER, THINK ABOUT . . .

- What were your first words? Although you probably do not recall uttering those words, maybe your parents or older siblings recollect your speaking to them. Were your first words recorded someplace, or does your family rely on an oral tradition, telling the family stories orally?
- How do you think children acquire language? Is language development primarily a matter of genetics (an inborn ability to learn languages), the types of experiences and support children receive from their parents and other people, or a combination of these factors?
- When do children begin to express their thoughts orally? Why do some children develop language early while others experience language delays?
- Have you ever been in a situation where everyone around you used a language you don't know? How did you feel? How did you communicate with these speakers?

BOX 2.1	**behaviorist perspective:** the view that language acquisition is a result of imitation and reinforcement
Definition of Terms	**cerebral cortex:** the largest part of the brain, composed of two hemispheres that are responsible for higher brain functions, including thought and language
	morpheme: the small unit of meaning in oral language. The word *cats* contains two morphemes: *cat* (name of a type of animal) and *s* (plural)
	myelineation: a process in which the neurons of the brain become coated with a white substance known as myelin, which facilitates the transmission of sensory information and promotes learning
	nativist perspective: the view that language development is a result of an inborn capacity to learn language
	neurobiological perspective: the view that language acquisition can be explained by studying the structural development of the brain
	neurons: the impulse-conducting cells that make up the brain
	otitis media: an inflammation of the inner part of the ear that can retard language acquisition
	phoneme: the smallest unit of sound in a language. There are approximately forty-four phonemes in English (2 4 letters)
	pragmatics: rules that affect how language is used in different social contexts
	semantics: the part of language that assigns meaning to words and sentences
	social-interactionist perspective: the view that language development is a result of both genetics and adult support
	synapses: connections between the neurons of the brain
	syntax: rules for arranging words into sentences

FOCUS QUESTIONS

■ What are the major views on how children's language develops? Which aspects of language development does each view adequately explain?

■ What are the major components of language?

■ How does the structure of an infant's brain develop? How does this structural development affect language acquisition?

■ What factors affect children's rate of language acquisition?

■ How does children's acquisition of a second language compare with their first language acquisition? What should adults do to make it easier for children to learn English as a second language?

Perspectives on Children's Language Acquisition

There are four views on how children learn language: behaviorism, linguistic nativism, social-interactionism, and the neurobiological perspective. We present a brief description of each perspective in this chapter. Our experiences as parents, teachers, and researchers lead us to believe that the social-interactionism perspective most realistically accounts for similarities and differences in young children's language development. Therefore, we present a more detailed description of what is presently known about children's language acquisition from this perspective. However, we also acknowledge the importance of the new neurobiological information provided by neuroscientists to help us understand the biology of language acquisition. Together, the social-interactionist and the neurobiological perspectives provide important insights for teachers and future teachers on how children acquire language.

Behaviorist Perspective

The behaviorist view suggests that nurture—the way a child is taught or molded by parents and the environment—plays a dominant role in children's language development. Through the first half of the twentieth century, this was the prevalent view. Researchers and teachers believed that all learning (language included) is the result of two basic processes—classical and operant conditioning (Skinner, 1957). Behaviorists attribute receptive language to associations that result from classical conditioning. For example, every time the baby is offered a bottle, the mother names the object, "Here's the bottle." After numerous repetitions with the adult presenting the action/object and phrase, the baby learns that the clear cylinder filled with food is called a bottle.

Behaviorists suggest that through operant conditioning, infants gradually learn expressive language by being rewarded for imitating the sounds and speech they hear. For instance, a baby spontaneously babbles and accidentally says or repeats the sound "mama." The mother responds joyfully, hugging and kissing the baby, saying "Yes, Mama!" The baby, given this reward, is reinforced and attempts to repeat the behavior. Once the behavior is repeated and rewarded often enough, the child connects the word sound to the object or event.

Nativist Perspective

The nativist view of learning and development, with its emphasis on nature, is at the opposite end of the continuum from the behaviorist perspective. According to the nativist view, a person's behavior and capabilities are largely predetermined. Nativists believe every child has an inborn capacity to learn language. If these theorists were using computer terminology, they would say that humans are hardwired for language. Noam Chomsky (1965) called this innate capacity a language acquisition device (LAD). Nativists posit that the LAD allows children to interpret phoneme patterns, word meanings, and the rules that govern language. For example, when children first begin to use past tenses, they often overgeneralize certain words, such as *goed* for *went*, or *thinked* for *thought*. Since *goed* and *thinked* are not words that children would hear adults say, these examples illustrate that children are using some type of internal rule system, not simple imitation, to govern their acquisition of language.

Nativists also believe that this innate language structure facilitates the child's own attempts to communicate, much the same way as the computer's wiring facilitates the use of a number of software programs. Nativists believe that language learning differs from all other human learning in that a child learns to communicate even without support from parents or caregivers. They view the environment's role in language acquisition as largely a function of activating the innate, physiologically based system. Environment, these theorists believe, is not the major force shaping a child's language development.

Social-Interactionist Perspective

Social interactionists do not come down on either side of the nature versus nurture debate; rather, they acknowledge the influence of genetics and parental teaching. They share with behaviorists the belief that environment plays a central role in children's language development. Likewise, along with nativists, they believe that children possess an innate predisposition to learn language. In addition, social interactionists stress the child's own intentional participation in language learning and the construction of meaning. The social interactionist's point of view emphasizes the importance of the infant's verbal negotiations or "verbal bouts" (Golinkoff, 1983; Golinkoff & Hirsh-Pasek, 1999) with caregivers. These negotiations occur partly because mothers or other caretakers treat children's attempts at speech as meaningful and intentional (Piper, 1993). An example is shown by eleven-month-old Dawn, standing by the garage door. Dawn is patting the door.

> ***Dawn:*** Bice!
>
> ***Mom:*** Do you want ice?

Dawn: [shaking her head] Biiisse.

Mom: [opening the garage door] Bise?

Dawn: [pointing at the bike] Bise.

Mom: You want to go for a bike ride?

Dawn: [raising her arms, nodding her head vigorously] Bice!

As Dawn's mother (and most mothers) begins to make sense of her child's speech, she also begins to understand her child's meaning and/or intent. Lev Vygotsky (1962) described this type of adult support, or scaffolding, as facilitating the child's language growth within the zone of proximal development, the distance between a child's current level of development and the level at which the child can function with adult assistance. In the preceding example, the mother's questions enable Dawn to successfully communicate using a one-word sentence, something she could not have done on her own. Parents also support children's efforts to learn language by focusing the child's attention on objects in the immediate environment and labeling each object and its action.

Neurobiological Perspective

The psychologists, linguists, and anthropologists who developed the three preceding perspectives of language acquisition had to infer the origins of language and brain activity from careful, long-term observations of external behavior. Over the past two decades, technological innovations have enabled neuroscientists to study the brain at a cellular level. Brain imaging techniques are noninvasive procedures that allow researchers to graphically record and simultaneously display three-dimensional, color-enhanced images of a living brain as it processes information. These data provide researchers with a better way to understand the organization and functional operations of the brain. The research in this area has virtually exploded in the past decade. Hundreds of studies of how the brain develops, processes, organizes, connects, stores, and retrieves language have been conducted and have added greatly to our understanding of human language.

According to this new perspective, the capacity to learn language begins with brain cells called neurons. Neurons emerge during the early phases of fetal development, growing at the fantastic rate of 250,000 per minute (Edelman, 1995). As neurons multiply, they follow a complex genetic blueprint that causes the brain to develop distinct but interdependent systems—brain stem and limbic system, cerebellum and cerebral cortex (MacLean, 1978). New brain-imaging technology has allowed scientists to locate specific areas in the brain that are dedicated to hearing, speaking, and interpreting language. Thus, the nativist linguistic theory of language acquisition is, in part, correct—the human brain has dedicated structures for language, and infant brains are born capable of speaking any of the three thousand-plus human languages (Kuhl, 1993, 1999; Gopnik, Meltzoff, & Kuhl, 2001). However, infants are not disposed to speak any particular language, nor are they born language proficient. The language that a child learns is dependent on the language that the child hears spoken in the home (Sylwester, 1995; Gopnik, Meltzoff, & Kuhl, 2001).

The recent discoveries in neurobiology support elements of the nativist, behaviorist, and social-interactionist views of language development. These biological findings reveal that language learning is a reciprocal dialogue between genetics (nature) and environment (nurture). Clearly, infants are born with key brain areas genetically dedicated to language functions. Yet for children to learn the language of their culture, it is necessary that they have consistent, frequent opportunities to interact with a persistent caregiver who models the language with the child. Likewise, neuroscientists agree that a child's language capacity is dependent on the quality of language input. Parents and caregivers who consistently engage in conversation with their infants actually help their children develop neural networks that lead to language fluency and proficiency (Kuhl, Tsao, Liu, Zhang, & de Boer, 2001; Healy, 1994, 1997; Kotulak, 1997; Sprenger, 1999). In Figure 2.1, we summarize the major concepts of these four perspectives of language acquisition.

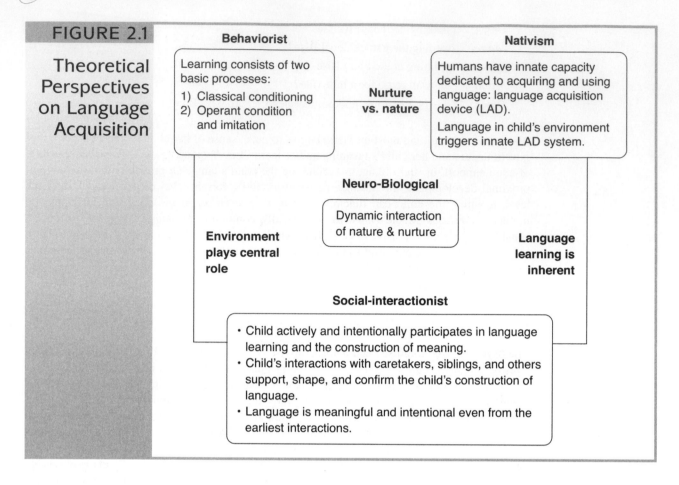

FIGURE 2.1

Theoretical Perspectives on Language Acquisition

Linguistic Vocabulary Lesson

Linguistics is the study of language. To better understand the complexities of linguistic acquisition, we provide a brief discussion of the components of linguistic structure: of phonology, morphology, syntax, semantics, and pragmatics.

Phonology

The sound system of a particular language is its phonology, and the distinctive units of sound in a language are its phonemes. Individual phonemes are described according to how speakers modify the airstream they exhale to produce the particular sounds.

Phonological development begins when sounds of speech activate neural networks in the infant's brain. This process begins during the last three months of prenatal development as babies are able to hear intonation patterns from their mother's voice (Shore, 1997; Hetherington & Parke, 2003).

Scientists have recently determined that since the mechanical aspects of the auditory system are in place prior to birth, the neural network that supports language acquisition has already started to develop. In fact at birth babies demonstrate a preference for the phonemes, rhythms, and tonal patterns of their native language (Werker & Tees, 2005; Vouloumanos & Werker, in press). (See More About 2.1.)

This type of research has suggested several findings (Gopnik, Meltzoff, & Kuhl, 2001; Vouloumanos & Werker, in press). Newborn infants recognize and prefer

- the sound of the human voice to all other sounds;
- the sound of their mother's voice (to all other female voices);
- the cadence/tonal qualities of their native tongue;
- familiar music (music they have heard frequently in the womb).

MORE ABOUT
2.1

How Scientists Assess Infant Knowledge

During the last twenty years developmental psychologists have determined creative ways to assess infants' knowledge. Developmental scientists have known for decades that infants are able to control their sucking movements long before they can control other motor movements, like reaching. Thus, these scientists use experimental methods that rely on infants' ability to control their sucking motions to assess what infants notice, perceive, and in some cases, what they know. This experimental method is one way to assess human infant cognition. For example, to assess newborn infants' recognition of their native versus an unfamiliar language, a researcher gives the infant a pacifier (which is attached to a computer) that can analyze the frequency and intensity of the infant's sucking. Over the years researchers have determined that infants suck harder and more frequently when they hear familiar voices, sounds, songs—this is called infant preference. When infants hear an unfamiliar voice, sound, or song, they slow down their sucking response and reduce the intensity of their sucking.

However, language use begins in earnest when infants engage in verbal interactions with caregivers. These early interactions allow babies to clearly hear sounds of their native language(s) and observe how the mouth and tongue work to create these unique sounds. Simultaneously, as babies babble, they gain motor control of their vocal and breathing apparatus. Interactions with caregivers allow babies an opportunity to listen, observe, and attempt to mimic sounds they hear and the mouth and tongue movements they see (Ramachandran, 2000). Through this process, babies begin to specialize in the sounds of their native language(s). The developmental window of opportunity (sometimes called the critical period) for mastering sound discrimination occurs within the first six months of an infant's life. By this time, babies' brains are already pruning out sensitivity to sounds that are not heard in their environment (Kuhl, 1993, 1999). This pruning is so efficient that children actually lose the ability to hear phonemes that are not used in their mother tongue. Children who consistently hear more than one language during this time may become native bi- or trilinguals, as they retain the ability to hear the subtle and discrete sounds.

Another important aspect of the English phonology is its prosody, or the stress and intonation patterns of the language. Stress refers to the force with which phonemes are articulated. Where the stress is placed may distinguish otherwise identical words (RECord [noun] versus reCORD [verb]). Intonation, on the other hand, refers to the pattern of stress and of rising and falling pitch that occurs within a sentence. These changes in intonation may shift the meaning of otherwise identical sentences:

IS she coming? (Is she or is she not coming?)
Is SHE coming? (Her, not anyone else)
Is she COMING? (Hurry up; it's about time)

Babies as young as four and five months begin to experiment with the pitch, tone, and volume of the sounds they make and often produce sounds that mimic the tonal and stress qualities of their parents' speech.

Morphology

As babies' phonological development progresses, they begin to make morphemes. Morphemes are the smallest unit of meaning in oral language. While it used to be thought that children didn't make word-meaning-to-sound connections until around their first birthday, the science of infant language acquisition has learned a great deal more about how infants and toddlers develop language. For instance, scientists (Tincoff & Jusczyk, 1999) now report that the sounds that give parents such a thrill—*Mama, Dada*—actually mark the very beginning of human word comprehension. It is now believed that the origins of language—linking sound patterns with specific meanings—stem from discrete associations infants make, beginning with socially significant people such as their parents, at six months of age. Real words are mixed with wordlike sounds (echolalia). As real words emerge, they can be categorized into the following:

Lexical—individual meaning-carrying words, such as *cat, baby*

Bound—units of sound that hold meaning (like *re, un*) but must be attached to other morphemes (*reorder, unbend*)

Derivational and inflectional—usually suffixes that change the class of the word; for example, noun to adjective—*dust* to *dusty;* verb to noun—*teaches* to *teacher*

Compound—two lexical morphemes that together may form a unique meaning, such as *football* or *cowboy*

Idiom—an expression whose meaning cannot be derived from its individual parts; for example, *Put your foot in your mouth* carries a very different meaning from the visual image it conjures up

Syntax

Syntax refers to how morphemes, or words, are combined to form sentences or units of thought. In English, there are basically two different types of order: linear and hierarchical structure. Linear structure refers to the object-verb arrangement. For example, *Building falls on man* means something very different than *Man falls on building.* Hierarchical structure refers to how words are grouped together within a sentence to reveal the speaker's intent. However, different languages have unique and inherent rules that govern syntax. A speaker of English might say: *The long, sleek black cat chased the frightened, tiny gray mouse.* A language with syntactical rules that differ from English could state it this way: *Chasing the gray mouse, tiny and frightened, was the cat, long, sleek, and black.*

Shortly after their first birthdays, most children are able to convey their intentions with single words. Have you ever heard a young child use the powerful words *no* and *mine*? More complex, rule-driven communication usually emerges between the ages of two and three, when children are able to construct sentences of two or more words.

Though children have prewired capacity for language rules (such as past tense), adult scaffolding or support plays a significant role in extending and expanding a child's language development. For instance, when Joe says *deenk,* his day care teacher can extend and clarify Joe's intentions: *Joe, do you want to drink milk or juice?* If Joe says *I drinked all the milk,* his teacher might tactfully expand his statement. *Yes, Joe, you drank all of your milk.* This type of subtle modeling is usually the most appropriate way to support children as they learn the conventional forms and complexities of their language. However, even when adults expand a child's speech, the child's own internal rule-governing system may resist modification until the child is developmentally ready to make the change. The following interaction between a four-year-old and an interested adult illustrates this phenomenon (Gleason, 1967):

Child: My teacher holded the baby rabbits and we patted them.

Adult: Did you say your teacher held the baby rabbit?

Child: Yes.

Adult: What did you say that she did?

Child: She holded the baby rabbits and we patted them.

Adult: Did you say she held them tightly?

Child: No. She holded them loose.

Semantics

"How would you differentiate among the following words that a blender manufacturer has printed under the row of buttons: stir, beat, puree, cream, chop, whip, crumb, mix, mince, grate, crush, blend, shred, grind, frappe, liquefy?" (Lindfors, 1987; p. 47). Semantics deals with the subtle shades of meaning that language can convey. Variations in language meanings generally reflect the values and concerns of the culture. For instance, dozens of Arabic words may be dedicated to describing the camel's range of moods and behaviors. The Polynesian language has many words that define variations in the wind; likewise, Inuit languages include many words for snow.

Knowledge of word meaning is stored throughout the brain in a vast biological forest of interconnected neurons, dendrites, and synapses. Beyond culture, children's ongoing personal experience allows them to connect words and meaning. Since words are symbolic labels for objects, events, actions, and feelings, a child may initially call all four-legged animals *kitty*. However, after several firsthand encounters with kitties (with the support of adults who can help label and describe the event) a child will likely develop the concepts and vocabulary to discriminate kitties from doggies, kittens from cats, and eventually Persians from Siamese.

Pragmatics

Sitting in his bouncer, two-month-old Marcus studies his mother's face as she talks to him. In a high-pitched voice, she exaggerates her words in a singsong manner: *Lookeee at Mommeeee. I see baabee Marceee looking at Mommeee.* Baby Marcus appears to mimic her mouth movements and responds to her conversations with smiles, wiggles, and very loud coos. After Marcus quiets, his mother knowingly responds to her baby's comments, *Yes, you're right, Mommeee does love her Marceee-Boy.*

When parent and child engage in singsong conversation of "parentese" and baby vocalizations, the basic conventions of turn-taking are learned, but rarely does the teacher or student realize that a lesson was being taught. Pragmatics deals with the conventions of becoming a competent language user. These include rules on how to engage successfully in conversation with others, such as how to initiate and sustain conversation, how to take turns, when and how to interrupt, how to use cues for indicating subject interest, and how to tactfully change subjects (Otto, 2006).

Pragmatics also refers to the uses of language (spoken and body) to communicate one's intent in real life. The message of a speaker's actual words may be heightened or may even convey the opposite meaning depending on the manner in which the words are delivered. This delivery may include inflection, facial expressions, or body gestures. Take, for example, this statement: *I'm having such a great time.* Imagine that the person who is saying this phrase is smiling easily and widely, with eyes making direct contact with the person with whom she is sharing her time. Now picture the person saying *I'm having such a great time* while sneering and rolling her eyes (see Figure 2.2). Though the words are identical, the intent of the two

The language development process begins when family and caregivers talk to infants.

FIGURE 2.2

Language Is More Than Words

"I'm having such a great time."   "I'm having such a great time."

speakers is obviously completely different. Further, pragmatics deals with an increasing conscious awareness of being able to accomplish goals through the use of language.

As children mature, they are able to use social registers—or the ability to adapt their speech and mannerisms to accommodate different social situations. This level of communicative competence can be observed in children as young as five as they engage in pretend play. During dramatic play children may easily switch roles—baby to parent, student to teacher, customer to waiter—by using the vocabulary, mannerisms, and attitudes that convey the role they wish to play.

In reviewing these linguistic structures—phonology, morphology, syntax, semantics, and pragmatics—it seems amazing that children acquire these components naturally. Parents rarely teach the intricate conventions directly. Instead, children acquire them by listening, imitating, practicing, observing, and interacting with supportive caregivers and peers.

Observing the Development of Children's Language

"One of the most remarkable cognitive achievements of early childhood is the acquisition of language" (Black, Puckett, & Bell, 1992, p. 179). By the time they enter school, most children have mastered the basic structures of language and are fairly accomplished communicators. Though individual variations do occur, this rapid acquisition of language tends to follow a predictable sequence.

This progression will be illustrated in two ways, first with a neurobiological focus on Joel's first two years of life, and then with a social-interactionist perspective that follows Dawn from infancy through kindergarten. Joel and Dawn are the children of educational researchers. Their development is like that of almost every other normal child throughout the world, except that it was documented by their researcher-parents. Dawn's and Joel's parents used a simple calendar-notation procedure to collect information about their children's language development. When Joel's and Dawn's parents reviewed the calendar each morning, new words were recorded. Thus, it became quite easy to document Joel's and Dawn's growth over time. When these busy parents had a moment, they recorded their recollections (vignettes) of an event and dated it. Often, at family celebrations, a video camera was used to record the events of Joel's and Dawn's use of language in great detail. Occasionally, videotapes also documented storytimes. By using the calendar vignettes and the videotapes, Dawn's and Joel's parents were able to marvel at their children's growth and development.

A Biological View of Development

motor skill

Brain-scanning technology, such as positron emission tomography (PET) and functional magnetic resonance imagining (MRI), have allowed scientists to observe and gain a better understanding of how infants' brains function and mature. This section reviews brain growth during the first two years of life. This information will be brought to life by observing Joel from birth through his second birthday. It is important to note that Joel's skills do not automatically develop at a certain point in brain maturation; but without a particular level of neural growth, Joel would not be able to accomplish his goals. Joel's development is a dynamic interaction of his intentions, muscle tone and coordination, and neural readiness. The information about brain development comes from several sources, including Golinkoff & Hirsh-Pasek (1999), Shore (1997), Lock (1993), Cowley (1997), Sporns and Tononi (1994), and Bradshaw and Rogers (1993). At birth, the human brain is remarkably unfinished. Most of the 100 billion neurons, or brain cells, are not yet connected. In fact, there are only four regions of the brain that are fully functional at birth, including the brain stem (which controls respiration, reflexes, and heartbeat) and the cerebellum (which controls the newborn's balance and muscle tone). Likewise, infants' sensory skills are rudimentary; for instance, newborns can only see objects within 12 to 18 inches of their faces. Still, newborns are able to distinguish between faces and other objects, and they recognize the sound of their parents' voices. Grace and Dan Bass have contributed Joel's case study to our text.

Right from the start, Joel was physically active. He spent his waking time swinging his arms, kicking his legs, practicing tongue movement, and strengthening his lungs by crying. There were subtle differences in his cries, which his mommy and daddy learned to recognize. There were cries associated with anger or frustration, such as when he hiccuped uncontrollably or couldn't find his thumb to suck. Coos of contentment were often heard when he cuddled with his parents and "ahs," which were sighs when he seemed particularly comfortable.

During the first month of life, the number of neural synapses or connections increase twenty times to more than 1,000 trillion. These neural connections are developed through daily verbal and physical interactions that the infant shares with parents, siblings, and other caregivers. Daily routines such as feeding and bathing reinforce and strengthen particular synapses, while neural networks that are not stimulated will eventually wither away in a process called neural pruning.

Joel began to socialize with people other than his parents as soon as he was born. There were always new faces peering down at him in his bassinet, new arms cuddling him, and new fingers for him to grasp. Joel seemed to scrutinize everything around him, and each new person he met commented on his alertness.

As the neuromuscular and sensory systems of the brain mature, babies begin to gain some control over their bodies. Motor control begins at the head and works downward (cephalocaudal) and from the center of body outward (proximodistal). At this time, babies are likely to reach their hands and kick their feet toward close objects.

Babies carefully observe parents, siblings, and other caregivers and often mimic the tongue and mouth movements they see. Babies also experiment with the range of new sounds they can make. These trills and coos are also bids for attention, as most babies have begun to make simple cause-and-effect associations, such as crying equals Mom's attention.

Throughout his infancy, Joel's parents sang to him. They played lullabies for him while he slept and talked to him during bath time. Joel kicked his feet and smiled to let them know that this pleased him.

During the second month, Joel's vocalizations grew, as his tongue became more adept and flexible. He frequently sought his parents' attention by adding stress to his "ehs." Multisyllable sounds, such as "eh-ah," "ey-ere," and "eh-um-mum" began. The "mmm" sound was especially dominant.

The cerebral cortex represents 70 percent of the brain and is divided into two hemispheres. Each hemisphere has four lobes—the parietal, occipital, temporal, and frontal. Each of these lobes has numerous folds, which mature at different rates as the chemicals that foster brain development are released in waves. This sequential development explains, in part, why there are optimum times for physical and cognitive development. For instance, at approximately three months, neural connections within the parietal lobe (object recognition and eye–hand coordination), the temporal lobe (hearing and language), and the visual cortex have begun to strengthen and fine-tune. This development allows babies' eyes to focus on objects that are more than two feet away from their faces. This new ability allows babies to recognize themselves in a mirror and begin to visually discern who's who.

> During his third and fourth months, Joel consistently responded to his parents with smiles and a face full of expression and recognition. His eyes widened and almost glowed when he was happy, and his laughing became more defined. Joel often greeted his parents with new and unique sounds that he created when he played with the shape of his mouth. Joel could deliberately alter his voice to become terse and choppy and now made raspberry sounds—an interesting combination of lips, tongue, drool, and exhaled breath.

The human brain triples its birth weight within the first three years of a child's life. This change is caused as neurons are stimulated and synapse connections increase, as the message-receiving dendrite branches grow larger and heavier. In addition, the long axons over which sensory messages travel gradually develop a protective coating of a white, fatty substance called myelin. Myelin insulates the axons and makes the transmission of sensory information more efficient. Myelineation occurs at different times in different parts of the brain. This process seems to coincide with the emergence of various physical skills and cognitive abilities. For instance, the neuromuscular development during the first four months of life is dramatic. Within the first four months, helpless infants develop the muscle tone and coordination that allows them to turn over at will. Babies develop a sense of balance and better eye–hand coordination as neural connections in the cerebellum and parietal lobe strengthen. This allows most six-month-old babies to sit upright with adult support and to successfully grasp objects within their reach. The ability to hold and inspect interesting items gives babies a lot to "talk" about.

> During his fifth and sixth months, Joel's laughter was more exuberant and he responded to pleasurable situations with squeals of delight. A new sound, "hmmm, hmmmm," uttered with some intensity, let his parents know that he wanted something. Joel chuckled when he played on his tummy and rolled over at will. These new physical achievements allowed him to observe and explore more of his world. During these activities, he made singsong noises and produced an extended "ahhhh" in a rattling growl. Other sounds at this time included loud screams, shrills, "ummmmm," "uh-uh-uh," and rasping his voice while breathing. Joel also began to use nonverbal actions as he shook his head from side to side in a negative fashion, as a response to spoken questions.

Between six and seven months, the brain has already created permanent neural networks that recognize the sounds of a child's native language(s) or dialect. Next, babies begin to distinguish syllables, which soon enables them to detect word boundaries (McNealy, Mazziotta, & Dapretto, 2006). Prior to this, *doyouwantyourbottle?* was a pleasant tune, but was not explicit communication. After auditory boundaries become apparent, babies will hear distinct words: *Do/you/want/your/BOTTLE?*

As sounds become words that are frequently used in context to label a specific object, the acquisition of word meaning begins. At this stage of development, babies usually recognize and have cognitive meaning for words such as bottle, mama, and daddy. Their receptive or listening vocabulary grows rapidly, though it will take a few more months before their expressive or oral language catches up.

> It is interesting to note that Joel's parents speak with wonderful southern accents. These sounds became a part of Joel's language development. "Bwatuh, bwatuh, bwatuh . . ." was Joel's first echolalia or wordlike sound. Joel uttered this often in a singsong conversationlike manner. In addition, Joel made streams of sound—"dadadada," "undat, undat," "um wah wah," "ba bow bow"—and followed these multisyllable sounds with screams and high squeals.

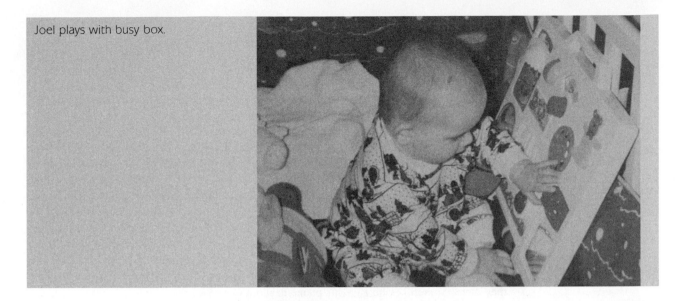

Joel plays with busy box.

Joel also observed social conventions; for instance, when his picture was taken, he made waving motions and occasionally exaggerated his smile into an extreme grimace. To seek his parents' attention, he began to produce a fake coughing sound. Joel's increased eye–hand coordination and manual dexterity allowed him to put everything he could reach into his mouth.

From about the eighth to the ninth month, the hippocampus becomes fully functional. Located in the center of the brain, the hippocampus is part of the limbic system. The hippocampus helps to index and file memories, and as it matures, babies are able to form memories. For instance, babies can now remember that when they push the button on the busy box it will squeak. At this point, babies' ability to determine cause and effect and remember words greatly increases.

By nine months, Joel was able to pull himself up to a standing position in his crib, crawled everywhere, and climbed on anything in his path. Joel enjoyed looking at himself in mirrors and always kissed his reflections. During bath time he splashed a lot, practically drenching his parents and anything next to the tub. Joel was proud of all his accomplishments, particularly the splashing!

At ten months, Joel could pull himself up to a standing position while holding on to the coffee table, but just as soon as he was standing, he would ease himself down to the floor. He practiced this up-and-down feat repeatedly. Joel developed a great fascination with toys with wheels. He pushed a large plastic fire truck about the house, making engine sounds as he went. Between "furniture cruising" and crawling, Joel was mobile enough to get into things that warranted extra attention, like daddy's coffee, mommy's purse, electrical cords, and outlets. He also began to open and close doors, including the glass stereo doors and mommy's jewelry box. For Joel's safety, the house now had to be childproofed. During all this exploration, Joel jabbered continuously, "yayayayaya."

Joel developed an intense interest in books; he enjoyed picking them up and looking at them alone, as well as with others. He made happy, loud noises as he worked to turn the thick pages by himself. At this time, Joel's favorite book was *Pat the Bunny,* and he liked to interact with each page. As he "read" this book with his mommy or daddy, he called out, "rar rar rar."

At the end of the first year, the prefrontal cortex, the seat of forethought and logic, forms synapses at a rapid rate. In fact, at age one, the full cortex consumes twice as much energy as an adult brain. This incredible pace continues during the child's first decade of life. The increased cognitive capacity and physical dexterity stimulates curiosity and exploration and a deep desire to understand how things work. Neural readiness, in combination with countless hours of sound play and verbal exchanges with loving caregivers, allows most children to begin speaking their first words.

Joel's first birthday marked other firsts—his first two teeth and his first steps. Joel loved squeezing into hidden crevices, playing a version of hide-and-seek. He enjoyed his dolls and stuffed animals and squealed with happiness when he hugged them. His oral language was developing slowly but surely.

At thirteen months, "blahdee" was the word/sound Joel used for *daddy,* and he used this word frequently. He continued to hide in small, tucked-away places, particularly under the computer desk. He also produced new strings of sounds, such as "ooh-blad-day-day-doo" and consistently responded to the request "come here" with "day-bah." During this time, Joel displayed word-like sounds, called vocables when he became fascinated with the telephone. He chattered and chattered on his play phone for long periods of time, even laughing during each conversation as if he had heard something funny. His vocalizations were conversationlike sounds and phrases, except for an initial greeting of "Heeey!" and the final "Bye." His relatives were aware of Joel's phone passion, so they sent him more play phones for various holidays. All of these phones were very important to Joel, and he always knew where they were. Sometimes he gave his phone to mom or dad so they could talk. These pretend conversations were fun for both Joel and his parents. His parents noted, however, that when his grandparent called and wanted to speak to Joel, he held the phone and listened in complete silence.

During his fourteenth and fifteenth months, Joel became much more interested in simple mechanics, such as swinging doors open and shut, rolling toys across the floor, and fitting belt buckles together. Balls, tractors, and trucks were great toys, but it was the remote controls for the television and satellite receiver that replaced phones as Joel's new play obsession. He began screeching when he wanted something, and he wanted the remote controls quite often. His serious devotion to the remotes became quite a nuisance for his parents as he delighted in turning the TV off and on and changing channels. Often, when he worked the TV controls, he would say "yah dad-dey." As he became more and more occupied with control buttons on all electronic devices in his home, he developed a preference for grown-up controls over baby electronic toys. Joel also began some teasing behaviors. He would pretend to hand something to his parents then snatch his hand back as they reached for it.

One of the most interesting features of Joel's language development from one year to eighteen months was that it was inconsistent and unpredictable. At about sixteen months, Joel began saying, with perfect enunciation, the word "everyday." He accentuated each syllable of this word and used it correctly in response to some statement or question. However, Joel only used this word for two weeks. Another instance of his verbal command occurred one evening as Joel and his daddy were playing. Joel picked up a book, handed it to his daddy, and said, "Read this." His daddy almost fainted, and his mommy was very excited and optimistic about this phrase that held meaning for his parents. However, it was the last time he used this phrase for several months. Another clearly spoken, context-appropriate, but one-time-only expression emerged: "It's hot in here. Let's go outside." Between fifteen and sixteen months Joel brought book after book to his parents. As they read, he pored over each detail. He wanted everything on the page to be named and discussed. When they stopped reading, he cried and fussed and sometimes threw the books if they tried to distract him. His parents wisely purchased baby books with thick, indestructible cardboard pages.

By eighteen months neural synapses have increased and strengthened and are beginning to transmit information quite efficiently; hence most toddlers begin to experience a language "explosion." Brain-imaging technology clearly reveals that the full cortex is involved in processing language. During this time children are able to learn as many as twelve words a day. Linguists call this phenomenon *fast mapping.*

Increased neural activity, plus verbal expression and physical skill, also gives rise to greater independence. At this time parents may hear "No!" quite often.

Though Joel could say *mommy* and *daddy,* he began to call his parents by their given names. Friends suggested that if Dan and Grace would call each other mommy and daddy, then Joel would too. However, this plan did not work. Joel's babysitter, friends at church and school, and the neighborhood children called his parents Dan and Grace, so Joel chose to do this also.

Joel's love of books continued. But now, instead of his parents pointing to and labeling everything on each page, they would ask Joel to point to specific characters or objects. Joel also read books to himself. He would sit on the couch with his books beside him, turn the pages, and "read" or "baby talk" about each page.

By nineteen months Joel had developed a stubborn streak. He became uncooperative at times and did not want to take a bath or sit in the shopping cart. He asserted his independence by pretending not to hear what his parents said to him. Sometimes he closed his eyes and turned his head away. Other times he flung himself on the floor and yelled, "NOOOOOO." His oral language continued to develop. If his mommy asked him if he was ready to go to bed, he would reply "nuht nuht"; when he fell, he muttered, "dab uh oh"; and when he saw a baby, he would say "uhh baby." Long strings of baby talk words began to flow from his lips, such as "dat ah kay, dat ah oh ee yah aye ah bladla beel cuh cuh a ta ah yel bloo day go go ich ah!"

During the next month, Joel's speech became much clearer. If he needed something, he muttered "ah nee," and if he wanted something, he said, "ah ownt." A passing tractor would immediately cause Joel to exclaim, "dat tractor!" If he wanted to know what something was he inquired, "ah is?" When he knew something his parents were telling him, he would interject, "ah no." Joel also became quite adapt at following simple requests; for example, when his parents asked him to get his favorite book, *Jamberry* (by Bruce Degen), Joel could go to the bookshelf, find the book, and bring it to them.

Though he loved changing channels, Joel did not seem interested in watching television. When he was about twenty-one months old, Joel's babysitter casually remarked that Joel had started to watch episodes of *Rugrats* and *Blue's Clues* with her four-year-old daughter. The babysitter mentioned that Joel would sometimes watch *Blue's Clues* for up to twenty minutes at a time. As a result of this conversation, Joel's mommy began to turn on *Barney* and *Elmo* to see what would happen. Indeed, Joel watched these programs but in an active way. Instead of sitting, he was up pointing and naming objects and characters on the screen, sometimes with real words and often with baby talk.

At twenty-two months, Joel pointed to each of the figures in his book, asking, "ah is?" which meant that he wanted his parents to name the objects. His parents were amazed at the minute details that caught Joel's eye, especially when he noticed something new after looking at the same books hundreds of times. For example, Joel noticed a little lighthouse in the top corner of a seascape or a ladybug walking on a small leaf at the bottom of a page. (See More About 2.2.)

<table>
<tr><td>MORE ABOUT
2.2</td><td>

Shared Visual Attention and Early Language Development

Wha dat? asked fifteen-month-old Briar, while pointing her finger at an elephant at the zoo. Her mother pointed to the elephant also and replied, That's an elephant, Briar. Isn't he big!

This scene, though quite common, is extraordinary. Young children across the world point and through various means ask parents/caregivers to label objects in their environment; typically most adults (or older siblings) oblige. Psychologists call this human event *shared visual attention,* and it appears to be necessary for children to develop vocabulary (Flom, Deak, Phill, & Pick, 2003; Namy & Waxman, 2000).

In research studies conducted by Amanda Woodward (2002) and her colleagues, young children were tested in two conditions. In both conditions, researchers introduced an unknown object and gave it a nonsense name. In the first condition, the researcher and child shared a joint visual gaze at the object while the researcher labeled it. In the second condition, the same child was introduced to another new object, but the researcher looked away while labeling the object. Later in the day the child was asked to locate the object from a group of similar objects. Results showed that children were quickly able to correctly identify and locate objects that were introduced in the first condition (joint visual gaze) but had difficulty identifying objects that were introduced in the second condition. These findings suggest that children need the support of others in highly specific ways to learn new vocabulary. In other words, the child and adult need to share a visual "embrace" when the object is labeled.

</td></tr>
</table>

At two years of age, most children have nimble fingers and are sturdy on their feet. Though they are generally aware of cause and effect, they are still unable to foresee potential problems. In other words, children's physical abilities may exceed their common sense. By this time, most children are able to use language to communicate their needs and accomplish their goals.

> Though he did not take his first step until his first birthday, at age two, Joel was coordinated and independent. He could go up and down steps with ease, jump from high places, run very fast without falling, climb, and get whatever he wanted by pushing furniture, using it as a ladder. Joel liked to mimic his parents. He worked on the computer and could turn it on and use the mouse, helped fold clothes and unload the dishwasher, and immediately held out his hands so that the blessing could be given when he sat down at the dinner table.
>
> At age two, Joel experienced an oral language explosion. He said many new words every day and attempted more words that still weren't perfected. Joel used sentences frequently, including "Mama, that a truck"; "That a big, big, truck"; "Are you sure?"; "Are you sure you sure?"; "I want juice (chips, truck, etc.)."

Joel's development is a wonderful example of the interaction of how the body and brain stimulate interactive development.

A Social-Interactionist View of Development

Dawn's development is viewed from a social-interactionist perspective. Her development is described in linguistic terminology. In her five-year case study, we observe how her parents and caregivers stimulate and support her efforts and how she uses language to gain attention and to accomplish her goals at a young age.

> During the first month of Dawn's life, most of her oral communication consisted of crying, crying, crying. The greatest challenge her parents faced was perceiving and interpreting the variations in her cries. It took about three weeks for them to understand that Dawn's intense, high-pitched cry meant she was hungry. Dawn's short, throaty, almost shouting cries indicated a change of diaper was necessary, while the whining, fussy cry, which occurred daily at about dinnertime, meant she was tired.
>
> During the second to third months after Dawn's birth, she began to respond to her parents' voices. When spoken to, Dawn turned her head, focused her eyes on her mother or father, and appeared to listen and watch intensely. Her parents and grandparents also instinctively began using an exaggerated speech pattern called parentese (often called baby talk). Until recently, parents were cautioned against using baby talk or parentese with their infants because it was believed to foster immature forms of speech. However, recent studies have demonstrated that this slowed-down, high-pitched, exaggerated, repetitious speech actually seems to facilitate a child's language development. Current research suggests that exaggerated speech allows babies many opportunities to observe how sounds are made and thus learn how to control their own vocal apparatus (Cowley, 1997; Field, Woodson, Greenberg, & Cohen, 1982; Healy, 1994; Shore, 1997). During these baby talk conversations, Dawn would often move her mouth, lips, and eyes, mimicking the facial movements of her parents. At the beginning of the fourth month, Dawn discovered her own voice. She delighted in the range of sounds she could make and sometimes chuckled at herself. At this point, Dawn (and most normally developing infants) could make almost all of the vowel and consonant sounds. She cooed and gurgled endlessly, joyfully experimenting with phonemic variations, pitch, and volume. When spoken to, she often began her own stream of conversation, called "sound play," which would parallel the adult speaker. At age six months, Dawn was also becoming an expert at imitating tone and inflection. For example, when her mother yelled at the cat for scratching the furniture, Dawn used her own vocal skills to yell at the poor animal, too.
>
> During her sixth month, Dawn's muscle strength, balance, and coordination gave her greater independent control over her environment as she mastered the fine art of crawling and stumble-walking around furniture. These physical accomplishments stimulated further cognitive development, as she now had the ability to explore the world under her own power.

At seven months, Dawn's babbling increased dramatically. However, the sounds she produced now began to sound like words, which she would repeat over and over. Though "Mmmmaaa Mmmmaaa" and "Dddaaaddaaa" sounded like "Mama" and "Dada," they were still not words with a cognitive connection or meaning.

In her eighth month, Dawn's babbling began to exhibit conversationlike tones and behaviors. This pattern of speech is called vocables. While there were still no real words in her babble, Dawn's vocalizations were beginning to take on some of the conventions of adult conversations, such as turn-taking, eye contact, and recognizable gestures. These forms of prelanguage are playlike in nature, being done for their own sake rather than a deliberate use of language to communicate a need or accomplish a goal.

At approximately nine months, Dawn first used real, goal-oriented language. As her father came home from work, she ran to him shouting in an excited voice, "Dada, Dada," and held her arms up to him. Dawn's accurate labeling of her father and her desire to be picked up were deliberate actions that revealed that Dawn was using language to accomplish her objectives.

Between age nine months and her first birthday, Dawn's expressive (speaking) and receptive (listening and comprehending) vocabulary grew rapidly. She could understand and comply with dozens of simple requests, such as "Bring Mommy your shoes" or the ever favorite label-the-body game, "Where is Daddy's nose?" In addition, Dawn's command of nonverbal gestures and facial expressions were expanding from waving "bye-bye" to scowling and saying "no-no" when taking her medicine. In addition, holophrastic words began to emerge, in which one word carried the semantic burden for a whole sentence or phrase. For example, "Keeths," while holding her plastic keys, purse, and sunglasses meant "I want to go for a ride," or "iith" meant "I want some ice." Dawn also used overgeneralized speech, in which each word embraced many meanings. For instance, "doll" referred not only to her favorite baby doll but to everything in her toy box, and "jooth" stood for any type of liquid she drank.

From one year to eighteen months, Dawn's vocabulary expanded quickly. Most of her words identified or labeled the people, pets, and objects that were familiar and meaningful to her. Clark's (1983) research suggests that young children between one and six will learn and remember approximately nine new words a day. This ability to relate new words to preexisting internalized concepts, then remember and use them after only one exposure, is called *fast mapping* (Carey, 1979).

Because chronological age is not a reliable indicator of language progression, linguists typically describe language development by noting the number of words used in a sentence, which is called *mean length of utterance* (MLU). At this point, Dawn was beginning to use two-word sentences such as "Kitty juuth." Linguists call these two- and three-word sentences "telegraphic speech," as they contain only the most necessary words to convey meaning. However, these first sentences may have many interpretations; for instance, Dawn's sentence "Kitty juuth" might mean "The kitty wants some milk," or "The kitty drank the milk," or even "The kitty stuck her head in my cup and drank my milk." Obviously the context in which the sentence was spoken helped her parents to better understand the intent or meaning of her communication.

Around age eighteen months to two years, as Dawn began speaking in sentences more frequently, the use of syntax became apparent. "No shoes" with a shoulder shrug meant she couldn't find her shoes, but "Shoes, no!" said with a shaking head meant Dawn did not want to put on her shoes.

Though Dawn's vocabulary grew, her phonemic competence did not always reflect adult standards. Many of her words were clearly pronounced (kitty, baby), while others were interesting phonemic attempts or approximations (bise for bike, Papa for Grandpa, bawble for bottle); yet others were her own construction (NaNe for Grandma). At this age, most children are unable to articulate perfectly the sounds of adult speech. Rather, they simplify the adult sounds to ones they can produce. Sometimes this means they pronounce the initial sound or syllable of a word (whee for wheel), and at other times, they pronounce only the final sound or syllable (ees for cheese). Another common feature is temporary regression, meaning that they may pronounce a word or phrase quite clearly, then later produce a shortened, less mature version. This, too, is a normal language developmental phase for all children. Thus it is important that parents accept their child's language and not become overly concerned with correcting their pronunciation.

Likewise, children's early attempts to use sentences need thoughtful support, not critical correction. Parents can best support their child's attempts to communicate through extensions and expansions. Extensions include responses that incorporate the essence of a child's sentence but transform it into a well-formed sentence. For example, when Dawn said, "ree stor-ee," her father responded, "Do you want me to read the story book to you?" When parents and caregivers use extensions, they model appropriate grammar and fluent speech and actually help to extend a child's vocabulary.

When parents use expansions, they gently reshape the child's efforts to reflect grammatically appropriate content. For example, when Dawn said, "We goed to Diseelan," instead of correcting her ("We don't say goed, we say went"), her mother expanded Dawn's language by initially confirming the intent of Dawn's statement while modeling the correct form, "Yes, we went to Disneyland."

The adaptations parents make when talking to young children—such as slowing the rate of speech, using age-appropriate vocabulary, questioning and clarifying the child's statements, and extensions and expansions—occur in all cultures. These early interactions with children and the gradual and building support is called parentese—or more gender specifically, motherese and fatherese. When parents use this form of support, they are actually helping their children gain communicative competence and confidence (Vygotsky, 1962; White, 1985). Between the ages of two and three years, Dawn's language had developed to the point where she could express her needs and describe her world to others quite well. In addition to using pronouns, she began to produce grammatical inflections, "-ing," plurals, past tense, and possessive inflections.

Dawn also loved finger plays such as "The Itsy, Bitsy, Spider" and "Grandma's Glasses"; poems such as "This Little Pig"; and songs such as "Jingle Bells," "Yankee Doodle," and the "Alphabet Song." She was also beginning to count and echo-read with her parents when they read her favorite stories, like *The Three Little Pigs*. Dawn would "huff and puff and blow your house down" as many times as her parents would read the story.

From ages three to five years, Dawn had become a proficient language user. She could make requests ("Please, may I have some more cake?") and demands ("I need this, now!") depending on her mood and motivation. She could seek assistance ("Can you tell me where the toys are?") and demonstrate concern ("What's the matter, Mama?"). She sought information about her world ("Why is the moon round one time and just a grin sometimes?").

Dawn's language development, though completely normal, is also a human miracle. Language plays a central role in learning, and a child's success in school depends to very large degree on his or her ability to speak and listen. Dawn's case study also confirms the critical role social interaction plays in language development. Thus, in the following section, we provide more information about ways parents and caregivers may support a child's language acquisition.

What Is Normal Language Development?

While the process of learning to talk follows a predictable sequence, the age at which children say their first word may vary widely from one child to another. Developmental guidelines describe specific behaviors and delineate the age at which most children demonstrate this language skill. This type of information helps parents and physicians anticipate normal physical and cognitive growth. While physical maturation is easy to observe, cognitive development is less obvious. Fortunately, children's language development provides one indication that their cognitive abilities are developing normally. In Table 2.1, we present the average ages for language development. While most children demonstrate language skills well within the normal age range, some do not. If a child's language is delayed more than two months past the upper age limits, caregivers should seek medical guidance, as delays may indicate problems (Shevell, 2005; Copeland & Gleason, 1993). Early identification of potential problems leads to appropriate intervention. While helpful, developmental guidelines are not perfect. To determine norms, data must be collected on specific populations. In most cases these data were collected on middle-income Caucasian children born in modern industrial-technological societies. Since this sample does not represent the world's population, the upper and lower age limits of these "universal" norms must be interpreted carefully (Cannella, 2002).

TABLE 2.1 Typical Language Development

About 90 percent of children will develop the following language skills by the ages indicated. If a child does not demonstrate these behaviors by these ages, it is important for parents to seek medical guidance.

Age in Months

0–3
- Communicates mostly through crying, as larynx has not yet descended
- Turns head to the direction of familiar voices
- Is startled by loud or surprising sounds

3–6
- Begins to make cooing sounds to solicit attention from caregivers
- Makes "raspberry" sounds
- Begins to play with voice
- Observes caregiver's face when being spoken to; often shapes mouth in a similar manner

6
- Vocalizes with intonation
- Responds to his or her name
- Responds to human voices without visual cues by turning head and eyes
- Responds appropriately to friendly and angry tones

12
- Uses one or more words with meaning (this may be a fragment of a word)
- Understands simple instructions, especially if vocal or physical cues are given
- Practices inflection
- Is aware of the social value of speech

18
- Has vocabulary of approximately 5–20 words
- Vocabulary made up chiefly of nouns
- Some echolalia (repeating a word or phrase over and over)
- Much jargon with emotional content
- Is able to follow simple commands

24
- Can name a number of objects common to his surroundings
- Is able to use at least two prepositions, such as *in, on, under*
- Combines words into a short sentence (largely noun-verb combinations)
- Approximately two-thirds of what child says should be understandable
- Vocabulary of approximately 150–300 words
- Rhythm, fluency often poor and volume, pitch of voice not yet well-controlled
- Can use pronouns, such as *I, me, you*
- *My* and *mine* are beginning to emerge
- Responds to such commands as "show me your eyes (nose, mouth, hair)"

36
- Is using some plurals and past tenses ("We played a lot.")
- Handles three-word sentences easily ("I want candy.")
- Has approximately 900–1,000 words in vocabulary
- About 90 percent of what child says is understandable
- Verbs begin to predominate, such as "let's go, let's run, let's climb, let's play"
- Understands most simple questions dealing with his environment and activities
- Relates his experiences so that they can be followed with reason
- Able to reason out such questions as "what do you do when you are hungry?"
- Should be able to give his sex, name, age

48
- Knows names of familiar animals
- Names common objects in picture books or magazines

(continued on next page)

| TABLE 2.1 | *(continued)* |

	■ Knows one or more colors and common shapes
	■ Can repeat four digits when they are given slowly
	■ Can usually repeat words of four syllables
	■ Demonstrates understanding of *over* and *under*
	■ Often engages in make-believe
	■ Extensive verbalization as he carries out activities
	■ Understands such concepts as *longer, larger,* when a contrast is presented
	■ Much repetition of words, phrases, syllables, and even sounds
60	■ Can use many descriptive words spontaneously—both adjectives and adverbs
	■ Knows common opposites: *big-little, hard-soft, heavy-light,* etc.
	■ Speech should be completely intelligible, in spite of articulation problems
	■ Should be able to define common objects in terms of use (hat, shoe, chair)
	■ Should be able to follow three commands given without interruptions
	■ Can use simple time concepts: morning, night, tomorrow, yesterday, today
	■ Speech on the whole should be grammatically correct
72	■ Speech should be completely intelligible and socially useful
	■ Should be able to tell a rather connected story about a picture, seeing relationships between objects and happenings
	■ Can recall a story or a favorite video.
	■ Should be able to repeat sentences as long as nine words
	■ Can describe favorite pastimes, meals, books, friends
	■ Should use fairly long sentences and some compound and complex sentences

Factors Contributing to Variations in Rate of Language Acquisition

Since the critical period for language development occurs within the first thirty-six months of a child's life, significant language delay may indicate specific medical or cognitive problems. Beyond medical problems, there are several factors that could modify the rate of normal language production. We review these factors in the following discussion.

Gender Differences

Are there differences in the rate and ways that boys and girls develop language fluency and proficiency? This question reflects another facet of the ongoing nature versus nurture debate. Observational research consistently reveals that a majority of girls talk earlier and talk more than the majority of boys. It is also true that the majority of late talkers are young boys (Healy, 1997; Kalb & Namuth, 1997). However, it is difficult to determine whether differences in the rate of language acquisition are biological or if biological differences are exaggerated by social influences. There is evidence for both views. For example, neurobiological research offers graphic images that illustrate how men's and women's brains process language somewhat differently (Corballis, 1991; Moir & Jessel, 1991). Though this research appears to support nature as the dominant factor in language differences, it is also important to consider how powerful a role nurture plays. Experimental research consistently documents differential treatment of infants based on gender. In other words, men and women tend to cuddle, coo at, and engage in lengthy face-to-face conversations with baby girls. Yet with baby boys, adults are likely to exhibit "jiggling and bouncing" behaviors but are not as likely to engage in sustained face-to-face verbal interactions. Perhaps girls talk earlier and talk more because they receive more language stimulation (Huttenlocher, 1991).

Socioeconomic Level

Numerous studies have long documented the differences in the rate of language acquisition and the level of language proficiency between low and middle socioeconomic families (Hart & Risley, 1995; Morisset, 1995; Walker, Greenwood, Hart, & Carta, 1994). These studies found that children, especially males, from low-income homes were usually somewhat slower to use expressive language than children from middle-income homes. These findings likely reflect social-class differences both in language use in general and in parent–child interaction patterns. For example, Betty Hart and Todd Risley (1995) estimate that by age four, children from professional families have had a cumulative total of 50 million words addressed to them, whereas children from welfare families have been exposed to only 13 million words. The children from professional families have had more than three times the linguistic input than welfare families' children; this gives them a tremendous advantage in language acquisition.

Results of long-term observations of middle-income and lower-income families concluded that all mothers spent a great deal of time nurturing their infants (e.g., touching, hugging, kissing, and holding), but that there were differences in the way mothers verbally interacted with their children. Middle-income mothers spent a great deal more time initiating verbal interactions and usually responded to and praised their infants' vocal efforts. Middle-income mothers were also more likely to imitate their infants' vocalizations. These verbal interactions stimulate neural-synapse networks that foster expressive and receptive language. It is still unclear why lower-income mothers do not engage their children in verbal interactions at the same level as middle-income mothers. The authors of these studies speculate that this may be a reflection of social-class differences in language use in general.

Cultural Influences

The rate of language acquisition may be somewhat different for children of different cultures. Since spoken language is a reflection of the culture from which it emerges, it is necessary to consider the needs verbal language serves in the culture. Communication may be accomplished in other meaningful nonverbal ways (González, Oviedo, & O'Brien de Ramirez, 2001; Bhavnagri & Gonzalez-Mena, 1997).

Likewise, some cultures do not view babies' vocal attempts as meaningful communication. Shirley Brice Heath (1983) describes a community in which infants' early vocalizations are virtually ignored and adults do not generally address much of their talk directly to infants. Many cultures emphasize receptive language, and children listen as adults speak.

Medical Concerns

Beyond gender, socioeconomic, and culture differences, other reasons that children's language may be delayed include temporary medical problems and congenital complications. Estimates of hearing impairments vary considerably, with one widely accepted figure of 5 percent representing the portion of young children with hearing levels outside the normal range. Detection and diagnosis of hearing impairment have become very sophisticated. It is possible to detect hearing loss and evaluate its severity in a newborn child.

Congenital Language Disorders

For most children, learning to communicate is a natural, predictable developmental progression. Unfortunately, some children have congenital language disorders that impair their ability to learn language or use it effectively. The origin of these disorders may be physical or neurological. Examples of physical problems include malformation of the structures in the inner ear or a poorly formed palate. Neurological problems could include dysfunction in the brain's ability to perceive or interpret the sounds of language.

Though the symptoms of various language disorders may appear similar, effective treatment may differ significantly, depending on the cause of the problem. For example, articulation problems caused by a physical malformation of the palate might require reconstructive surgery, while articulation problems caused by hearing impairment might require a combination o

MORE ABOUT 2.3

Typical Pronunciation Development

Three-year-old Annie points to a picture of an elephant and says, "Yes, that's a ella-pant."
Two-year-old Briar sees her favorite TV show and shouts, "It's da Giggles!" (Wiggles).
Two-and-a-half-year-old Robbie asks his grandma, "Gigi, can I have some tandy?" (candy).

Parents both delight in and worry about these darling mispronunciations, which are a normal part of the language development process. Most mispronunciations are usually caused by a combination of children mishearing sounds and misarticulation of new words. Most of these mispronunciations self-correct with maturation.

auditory amplification and speech therapy. Two of the most common symptoms of congenital language disorders are disfluency and pronunciation.

DISFLUENCY. Children with fluency disorders have difficulty speaking rapidly and continuously. They may speak at an abnormal rate—too fast or too slow; in either case, their speech is often incomprehensible and unclearly articulated. The rhythm of their speech may also be severely affected. Stuttering is the most common form of this disorder. Many children may have temporary fluency disruptions or stuttering problems as they are learning to express themselves in sentences. Children who are making a transition to a second language may also experience brief stuttering episodes. It is important for parents or teachers to be patient and supportive, as it may take time to distinguish normal developmental or temporary lapses in fluency from a true pathology. Stuttering may have multiple origins and may vary from child to child. Regardless of cause, recently developed treatment protocols have been effective in helping stutterers. (Dodd & Bradford, 2000).

PRONUNCIATION. Articulation disorders comprise a wide range of problems and may have an equally broad array of causes. Minor misarticulations in the preschool years are usually developmental and will generally improve as the child matures. Occasionally, as children lose their baby teeth, they may experience temporary challenges in articulation. However, articulation problems that seriously impede a child's ability to communicate needs and intentions must be diagnosed. Causes of such problems may include malformation of the mouth, tongue, or palate; partial loss of hearing due to a disorder in the inner ear; serious brain trauma; or a temporary hearing loss due to an ear infection (Copeland & Gleason, 1993; Forrest, 2002).

It is important to remember that some children may simply show delayed language development; this may mean that a child is gaining control over speaking mechanisms at a slower rate than same-age peers or has had limited opportunity to hear speech or interact with others. Children who are learning a second language may also appear to have articulation difficulties when they attempt to use their second language. As we explain in Special Feature 2.1, anyone learning a new phonemic system will experience some difficulty in expressing new sound combinations. "Bilingual children should be assessed in their native language and referred for therapy only if an articulation disorder is present in that language" (Piper, 1993, p. 193). Caregivers and teachers need to be careful not to confuse the normal course of second-language acquisition with speech disorders.

SPECIAL FEATURE 2.1

Young Children's Second-Language Development

Sarah Hudelson and Irene Serna

Have you ever been in a situation where everyone around you is using a language that you don't know? How did you feel when the language around you sounded like gibberish? How did you respond? Were there some strategies that you used to cope? Think about yourself in this kind of situation as you read about young children learning a second language.

Years ago there was concern that young children would be cognitively damaged by such early exposure to two languages, that there would be considerable confusion on the child's part and that normal language development would be delayed (Hakuta, 1986). Recent investigations, however, have made it clear that

SPECIAL FEATURE 2.1 *(continued)*

this is not the case. There is now ample evidence that young children raised from birth with two languages develop language at rates comparable to monolingual children. They begin to use single words and multilingual word combinations at the same time as monolingual children. Young bilingual children develop separate language systems and use them appropriately (Hakuta, 1986). Depending on the frequency of use, one language may develop more fully than the other. It is also common for young bilinguals to borrow words from one language and use them in speaking the other language in order to communicate their intentions. But fluency in two languages is a common occurrence among young children (see Goodz, 1994, for a recent review of research on preschool bilingualism). It is certainly possible that some of the young children in your pre-kindergarten or primary grade classrooms will be bilingual in English and another language.

It is even more probable, however, that your classroom will contain some children whose native language is other than English—Spanish, French, Russian, Polish, Croatian, Arabic, Vietnamese, Chinese, Khmer, Japanese, Urdu, Navajo, Hopi, Apache, to name a few. There are currently millions of young children in this country who are being raised in households where a language other than English is spoken (Waggoner, 1992). Thus, these learners bring to school understandings of what language is, what language can do, what language is for, and how to use language appropriately in their own communities (Lindfors, 1987).

When young speakers of languages other than English enter school, they may be fortunate enough to be placed in bilingual classrooms, where children and adults make use of the native language for learning and where the English language and academic instruction through English are introduced gradually. Or they may find themselves in settings where English is the basic language of the class and of instruction. In either case, children find themselves in the position of acquiring English as a second or additional language (ESL). What this means is that children must develop new ways of expressing themselves, new ways of talking about their experiences, new ways of asking questions, new ways of using language to help them learn. They must also learn to behave appropriately in settings, including school, where the new language is used. This is hard work that involves them in striving both to understand the language around them and to use that language for themselves and with others (Lindfors, 1987; Tabors & Snow, 1994). The perspective on child second-language acquisition that most researchers and educators take is similar to the social-interactionist perspective articulated in Chapter 2. That is, in learning a new language children engage in the creative

construction of the rules of the new language, and this creative construction occurs within the context of multiple social interactions as children use the new language with others (Allen, 1991). The discussion that follows summarizes some essential points about children's ESL acquisition. Most of the understandings presented have been formulated through careful observation of children and teachers in pre-kindergarten and primary grade settings.

Nora, a first-grade, Spanish-speaking child whose acquisition of English was studied by respected researcher Lily Wong Fillmore (1976), provides a good demonstration of the child as creative constructor. Early in first grade, Nora memorized such phrases as "Do you wanna play?" and used them to initiate contact with English-speaking children. Soon she began to use the phrase "How do you do dese?" as a general formula to ask for information and help. After a while she added elements to the formula so that she could ask such questions as: "How do you do dese little tortillas? How do you do dese in English?" Gradually she was able to vary the sentence after the word *you* to produce: "How do you like to be cookie cutter? How do you make the flower? How do you gonna make these?" She was also able to use *did* as in "How did you lost it?" Later still she was able to use *how* in sentences very different from the original formula; for example, "Because when I call him, how I put the number?" (pp. 246–247) These efforts illustrate how Nora, over time, constructed and reconstructed her English to convey her meanings and accomplish her purposes.

Tabors and Snow (1994) have documented a general sequence in young children's ESL acquisition that appears to be fairly common. When they first encounter the new language, many young learners will continue to use their native language when speaking to English speakers. This behavior is often followed by a period when they do not talk at all but instead attempt to communicate nonverbally through gestures, mimes, and cries or whimpers to attract attention. Young ESL learners also have been observed to engage in spectating—paying close attention to the actions and utterances of English speakers (so that they can connect words to activities)—and rehearsing—practicing the new language to, by, and for themselves, repeating words, phrases, and sounds in English at a very low volume. Following the nonverbal period, children begin to use formulaic expressions in English (e.g., "What's that?" "Wanna play?" "I want that." "I don't know." "Gimme!"), which may get them into the action with other children. From formulas, as Nora demonstrated, children gradually begin productive language use, moving beyond memorized utterances and formulaic expressions to creative construction. Although this sequence has been described as if it were discrete

(continued on next page)

and unidirectional, this is not necessarily so for all learners.

There are tremendous individual differences in children's second-language learning. Learners differ in the rate at which they learn the second language. They differ in their willingness to learn English and in their avoidance or nonavoidance of the new language. They differ in the language-learning strategies they use. They differ in whether their stance is more participator or observer. The least successful English learners seem to be those who avoid contact with English speakers and who do not engage with what is going on around them in English (Fillmore, 1976; Saville-Troike, 1988). Some research has suggested that the best ESL learners are those children who are most eager to interact with English speakers, who are most willing to participate and use whatever English they have at a particular point in time, who are risk takers and are not afraid to make mistakes, and who identify with English speakers (Fillmore, 1976; Strong, 1983). However, researchers also have discovered that quiet children who pay close attention to what is going on around them (the careful observer stance) may also be quite effective language learners (Fillmore, 1983; Flanigan, 1988). So not all young children learn a second language in exactly the same way.

What is crucial to children's successful second-language acquisition is the learner's choosing to work at communicating with people who speak the new language. Young ESL learners find themselves in environments where English is used. But they must choose to work at learning the new language; they must want to interact with others in English if acquisition is to occur. Interaction is critical in two ways: (1) it gives learners opportunities to try out the new language to see if they can make themselves understood; and (2) fluent English speakers respond to the learner's efforts, providing both additional language input and a gauge on how well the learner is communicating. This language give and take is critical to continued learning (Ellis, 1985; Tabors & Snow, 1994).

In the ESL setting both adults and other children may act as language teachers for children. Adults tend to modify or adapt their ways of speaking to what they think the ESL learner will understand and respond to. Studies of primary teachers working with ESL learners have reached the following conclusions: As with "baby talk" in native language settings, effective teachers tend to speak more slowly, using clear enunciation, somewhat simplified sentences, and exaggerated intonation. They often use repetitions or restatements of sentences. They also contextualize their speech by using objects and physical gestures so that learners may use nonlinguistic cues to figure out what has been said. Finally, adults make concerted efforts both to encourage the ESL child to talk and to understand what the learner is saying. In their efforts to understand children, adults frequently

expand children's incomplete sentences or extend what they have said (Enright, 1986; Fillmore, 1982, 1983; Washington, 1982). Through all of these provisions of "comprehensible input" (Krashen, 1982), adults are responsive persons with whom to try out the new language.

Fluent English-speaking children are also important language models and teachers for their ESL counterparts. During interactions, English-speaking children may assist their non-English-speaking peers by gesturing, correcting, giving feedback, engaging in language play, and encouraging the second-language learner to talk (Ventriglia, 1982). But children do not make the consistently concerted efforts that adults do to be understood by and to understand ESL learners unless they have been coached to do so (see Tabors & Snow, 1994). They may tire of the teacher role and move away from it more quickly than an adult would. And children do not tend to focus as exclusively on understanding the ESL child as adults do; what is often most important is carrying out whatever activity they happen to be engaged in (Fillmore, 1976; Peck, 1978). But given that children often (but not always) are more interested in interacting with other children than they are with adults, other children provide strong incentives for ESL children to use their developing English and to make themselves understood. The desire to communicate is at the heart of young children's second-language learning.

Earlier we distinguished bilingual from ESL classrooms. In spite of research evidence that speaks to the efficacy of teaching children through their native language, a major issue with regard to non-English-speaking learners has been the role that languages other than English play in children's learning. The commonsense belief that the most efficient way to encourage English language proficiency is to use only English is still adhered to by numbers of early childhood educators (see Fillmore, 1991). This has meant that numbers of Head Start and kindergarten programs have embraced the idea of an early school introduction of, and sometimes school immersion in, English—with the understanding that parents will continue to use their native languages at home so that young children continue to develop linguistic abilities and communicative competence in their home tongues while acquiring English (Tabors & Snow, 1994). Theoretically, this situation should result in young children becoming bilingual, but using their two languages in different settings.

Unfortunately, the reality is that early introduction to English in school has often meant that non-English-speaking children refuse to communicate in their native languages and try to use English exclusively. In a study of the home language practices of more than 300 immigrant preschoolers, Fillmore (1991) discovered that these young learners, whether they were enrolled in bilingual or English-only classrooms, were

SPECIAL FEATURE 2.1 *(continued)*

particularly vulnerable to language loss. The longer they stayed in school, the more they relied on English for communication, even at home. This jeopardized non-English-speaking parents' abilities to interact verbally with their children and socialize them.

Fillmore raises the issue of whether English-language acquisition has to come at the expense of other languages. Her data point out the potentially devastating consequences of children's refusal to speak their native languages. Parents anguish over how to communicate with their children, how to pass on family and community histories, how to transmit cultural expectations, how to discipline them, and so on if they are unable to communicate with them. We believe that not only early childhood educators but all educators, whether bilingual or not, must wrestle with the reality of how to respect and value children's home languages and cultures.

In many important ways, second-language acquisition in young children is quite similar to first-language acquisition. This general statement means that adults working with second-language learners need to focus both on making themselves understood by children and on understanding children and encouraging them to use their new language. Adults need to focus on the learners' communicative intentions, not on the conventionality of their utterances. Adults also need to be sensitive to individual differences in children's rates of second-language learning and accepting of these differences. Children should be encouraged but not forced to use the new language, and children should not be belittled for hesitancy in trying out English. Adults need to recognize that children are learning English even if they are not responding verbally. Adults need to encourage other children who are native speakers of English to have patience with ESL learners and to assist them in their learning. Finally, adults should value the native languages that children bring to school with them and encourage them to continue to use their native languages.

Summary

Children's acquisition of oral language is truly remarkable. By the time they enter kindergarten, most children have mastered the basic structures and components of their native language, all without much stress or effort. How did the information contained in this chapter compare with what you were able to discover about your own first words and early language learning? Which of the four perspectives described above comes closest to your view about children's language development?

To summarize the key points about oral language development, we return to the guiding questions at the beginning of this chapter:

■ *What are the major views on how children's language develops? Which aspects of language development does each view adequately explain?*

Four competing perspectives have been used to explain how children acquire language. The behaviorist perspective emphasizes the important role of reinforcement in helping children learn the sounds, words, and rules of language. This view handily explains the imitative aspects of initial language learning. Nativists stress the importance of children's inborn capacity to learn language and suggest that a portion of the brain is dedicated to language learning. Nativist theory explains how children "invent" their own two- and three-word grammars and overgeneralize rules for past tense ("He goed to the store") and plural ("I saw two mouses today!"). The social-interactionist perspective emphasizes the importance of both environmental factors and children's innate predisposition to make sense out of language and use it for practical purposes. According to this view, children learn about language by using it in social situations. The social-interactionist view highlights the role of parental support in language acquisition. Finally, new technology has allowed scientists to observe how the brain perceives, interprets, and expresses language. These developments have led to a new perspective on children's language learning, the neurobiological view, which complements the three earlier views on language development. This perspective explains how the structural development of the brain is related to language acquisition. It helps explain why children's experiences during infancy have such a crucial effect on later language learning.

■ *What are the major components of language?*

The major components of language are (1) phonology—the sounds that make up a language; (2) morphology—the meaning-bearing units of language, including words and affixes; (3) syntax—the rules for ordering words into sentences; (4) semantics—the shades of meaning that words convey; and (5) pragmatics—the social rules that enable language to accomplish real-life purposes.

■ *How does the structure of an infant's brain develop? How does this structural development affect language acquisition?*

At birth, the human brain is remarkably unfinished. Most of the 100 billion neurons or brain cells are not yet connected. During the first month of life, the numbers of neural synapses or connections increases twenty times to more than 1,000 trillion. As a child matures, the actual number of neurons remains stable; however, the number of synapse connections increases, and the message-receiving dendrite branches grow larger and heavier. At age one, the full cortex consumes twice as much energy as an adult brain. This neural readiness, in combination with countless hours of sound play and verbal exchanges with loving caregivers, allows most children to begin speaking their first words at this age.

By eighteen months, neural synapses have increased and strengthened and are beginning to transmit information efficiently. Hence most toddlers begin to experience a language explosion, particularly in the areas of vocabulary and syntax. During this time, children are able to learn as many as twelve words a day. Thus, the neurobiological perspective reveals how the rapid development of the brain during the first few years of life makes it possible for children to acquire language so quickly and efficiently. This perspective also explains why the first thirty-six months are a critical period for language development.

■ *What factors affect children's rate of language acquisition?*

While language development follows a predictable sequence, the rate at which children acquire language varies tremendously. Gender, socioeconomic level, and cultural influences all can affect the rate of language acquisition. A child's language learning can also be impeded by illnesses, such as otitis media, and by a variety of congenital problems of a physical and/or neurological nature. Parents and caregivers are cautioned to seek a medical diagnosis if language development is significantly delayed, as early identification and treatment can often avoid irreparable disruption of the language acquisition process.

■ *How does children's acquisition of a second language compare with their first language acquisition? What should adults do to make it easier for children to learn English as a second language?*

In many ways, second-language acquisition in young children is similar to their acquisition of the first language. In learning a new language, children engage in the creative construction of the rules of the new language, and this creative construction occurs within the context of multiple social interactions as children use the new language with others.

Adults working with second-language learners need to focus both on making themselves understood by children and encouraging these children to use their new language. Adults need to focus on the learners' communicative intentions, not on the conventionality of their utterances. Children should be encouraged but not forced to use the new language, and children should not be belittled for hesitancy in trying it. Adults need to recognize that children are learning English even if they are not responding verbally. Adults need to encourage other children who are native speakers of English to have patience with ESL learners and to assist them in their learning. Finally, adults should value the native languages that children bring to school with them and encourage them to continue to use their native languages.

LINKING KNOWLEDGE TO PRACTICE

1. Interview two parents and two early childhood teachers regarding how they believe children learn language. Consider which theory of language acquisition best matches each interviewee's beliefs.

2. Interview a school nurse or health care aide about the numbers of children she or he sees who are affected by illnesses and congenital problems. From the health care worker's perspective, what effect do these medical problems have on children? How often should children be screened for auditory acuity? If a family has limited financial recourses, what agencies can provide medical services?

3. Observe a second-language learner in a preschool or day care setting. Does the second-language learner comprehend some of the talk that is going on in the classroom? How does the child communicate with other children? How does the teacher support the child's second-language acquisition? Are other children helping? Does the second-language learner have any opportunities to use his or her native language?

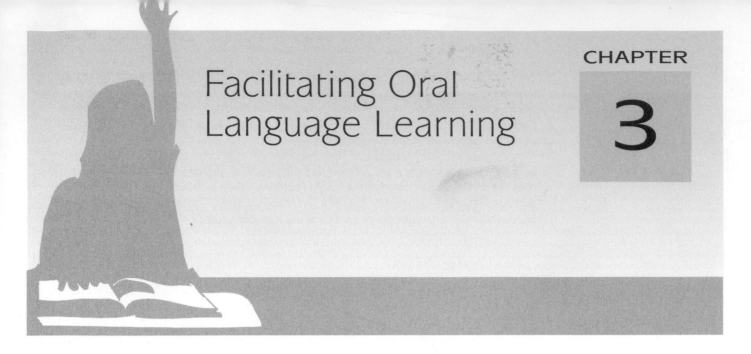

Facilitating Oral Language Learning

Four-year-old Evan, from Arizona, was visiting his grandmother in Vermont during the Christmas holiday. Upon opening the drapes one morning, he viewed snow-covered trees and fields. Evan gasped, "Grammie, who spilled all the sugar?" His grandmother responded, "Evan, that's very clever. It sure looks like sugar. Actually, it's snow."

Clearly, Evan's unfamiliarity with snow didn't prevent him from drawing a clever comparison. His grandmother responded by first showing appreciation for Evan's deduction and then providing the correct word, *snow.* Evan had a great opportunity to learn about the qualities of snow through conversations with his parents, grandparents, and older sister as they played together in the snow. During these adventures, they offered appropriate words for and information about all the new sights, sounds, tastes, smells, and feelings. By the end of the week, Evan knew the difference between wet and powder snow. He made snow angels, helped build a snowman and snow fort, engaged in a snowball war, and had an exhilarating ride on a sled. The new experiences he shared with older and more snow-experienced language users allowed Evan to build new vocabulary and cognitive understandings.

Chapter 2 discussed how infants and young children learn their native language through complex social interactions with parents, siblings, and other caregivers. These individuals are essentially a child's first and most important teachers. Throughout the preschool years, the family plays a significant role in helping children become accomplished language users. In this chapter, we examine the talk that goes on in homes and describe ways parents can support and enrich language development. Next, we discuss the many ways teachers can create learning environments that invite the types of rich oral interactions that promote language acquisition and enhance learning in all areas of the curriculum.

BEFORE READING THIS CHAPTER, THINK ABOUT. . .

- Your home language environment when you were a young child. Did you engage in lengthy conversations with your parents and siblings? Did you have an appreciative audience when you told stories about your own experiences? Did your family discuss the videos/DVDs/television shows that you watched?
- The conversations that took place in your classroom when you were in school. Were these mainly teacher-centered exchanges in which you and your classmates responded to questions asked by the teacher, or did you have the opportunity to engage in two-way conversations with the teacher and other students?

■ Sharing or show-and-tell. What did you like about this activity? Was there anything that you did not like about it?

■ The make-believe play you engaged in when you were a child. What were some of the favorite roles and themes that you acted out during this play?

FOCUS QUESTIONS

■ How can parents best facilitate their children's oral language development?

■ What is the initiation, response, evaluation (IRE) pattern of class talk? What problems are associated with this type of discourse? How can teachers provide children with more stimulating conversations in the classroom?

■ How do group activities, learning centers, and dramatic play promote oral language acquisition?

■ What can teachers do to promote language-rich dramatic play?

■ How can sharing or show-and-tell be turned into a valuable oral language activity?

■ How can teachers effectively assess children's oral language development?

■ What can teachers do to optimize oral language experiences for bilingual and second-language learners?

Home Talk: A Natural Context for Learning and Using Language

Evan's family helped him understand and label his new experience with snow. Their language support was natural and was guided by Evan's constant questions: "Why doesn't this snow make a snowball? Why can't I make an angel on this snow?" Evan's learning while he played was nothing new or extraordinary; he has received language support from his parents and sibling from the moment he was born. His parents and older sister intuitively supported his attempts to communicate. When Evan was an infant his parents, like most parents, naturally used parentese. That is, they talked to him in higher-pitched tones, at a slower rate of speech, and with exaggerated pronunciation and lots of repetition of phrases. Parentese helped Evan hear the sounds and words of his native language. Between the age of eighteen months and three years, as Evan's

BOX 3.1	**active listening:** the listener combines the information provided by the speaker with his or her own prior knowledge to construct personal meaning
Definition of Terms	**anecdotal record:** a brief note describing a child's behavior
	checklist: an observation tool that specifies which behaviors to look for and provides a convenient system of checking off when these behaviors are observed
	dramatic play: an advanced form of play in which children take on roles and act out make-believe stories and situations
	initiation, response, evaluation (IRE): a pattern of classroom talk in which the teacher asks a question, a student answers, and the teacher either accepts or rejects that answer and then goes on to ask another question
	metalinguistic awareness: the ability to attend to language forms in and of themselves. For example, a child may notice that two words rhyme with each other
	metaplay language: comments about play itself ("I'll be the mommy, and you be the baby.")
	personal narrative: a story told in the first person about a personal experience
	pretend language: comments that are appropriate for the roles that children have taken in dramatic play. For example, a child pretending to be a baby might say "Waah! Waah!"
	rubric: a scoring tool with a list of criteria that describe the characteristics of children's performance at various proficiency levels
	scaffolding: temporary assistance that parents and teachers give to children to enable them to do things that they cannot do on their own

communicative competence grew, his family intuitively adjusted their verbal responses so that he could easily learn new vocabulary and grammatical structures.

In fact, the most important component of learning language is actually engaging children, even infants, in conversational bouts. In Chapter 2 we discussed how families provide the rich social context necessary for children's language development. The thousands of hours of parent–child interactions from the moment of birth through the preschool years provide the foundation for language. As children acquire language, they are able to share with others what they feel, think, believe, and want. While most children begin to use their expressive vocabulary in the second year of life, research has long documented that children differ in their ability to learn and use new words (Smith & Dickinson, 1994). In an effort to understand what accounts for these differences, researchers Betty Hart and Todd Risley (1995) documented parent and child interactions during the first three years of children's lives. The research team observed forty-two families from different socioeconomic and ethnic backgrounds one hour each month for two-and-a-half years. Their data revealed vast differences in the amount of language spoken to children. Children from welfare homes heard an average of 616 words an hour; children from working-class families heard 1,251 words an hour; while children from professional homes heard 2,153 words per hour! If one thinks of words as dollars, the children from these different socioeconomic homes would have significantly disparate bank accounts. Further, this long-term study revealed that early language differences had a lasting effect on children's subsequent language accomplishments both at age three and at age nine. In other words, talk between adults and children early in life makes a significant difference. To look at an example of how this language difference begins to multiply, observe the following interaction between three parents and their babies, regarding preparing to eat a meal.

Mom 1: Okay, Crystal, let's eat.

Mom 2: Okay, Paulie, it's time to eat our lunch. Let's see what we are having? Yes, let's have carrots.

Mom 3: Okay, Teryl, it's lunchtime. Are you hungry? Mommy is so hungry! Let's see what we have in the refrigerator today. What is this? It's orange. Could it be peaches? Could it be apricots? Let's see!! See the picture on the jar? That's right, it's carrots.

Unfortunately, many parents do not realize how important these verbal interactions or conversations are to helping children learn to talk and build vocabulary (Rhodes, Enz, & LaCount, 2006).

Encouraging Personal Narratives

Evan's family played a vital role in helping him interpret, label, and recall his new experiences with snow. Back in Arizona, Evan had many stories to tell his teacher and playmates at preschool. For the next several months, each time he spoke with his grandparents, he relived his snow-day tales. The stories, or personal narratives, that Evan told helped him make sense of this new experience, broadened his vocabulary, and reinforced his expressive language skills. Likewise, each time Evan told the story about how the snowball he threw at his sister knocked off the snowman's nose and made his dad laugh, he deepened his memory of the event.

Children's personal narratives are a window into their thinking. Their language also reveals how they use current knowledge to interpret new experiences. Evan's first interpretation of a snowy field was to relate it to a recent incident with a broken sugar bowl. These verbal expressions of new mental constructions can be both fascinating and humorous. Likewise children's personal narratives offer insight into their language development and overall intellectual, social, and emotional growth (Dodici, Draper, & Peterson, 2003).

Though children instinctively know how to put experiences, feelings, and ideas into story form, parents and caregivers can encourage their children's language development by offering many storytelling opportunities and attentively listening while children share their accounts of events (Canizares, 1997). Though nothing can replace quiet and private time to listen to children, many working parents report that they use the time in the car, bus, or subway going to and from day care and/or errands to listen carefully to their children.

Reading storybooks builds early vocabulary.

Children often share what they know or have learned in story form. This is because the human brain functions narratively—for most of us it is much easier to understand and remember concepts when we are given information in story form rather than as a collection of facts. Since the human brain retains information more efficiently in story form, parents can explain new information using stories. For example, when five-year-old Tiffany wanted to know how to tie her shoelaces, her daddy told her the following story:

> Once upon a time, there were two silly snakes [the shoelaces] who decided to wrestle. They twisted around each other and tied themselves together very tightly [first tie]. The snakes became scared and tried to curl away from each other [the loops]. But the snakes tripped and fell over each other and tied themselves in a knot.

Reading Storybooks

Research reveals a connection between the amount of time adults spend reading storybooks to children and the level of children's oral language development. The stories, pictures, and accompanying adult-to-child interactions facilitate language use and increase expressive and receptive vocabulary. Further, children who have been read to frequently are better able to retell stories than children who have had few opportunities to engage in story time (Barrentine, 1996; Durkin, 1966). Children are able to learn new vocabulary during storybook time as they point to pictures they see in the book and when an attentive adult labels the picture or illustration. This interaction is called shared visual attention (See Chapter 2, More About 2.2) and is the basis of a great deal of vocabulary development (Woodward & Guajardo, 2002; Corkum & Moore, 1998). Sharing simple storybooks with interesting illustrations is one way parents can increase their children's vocabulary. As the parent, sibling, or caregiver reads the storybook to a child, the opportunity to label many wonderful new and rare sights is almost unavoidable! The following conversation took place between Josh (four) and Jared (two) while they were reading *I Know a Rhino* (actually talking about the pictures).

Josh: See the Rhi-na-ser-rus, Jared? They really don't drink coffee but it's funny.

Jared: Me, turn page.

Josh: Okay, see the pig? Jared, point to the muddy pig. You found him.

> *Josh:*   Now see? Okay, you tell me? What it is?
>
> *Jared:*   Monkey!
>
> *Josh:*   Well, it says ape but they are the same things, monkey and ape. Yup, the same thing, but say ape. Okay?
>
> *Jared:*   Ape monkey.

The interactions between these two brothers show how quickly vocabulary is developed through story time. (See also Chapter 4.) Plus, just how often will a Rhi-na-ser-rus just show up at your home?

Caregivers may also encourage discussion and comprehension by asking open-ended questions about the story. Children often relate to the characters and story lines and, when encouraged, they reveal interesting views. The following conversation occurred when Dominique was four years old, after a reading of *Goldilocks and the Three Bears*.

> *Mom:*   What part of the story did you like the best?
>
> *Dominique:*   When Goldilocks kept messing up baby bear's stuff.
>
> *Mom:*   Who did you like best in the story?
>
> *Dominique:*   Baby bear.
>
> *Mom:*   Why?
>
> *Dominique:*   'Cause baby bear is like me. All of his stuff is wrecked up by Goldilocks, like Sheritta [her eighteen-month-old sister] messes up mine.

Notice that Dominique's mother asked open-ended opinion questions and accepted her child's responses. This type of question encourages oral responses and children's personal interpretation of the story. Adults should refrain from asking interrogation or detail questions, such as "What did Goldilocks say when she tasted the second bowl of porridge?" Detail questions tend to make story time avoidable, not enjoyable.

As children snuggle in a parent's lap or beside their parent in a chair or bed, story time creates a comforting, private time to talk together. In addition to providing wonderful language opportunities, story time also establishes a foundation for children to become successful readers. (See Chapters 4 and 5.)

In today's culturally, linguistically, and socioeconomically diverse society, teachers may find that some of their students' parents may not have the ability to read to their children or the financial means to purchase storybooks. Even more parents are unsure how to successfully engage their children in story time. Teachers may need to help parents by serving as a resource. In Chapter 11, readers will discover a number of concrete suggestions for ways to help teachers provide a range of supports families may need.

Television as a Language Tool

> *Deeply engrossed in a Discovery video titled* Birds, *three-year-old Annie cheers when a duck slowly hatches from its egg. She watches this video several times, frequently asking questions about "How did the duck get into the egg?"*
>
> *In the middle of the night several evenings later, Annie's father awakens to noises coming from the family room. As he walks into the living room he realizes that Annie has begun to play the* Birds *video in the VCR. He also observes that her hands are full of eggshells and yolks. She asks, "Daddy, where's the baby duck?"*

As you can see, Annie's interest in ducks, eggs, and the mysteries of hatching were clearly sparked by her observation of a science video. Children today have a wide range of electronic media to watch and interact with. Television, the oldest medium, is still the most influential and easily accessible, and opens the door for cable programming, videos, and DVDs. Parents have the choice to view television as a hazard to their child's intellectual development or they can explore its potential as an inexpensive tool that can broaden their child's curiosity and vocabulary (Foley & Enz, 2004).

Television has been a major influence in family life in almost all U.S. households since the 1950s. In the 1980s, the availability of video rentals and inexpensive video players, video movies and storybooks, cartoons, and games added yet another dimension to television watching. During the 1990s it was estimated that 99 percent of U.S. homes had at least one television set. The latest research reveals that the television/video player/DVD player is usually in the part of the home where most family interactions occur (Miller, 1997). Hence, the average child between two and five years of age will spend twenty-seven hours a week viewing television programming (Lemish, 1987). Anything that occupies children for so many hours a week deserves careful consideration. So what are some of the key elements a parent needs to consider when determining how to use the powerful medium?

TIME. Research regarding the amount of time young children watch television and the effect of viewing on later academic success is inconclusive, though the data clearly suggest that watching for many hours per day or week has a negative effect on children's academic performance. Susan Neuman (1988) suggests that more than four hours of television viewing a day has a negative effect on children's reading achievement. Likewise, Angela Clarke's and Beth Kurtz-Costes's (1997) study of low-socioeconomic African American preschool children shows that children who watched the most television (between thirty and fifty-five hours per week) exhibited poorer academic skills than their peers who watched fewer than twenty-five hours per week. On the other hand, moderate amounts of television viewing may be beneficial. The Center for the Study of Reading landmark report, "Becoming a Nation of Readers," suggests that there is actually a positive link between watching up to ten hours of television a week and reading achievement (Rice, Huston, Truglio, & Wright, 1990). Clarke and Kurtz-Costes (1997) suggest that the variation in researchers' findings may be due in part to the home climate. They suggest that *who* watches television with young children and *how* television is watched may have a greater effect on children's learning than simply the *amount* of television viewing.

CHOOSING PROGRAMMING FOR YOUNG CHILDREN. Selecting appropriate children's programming has become more challenging in recent years. In addition to regular public access, cable service may offer as many as 100 options to choose from each hour of the day. And while there are a number of proven classics—such as *Sesame Street, Reading Rainbow,* and *Mister Rogers*—children's programs change from year to year. One way parents can determine the quality of children's programming is through considering children's needs. Diane Levin and Nancy Carlsson-Paige (1994) created a list of children's developmental needs and suggested program criteria to accommodate these concerns. Figure 3.1 presents A Developmental Guide for Assessing Television Programming adapted from their work.

ACTIVE VIEWING

> *"What do you think Dora will do, Shelly? Swiper took her cousin's present! What would you do?" asks mom to her three-year-old daughter Shelly, who adores all things* Dora the Explorer. *Shelly replies, "Follow the triangula (Spanish for triangle)." Shelly's mom marvels; her preschooler is learning her shapes in English and in Spanish!*

Research suggests that when parents watch high-quality programming with their children, the opportunities for vocabulary development and story comprehension are tremendous (Close, 2004). Young children are extremely impressionable, and television's visual imagery is a powerful force in their lives. Electronic programming also provides exceptional opportunities for shared visual attention, which may greatly stimulate vocabulary development in much the same way as a storybook (Walker, 2004). Therefore, it is important for parents to help guide and mediate the viewing process. Susan Miller (1997) suggests a number of ways parents and caregivers may interact with children as they view television.

■ *Watch television together*—Help children interpret what is seen on the screen.
■ *Talk about the programs*—Conversations initiated by television programming offer opportunities to discuss a wide variety of issues.

FIGURE 3.1	To help children develop:	Programming qualities to promote:
A Developmental Guide for Assessing Television Programming Adapted from Levin, D. & Carlsson-Paige, N. (1994). Developmentally appropriate television: Putting children first. *Young Children, 49*, 38–44.	A sense of trust and safety	A world where people can be trusted and help each other, where safety and predictability can be achieved, where fears can be overcome
	A sense of autonomy with connectedness	A wide range of models of independence within meaningful relationships and of autonomous people helping each other
	A sense of empowerment and efficacy	Many examples of people having a positive effect on their world without violence
	Gender identity	Complex characters with wide-ranging behaviors, interests, and skills; commonalities between the sexes in what each can do
	An appreciation of diversity among people	Diverse peoples with varied talents, skills, and needs who treat each other with respect, work out problems non–violently, and enrich each others' lives
	The foundations of morality and social responsibility	Complex characters who act responsibly and morally toward others—showing kindness and respect, working out moral problems, taking other people's points of view
	Imagination and opportunities for meaningful play	Meaningful content to use in play, which resonates deeply with developmental needs; shows not linked to realistic toys so that children can create their own unique play

- *Observe children's reactions*—Ask children to label or describe their feelings.
- *Foster critical thinking*—Ask children what they think about a program. Would they have handled the problem differently? Did they agree with the character's actions?
- *Extend viewing activities*—Children are often motivated to learn more about a topic or activity once television has sparked their interest.

For instance, Annie's interest in the hatching sequence in the video inspired her to find her *Egg Becomes Chick* book. She pored over this early science text, which features actual photographs of the development of a chick inside the egg. A trip to the zoo in early spring also provided her with the opportunity to see more chicks being hatched in a large incubator.

In short, television/videos/DVDs can be a powerful tool in children's learning, but how much, what, and how children view television programs should be carefully considered.

School Talk: A Structured Context for Learning and Using Language

While most children arrive at preschool/kindergarten capable of conversing with both adults and peers, the words they know and use vary significantly (Hart & Risley, 1995). There is evidence that these early differences will not go away without direct intervention—explicit and consistent vocabulary instruction (Hart & Risley, 1995; Biemiller, 2001). Sadly, research indicates that in most schools, there is little emphasis on the acquisition of new vocabulary (Rupley, Logan, & Nichols, 1999). Research has also found that low vocabulary knowledge (relative to peers at the end of kindergarten) typically means low vocabulary knowledge throughout a child's entire schooling (Baumann & Kame'enui, 2003).

The good news is that vocabulary can easily develop through direct instruction of word meanings (Biemiller, 2001) and through incidental learning from contexts that provide rich verbal opportunities (Roskos, Tabors, & Lenhart, 2004; Weizman and Snow, 2001). Teachers, therefore, are responsible for promoting language learning by engaging in conversations with students, encouraging children to converse with each other (Roser, 1998), and most importantly, teaching vocabulary in a direct, meaningful, and consistent manner (Biemiller, 2001).

Language Opportunities in School—Building Explicit Opportunities

Day care, preschool, and kindergarten teachers must consistently work to enhance children's language development. Fortunately, the school day offers numerous opportunities for both direct instruction and incidental oral interactions. However, teachers of young children must be diligent and mindful to create vocabulary learning moments. Kathy Roskos, Patton Tabors, and Lisa Lenhart (2004) suggest that teachers who are also playful, planful, and purposeful are successful in helping children to develop oral language competence and simultaneously expand their vocabulary.

Trade Secret 3.1 demonstrates how Ms. V., a kindergarten teacher, playfully, planfully, and purposefully employs classroom routines to intentionally offer explicit vocabulary instruction.

Teacher Discourse

Over every school day, there are dozens of possibilities for verbal interactions (Smith & Dickinson, 1994). Unfortunately, research indicates that this opportunity is often overlooked in traditional transmission-oriented classrooms. Studies have shown that in many classrooms the teacher dominates the language environment; this does little to promote the children's oral language growth (Buzzelli, 1996; Cazden, 1988; Howard, Shaughnessy, Sanger, & Hux, 1998; Wells, 1986). For example, these studies suggest that in some classrooms:

- teachers spend most of the time talking *to* rather than talking *with* children.
- teachers dominate discussions by controlling how a topic is developed and who gets to talk.
- children spend most of their time listening to teachers.
- when children do talk, it is usually to give a response to a question posed by the teacher.
- teachers tend to ask testlike, closed-ended questions that have one right answer (that the teacher already knows).

The typical pattern of classroom discourse is characterized by teacher initiation, student response, and teacher evaluation. In the IRE pattern, the teacher asks a question, a student answers, and the teacher either accepts or rejects that answer and goes on to ask another question (Galda, Cullinan, & Strickland, 1993). For example, before the following discussion, the kindergarten children had listened to *The Three Little Pigs*.

> *Teacher:* What material did the pigs use to build their first house?
>
> *Bobbie:* They used sticks.
>
> *Teacher:* Yes. That is correct; the pigs used sticks for the first house. What did the pigs use to build the third house?
>
> *Manuel:* They used cement.
>
> *Teacher:* No. Who remembers what the book says? Jon?
>
> *Jon:* Bricks.
>
> *Teacher:* Yes. The pigs used bricks.

Notice how the teacher's questions are not real questions; rather they test whether the children recalled specific details of the story. Note also that children have no opportunity to construct their own meaning of the story by combining text information with their prior knowledge. For example, Manuel's answer, *cement,* suggests that Manuel was making inferences based on prior experience. The teacher's negative response to Manuel's comment probably communicates to him that it is incorrect to make inferences when reading. This sends a message to children that one should recall exactly what is said in the text. Finally, notice that there is absolutely no interaction from child to child. The turn-taking pattern is teacher–child–teacher–child.

These types of IRE interactions are sometimes appropriate because teachers do need to get specific points across to students (Buzzelli, 1996; Dyson & Genishi, 1983). However, problems ensue if this is the only type of talk that is taking place in the classroom. IRE discussions do not provide the type of language input and feedback that "advance children's knowledge of language structure and use" (Menyuk, 1988, p. 105). In addition, these teacher-dominated exchanges do not allow children to negotiate and build meaning through dialogue (Hansen, 1998).

TRADE SECRET 3.1

Explicit Vocabulary Instruction

Ms. V. is working with predominantly English-speaking kindergarten children from lower socioeconomic homes. Most of these children are able to share their wants and needs and express their feelings, but Ms. V. has noticed that most of the children have limited vocabularies. Her *purpose* is to help them build expressive vocabulary. The scenario below describes Ms. V.'s explicit vocabulary activities beginning with a game she *plays* with the children once or twice a week. She usually *plans* her target words to extend a storybook or a social studies or science lesson. Ms. V. begins by explicitly introducing new vocabulary words to the children the minute they enter the classroom today.

- ◆ **Morning greeting**—"Martine, you are clever," whispers Ms. V. into Martine's ear. Moving to Jorge, she again whispers, "Jorge, you are so smart." Kevin is next; Ms. V. whispers, "Kevin, you are so bright." And she repeats the procedure with several more children, as the class assembles for group time.
- ◆ **Group time**—Ms. V. continues to extend the new words *clever, smart,* and *bright* during group time. She tells the class, "I whispered a word to many of you this morning as you came in the door. But I didn't use exactly the same word. So listen closely! If I told you that you were clever, please stand up!" Four children stand. "Great. This is the word *clever* (holding a word card that will later go on the vocabulary word wall). "If I told you that you were smart, stand up!" If I told you that you were bright, stand up!" She asks the children to repeat the words on the card as she points to them on the chalkboard. Then she asks the children, what do you think is the meaning of these words? Turn to your neighbor and tell them what *smart* means. Can some of you share your ideas? Do you agree? Smart means knowing a lot of things? Okay, what does clever mean? Tell another partner. Children begin to offer their ideas; Ms. V. listens and nods. She says, "Jason and Gabby think *clever* also means someone knows a lot of stuff but they might be sort of tricky. What do the rest of you think?" Now the children discuss

bright. Two young ladies, Hannah and Emma, suggest *bright* may have something to do with knowing a lot of stuff, but it also means really colorful, like Rainbow Brite dolls. Ms. V. takes a large piece of construction paper and asks the children if they can agree that bright, clever, and smart all mean knowing a lot. The children agree, and she writes this common definition on the paper and then puts the three words below. She asks the children if there are any other words they can think of that also mean knowing a lot of stuff. Connor suggests *brilliant.* "Ron said that Hermione [Harry Potter] is brilliant when she had a really good idea." Ms. V. congratulates Connor on being very clever! Ms. V. adds *brilliant* to the list. She reminds the students that today they are going to try to use their new words and listen to see if Ms. V. uses them.

- ◆ **Activity time**—During centers, Ms. V. roams the room and catches the children being clever, smart, brilliant, bright. Each time she uses the words the children repeat it loudly. Each time a child uses the word (correctly) in a sentence the other children in the center clap. Using these new words is exciting and immediately reinforced.
- ◆ **Snack time**—During snack time today the children's comments are full of the target words. *This snack will make us brilliant! Milk is a drink for smart kids.* Clever kids eat carrots. The children are pleased when Ms. V. claps for their efforts.
- ◆ **Story time**—Today the children hear *The Gingerbread Boy* by P. Galdon. After Ms. V. reads the story, she asks the children to describe the different characters. Elija suggests, "The Gingerbread Boy thought he was smart, but really he wasn't because he kept teasing everyone else." Ariel comments, "The fox was clever—smart and tricky—since he caught the Gingerbread Boy." Gabby exclaims, "Wow, brilliant! "
- ◆ **Outdoor play**—On the playground Tony is heard shouting, "I'm the smartest"; under her breath Kara responds by saying to her teacher, "No, he's just fast; that doesn't mean he knows a lot."

Ms. V.'s clever use of words was brilliant, don't you think? A few moments of preparation and a great deal of determination are helping her bright young students become even smarter.

What can early childhood teachers do to provide children with more stimulating experiences with language? We offer three recommendations:

(1) Engage children in reciprocal discussions and conversations.
(2) Provide ample opportunities for activity-centered language that invite (and, at times, require) children to use language to get things done.
(3) Provide language-centered activities that focus children's attention on specific aspects of language.

In the sections that follow, we present guidelines for implementing each of these recommendations.

Reciprocal Discussions and Conversations

Teachers' verbal interaction styles set the general tone for classroom language environments. The worst-case scenario occurs when a teacher insists on absolute silence except during teacher-led initiation, response, evaluation discussions. Such environments definitely limit continued oral language development (Dickinson & Tabors, 2001). Other teachers provide ideal language environments by engaging students in genuine conversations; conducting stimulating reciprocal discussions; and allowing children to converse with each other at a moderate volume during classroom learning activities, using "inside voices" (soft voices that do not disrupt classroom learning).

Teachers have many opportunities to talk with children throughout the school day, ranging from one-to-one conversations to whole-group discussions. Following is an example of an effective conversation between Ms. E., a preschool teacher, and Roberto, age four:

Roberto: See my new backpack, Teacher?

Ms. E.: What a neat backpack, Roberto. Show it to me.

Roberto: It has six zippers. See? The pouches hold different stuff. Isn't it neat?

Ms. E.: I like the different-size pouches. Look, this one is just right for a water bottle.

Roberto: Yeah. The arm straps are great too. See, I can make 'em longer.

Ms. E.: Yes [nods and smiles]. It fits your arms perfectly. Where did you get this nifty backpack?

Roberto: We got it at the mall.

Ms. E.: What store in the mall?

Roberto: The one that has all the camping stuff.

Ms. E.: The Camping Plus store?

Roberto: Yeah. That's the one.

Notice how Ms. E. allowed Roberto to take the lead by listening carefully to what Roberto said and by responding to his previous statements. She let him do most of talking, using back-channeling (nodding and smiling) to keep the conversation going. Ms. E. asked only three questions, and they were genuine—she wanted to know where Roberto purchased the backpack.

Reciprocal conversations are not restricted to one-to-one situations. Teachers can also engage children in genuine discussions pertaining to ongoing instructional activities. Cory Hansen (1998) gives an example of group discussion of George MacDonald's 1872 classic, *The Princess and the Goblin* (Puffin Books). The book is being discussed by a group of kindergarten students in Chris Boyd's classroom.

Previously in the story, the grandmother had given the princess a gift of a glowing ring from which a thread would lead her to comfort if she were frightened. The princess assumed it would lead her to her grandmother, but one night it led her deep into a cave and stopped at a heap of stones. The chapter (Irene's Clue) ends with the princess bursting into tears at the foot of the rocks. Curdie, the fearless miner's son, was missing.

Joseph: I think that Curdie's on the other side of the rocks.

Mrs. B.: Where'd you get the clue for that?

Anna: Because the strings led her to the mountain. That means it was close to Curdie because Curdie lived by the mountain.

Kim: Maybe Curdie's on the other side of the stones!

Jamal: I think her grandmother was a goblin since she could have went through the rocks.

Jordan: I know. Maybe—when she was falling asleep on the other side—but how could the goblins be that fast?

Anna: Because they're magic.

Richard: I know how Curdie got to the other side . . .

Chorus: Children begin to talk in small groups simultaneously.

Joseph: Maybe Curdie's in the heap of stones.

Mrs. B.:   What makes you say that?

Joseph: Because in the last chapter—Curdie's Clue—it said they piled the rock—a big stone in the mouth of the cave.

Kim: The grandmother said the ring always led to the grandmother's bedroom so she. . .

Anna: No it didn't. It said, "This will take me to you—wherever it takes you, you go." And the grandmother said, "Wherever it takes you, you will go."

Mrs. B.:   Can you think of any reason why the princess should go to the cave?

Joseph: Because it said, "You must not doubt the string."

Adam: The grandmother said the thread would lead to her but it ended up leading her to Curdie.

Alondra: I think the grandmother knows about Curdie.

Kim: It's because her grandmother wanted her to save Curdie!

Anna: That was the clue.

Jamal: To get Curdie out cuz she know about him.

Joseph: Yeah.

(Hansen, 1998, pp. 172–173)

Here, Mrs. B. let the students take the lead by listening closely to what they said and responding to their comments. Her questions were genuine (she did not know what the children's responses would be) and were open ended in nature ("What makes you say that?"). By welcoming the children's viewpoints, she encouraged them to bring their personal interpretations to the story. Also note that the children talked to each other; they engaged in real conversations. The teacher facilitated this child–child turn-taking pattern by encouraging the students to respond to each other's ideas.

Ms. E.'s and Mrs. B.'s effective use of reciprocal questions allowed children to engage in authentic discussion with the teacher and each other. Obviously, the way a teacher interacts with young children influences the way children communicate. Therefore, it is important for teachers to reflect on the quality of their conversations and discussions with young children.

Contexts for Encouraging Language: Providing Incidental Opportunities

We know that what children say and do is greatly influenced by where they are and what is around them. For example, as Evan played in the snow, he learned snow-related vocabulary with his family. Teachers must create dynamic learning environments that are contexts for language development. In other words, the curriculum must give children something to talk about. These contexts are perfect opportunities for incidental language learning between young students and their teacher. Incidental (sometimes called milieu —which means in the environment) language opportunities occur and can be reinforced when children are engaged in language-rich contexts that spark children's interests (Kaiser, Yoder, & Keetz, 1992). In the following section, we describe how teachers might use group activities, learning centers, and dramatic play to expand children's learning and opportunities to use language.

GROUP ACTIVITIES.   Teachers can support language by involving children with group activities that encourage, and at times necessitate, verbal interaction. What sort of activities would require children to talk? As Celia Genishi (1987) points out, "almost every object or activity presents an opportunity for talk when teachers allow it to" (p. 99). In the following vignette, we provide an illustration of a whole-group activity that required a rather large group of multilingual, four-year-old children to reveal and assert needs and wants and connect with themselves and others. Likewise researchers Susan Burns, Peg Griffin, and Catherine Snow suggest that "sociodramatic play activities give children a chance to develop language and literacy skills, a deeper understanding of narrative, and their own personal responses to stories" (1999, p. 72).

The children have been learning about manners and balanced meals. As part of a culminating activity, the entire room has been transformed into a restaurant. Twelve little tables are draped with tablecloths, and each table has a vase of flowers. Today the teachers are waitresses, and a few parents have volunteered to cook real food. The children must choose between the Panda Café (spaghetti, meatballs, garlic toast, juice or milk) or the Café Mexico (burrito, chips, salsa, juice or milk). Each café has a menu with words and pictures. The children must select the specific items they wish to eat and give their orders to the waitress. The waitress takes the children's orders on an order form and gives the form to the cooks. The cooks fill the orders exactly as the children request. Then the waitress returns with the food and the order form and asks the children to review the order.

Teacher: What café would you like, sir?

Roberto: [Points to menu.]

Teacher: Which café? You must tell me.

Roberto: The Café Mexico.

Teacher: Right this way, sir. Here is your menu. Take a moment to decide what you want to eat. I'll be right back to take your order.

Roberto: [Looks over the menu and shares his choices with his friend by pointing to the items he wants.]

Teacher: Okay, sir. What would you like?

Roberto: [Points to the items on the menu.]

Teacher: Please, sir. You will have to tell me.

Roberto: [Hesitates for a few seconds.] I want the burrito and chips and juice.

Teacher: Do you want salsa? [She leans over so he can see her mark the items on the order form.]

Roberto: No. [firmly.]

Notice how the teachers organized this activity so that the children had to verbally express their needs multiple times throughout the restaurant adventure. In addition, the children had many opportunities to see how print is used in real life. However, teachers are not the only valuable source of language input. Children can also gain valuable oral language practice from talking with peers who are not as skilled as adults in initiating and maintaining conversations. To encourage peer-to-peer interactions, these teachers also created a miniature version of the restaurant in a dramatic play learning center. In this center, Roberto and his classmates will be able to play restaurant together for a few weeks.

LEARNING CENTERS.   Since children's learning and language are greatly influenced by their environment, good teachers guide children's language development through the deliberate structuring of the classroom environment. For example, the teachers in the previous vignette created a restaurant to encourage talk about food, ordering meals, taking orders, cooking meals, and the like. Later, as the children interacted together in the restaurant dramatic play center, they continued to help each other build and reinforce their knowledge of restaurants. In classrooms that use dramatic play-learning centers, the teacher's role is to set up the environment, observe as children interact with the materials, supply help and guidance when needed, and engage in conversations with the children about the materials they use in their learning. A good deal of the teacher's effort is expended on the setting-up or preparation phase. Centers are created when the teacher carves the classroom space into defined areas. (See Chapter 10 for ideas on how to carve classroom space into learning centers.)

Readers seeking more information on establishing centers will find *The Creative Curriculum for Early Childhood Education* (Dodge & Colker, 1992) useful. This book presents detailed, easy-to-follow instructions for setting up popular interest areas (centers). It also contains practical tips on schedules, routines, and other aspects of classroom management, plus good suggestions for encouraging parental involvement.

DRAMATIC PLAY.   Another context for activity-centered language is dramatic play. Dramatic play occurs when children take on roles and use make-believe transformations to act out situations and play episodes. For example, several children might adopt the roles of family members and pretend to prepare dinner, or they may become superheroes who are engaged in fantastic adventures. This type of play—also called sociodramatic, make-believe, pretend, or imaginative play—reaches its peak between the ages of four and seven.

Although to some dramatic play appears simple and frivolous at first glance, close inspection reveals that it is quite complex and places heavy linguistic demands on children (Bredekamp, 1999; Fessler, 1998). In fact, Jerome Bruner (1983, p. 65) reported that "the most complicated grammatical and pragmatic forms of language appear first in play activity." When children work together to act out stories, they face formidable language challenges. They not only need to use language to act out their dramas, they must also use language to organize the play and keep it going. Before starting, they must recruit other players, assign roles, decide on the make-believe identities of objects (e.g., that a block of wood will be used as if it were a telephone), and plan the story line. Once started, language must be used to act out the story, keep the dramatization heading in the right direction (e.g., be sure that everyone is doing things appropriate to their role), and re-energize the play if it is becoming repetitious and boring. To accomplish these tasks, children must use two different types of language: (1) pretend language that is appropriate for their roles, and (2) metaplay language about the play itself. Children switch between their pretend roles and their real identities when making these two types of comments.

In order to take full advantage of dramatic play's potential as a medium for language development, attention needs to be given to three factors: (1) the settings in which play occurs, (2) the amount of time allocated for play activities, and (3) the type of teacher involvement in play episodes.

Play Settings. It is important to remember that children play best at what they already know. Therefore, dramatic play settings need to be familiar to children and consistent with their culture (Neuman, 1995). For example, the domestic play themes, such as parents caring for a baby or a family eating a meal, are very popular with young children because these are the roles and activities with which they are most familiar. For this reason, we recommend that preschool and kindergarten classrooms contain a housekeeping dramatic play center equipped with props that remind children of their own homes. Not only do such centers encourage dramatic play, but they

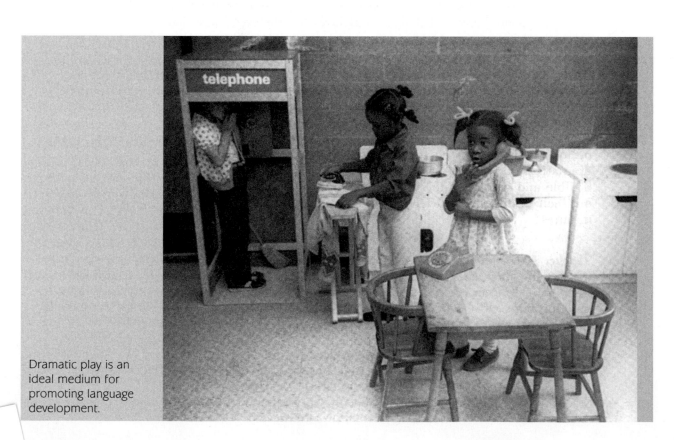

Dramatic play is an ideal medium for promoting language development.

also provide a context in which children can display the types of literacy activities they have observed at home.

The range of children's play themes and related literacy activities can be greatly expanded by adding a theme center to the classroom. These centers have props and furniture that suggest specific settings familiar to children, such as a veterinarian's office, restaurant, bank, post office, ice cream parlor, fast-food restaurant, and grocery store. (Table 6.1 contains lists of literacy materials that can be used in a variety of theme centers.) For example, a veterinarian's office might be divided into two areas: a waiting room with a table for a receptionist and chairs for patients and an examination room with another table, chairs, and a variety of medical props (doctor's kit, scales, etc.). Stuffed animals can be provided as patients. Theme-related literacy materials—appointment book, patient folders, prescription forms, wall signs, and so on—should also be included to encourage children to reenact the literacy activities they have observed in these settings. Children will use their knowledge of visits to the doctor to engage in play with their peers. The following scenario illustrates how three preschoolers verbalize their knowledge of what occurs at the animal hospital.

> *Sergio:* [The vet is looking at the clipboard.] It says here that Ruffy is sick with worms.
>
> *Marie:* [owner of a toy kitty named Ruffy] Yep, uh-huh. I think she ate bad worms.
>
> *Sergio:* That means we gotta operate and give Ruffy big horse pills for those worms.
>
> *Joy:* [the nurse] Okay, sign here. [Hands Marie a big stack of papers.] Sign 'em all. Then we'll operate. But you gotta stay out in the people room. You could faint if you stay in here.

Chari Woodard (1984), a teacher who has had considerable success with theme centers in her university's laboratory preschool, recommends that one theme center be introduced at a time and left for several weeks. Then the center can be transformed into another theme. She also advises locating these centers near the permanent housekeeping center so that children can integrate the theme center activities with their domestic play. Children acting as parents for dolls, pets, or peers in the housekeeping area might, for example, take a sick baby to the doctor theme center for an examination. Or children might weld or examine cars in the classroom garage (Hall & Robinson, 1995). Woodard found that children, particularly boys, began engaging in more dramatic play when the theme centers were introduced.

Time. Dramatic play requires providing a considerable amount of time for children to plan and initiate. If play periods are short, children have to stop their dramatizations right after they have started. When this happens frequently, children tend to switch to less-advanced forms of play, such as functional (motor) play or simple construction activity, which can be completed in brief sessions.

Research has shown that preschoolers are much more likely to engage in rich, sustained dramatic play during thirty-minute play periods than during shorter fifteen-minute sessions (Christie, Johnsen, & Peckover, 1988). Our experience indicates that even longer periods are needed. For example, Billie Enz and Jim Christie (1997) spent a semester observing a preschool classroom that had forty-minute play periods. Very often, the four-year-olds had just finished preparing for a dramatization when it was time to clean up. Fortunately, the teachers were flexible and often let the children have an extra ten to fifteen minutes to act out their dramas. We recommend that whenever possible, center time last for at least sixty minutes.

Teacher Involvement. For many years, it was believed that teachers should just set the stage and not get directly involved in children's play activities. This hands-off stance toward play has been seriously challenged by a growing body of research that suggests that classroom play can be enriched through teacher participation. Teacher involvement has been found to assist nonplayers to begin to engage in dramatic play, to help more proficient players enrich and extend their dramatizations, and to encourage children to incorporate literacy into their play episodes (Enz & Christie, 1997; Roskos & Neuman, 1993). However, teachers need to use caution because overzealous or inappropriate forms of involvement can interfere with ongoing play and sometimes cause children to quit playing altogether (Enz & Christie, 1997).

The simplest and least intrusive type of teacher involvement in play is observation. By watching children as they play, teachers demonstrate that they are interested in the children's play and that play is a valuable, worthwhile activity. Observation alone can lead to more sustained play. Bruner (1980) reported that preschoolers' play episodes lasted roughly twice as long when a teacher was nearby and observing than when children played completely on their own. In addition, the children were more likely to move toward more elaborate forms of play when an adult was looking on.

Observation can also provide clues about when more direct forms of teacher involvement in play are appropriate. A teacher may find that in spite of conducive play settings, some children rarely engage in dramatic play. As we explain in Special Feature 3.1, this pattern of play behavior is atypical for four- and five-year-old children. Or the teacher may notice that there is an opportunity to extend or enrich an ongoing play episode, perhaps by introducing some new element or problem for children to solve (Hall, 1999). Both situations call for active teacher involvement.

Chapter 6 describes three roles that are ideal for initiating and extending dramatic play: the stage manager role, in which the teacher supplies props and offers ideas to enrich play; the coplayer role, in which the teacher actually takes on a role and joins in the children's play; and the play leader who stimulates play by introducing, in a role, some type of problem to be resolved. For more information about these roles and other roles that teachers can adopt during play, see Jones and Reynolds (1992).

In addition to promoting language acquisition, dramatic play encourages children to help each other learn academic skills and content (Hansen, 1998; Christie & Stone, 1999), make friends, and develop important social skills (Garvey, 1977). Peer-to-peer interaction is particularly important for the growing numbers of students who are learning English as a second language and need help with more basic aspects of oral language (Fessler, 1998). For these reasons, dramatic play centers need to be a prominent feature in early childhood classrooms.

Language-Centered Activities

Beyond creating contexts that encourage language and facilitate verbal interactions, teachers can also provide activities that focus specifically on language. Read-alouds, sharing, storytelling, and language play all fall into this category. The first of these, teacher read-alouds, is the subject of an entire section of Chapter 5. Storybook reading can be an ideal context for promoting attentive listening and oral discussion skills. We discuss the remaining four language-centered activities below.

SHARING. Sharing, or show-and-tell, is a strategy designed to promote students' speaking and listening abilities. Traditionally, sharing has been a whole-class activity in which one child after another gets up, takes center stage, and talks about something of her or his own choosing—often some object brought from home (Gallas, 1992). Children in the audience are expected to quietly listen and not participate.

In this traditional format, sharing is not a very productive language experience for the child who is speaking or for those who are listening. The large group size can intimidate the speaker and reduce participation—only a small percentage of students get to share on a given day. Or if many students share, it becomes a very drawn-out, boring affair. The lack of participation on the part of the audience leads to poor listening behavior. Listening is an active, constructive process in which listeners combine information provided by a speaker with their own prior knowledge to build personal meaning. Mary Jalongo (1995) relates a teacher's definition of listening that captures the essences of active listening: "It is hearing and making and shaping what you heard—along with your own ideas—into usable pieces of knowledge" (p. 14). The passive role of the audience in traditional sharing works against this process.

With two modifications, sharing can be transformed into a very worthwhile language activity. First, group size should be "small enough to reduce shyness, encourage interaction, permit listeners to examine the object, and afford everyone a long enough turn without tiring the group" (Moffett & Wagner, 1983, p. 84). Groups of three to six students are ideal for this purpose. Second, listeners should be encouraged to participate by asking questions of the child who is sharing. "Let the sharer/teller begin as she will. When she has said all that initially occurs to her, encourage the audience by solicitation and example to ask natural questions" (Moffett and Wagner, 1983, p. 84).

SPECIAL FEATURE 3.1

Age Trends in Children's Play

Researchers have been very interested in how children's play changes with age. Typically, they have used cross-sectional research methods, observing children of different ages during indoor free-choice periods. The children's behavior was systematically observed and categorized, often with Smilansky's (1968) play categories:

1. *Functional play*—Repetitive movement with or without objects. Examples include (a) running and jumping, (b) stacking and knocking down blocks, (c) digging in a sand box, and (d) bouncing a ball against a wall.
2. *Constructive play*—Using objects (blocks, Legos, Tinkertoys) or materials (sand, Play-Doh, clay) to build something.
3. *Dramatic play*—Taking on a role and using make-believe transformations to act out a situation or a story.
4. *Games with rules*—Engaging in games that require the recognition of, acceptance of, and conformity with preestablished rules.

Kenneth Rubin, Greta Fein, and Brian Vandenberg (1983) summarized the results of this observational research and identified several major age trends with respect to the cognitive play categories. Functional play is the most prevalent form of play during the first three years of life. Starting at around eighteen months of age, both constructive and dramatic play appear and begin to increase. Between the ages of four and six years, constructive play is the modal form of play activity, accounting for almost half of the play observed in preschool and kindergarten classrooms (due, in part, to the abundance of constructive materials in school settings). During this same period, dramatic play continues to increase at the expense of functional play, rising to approximately 20 to 30 percent of all play by age six years. As children enter the primary grades, dramatic play declines in frequency. Dramatic play thus appears to follow an inverted-U developmental progression, first appearing between the ages of one and two years, increasing during the preschool years, peaking at about age six years, and then declining during middle childhood.

Several aspects of dramatic play change during the preschool period: Dramatic play becomes more social with age (Fenson, 1984). Because of limited social skills, children's first attempts at pretending are usually solitary. By age three or four years, many children have learned to share, compromise, and cooperate with others, and they soon begin to engage in group dramatizations with other children. The story lines children enact in their pretend play become more complex with age (Fenson, 1984), changing from isolated events (e.g., feeding a doll) to complex, interrelated episodes (e.g., cooking a make-believe meal, serving it to guests, and then eating the meal while conducting polite conversation).

The roles and themes children enact change with age, becoming more creative and unusual (Garvey, 1977). Initially, children adopt highly familiar roles, such as family members, and act out very routine types of domestic activity, such as preparing dinner or going shopping. As they mature, children begin taking on less familiar roles, such as occupations (e.g., mail carrier) and fictional characters (e.g., Batman), and they begin to introduce unusual elements into their dramatizations (e.g., an earthquake may occur during a shopping trip).

As a result of this research, teachers now have a clearer picture of how dramatic play changes with age. Dramatic play begins around age two years and is marked by solitary make-believe, isolated actions, and familiar roles. By the time dramatic play reaches its peak at around age six years, it has evolved into a complex endeavor that involves groups of children, interrelated action sequences, and highly imaginative roles and themes.

These age trends can help teachers interpret the play they observe in the classroom. While the beginnings of dramatic play begin to appear by two years of age, most children do not engage in fully elaborated group dramatic play until age four years or beyond. Therefore, teachers should not worry when two- and three-year-olds rarely engage in dramatic play. Teachers should also not be concerned when children of this age engage in dramatic play by themselves or if their dramatizations are limited to simple, isolated actions. However, if these characteristics persist at ages four or five years, teachers may want to take steps to facilitate children's play development.

The teacher's role is to model questioning that encourages elaboration and clarification ("When did you get . . .?" "What happened next?" "What's that for?"). After asking one or two questions, teachers should pause and encourage the audience to participate. Prompts, such as "Does anyone have questions for Suzy?" may sometimes be needed to get the process started. Once children realize that it is acceptable for them to participate, prompting will no longer be necessary.

This peer questioning stimulates active listening by giving the audience a reason to listen to the child who is sharing. Children know that in order to ask relevant questions, they are going to have to listen very carefully to what the sharer has to say. The child who is sharing benefits as well. Children can be encouraged to elaborate their brief utterances or to organize their content more effectively and to state it more clearly (Moffett & Wagner, 1983).

Teachers can add variety to sharing by occasionally giving it a special focus, such as by asking children to bring something that

(1) has a good story behind it, which encourages narrative discourse;
(2) they made or grew, which facilitates explanation or description; or
(3) works in a funny or interesting way, which fosters expositive communication.

STORYTELLING. Chapter 4 discusses many of the values of reading stories to children. Telling stories to children is also very worthwhile. The direct connection between the teller and audience promotes enjoyment and active listening. Marie Clay (1989) describes some of the values of storytelling:

> Storytelling is more direct than story reading. Facial expressions, gestures, intonations, the length of pauses, and the interactions with the children's responses create a more direct contact with the audience, dramatic in effect. The meaning can be closer to the children's own experiences because the teller can change the words, add a little explanation, or translate loosely into a local experience. (p. 24)

Because of the literate and technological nature of our culture, many teachers lack experience with storytelling. This, in turn, can lead to avoidance of telling stories. For this reason, we include tips for getting off to a good start with storytelling in Chapter 4. Here we focus on children as storytellers.

The first stories that children tell usually involve real-life experiences—they relate something that has happened to them. Sharing, discussed in the previous section, can be an ideal context to allow children to tell these types of stories in the classroom. Small-group, interactive sharing provides feedback that enables children to tell clearer, better-organized stories about personal experiences (Canizares, 1997).

Some children need assistance in broadening the range of their storytelling to imaginative, fictional stories. The following suggestions can help with this task:

- Open up the sharing period to include fantasy stories. Once teachers begin permitting their children to tell "fictional" stories, the children may begin sharing imaginative, creative stories that feature language that is much richer than that used in their show-and-tell sharing (Gallas, 1992).
- Encourage children to retell the stories contained in their favorite storybooks. Books remove the burden of creating an original story to tell. Story retelling has other benefits for children, including enhanced oral fluency and expression and improved story comprehension (Morrow, 2005).
- Dramatic story retelling through puppetry. Many children will share their thoughts through the safety of a puppet character. Again, the story can be an original or a retell of a favorite story (Lowe & Matthew, 2000).
- Have children make up words for the stories in wordless picture books, such as *Pancakes for Breakfast* by Tomie dePaola (1978). Here again, the book is providing the content for the child's story.
- Link storytelling with play and writing. Vivian Paley (1990) has developed a strategy in which children come to a story table and dictate a story that the teacher writes down. During this dictation, the teacher asks the children to clarify any parts of the story that are unclear or difficult to understand. The teacher reads the story plays to the class. Finally, children serve as directors and invite classmates to join in acting out their stories. Children enjoy watching their stories dramatized, motivating them to create additional imaginative stories.

LANGUAGE PLAY. In addition to using language in their dramatic play, children also play with language. This intentional "messing around" with language begins as soon as children have passed through the babbling stage and have begun to make words (Garvey, 1977). This play involves the phonological, syntactic, and semantic aspects of language. By age two, language play becomes quite sophisticated. Ruth Weir (1962) placed a tape recorder in her two-and-a-half-year-old son Anthony's crib and turned it on after he had been placed in his crib for the evening. During this presleep time, Anthony engaged in an extensive amount of systematic language play. He experimented with speech sounds ("Babette . . . Back here . . . Wet"), substituted words of the same grammatical category ("What color. What color blanket. What color mop. What color glass."), and replaced nouns with appropriate pronouns ("Take the monkey. Take it." and "Stop it. Stop the ball. Stop it."). These monologues constituted play because language was being manipulated for its own sake rather than being used to communicate.

Young children also make attempts at humor, playing with semantic aspects of language. Kornei Chukovsky (1976) explains that "hardly has the child comprehended with certainty which objects go together and which do not, when he begins to listen happily to verses of absurdity" (p. 601). This, in turn, leads children to make up their own nonsense. Chukovsky uses his two-year-old daughter as an example. Shortly after she had learned that dogs say "bow wow" and cats say "miaow," she approached him and said, "Daddy, 'oggie—miaow!" and laughed. It was his daughter's first joke!

Children gain valuable practice while engaging in these types of language play. They also begin to acquire metalinguistic awareness, the ability to attend to language forms as objects in and of themselves. Courtney Cazden (1976) explains that when language is used for its normal function—to communicate meaning—language forms become transparent. We "hear through them" to get the intended message (p. 603). When children play with language, the situation is reversed. The focus is on the language—the grammatical rules and semantic relationships they are manipulating.

The type of language play children engage in is also age related (Geller, 1982). At age three, children like to repeat traditional rhymes ("Mary Had a Little Lamb"). They eventually begin to make up their own nonsense rhymes, playing with sound patterns ("Shama sheema / Mash day 'n' pash day . . ."). By ages five and six, children delight in verbal nonsense ("I saw Superman flying out there!") and chanting games ("Cinderella, dressed in yellow / Went upstairs to kiss her fellow / How many kisses did she get? / 1, 2, 3, 4, 5, . . .")—forms themselves rather than meaning. The obvious educational implication is that language play should be encouraged and supported at school (Cazden, 1976). Judith Schwartz (1983) recommends that teachers try three things to stimulate their students to play with language.

(1) Create a climate that allows play to flourish—a classroom atmosphere in which "children and teacher laugh easily and often."
(2) Serve as a model by sharing humorous anecdotes, word play, folk literature, jokes, and stories with children and by using gentle humor in interpersonal relationships with children.
(3) Value each child's contributions by allowing many opportunities for sharing oral and written language play.

SONGS AND FINGER PLAYS. Sitting on the floor with a small group of preschoolers, Ms. K. begins:

Where is Thumbkin?
Where is Thumbkin?
Here I am! Here I am!
How are you today, sir?
Very well, I thank you.
Run away, Run away.

The three- and four-year-old children quickly join in and immediately start the finger movements that accompany this familiar song. Very young children love to sing. The human fondness for a catchy tune and a snappy, clever rhyme begins early. Beginning in infancy and continuing on throughout their childhood, they are experimenting with their voices and the sounds that they can make. Singing encourages risk-free language play, especially for children who are learning a second language (Freeman & Freeman, 1994; Jackman, 1997). Singing songs in a new language allows children to make safe mistakes as they experiment with the new phonemic system—similar to the way toddlers may begin to sing jingles they hear on the television long before they can actually speak in full sentences. As noted in a recent report by Catherine Snow and her colleagues (1998), singing songs is an important literacy activity.

Therefore, teachers of young children would be wise to build in singing as part of their language arts curriculum (Collins, 1997). In particular, children enjoy songs that

- offer repetition and chorus, such as "Polly Put the Kettle On," "Mary Had A Little Lamb," or "Here We Go Round the Mulberry Bush";
- provide repeated words or phrases that can be treated like an echo, such as "Miss Mary Mack" or "She'll Be Comin' Round the Mountain";
- require sound effects or animal noises, such as "If You're Happy and You Know It" or "Old MacDonald Had a Farm";
- tell a story, such as "Hush, Little Baby," "Humpty Dumpty," or "Little Bo Peep"; and
- ask questions, such as "Where Is Thumbkin?" or "Do You Know the Muffin Man?"

In addition to singing, many songs or poems include finger plays. Do you recall "The Itsy-Bitsy Spider" and how your fingers became the spider who climbed up the waterspout? Children's minds are fully engaged when they act out the words of a song or poem with their fingers (Collins, 1997).

Many preschool and kindergarten teachers write the songs the children love to sing on chart paper or purchase the big book format of these beloved songs. As the children sing, the teacher uses a pointer to underline each word. The follow-the-bouncing-ball approach to teaching reading is quite effective with some children (Segal & Adcock, 1986). Singing is a wonderful way for children to play with and enjoy language.

However, not all children are equally able to engage in language play. Many children—for many reasons—have difficulty with language expression and oral comprehension.

Children who are learning a second language need many opportunities to practice their new language in a safe classroom environment.

Assessment: Finding Out What Children Know and Can Do

In Chapter 1 we introduced you to three terms: *benchmarks,* which are skills or knowledge that children are expected to demonstrate at certain developmental levels (e.g., by the end of the preschool years or by the beginning of kindergarten children will know and be able to . . .); *content standards*, which detail the knowledge and skills that children must obtain in a specific content area (e.g., the child should be able to express their needs and wants); and *performance standards,* which reflect the way students need to demonstrate their new knowledge or skill (e.g., the child will be able to request materials or support). All of these terms relate directly to how children are assessed.

Accurately assessing children's knowledge about and use of oral language is highly complex. Good assessment begins with realistic expectations, determined by child development experts, of what most children know and should be able to do. Performance standards serve as guidelines to help teachers develop learning opportunities and curriculum- and target-specific instruction. Likewise, when children do not meet the performance standards, this information helps teachers to provide additional support and instruction. If children still do not respond, teachers begin to investigate why the child is not making adequate progress. For instance, if a child is not able to express himself clearly, he may have hearing difficulties or articulation problems that may require medical intervention or specialized instruction.

Most states now have identified the skills, knowledge, and social dispositions that young children should be able to demonstrate within appropriate home, day care, or preschool settings. (See Figure 3.2 on page 68 for an example.)

By the time most children are preschoolers, their oral language is quite rich and complex. This complexity makes assessment difficult. The only way to truly capture the full richness of children's language is to tape-record their conversations and then make a verbatim transcription of what is said, along with a detailed description of the context in which the language occurred. The transcript can then be analyzed to determine the mean length of sentences used, which forms of language the child used, the pragmatic rules followed, and so forth (see Genishi & Dyson, 1984).

Optimizing Oral-Language Learning Experiences for Bilingual and Second-Language Learners

Sarah Hudelson and Irene Alicia Serna

In Chapter 2, several general points were made about young children's second-language acquisition. Second-language development was discussed from the perspective of creative construction, suggesting that learners, at their individual rates and using their individual styles, engage in figuring out how their new language works much as they had to figure out how their native language works. The focus was on the social-interactionist perspective on language acquisition, noting that children learn a second language as they interact with others (adults and other children) in that language. This means that teachers and English-speaking children in classrooms are all language teachers. Also, as noted earlier, there is evidence that teachers of second-language learners use language in ways that are similar to the talk parents use with their young children. This observation suggests that the attributes of parental talk discussed at the beginning of Chapter 3 also would apply to adults working with second-language learners.

With this general perspective in mind, the specific recommendations for promoting oral language articulated in this chapter are discussed as they relate to educators who work in bilingual and second-language settings.

THE USE OF RECIPROCAL DISCUSSIONS AND CONVERSATIONS WITH BILINGUAL AND SECOND-LANGUAGE LEARNERS

Environments that promote genuine conversations and discussions—both among children themselves and between children and adults—are critical to the language growth of bilingual and second-language learners. Teachers' understandings and attitudes are central to the establishment of these linguistic contexts. In bilingual education settings, where the philosophy is to use both the children's native language and English as vehicles for learning, teachers provide nonnative-English-speaking children with opportunities to extend both native and English language ability by using both languages in academic settings. As they provide these opportunities, bilingual teachers must decide how to allocate the use of the two languages in the classroom. Such allocation often depends on program design and goals, and on the language abilities of specific teachers and children (Lessow-Hurley, 1990).

Bilingual teachers may use one language for certain content or activities (such as language arts and mathematics) and the other language for other con-

tent and activities (such as science and art). Instead, one language may be used for part of the day and the other language for the rest of the time. Alternatively, the teacher and the children may use both languages freely, alternating between them in the ways that bilingual people often do (Jacobson & Faltis, 1990). In some settings, more of the native language is used in conversations and discussions when children are less comfortable in English. As the children gradually become more fluent in English, more time is spent in English. In other settings, teaming occurs, with one teacher using only a language other than English for instruction and the other educator using only English. Across these settings, the message that teachers send to children is that of valuing and using both languages and that it is possible to learn English without sacrificing their home language. In many classrooms, teachers also encourage English speakers to try to learn some of the non-English language, just as they encourage non-English speakers to use English (Reyes, Laliberty, & Orbansky, 1993; Turner, 1994).

Many elementary school teachers, however, are not bilingual and will therefore use only English in their teaching, even though several of their students may use languages other than English. In these settings, it is necessary for teachers to make adjustments in their ways of talking and presenting content, in order for children who are still learning English to participate more fully. These adjustments are also the case for bilingual teachers when they are working in the learners' second language. Teachers need to make adjustments in the following ways:

- Teachers need to organize class environments that are rich with materials and that provide opportunities for collaborative, hands-on experiences (Enright, 1986; Enright & McCloskey, 1988).
- Teachers need to adjust their own speech when speaking with and responding to second-language learners—focusing on the here and now, slowing down their delivery, simplifying their syntax and repeating and rephrasing, attending carefully to children's understandings or confusion, focusing on the child's meaning over correctness, and extending and expanding the second-language learner's language (Enright, 1986; Freeman & Freeman, 1994; Lindfors, 1987).
- Teachers need to structure opportunities for second-language learners to experiment with English and need to encourage learners to do so (Ernst, 1994). Early on, second-language learners may do better in situations where teachers are involved directly. As these children become more fluent, they need to interact with their peers in English and to use the new language for academic content (Willett, 1995).
- Teachers need to acknowledge that mistakes are a natural and necessary part of language learning and

(continued on next page)

to set up environments that encourage risk taking and allow mistakes (Freeman & Freeman, 1994b).

- Teachers need to provide learners with feedback on their efforts within the context of their engagement with content.
- The focus needs to be on the learners' ability to communicate, not simply on the accuracy of grammatical forms (Freeman & Freeman, 1994b).
- Teachers need to allow children to use languages other than English as a way to negotiate content before expressing their understandings in English (Freeman & Freeman, 1994b; TESOL, 1996).
- Teachers may need to sensitize native or fluent English-speaking children to the struggles of children who are working both to learn English and to use English to learn. This may be done, for example, through using a language other than English to teach a lesson or to read a story to English-speaking children and then discussing how the children felt, what problems they had in understanding, and how they could help others in similar situations (Rudnick, 1995).

Keeping the factors just mentioned in mind should mean that children who are learning English as a second language have more opportunities to participate in classroom activities, conversations, and discussions.

THE USE OF CONTEXTS FOR ACTIVITY-CENTERED LANGUAGE WITH BILINGUAL AND SECOND-LANGUAGE LEARNERS

Children, including English-language learners, learn a lot of language from each other and often prefer to interact with peers instead of with adults. English learners will learn the new language most naturally when they need to use it to engage with others, at least with some others who are more proficient in English than they are (TESOL, 1999). In a school setting, such engagement logically springs from interesting and meaningful content that children examine in collaboration with others in thematic units, in centers, and in paired and group projects. One challenge many teachers may face is how to structure activities to promote collaboration, including verbal interactions. An added challenge is how to structure groups to maximize the participation of children who are learning English.

Teachers whose classes include second-language learners need to give serious consideration to the linguistic abilities of children as they form groups. There are times when children organize their own groups. There is evidence that ESL learners who choose to work with others still learning the language can be successful at negotiating content and using English to learn, especially if the learners come from different native language backgrounds and are in the numerical minority in a classroom (Willett,

1995). At other times, however, teachers may assign children to work or play with others. At these times, particularly if the teachers have an agenda of language development along with academic learning, teachers may group heterogeneously in terms of language ability, making sure that groups contain more- and less-able users of English. In this way, the less-proficient speakers learn from those with more proficiency. However, factors other than language proficiency may also need to be taken into account when organizing groups. Jerri Willett, for example, has reported that a teacher grouped two English speakers with a Spanish speaker, thinking that the English speakers would work with the other child and thus facilitate his English development (1995). However, the two English speakers were girls, and they resisted collaborating with the Spanish-speaking boy, refusing to interact with him. Collaboration became a reality only when this young child worked (and played) with other boys.

In settings where many of the learners come from one home language (e.g., Spanish), groups may be formed that include at least one native English speaker, one child who is bilingual, and one child who speaks Spanish fluently but is not yet fluent in English. In these groupings, the bilingual learner often acts as a language broker, assisting the other children in communicating with each other (Fournier, Lansdowne, Pastenes, Steen, & Hudelson, 1992). This assumes that children are free to use languages other than English in the classroom, even if children ultimately share their work in English.

THE USE OF LANGUAGE-CENTERED ACTIVITIES WITH BILINGUAL AND SECOND-LANGUAGE LEARNERS

In bilingual and second-language classrooms, many activities that teachers organize focus specifically on language. This chapter discusses the language-centered practices of read-aloud experiences, sharing, storytelling, and language play, all of which need to be considered for bilingual and ESL learners. Each language-centered practice is discussed in turn.

Read-Aloud Experiences

Reading aloud is a central component of instruction, not a frill. It is central to both first- and second-language development. Reading aloud should be done in children's home languages, as well as in English, even if there is not a formal bilingual program in place. In some Spanish–English bilingual classrooms, teachers group children by language for one read-aloud experience daily, so that the Spanish-dominant children listen and respond to Spanish-language literature and the English-dominant children do the same in English. At other times, the children are mixed, and both languages are used to negotiate story content.

SPECIAL FEATURE 3.2 (continued)

Sharing

Sharing is employed by many teachers because it gives children an opportunity to talk about aspects of their own lives and encourages them to listen to each other. There is evidence that successful participation in such classroom activities is important for ESL learners' linguistic development and for their ability to negotiate in mainstream classrooms (Ernst, 1994). However, children who are just learning English may be much less confident in using the new language than their English-speaking peers. They may speak more slowly, with more hesitations. They may not articulate as native speakers do. Their verbalizations may be incomplete or unconventional syntactically. This may make it more difficult for them to share their experiences and to get and maintain the attention of their peers. Given these realities, teachers may need to take an active role in facilitating the participation of ESL children. This role may include negotiating with others opportunities for ESL learners to talk, assisting children in articulating what they want to contribute, and sensitizing other children to their struggles to express themselves (Ernst, 1994; Rudnick, 1995).

Storytelling

It has been our experience working with bilingual and second-language learners from many different backgrounds that many of them come from cultures where oral stories abound and storytelling traditions are strong (Au, 1993). Therefore, storytelling should occupy a prominent place in classrooms that are populated by numbers of culturally and linguistically diverse students. When teachers are telling stories, they need to incorporate stories that reflect the heritages of the children with whom they work (see, for example, Bishop, 1994; Bosma, 1994; Harris, 1992; and Miller-Lachman, 1995, for animal stories, fables, folktales, legends, and myths that might be used). Children need to be encouraged to tell stories from their cultural backgrounds. Parents may also be invited to classrooms to participate in storytelling. Storytelling opens up multiple possibilities for understanding diverse worldviews.

Language Play

Across cultures, children engage in language play (Lindfors, 1987). One of the oral traditions of many cultures is the sharing of rhymes, songs, riddles, games, tongue twisters, jokes, and so on across generations and among children. Teachers should make deliberate plans to use these forms, both to foster appreciation for other languages and cultures and to provide children with opportunities to manipulate the sounds of familiar and new languages. For example, teachers can make written records of these rhymes, songs, and finger plays in Spanish and English and can use them repeatedly in daily routines such as opening exercises, transitions between activities, introduction to read-aloud time, and school closing. Because children usually chant these forms in chorus, practice with the sounds of the new language takes place in a risk-free environment.

Unfortunately, such endeavors are very time consuming and not practical in most teaching situations.

A number of more practical options are available for assessing children's oral language abilities. To illustrate these options, we use an incident recently observed by two of the authors in a university preschool. Julia is a four-year-old Korean girl who has been in the United States for about eight months. She participates in classroom activities, especially dramatic play, but rarely speaks either in Korean (she is the only child from Korea in the class) or in English. Chari, Julia's teacher, is playing with several other children at the time of the incident. Chari takes on the role of a customer and asks to use the toy phone in a post office theme center. She picks up the phone and makes a pretend phone call to Buddy, whose behavior is becoming very raucous. Chari says, "Ring, ring, ring . . . Buddy, there's a package waiting here for you in the post office." This is successful in redirecting Buddy away from the rough-and-tumble play that he had been engaging in. Julia is playing by herself in the housekeeping center, pretending to be a parent taking care of a baby (a doll). Julia overhears Chari's pretend phone call to Buddy, but she continues with her solitary play. A few minutes later, Julia picks up a toy phone in the housekeeping center, and says: "Ring, ring . . . Miss Chari, will you come over to my house?" This is Julia's first complete sentence used in the classroom!

As you review Figure 3.2, what skills has Julia demonstrated?

Chari has several options for recalling Julia's language breakthrough. She might use a checklist. Figure 3.3 is a checklist used in a multilingual classroom. This checklist focuses on Michael Halliday's (1975) functional uses of language (see Table 2.1). Such checklists are easy to use and require little time. This checklist can be easily modified to fit other situations (for example, for a monolingual classroom, the language columns could be eliminated) or to focus on

FIGURE 3.2 Arizona's Young Learners Standards—Oral Language Development

STRAND 1: ORAL LANGUAGE DEVELOPMENT—Preschool

Concept 1: Listening and Understanding—The child listens with understanding to directions, stories, and conversations. During the preschool years, children learn language more quickly than at any other time in their lives. Associating language with pleasant and stimulating experiences nurtures this development. Young children's sense of words and sentences, sensitivity to tone, and understanding of ideas communicated, influences their abilities to listen and to comprehend. Listening involves paying attention to adults and peers as they share their ideas, feelings, and needs. Listening is a blend of building relationships and processing information.

Indicators:

Comprehends finger-plays, rhymes, chants, poems, conversations, and stories.

Follows directions that involve

■ One step

■ Two steps

■ A series of unrelated sequences of action

Examples in the Context of Daily Routines, Activities, and Play:

■ Child responds by gestures, actions, and language.

■ Child points to blocks when asked, "Where would you like to play?"

■ Child claps when prompted with, "If you're happy and you know it, clap your hands."

■ Child places toy truck on shelf when adult says, "Please put the truck on the shelf."

■ Child follows directions when an adult says, "Please wipe your nose and toss the tissue in the trash."

■ Child responds to directions, "Put the block on the table, put your paper in the cubby, and line up to go outside."

Concept 2: Speaking and Communicating—The child uses verbal and nonverbal communication to share ideas for a variety of purposes (e.g., ask questions, express needs, and obtain information). Children develop language by engaging in conversations with others and listening and responding to rhymes, chants, songs, stories, and poems. Children who are encouraged to share their personal experiences, ideas, feelings, and opinions develop confidence using increasingly complex language.

Indicators:

Communicates needs, wants, and thoughts, through nonverbal gestures, actions, or expressions.

Recites finger plays, rhymes, songs, or short poems.

Makes relevant responses to questions and comments from others.

Is understood when sharing experiences, ideas, and feelings with others through the use of language and gestures.

Initiates conversations.

Uses appropriate **tone** and **inflection** to express ideas, feelings, and needs.

Sustains or expands conversations.

Recognizes when the listener does not understand and uses techniques to clarify the message.

Examples in the Context of Daily Routines, Activities, and Play:

Child leads adult to the bookshelf and points to a book.

■ Child sings the words of the song "The Wheels on the Bus."

■ Child says, "I want to paint" when asked, "What would you like to do next?"

■ When talking about puppies, child tells or uses sign language to indicate that her dog had puppies. Another child asks, "How many puppies are there?"

■ Child approaches peers and asks, "What are you building?"

■ Child comforts a crying child and softly speaks, "It's going to be okay."

■ After zipping his jacket, child exclaims, "I did it!"

■ When someone is talking about a trip to a park, another child adds, "I went to the park too. We had a picnic."

■ When child realizes he has been misunderstood, he uses a gesture and/or a different word to clarify the intended message.

Example Arizona's Early Learning Standards—2005 Arizona.

Kindergarten Standard—*Oral language development is an important set of skills encompassing both the understanding of what is said and the use of speech to engage in conversation and express ideas, wants, and needs. These skills begin developing at birth and continue progressing throughout a child's pre-K years and beyond. The abilities to listen with understanding and communicate clearly are important precursors, or forerunners, that provide the foundation necessary for developing prereading and prewriting concepts.*

FIGURE 3.3

Oral
Language
Checklist

Child's Name	Language			Partner(s)			Location								Function						
	English	Spanish	Other	Child	Several Children	Adult	Library	Writing	Listening	Housekeeping	Theme (play)	Blocks	Math/Sci	Art	Instrumental	Regulatory	Interaction	Personal	Heuristic	Imaginative	Informative
Julia	✓									✓										✓	

other aspects of language. Such instruments provide a broad view of the language that children use in the classroom. However, much of the richness of the children's actual language is lost.

Chari might use a less-structured observation-recording form, such as the one illustrated in Figure 3.4. Forms like this allow teachers to record more detailed information about children's language behaviors. Typically such forms have columns for children's names, samples of their speech, and other variables that might be of interest to the teacher. Chari is interested in knowing the context within which her children's language samples are collected and the language forms illustrated. Hence, she added two columns to the observation-recording form she uses in her classroom. Notice that she does not put lines on her observation-recording form. This is intentional. No lines means that Chari can record as much information about each incident as necessary for her to recall each language event. Compare the information on this form to that recorded on the checklist. Notice how the observation-recording form captured much more of the essence of Julia's language accomplishment than did the checklist.

Chari might use an anecdotal record. Anecdotal records are even less structured than an observation-recording form (Figure 3.5). Here, the teacher writes a brief description of the language incident on a piece of paper, index card, or sticky note. Later, Chari can file these anecdotes in individual folders for each of her children. This unstructured format allows Chari to make the most detailed description of Julia's.

As suggested earlier, teachers may elect to make audio or video recordings of children's language activity. Genishi and Dyson (1984) have developed guidelines for making audio recordings. These are adapted to include video recordings:

FIGURE 3.4

Oral Language Observation Recording Form

Child's Name	Context	What Was Said	Language Forms
Julia	Playing role of mother in house keeping center.	Ring, ring... Miss Chari... Will you come to my house?	Complete sentence!

■ Select an activity setting that encourages language interaction. (Dramatic play areas are a good place to start.)

■ If you are using a tape recorder, place it in the target setting and turn it on, checking first to make sure that the equipment is working. If using a video camcorder, place the camera on a tripod and adjust the zoom lens so that it covers the main area where children will be interacting. Turn the camera on, and check it occasionally to make sure that the camera angle is capturing the significant action.

■ Do a trial recording to make sure that the equipment is working correctly and that the children's language is being clearly recorded. This trial will also help desensitize the children to the equipment.

■ Listen or view the recordings as soon as possible so that your memory can help fill in the gaps in unintelligible parts of the recordings.

An effective way to analyze the data contained in audio and video recordings is to use a rubric to judge the quality of individuals' oral language behavior. A rubric is a set of criteria that describe student performance in terms of proficiency levels (O'Neil, 1994).

Summary

This chapter began with a review of the many ways parents can support their child's language development within the home. The remainder of the chapter described ways that teachers can provide young children with stimulating oral language experiences that promote active listening and more precise, sophisticated speech. How did your own experiences at home and at school compare with those described in this chapter? Did you recall other types of beneficial oral language activities that were not covered?

To summarize the key points about facilitating oral language learning, we return to the guiding questions at the beginning of this chapter:

■ *How can parents best facilitate their children's oral language development?*

Parents can promote their children's oral language by scaffolding their language, encouraging them to tell personal narratives about their experiences, reading stories to them on a regular basis, and monitoring their children's television viewing and encouraging active viewing.

FIGURE 3.5

Anecdotal Record

Julia   4/6/95

Julia observed me making a prentend phone call to Buddy from the post office center. Several minutes later she picked up the toy phone in the housekeeping center and said "Ring, ring .. Miss Chari, will you come to my house?" It was her first complete English sentence!

■ *What is the initiation, response, evaluation (IRE) pattern of class talk? What problems are associated with this type of discourse? How can teachers provide children with more stimulating conversations in the classroom?*

The IRE pattern of discourse occurs when the teacher asks a question, a student answers, and the teacher either accepts or rejects that answer and goes on to ask another question. These types of question-and-answer exchanges do not provide the type of language input and feedback needed to advance children's language skills. Teachers can provide richer oral language experiences for children by engaging them in reciprocal conversations and discussions—listening closely and responding to their comments; asking genuine, open-ended questions; welcoming the interjection of personal experiences; and encouraging child–child turn-taking.

■ *How do group activities, learning centers, and dramatic play promote oral language acquisition?*

These types of activities create language content (i.e., give children something to talk about). In addition, children must use language to participate successfully in these types of activities.

■ *What can teachers do to promote language-rich dramatic play?*

Teachers can promote language-rich play by providing (1) settings equipped with theme-related, culturally relevant props; (2) scheduling lengthy play periods; and (3) being actively involved in children's play activities.

■ *How can sharing or show-and-tell be turned into a valuable oral language activity?*

Traditional sharing involves having one child speak to the entire class. This activity can be transformed into a valuable oral language activity by limiting group size and encouraging children in the audience to actively participate by asking questions and making comments.

■ *How can teachers effectively assess children's oral language development?*

Teachers should observe children interacting during regular classroom activities and use checklists, observation sheets, and/or anecdotal records to document significant milestones in their oral language acquisition.

■ *What can teachers do to optimize oral language experiences for bilingual and second-language learners?*

The same strategies recommended for native English speakers are also appropriate for use with bilingual and second-language learners. The major adaptations that are needed are (1) exposing children to books and other print in the child's native language, and (2) allowing children lots of opportunity to speak, listen, read, and write in their native language.

LINKING KNOWLEDGE TO PRACTICE

1. Visit an early childhood classroom and observe children interacting in a dramatic play center. Note the theme that the children are acting out and the roles that they are playing. Record examples of both metaplay language and pretend language.
2. Observe children engaging in a sharing (show-and-tell) activity. Describe the teacher's role and the children's behavior (both the speaker and the audience). Did this sharing time involve most of the students in active listening?
3. Make an observation-recording form similar to the one in Figure 3.3. Visit an early childhood classroom and observe a small group of children interacting at a learning center. Use the observation-recording form to record several significant utterances from each child. What do these behaviors indicate about each child's language development?

Sharing Good Books with Young Children

The four-year-olds in Ms. Andrea Jackson's classroom are gathered together in the Circle Time area. They are ready for story time. Ms. Jackson begins by showing the children the back of the book. "Today I'm going to read you a story that is one of my favorites, Click, Clack, Moo Cows That Type. *Am I ready to begin reading?" Several children respond, "You have to turn the book the other way." Ms. Jackson turns it upside down. "No! To the front!" Ms. Jackson responds, "You are so right! Here is the front of the book." She reads the title, pointing to each word. "Doreen Cronin is the author of this book. What is an author?" Germaine responds, "The author writes the story and the illustrator draws the pictures." Several children express their agreement with Germaine's explanation. Ms. Jackson confirms, "You are so right! Doreen Cronin wrote this story, and the pictures are by Betsy Lewin. Take a look at the picture on the front of this book. Tell me what you see." The children label the picture—cows, chicken, bird. Ms. Jackson labels the chicken as a hen and the bird as a duck. As Ms. Jackson predicted, none of the children label the typewriter. She reaches behind her, pulls the cover off an old typewriter, and places it on a stand so all the children can see it. "What is this?" she asks. Quintella responds, "An old computer." Ms. Jackson asks him to explain his thinking. He notes that it has a "keyboard a little like the [classroom's] computer." Ms. Jackson compliments him on his observation. She explains, "Before computers, people typed their messages on this machine. It's called a typewriter. Say that with me. Typewriter." She hits a couple of keys so that the children can hear the click and the clack. "I'll leave this typewriter out during center time so that you can try typing a message on a typewriter. [She puts special stress on the word.] We'll take a poll to see which you like best, a typewriter or a computer." She opens the book to the title page and rereads the title. She turns to the first page. "Now, this is a story about cows who like to do what?" The children respond, "Type." Ms. Jackson asks, "On what?" The children respond, "A typewriter!" Ms. Jackson asks, "So if this story is about cows, who might this man be?" She points to the picture of the farmer. The children respond, "A farmer!" Ms. Jackson asks, "Does he look happy or sad?" Anarundle thinks sad "because his mouth is upside down." Ms. Jackson expands, "His mouth is upside down. He is frowning." She reads the text. "So was Anarundle right? Is the farmer sad?" The children think so. "Why?" she asks. Germaine says, "Farmer Brown is not happy because the cows are typing and making noise." Ms. Jackson says, "Let's see." On each page, the children and the teacher talk about the text. The teacher explains unfamiliar words, like "strike," "impatient," "furious," "ultimatum," and "diving board." They figure out that Farmer Brown is probably really unhappy when the cows type a note telling him that they won't give him milk and another note that the hens won't give him eggs unless they get the electric blankets they requested. "He's getting madder and madder." They talk about why Farmer Brown typed his note to cows and hens. "What do you think he hoped would happen?" They talk about how Farmer Brown's problem with the cows and hens was solved. They talk about how Farmer Brown probably felt when he heard the ducks typing "click, clack, quack." They talk about whether or not the ducks had a good idea. "Would they get their diving board?" Ms. Jackson asks. As Ms. Jackson turns the last page, a wordless page, she asks the children, "What do you think the ducks might be saying?" De'Zebbra responds, "Hooray! We got our diving board!" As Ms. Jackson closes the book, she asks, "Have you ever written a note or letter asking for something? Did you get what you wanted?" Ms. Jackson elaborates. "Yesterday, I wrote a note to your families asking them if they could send in celery and cream cheese for our cooking activity tomorrow. Look at that shelf over there. Did my note work? Did I get what I wanted?" These four-year-olds struggle to share examples from their experiences. Ms. Jackson says, "I put some special note-writing paper in the Writing Center today. Maybe you want to write someone about something you want or need. Maybe you want to type your note on the typewriter that I'll put in the Writing Center. [Later in the day, Ms. Jackson receives the following typed message: I ned nu mrkrz. (I need new markers.) The next day she brings in new markers, reads the child's message, and shows the children the new markers. Guess what happened that day during Center Time.]*

As early as 1908, Edmond Huey wrote about children's acquisition of reading and noted that "the key to it all lies in the parents reading aloud to and with the child" (p. 332). Today, after decades of research on the teaching of reading, we continue to agree with Huey. More recently Marilyn Adams (1990) summarized what many educators believe and research supports: "The single most important activity for building the knowledge and skills eventually required for reading appears to be reading aloud to children" (p. 46). Even more recently, reading to children has been characterized as "a cornerstone of literacy development and classroom practice" (Brabham & Lynch-Brown, 2002, p. 465). This single act—parents' and teachers' reading aloud to children—has received more research attention than any other aspect of young children's literacy development.

What do we know about the benefits of parents' or other adults' reading aloud to young children? Come peek in on one of Joseph's storybook-reading events with his father, Mike (Mowery, 1993). The reading begins with Mike inviting eighteen-month-old Joseph to pick "one [a book] that Daddy hasn't read in a while"—and Joseph eagerly climbing up into his father's lap. Already *Joseph knows that books are enjoyable;* he even has favorites. Dad waits for Joseph to snuggle in and turn the book so it is ready to be opened. Already *Joseph knows how to hold the book and knows that it needs to be held in a certain way to open*—skills Marie Clay (1985) would call important concepts about print. Joseph quickly moves beyond the title page; *he knows the story begins on the page with more print*—another concept about print. He looks up at Mike, perhaps signaling "ready." *He knows what his father will do (read and talk), and he knows what he should do (listen and talk).* Sometimes Mike says, "What's this?" as he points to a picture in the book. Joseph does his best to label the picture. And Mike says, "Hey, it's a ____! And this is a ____." And Joseph says, "Hey! ____!" *Joseph increases his vocabulary as he labels pictures in books* and as he hears words read aloud in the context of a story.

Today Mike reads a story that is one of Joseph's favorites, but one Mike has grown weary of reading. To hurry the reading along, Mike creates a sentence to accompany the picture on a page. Joseph says, "NO! NO! READ!" and he points to the words on the page. *Already Joseph knows about the stability of words in books; they tell the same story each time. He also seems to know that his father reads the words on the page, not the pictures.* This is an atypical skill for an eighteen-month-old. As soon as Mike finishes reading the book, Joseph looks up at him and says sweetly, "Read it again, Daddy." *Joseph is learning to love books,* one of the most important gifts his family can give him. The National Education Goals Panel (1997) summarizes:

Early, regular reading to children is one of the most important activities parents can do with their children to improve their readiness for school, serve as their child's first teacher, and instill a love of books and reading. Reading to children familiarizes them with story comprehension such as characters, plot, action, and sequence ("Once upon a time . . .," ". . . and they lived happily ever after"), and helps them associate oral language with printed text. Most important, reading to children builds their vocabularies and background knowledge about the world. (p. 20)

Helen Ezell and Laura Justice (2005) add to the list of reasons why adults should read books to children. Through storybook reading, children are exposed to:

- linguistic concepts, such as descriptive adjectives (e.g., grumpy, fierce, scary);
- sound structure and grammar of their language;
- pragmatic rules that govern the use of language;
- how narratives are organized;
- alphabet and the way in which letters and sounds map on to one another.

Margaret McKeown and Isabel Beck (2006, p. 284) add one more idea to this impressive list of the benefits of reading storybooks to young children:

Book language is decontextualized, removed from everyday tangible and familiar experiences within the immediate context. In order to make sense of text they hear, listeners need to build ideas from words alone. Participating in decontextualized language, forming ideas about what was in a book, and expressing them in ways that make sense to others are the ingredients of building communication competence.

The importance of experiences with decontextualized language to young children's development is a common theme in today's storybook-reading literature. Storybook reading, then, is very important for children's language and literacy development.

This chapter is about how to share books with young children. We begin by explaining how teachers can set up inviting library centers in their classrooms and how they can effectively read stories to young children. Finally, we discuss how story-reading sessions can be an ideal context for assessing children's literacy growth.

BEFORE READING THIS CHAPTER, THINK ABOUT . . .

- The favorite books from your childhood. Did you have one or two favorite books that you liked to have your parents, siblings, or other adults read to you or a favorite book that you liked to read on your own?
- When your teachers read stories to you in school. Does any one teacher stand out as being particularly skilled at storybook reading? If so, why?

FOCUS QUESTIONS

- How can teachers set up a well-designed library center?
- What are the characteristics of effective adult storybook reading?
- What are some of the ways children can respond to and extend the stories that they have been read?
- How can teachers use storybook-reading sessions to assess children's literacy development?

Making Books Accessible to Young Children

The careful selection of quality picture storybooks can play an important role in young children's development. According to Charlotte Huck, Barbara Kiefer, Susan Hepler, and Janet Hickman (2004), quality picture storybooks can

enlarge children's lives, stretch their imaginations, and enhance their living. The phenomenal growth of beautiful picture books for children of all ages is an outstanding accomplishment of

BOX 4.1 Definition of terms	**author study:** teacher reads a set of books by one author and invites children to discuss and compare the books
	creative dramatics: children act out a story with no printed script or memorized lines
	decontextualized language: language that is removed from everyday tangible and familiar experiences within the immediate context; no supports from the immediate environment to help get the point across
	interactive reading: important interactions that occur between adults and children during storybook reading
	read-aloud (shared reading): adult (parent, teacher) and child reading of and talking about a book or an adult reading and talking about a book to a group of children
	shared big-book reading: teacher reading of an enlarged book—a book different from the typical book read to children in size only—to a group of children

the past fifty years of publishing. Children do not always recognize the beauty of these books, but early impressions do exert an influence on the development of permanent tastes for children growing up. (p. 250)

To help teachers make appropriate selections of quality books, we suggest two resources. First, we suggest readers consider obtaining a copy of Charlotte Huck, Barbara Kiefer, Susan Hepler, and Janet Hickman's book, *Children's Literature in the Elementary School*. Though the title says "elementary school," the book is a rich resource for teachers of children of all ages. It alerts readers to a multitude of titles of outstanding literature, noting the likely age of children who would enjoy the book most. At the end of each chapter, readers will find pages and pages of recommended titles. This book is a *must* for every teacher's professional library.

A second resource we suggest is the Internet. One of our favorite Web sites is the American Library Association's *Great Web Sites for Kids*. This site links readers to numerous other sites, each coded for its appropriateness for preschool children (www.ala.org/gwstemplate. cfm?section=greatwebsites&template=/cfapps/gws/default.cfm). Another excellent Internet resource is the Children's Book Council Web site. In the "Booklists" section, for example, readers will find a list of recommended books for children ages 0 to 3 and thematic annotated reading lists for all ages, which are update bimonthly (www.cbcbooks.org). A third resource, the Cooperative Children's Book Center, has created bibliographies and lists of recommended books on a wide range of themes and topics. This Web site has a special section for early childhood care providers. (See www.education.wisc.edu/ccbc/books/bibBio.asp?publications=true.) Further, most trade book publishers have individual Web sites that showcase their authors' books. Several of these sites have an advanced search feature that allows searches by title, author, illustrator, subject, or age group. Several of the Web sites referenced above sort their book recommendations by age (e.g., ages 0 to 3, 3 to 5). This is very helpful to teachers because children of different ages, or stages of development, need books with different features. In Special Feature 4.1, Billie Enz and two colleagues provide a few book suggestions for children from birth through age three based on developmental characteristics.

Certainly, teachers should share literature representative of various cultures. Again we recommend the Internet for the most up-to-date information on multicultural books. For example, www.cbcbooks.org is a Web site of annotated bibliographies organized by genre (e.g., realistic fiction, nonfiction, biography, fantasy) and culture (e.g., African American, Latino/Hispanic American, Korean American, Japanese American, Jewish American, Native American). Middle East is a new addition to this Web site.

A variety of sites can be found using the descriptors "multicultural children's literature" with any of the major search engines (Yahoo, Lycos, Excite, Alta Vista, etc.). For example, a recent search located the site Internet School Library Media Center (ISLMC) Multicultural Page. The ISLMC advertises itself as "a meta site which brings together resources for teachers, librarians, parents and students." Linda Labbo (2005) and Linda Robinson (2003) remind teachers that in this new millennium access to "just" books is no longer sufficient. Young children also should have access to "appropriately designed computer programs and Internet

Reading by Ages and Stages

Dawn Foley, Monique Davis, and Billie J. Enz

Certain types of books are better for young children at different ages and stages.

BIRTH TO ONE YEAR

High Contrasting Colors (Black/White/Red) (Birth to Six Months)

Studies have shown that babies prefer these colors in the early weeks of life up until six months of age. Their vision is not fully developed, and they respond best to bold contrasting colors and graphics.

White on Black. Hoban, T. (1993). New York: Greenwillow Books.

Black on White. Hoban, T. (1993). New York: Greenwillow Books.

What Is That? Hoban, T. (1994). New York: Greenwillow Books.

Who Are They? Hoban, T. (1994). New York: Greenwillow Books.

Baby Animals Black and White. Tildes, P. (1998). Watertown, MA: Charlesbridge Publishing.

Colors (Five Months to One Year)

Babies gain visual perception much more quickly than was once believed. It is important to select books with a single object on each page so as to not overstimulate children. Children less than eighteen months often have difficulty understanding complicated illustrations that adults recognize instantly. Books with one color image are the best.

Spot Looks at Colors. Hill, E. (1986). New York: Putnam Publishing Group.

Red, Blue, Yellow Shoe. Hoban, T. (1986). New York: Greenwillow Books.

Brown Bear, Brown Bear. Carle, E. (1992). New York: Henry Holt & Company LLC.

I Love Colors. Miller, M. (1999). New York: Little Simon.

Happy Colors. Weeks, S. (2001). New York: Reader's Digest Children's Books.

Little Blue and Little Yellow. Lionni, L. (1995). New York: Mulberry Books.

Textured Books

These books encourage babies to reach out and touch the pages. Shared reading, then, becomes an enjoyable tactile experience. Texture also allows babies to use their sensory exploratory approach to learning about the objects around them.

Touch and Feel: Baby Animals. (1999). New York: Dorling Kindersley Publishing.

Touch and Feel: Kitten. (1999). New York: Dorling Kindersley Publishing.

Touch and Feel: Puppy. (1999). New York: Dorling Kindersley Publishing.

That's Not My Teddy. Watt, F. & Wells, R. (1999). London: Usborne Publishing Ltd.

That's Not My Puppy. Watt, F. & Wells, R. (1999). London: Usborne Publishing Ltd.

Kipper's Sticky Paws. Inkpen, M. (2001). London: Hodder Children's Books.

Touch and Feel: Pets. (2001). New York: Dorling Kindersley Publishing.

Night, Night Baby. Birkinshaw, M. (2002). London: Ladybird Books.

Object Labeling (Familiar and Environmental) with Texture

Babies are beginning to learn and explore their world. Object labeling allows them to get to know their environment. These kinds of books encourage the readers to point to and name the objects in the book.

Touch and Feel: Home. (1998). New York: Dorling Kindersley Publishing.

Touch and Feel: Clothes. (1998). New York: Dorling Kindersley Publishing.

Match Shapes with Me. Hood, S. (1999). New York: Reader's Digest Children's Books.

Baby Faces. Miller, M. (1998). New York: Little Simon.

Touch and Feel: Shapes. (2000). New York: Dorling Kindersley Publishing.

Buster's Bedtime. Campbell, R. (2000). London: Campbell Books.

Touch and Feel: Bedtime. (2001). New York: Dorling Kindersley Publishing.

The Going to Bed Book. Boynton, S. (1995). New York: Little Simon.

Froggy Gets Dressed. London, J. (1992). New York: Scholastic.

ONE TO TWO YEARS

Interactive/Lift the Flap Books

These kinds of books encourage babies to reach out and touch the pages. Again, they experience and enjoy reading as a tactile experience. Texture also allows babies to build on their sensory exploratory approach to learning about the objects around them.

Where is Baby's Belly Button? Katz, K. (2000). New York: Little Simon.

Fit-A-Shape: Shapes. (2000). Philadelphia, PA: Running Press.

Fit-A-Shape: Food. (2001). Philadelphia, PA: Running Press.

(continued on next page)

Where's My Fuzzy Blanket? Carter, N. (2001). New York: Scholastic Paperbacks.

Where is Baby's Mommy? Katz, K. (2001). New York: Little Simon.

Fit-A-Shape: Clothes. (2001). Philadelphia, PA: Running Press.

The Wheels on the Bus. Stanley, M. (2002). Bristol, PA: Baby's First Book Club.

Touch and Talk: Make Me Say Moo! Greig, E. (2002). Bristol, PA: Sandvick Innovations.

Quack, Quack, Who's That? Noel, D. & Galloway, R. (2002). London: Little Tiger Press.

Labeling Familiar People, Emotions, and Actions

These kinds of books encourage the reader to point to and name the objects in the book. In addition, readers can encourage the child to say the name of the objects in the book.

Winnie the Pooh: Feelings. Smith, R. (2000). New York: Random House Disney.

WOW! Babies. Gentieu, P. (2000). New York: Crown Publishers.

Faces. Miglis, J. (2002). New York: Simon Spotlight.

Feelings. Miglis, J. (2002). New York: Simon Spotlight.

Where the Wild Things Are. Sendak, Maurice (1988). New York: Harper Trophy.

Alexander and the Terrible, Horrible, No Good, Very Bad Day. Viorst, J. (1987). New York: Aladdin Library.

The Selfish Crocodile. Charles, F. & Terry, M. (2000). New York: Scholastic.

Glad Monster, Sad Monster: A Book about Feelings. Emberley, E. & Miranda, A. (1997). New York: Scholastic.

No David! Shannon, D. (1998). New York: Scholastic Trade.

Rhyme and Rhythm

Between twelve and eighteen months, children discover that words have meaning. With this in mind, book selections should stimulate the children's sight and hearing. Books with rhymes are excellent because they introduce the children to sounds and syllables and to the rhythm and rhyme of language.

Each Peach Pear Plum. Ahlberg, A. & Ahlberg, J. (1978). London: Penguin Books Ltd.

Moo, Baa, La La La. Boynton, S. (1982). New York: Little Simon.

Down by the Bay. Raffi, & Westcott, N. B. (1990). New York: Crown Publishers.

Five Little Ducks. Raffi (1999). New York: Crown Publishers.

Five Little Monkeys Sitting in a Tree. Christelow, E. (1993). St. Louis, MO: Clarion.

This Old Man. Jones, C. (1990). New York: Houghton Mifflin Co.

The Itsy Bitsy Spider. Trapani, I. (1993). Watertown, MA: Charlesbridge Publishing.

Find the Puppy. Cox, P. (2001). London: Usborne Publishing Ltd.

Find the Kitten. Cox, P. (2001). Newton, MA: EDC Publications.

Five Little Monkeys Jumping on the Bed. Christelow, E. (1998). New York: Houghton Mifflin.

TWO TO THREE YEARS

Encourage Scribbling

Children who are encouraged to draw and scribble "stories" at an early age will later learn to compose more easily, more effectively, and with greater confidence than children who do not have this encouragement.

Crayon World. Santomero, A. (1999). New York: Simon Spotlight.

Figure Out Blue's Clues. Perello, J. (1999) New York: Simon Spotlight.

Blue's Treasure Hunt Notebook. Santomero, A. (1999). New York: Simon Spotlight.

Harold's Fairy Tale: Further Adventures with the Purple Crayon. Johnson, C. (1994). New York: Harper Trophy.

Harold's Trip to the Sky. Johnson, C. (1981). New York: Harper Collins.

A Picture for Harold's Room. Johnson, C. (1985). New York: Harper Trophy.

Harold and the Purple Crayon. Johnson, C. (1981). New York: Harper Collins.

Get in Shape to Write. Bongiorno, P. (1998). New York: Pen Notes.

Messages in the Mailbox: How to Write a Letter. Leedy, L. (1994). New York: Holiday House.

Let's Learn to Write Letters: A Wipe-It-Off Practice Book. Troll Books (1994). Memphis, TN: Troll Association.

Let's Learn to Write Numbers: A Wipe-It-Off Practice Book. Troll Books (1994). Memphis, TN: Troll Association.

Environmental Print

Children of this age are beginning to attend to print in the environment. Readers might select books that they "read" with the children. With the supportive surrounding context, many children can read many words found in their environment (e.g., STOP, EXIT).

M & M's Counting Book. McGrath Barbieri, B. (1994). Watertown, MA: Charlesbridge Publishing.

The Pokéman Book of Colors. Muldrow, D. (2000). New York: Golden Books Company, Inc.

SPECIAL FEATURE **4.1** *(continued)*

The Pokéman Counting Book. Muldrow, D. (1999). New York: Golden Books Company, Inc.

The Cheerios Play Book. Wade, L. (1998). New York: Little Simon.

The Cheerios Animal Play Book. Wade, L. (1999). New York: Simon and Schuster Merchandise.

Pepperidge Farm Goldfish Fun Book. McGrath, B.B. (2000). New York: Harper Festival.

Kellogg's Froot Loops! Counting Fun Book. McGrath, B.B. (2000). New York: Harper Festival.

The Sun Maid Raisins Playbook. Weir, A. (1999). New York: Little Simon.

The Oreo Cookie Counting Book. Albee, S. (2000). New York: Little Simon.

Pepperidge Farm Goldfish Counting Fun Book. McGrath, B.B. (2000). New York: Harper Festival.

sites . . . [to] support [their] . . . engagement with ideas, words, and various genres of text" (Labbo, 2005, p. 288). Robinson suggests that early childhood teachers choose storybook software with a high degree of interactivity, allowing children control over such features as the pace of the presentation, the turning of the "page," and the reading of the text word by word or line by line. Once appropriate selections have been made, the teacher's challenge is to organize the books to make them accessible to their students—to encourage them to voluntarily read, read, read.

Classroom Library Centers

A key feature of a classroom for young children is a well-stocked, well-designed library center. Classroom libraries promote independent reading by providing children with easy access to books and a comfortable place for browsing and reading. Children have been found to read more books in classrooms with libraries than in ones without libraries (Morrow & Weinstein, 1982). As Stephen Krashen (1987, p. 2) has pointed out, this finding supports "the common-sense view that children read more when there are more books around."

Fifteen-month-old Emma reads one of her favorite books.

However, the mere presence of a classroom library is not enough to ensure heavy use by young children. The library must contain an ample supply of appropriate and interesting books for children to read. Design features are also important. Lesley Morrow and Carol Weinstein (1982) found that children did not choose to use "barren and uninviting" library corners during center time. However, when the design features of centers were improved, children's library usage increased dramatically.

BOOKS. In order to attract and hold children's interest, a classroom library must be stocked with lots of good books to read. Experts recommend that classroom libraries contain five to eight books per child (Fractor et al., 1993; Morrow, 2005). According to these guidelines, a class of twenty children would require 100 to 160 books. These books should be divided into a core collection and one or more revolving collections. The core collection should be made up of high-quality literature that remains constant and available all year. These should be books that appeal to most of the children in class and that most children will enjoy reading on more than one occasion. Lesley Morrow (2005) also recommends that the books be color coded according to type. For example, all animal books could be identified with blue dots on their spines so they can be clustered together on a shelf marked *Animals*. Each category would be distinguished by a different color. Morrow suggests that color coding "introduces children to the idea that books in libraries are organized so as to be readily accessible" (p. 253).

Revolving collections change every few weeks to match children's current interests and topics being studied in class. For example, if several children become hooked on an author, such as Tomie de Paola or Maurice Sendak, collections of the author's books could be brought into the library to capitalize on this interest. If the class were studying seeds and plants, then picture storybooks and informational books relating to these topics could be added. When student interest shifts to a new author or when a new topic is under investigation, the old sets of revolving books are replaced with new ones.

Quality and variety are also of utmost importance in selecting books for the classroom library (Fractor et al., 1993). In order to motivate voluntary reading and to instill positive attitudes toward written texts, books must catch children's attention, hold their interest, and captivate their imaginations. Only high-quality literature will achieve these goals.

A well-designed library center invites children to read books.

PHYSICAL CHARACTERISTICS.   A number of physical features have been identified that make libraries attractive to children and that promote book reading (Morrow, 1982, 2005):

◆ *Partitions*—Bookshelves, screens, large plants, or other barriers set the library center apart from the rest of the classroom. This gives children a sense of privacy and provides a cozy, quiet setting for reading.

◆ *Ample space*—There should be enough room for at least five or six children to use the library at one time.

◆ *Comfortable furnishings*—The more comfortable the library area, the more likely it is that children will use it. Soft carpeting, chairs, old sofas, bean bags, and a rocking chair all help create a comfortable atmosphere for reading.

◆ *Open-faced and traditional shelves*—Traditional shelves display books with their spines out, whereas open-faced shelves display the covers of books. Open-faced shelves are very effective in attracting children's attention to specific books. Researchers have found that when both types of shelves are used, kindergartners chose more than 90 percent of their books from the open-faced displays (Fractor et al., 1993). Traditional shelves are also useful because they can hold many more books than open-faced shelves. Many teachers rotate books between traditional and open-faced shelves, advertising different books each week.

◆ *Book-related displays and props*—Posters (available from such sources as the Children's Book Council, 67 Irving Place, New York, NY 10003; the American Library Association, 50 East Huron Street, Chicago, Illinois 60611; and the International Reading Association, 800 Barksdale Road, Newark, Delaware 19711), puppets, flannel boards with cutout figures of story characters, and stuffed animals encourage children to engage in emergent reading and to act out favorite stories. Stuffed animals also are useful as listeners or babies for children to read to.

◆ *Labels for the center*—Like cordoning off the area from the classroom space, symbolic cues help define the space and identify appropriate activities for young children. Using both print, "Library Corner," and symbols associated with the library—book jackets, a photograph of a child looking at a book—helps even the youngest child read the label for the corner.

◆ *Writing center*—Some teachers like to place a writing center near the library corner. This accessibility seems to prompt young children to make illustrations and write in their personal script or dictate a sentence to an adult about the stories they are reading. A description of one young writer's behaviors illustrates how children might use the library corner to support their efforts in such a writing center. Allen, a kindergartner, sits looking into space, thinking, in the writing center. He collects a Post-it Note and writes "dot toht" ("Don't touch"), attaches it to his blank paper, and wanders into the library corner. Shortly, he returns, sits, and instantly begins writing a story about a caterpillar, with one word per line. His teacher surmised that while in the library corner Allen was engaging in prewriting, thinking about his topic and using Eric Carle's (1969) *The Very Hungry Caterpillar* as his writing model (see Figure 4.1).

To this list, Miriam Smith and David Dickinson add:

◆ *Listening center*—The Literacy Environment Checklist from the Early Language and Literacy Classroom Observation Toolkit (Smith & Dickinson, 2002) is used often to assess the quality of the literacy environment in preschool classrooms. Users examine the classroom's layout, looking for such items as a partitioned library area with comfortable furnishings and open-faced and traditional bookshelves and books ranging in difficulty level (e.g., wordless picture books to books with multiple paragraphs on each page). Smith and Dickinson expect this area also to contain a listening station, typically a table large enough for four to eight children to gather around a cassette or CD player, put on headphones, and listen to taped stories. The teacher provides multiple copies of the book on tape or CD so that children can turn the pages of the book as the story unfolds.

Remember, the better designed the library corner, the more use children will make of it—that is, more children will choose to participate in book reading and literature-related activities during free-choice periods. Therefore, a classroom library corner that is voluntarily used by few children is suspected to be a poorly designed center. What might an

FIGURE 4.1

Allen's Story

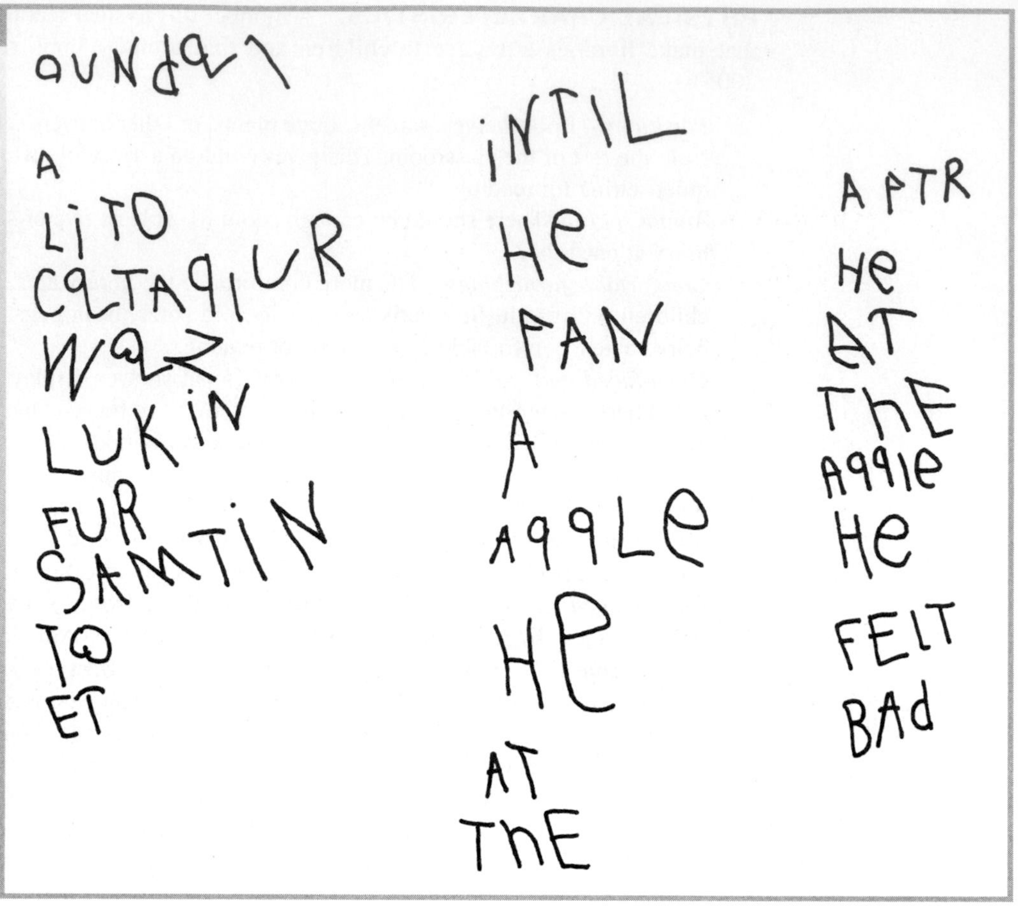

oVNDaL

A

LiTO

CILTAGIUR

WaZ

LUKIN

FUR

SAMTIN

TO

ET

iNTIL

HE

FAN

A

AggLe

HE

AT

TnE

A PTR

HE

AT

THE

Aggie

HE

FELT

BAd

enticing library corner look like? We provide a drawing of a possible library corner for an early childhood classroom in Figure 4.2.

Classroom Lending Library

We have already said it once: Reading aloud to young children is believed to be the single most important activity for building the knowledge and skills eventually required for their success in learning to read. Therefore, teachers regularly recommend that parents read to their young children. Unfortunately, many parents face great financial hardships and cannot provide high-quality reading materials in their homes (Becker & Epstein, 1982). While many communities house excellent public libraries with quality children's literature sections, these same parents often find it difficult to carve out time from their busy schedules to visit the library; working two or three jobs to meet pressing financial needs understandably takes priority. Therefore, for parents to fulfill their roles as partners in literacy programs, teachers must work with these families to offer easy access to books (Brock & Dodd, 1994).

Many early childhood teachers have attempted to get quality literature into the homes of all their young students through the creation of classroom lending libraries. These libraries allow children to check out a book every day, thus ensuring that all parents have an opportunity to read to their children frequently.

A first step in the creation of a lending library is the acquisition of books. Because the children will exchange a book for a different book each week, a teacher in a twelve-month child care program with twenty children in her classroom would need at least fifty-two books in the classroom lending library. For a new teacher, that is a lot of books, especially when that new teacher is also building the classroom library. Terrell Young and Barbara Moss (2006) make the following suggestions about how to acquire books without spending too much:

FIGURE 4.2 Library Center

- Use bonus points from classroom book clubs.
- Attend garage sales to purchase books at bargain prices.
- Ask older children to "adopt" the class, passing on the gently used books they have outgrown to younger children.
- Prepare a "wish list" for parents who are willing to purchase classroom reading materials.
- Look for organizations that provide small grants to teachers to buy books.

The rules that accompany the classroom lending library are simple. A child may borrow one book each week. When the book is returned, the child may check out another book. Teacher Carolyn Lingo puts a book and an activity appropriate for the book in a bag for her young learners. For example, one of her book bags is built around *Mouse Paint* (Walsh, 1989). The materials in the book bag include small vials of paint, a smock, newspaper to cover the table, a paint brush, and mixing cups. First the parent and child read the book together. Then they pretend they are the mice in the book; they are to mix the yellow, blue, and red paints, just like the mice in the book did. What happens?

Sharing Literature with Children

Teachers can share literature with young children in several ways: by reading stories aloud, by engaging children in shared reading, and by encouraging them to respond to literature in a variety of ways.

Effective Story-Reading Strategies

In the earlier edition of this book, the following vignette introduced this chapter:

The four-year-olds in Ms. Jensen's class sit expectantly in a semicircle on the floor, waiting for one of their favorite activities—story time. They know that every day at this time their teacher will read them an interesting and entertaining story. "Today, I'm going to read you one of my all-time favorites, Where the Wild Things Are *by Maurice Sendak. Look at the strange creatures on the cover! What do you think this story will be about?" After fielding several predictions and comments from the children, Ms. Jensen reads this classic story with expression and a sense of drama. The children listen raptly to each page as Max, the main character, takes a fantastic journey to an island populated with fierce monsters. The children like the way Max manages to take control of the huge beasts (symbols for adults?) and becomes king of the island, but they are also relieved when Max decides to give up his newly found power and return to the comforts of home. When the story is finished, Ms. Jensen invites the children to discuss the parts that they liked best and to tell what they would have done if they were in Max's place. She then shows the children some stick puppets that represent Max, his mother, and some of the monsters. She invites the children to reenact the story during free-choice activity time.*

Compare Ms. Jensen's reading of *Where the Wild Things Are* to Ms. Jackson's reading of *Click, Clack, Moo Cows That Type,* the vignette at the beginning of the chapter. Ms. Jensen just read *Where the Wild Things Are* to her children. Just reading books with children is beneficial. But Laura Justice and Khara Pence's (2005) review of the storybook-reading literature led them to conclude that just reading books with children

> is not as effective as embedding particular types of strategies or interactive behaviors into reading to systematically build children's skills in specific areas . . . Research of the last decade has shown unequivocally that storybook reading interactions between children and adults can be manipulated to maximize children's gains. . . . For instance, adults can point to print and track the print when they read to help develop children's interest in print and awareness of print forms and functions. Likewise, adults can pause during reading sessions when they encounter unfamiliar words to define and talk about those words; this strategy builds children's vocabulary knowledge.
>
> (Justice & Pence, 2005, p. ix)

The verbal interaction between adult and child that occurs during story readings has a major influence on children's literacy development (Justice & Ezell, 2000; Wasik & Bond, 2001; Whitehurst et al., 1994). Getting children to talk about the text or think about what is going on in the story is central to children's literacy growth.

ADULT BEHAVIORS WHILE READING. The majority of researchers have concentrated on the human interactions during story reading. From this research, we learn about turn-taking in story reading. Through story reading, very young children are guided into the turn-taking pattern inherent in all conversation: the adult (in this research the adult is usually a parent) talks, then the child talks, then the adult talks, and so forth.

It is within this verbal exchange that the dyad (parent and child) engages in its most significant negotiations: negotiating the meaning of the story. Obviously the adult's understanding exceeds the child's understanding of the text. Through scaffolding, the adult gently moves the child toward the adult's understanding of the text. That is, the adult questions the child about the text's meaning. The child replies, and this reply gives the adult a cue. Based on the child's response, the adult adjusts the kind of support (the scaffold) provided. To aid the child's construction of the meaning, the adult behaves in three ways: (1) as a co-respondent who shares experiences and relates the reading to personal experiences, (2) as an informer who provides information, and (3) as a monitor who questions and sets expectations for the reading session (Roser & Martinez, 1985).

Adults play these roles differently depending on the child's response and age.

◆ With a baby or toddler (twelve months or younger), the adult tends to do most of the talking. Mostly adults label the pictures. "Look, Licky, a train! Yup, that's a train—choo, choo!" Typically adults point as they label.

◆ Between the ages of twelve and fifteen months, adults tend to ask the child rhetorical questions (e.g., DeLoache, 1984): "And that's a kite. Isn't that a kite, Josh?" The questions function to reinforce the picture's label; the adult does not really expect the child to answer. The adult's playing of both roles, asking the question and giving the answer, provides the toddler with experience in the question–answer cycle before the child is required to participate verbally in the exchange.

◆ Beginning around fifteen months, the adult's expectations shift, and the child is expected to be a more active participant in the story reading. As the child acquires more facility with language, the adult expects the child to answer more of the questions posed. First, the adult asks the child to provide the label for the picture. The adult says things like "Look!" or "What's that?" or "It's a what?" If the child hesitates, the adult intervenes and provides the answer. When the child seems to be correct (Joseph says, "Pithee" in response to his father's query), the adult typically repeats the label or positively reinforces the toddler's response (Joseph's father says, "Yeah. These are peaches."). When the child shows competence at this task, the adult ups the ante, requesting perhaps a description, like asking for information about the color.

Researchers have discovered that this story-reading sequence (adult question, child response, adult feedback) is just like the typical interaction sequence between teacher and student in many classrooms (Mehan, 1979). Hence, these story readings also begin children's socialization into the response pattern typical of many classrooms.

Researchers like Marilyn Cochran-Smith (1984) and Denny Taylor and Dorothy Strickland (1986) discovered that adults from all socioeconomic levels do the same thing when they introduce a child to a new concept in a book. They try to make the concept meaningful for the child by linking the text to the child's personal experiences. For example, Ann Mowery (1993, p. 46) describes how, when young Joseph and his father read *Wish for a Fish,* Joseph's father made numerous text-to-life connections: "That sure looks like where we go, doesn't it?" "See, that's a can of worms just like what we fish with." "That's a bobber just like ours." "That boy is waiting quietly for a fish. You usually play with the worms and throw rocks, don't you?"

When children approach about three years of age, adult story readers tend to increase the complexity of the questions. Now they question the child about the characters and the story's meaning—and they expect the child to raise questions about the characters and the story's meaning. It is this talk surrounding the reading that researchers judge to be the most valuable aspect of the storybook-reading activity for enhancing children's language development. David Dickinson and Miriam Smith's (1994) and Bill Teale and Miriam Martinez's (1996) careful analyses of the teacher/student book-reading interactions suggest that the best talk is the kind that invites children to reflect on the story content or language. The focus of teacher/student talk is: What are the important ideas in this story?

CHILD BEHAVIORS DURING READING.   What do children do when they are being read to by a caring adult? Several researchers (e.g., Baghban, 1984; Morrow, 1988) have studied young children's behavior, often their own children, during adult–child readings. These researchers tell us that even infants focus on the book. They make sounds even before they are speaking, as if they are imitating the reader's voice. They slap at the picture in the book. A little older child with some language facility begins to ask questions about the pictures. They play the "What's that?" game, pointing and asking "What's dat? What's dat? What's dat?" almost without pausing for an answer.

CULTURAL VARIATIONS IN STORY READING.   Do children from nonmainstream families have similar early childhood home reading experiences? Shirley Brice Heath's answer to this question is no. In her book *Ways with Words* (1983), Heath provides a rich description of the literacy experiences of working-class African American, working-class Caucasian, and mainstream families in the Piedmont area of the Carolinas. From her research, Heath learned that the parents from mainstream families read to their children well into elementary school; use a wide variety of complex questioning strategies to develop their children's understanding of story, plot event sequence, and characterization; and look for ways to connect the text information to their children's experiences. Parents from the working-class Caucasian families also read to their children, but what they do while they read is different. They stress the sequence of the stories and ask children literal meaning questions ("What did the little boy do then?" "What's the hen's name?"). Further, they make few attempts to connect the events described in the books to their children's experiences. Finally, Heath learned that the African American families tell lots of stories, but reading is strictly for functional purposes. These families read forms, recipes, and the newspaper. They tend not to read books to their children. Of course, Heath's work cannot be generalized to all mainstream, Caucasian working class, or African American families. As Teale (1987) notes, there is a great deal of variation among and within social and cultural groups. Teachers need to learn from their students' parents about the experiences their young children have had with books.

We believe that children who have had experiences with books and have experienced dialogic interactions with adults with books are advantaged over children who have no experiences with books and whose parents or early teachers have not shared books with them. Therefore, we strongly encourage teachers and parents of young children to read, read, read to their children—and to talk, talk, talk while reading about the important content, allowing children sufficient time to reflect on the content.

CLASSROOM READ-ALOUDS. When a parent and a child read together, they cuddle. Like eighteen-month-old Joseph, whom readers met at the beginning of this chapter, the child typically sits in the parent's lap or snuggles under the parent's arm. Many parents establish a bedtime reading ritual, cuddling with the child for a quiet reading time before the child goes to bed. Parents report enjoying this ritual as much as the child, and it establishes a mind-set that encourages the child to read before going to sleep when the child can read independently. Teachers of the very youngest children, infants, and toddlers should follow parents' lead and apply what is known about how parents read to infants and toddlers to their reading to their young students. The low teacher–child ratio recommended by the National Association for the Education of Young Children for infant (one adult to one infant) and toddler (one adult to four toddlers) programs helps permit this kind of adult–child interaction—though with toddlers, such one-on-one reading together requires some careful arranging (Bredekamp, 1989). We recommend that teachers create a daily reading ritual, perhaps just before nap time. Some day care centers connect with church groups or nearby residential facilities for elderly citizens for the explicit purpose of adults coming to the center just before nap time to read to the children. Now, like at home, every child can have a lap, a cuddle, and a "grandparent" all alone.

We are concerned when we hear infant and toddler teachers say, "Read to the kids in my classroom? You must be kidding!" We are even more concerned when we read that this response about reading to young children is not uncommon (Kupetz & Green, 1997). Barbara Kupetz and Elise Green describe the benefits of reading to infants and toddlers:

■ It helps infants' eyes to focus.
■ It increases infants' recognition of objects and their ability to label objects and understand basic concepts.
■ It enhances infants' listening skills.
■ It stimulates their imaginations.
■ It builds infants' sensory awareness.
■ It extends infants' experiences.
■ It establishes the physical closeness so critical to young children's emotional and social development.

These two former early childhood teachers acknowledge that it takes organization and working together to structure the infants' and toddlers' day to include story reading. "Reading to infants and toddlers is certainly not a large-group activity. It can effectively occur only in very small groups or in one-to-one pairing" (p. 23). Like us, they recommend the center attempt to make appropriate extra-adult arrangements in order to ensure the inclusion of this important activity in infants' and toddlers' days.

The older the young child, the larger the permitted-by-law number of children in the group. The typical kindergarten class, for example, is often one teacher and twenty (unfortunately, sometimes even more) children. Teachers of these children are challenged to keep read-alouds enjoyable, pleasurable experiences. Of course, selecting age- and interest-appropriate books is important. Read-aloud experiences are one means to ensure that high-quality literature is accessible to all students, something that is especially important for children who have had few storybook experiences outside school. The *how* of reading is also important. Now there are too many children for everyone to cuddle next to the adult reader. Yet physical comfort is important. Having a special carpeted area for reading to the group is important. Often this area is next to the library center. Nancy asks her young learners to sit in a semicircle. Patty asks her young learners to sit on the X marks she has made using masking tape on the carpet. Lolita asks her three-year-olds to sit or lie wherever they like in the small carpeted area—as long as they can see the pictures. Each day a different child gets to snuggle with her. In each of these classrooms, the teacher sits at the edge of the circle or the carpet on a low chair, holding the picture book about at the children's eye level. The chair the teacher sits in to read from is a special chair, used both for teacher read-alouds and for the children to read their own writing to the class. Each teacher calls this chair *the author's chair*. Nancy, Patty, and Lolita have mastered reading from the side. Thus the children can see the illustrations while the teacher reads.

These teachers know the story they are about to read. They have carefully selected it and read it through, practicing how it will sound when read aloud, in advance. They know how to read it with excitement in their voices. They are careful not to overdramatize, yet they use pitch and stress to make the printed dialogue sound like conversation. They show that they enjoy the story. Each of these teachers recalls how, in her teacher preparation program, she was required to videotape or audiotape herself reading to a group of children. Then she complained; now she realizes how important it is to continually reflect on one's practice. After listening to a tape of her story reading, Nancy, a kindergarten teacher, says, "We all think we are fine readers. But just listen to me! I love this story, but you'd never know it from the way I sound! My intonation is the same on every page. Also, I *meant* to tell them the name of the author and the illustrator. Oops!" There is value in listening to yourself read—even for veteran teachers.

Nancy suggests one criterion of an effective read-aloud with young children: read with expression. The following suggestions are recommended by several groups of researchers based on their survey of research studies, reading methods textbooks, and books and articles about reading to children.

- ◆ *Read to students every day*—Research done during the 1980s indicated that only 50 to 60 percent of teachers read aloud to their classes on a regular basis (Lapointe, 1986; Morrow, 1982). A more recent study by James Hoffman, Nancy Roser, and Jennifer Battle (1993) presents a much more positive picture. These researchers found that, on a given day, 84 percent of kindergarten teachers read to their classes.
- ◆ *Select high-quality literature*—A key element to a successful read-aloud experience is the book that is being read. Try to find books that will appeal to the children's interest, evoke humor, stimulate critical thinking, stretch the imagination, and so on. While a good story is always effective, also try to include informational books and poetry written for young audiences.
- ◆ *Show the children the cover of the book*—Draw the children's attention to the illustration on the cover ("Look at the illustration on this book!"). Tell the children the title of the book, the author's name, and the illustrator's name. ("The title of this book is . . . The author is . . . The illustrator is . . .") Tell the children that the author is the person who wrote the book and the illustrator is the person who drew the pictures. Later, ask the children what the author and the illustrator do. Draw your finger under the title, the author's name, and the illustrator's name as you read each. Remind the children that the title, author's name, and illustrator's name are always on the front of the book. Remember that these are new concepts for young children.
- ◆ *Ask the children for their predictions about the story*—("What do you think this story might be about?") Take a few of the children's predictions about the story's content. ("Let's read to see what this story is about.")
- ◆ *Or provide a brief introduction to the story*—This can be accomplished in a number of ways. You might provide background information about the story ("This story is going to

be about . . ."), connect the topic or theme of the story to the children's own experiences, draw the children's attention to familiar books written by the same author, draw the children's attention to the book's central characters, clarify vocabulary that might be outside the children's realm of experiences, and so on. Keep the introduction brief, but sufficient to build the children's background knowledge, so there is ample reading time.

◆ *Identify where and what you will read*—Two important concepts about print for young children to learn are that readers read the print on the pages, not the pictures, and where readers begin reading. Begin read-alouds by identifying where you will start reading and what you will read. Repeating this information often ("Now, I'll begin reading the words right here") weaves this important information into the read-aloud. Be sure to point to the first word on the page as you say where you will begin. Eventually the children will be able to tell you where to begin reading. After many exposures to this important concept, you might playfully ask, "Am I going to read the words or the pictures in this book?" "Where should I begin reading?"

◆ *Read with expression and at a moderate rate*—When teachers read with enthusiasm and vary their voices to fit different characters and the ongoing dialogue, the story comes alive for children. It is also important to avoid reading too quickly. Jim Trelease (2006), a leading authority, claims that this is the most common mistake that adults make when reading aloud. He recommends reading slowly enough that children can enjoy the pictures and can make mental images of the story.

◆ *Read stories interactively; that is, encourage children to interact verbally with the text, peers, and the teacher during the book reading*—In interactive reading, teachers and children pose questions throughout their book reading to enhance the children's meaning construction and to show how one makes sense of text (Barrentine, 1996). Teachers encourage their students to offer spontaneous comments, to ask questions, to respond to others' questions, and to notice the forms and functions of print features (words, punctuation, letters) as the story unfolds. They use the during-reading book discussions to help children understand what to think about as a story unfolds. With a group of colleagues, Jerry Harste (1984) identified the range of information that teachers can demonstrate to children through interactive read-alouds, including the relationship between page turning and moving through the story, how readers read, how readers self-correct while reading and monitor their construction of meaning, and why readers change voice inflections while reading. According to Brian Cambourne (1988), children learn through active engagement with literacy events, not through passive absorption. Interactive storybook reading provides an opportunity for such needed engagement. In summarizing the literature on interactive storybook reading, Laura Justice and Khara Pence (2005) say:

> Adult-child interactive storybook reading . . . . is . . . one of the most potent and frequent contexts for . . . incidental language and literacy learning of young children. [Interactive] book reading is seen as particularly powerful because it is a context that is meaningful, interesting, and motivating to young children. Hypothetically, children's language and literacy are advanced with such interactions as a function of both adult and child contributions; the adult deliberately encourages and scaffolds the child's engagement and participation while the child extracts meaning and constructs knowledge (p. 7–8).

In their book *Scaffolding with Storybooks: A Guide for Enhancing Young Children's Language and Literacy Achievement*, Justice and Pence describe how to use specific storybooks and interactive storybook-reading strategies to assist children in developing print knowledge, word knowledge, phonological knowledge, alphabet knowledge, narrative knowledge, and world knowledge. The multiple examples of the "extratextual conversation" language (what does it really sound like when teachers engage in conversations with their students during storybook reading?) scaffold teachers new to interactive storybook-reading strategies as they work to change or develop their storybook-reading behavior from "just" reading to reading interactively.

Several research teams (McKeown & Beck, 2006; Whitehurst et al., 1988) have developed specific interactive-style read-aloud approaches. Grover Whitehurst and his colleagues (Whitehurst et al., 1988) call their interactive reading approach "dialogic reading."

Dialogic reading is often used by teachers of young children. In Trade Secrets 4.1, Silvia Palenzuela describes how preschool teachers in an Early Reading First project are using this approach with their young children.

◆ *Read favorite books repeatedly*—Not every book you read has to be a book the children have never heard before. In fact, repeated readings of books can lead to enhanced comprehension and better postreading discussions (Martinez & Roser, 1985; Morrow, 1988) and increased likelihood that the children will retain the new vocabulary word, both expressive (words the children produce) and receptive (words the children understand) (Justice, 2002; Penno, Wilkinson, & Moore, 2002). In addition, reading a book three or more times increases the likelihood that young children will select that book during free-choice time and will try to reenact or read it on their own (Martinez & Teale, 1988). Of course, the benefits of repeated reading need to be balanced against the need to expose children to a wide variety of literature.

◆ *Allow time for discussion after reading*—Good books arouse a variety of thoughts and emotions in children. Be sure to follow each read-aloud session with a good conversation, with questions and comments ("What part of the story did you like best?" "How did you feel when . . . ?" "Has anything like that ever happened to you?" "Who has something to say about the story?"). This type of open-ended question invites children to share their responses to the book that was read. After listening to a book read-aloud, children want to talk about the events, characters, parts they liked best, and so forth. As children and teacher talk about the book together, they construct a richer, deeper understanding of the book. Reader response theorists, like Louise Rosenblatt (1978), provide theoretical support for the importance of teachers' talking with children about shared books. Rosenblatt believes that as children listen to stories, they are constructing meaning based on the previous experiences they bring to the text and their purpose for listening. Listeners focus on two kinds of information: remembering information (e.g., the story's main idea, the three main events) and connecting through personal images, ideas, feelings, and questions evoked while listening. Through good conversations about books, teachers and children can explore ideas of personal importance and thus can analyze and interpret the book. Teachers want to work toward being a member of the book circle, one of the discussants who takes turns talking with the children. When the teacher does ask questions, they are open-ended questions that encourage children to interpret, extend, and connect with the text. In Trade Secrets 4.2, Cory Hansen describes how Chris Boyd engages her kindergartners in discussions that help them jointly construct deeper meaning for the stories they are read. Chris's strategy lays the foundation for literature study groups in the primary grades.

SHARED BIG-BOOK EXPERIENCE.   Teachers usually read picture books to their classes by holding the books so that the children can see the illustrations, pausing to elicit students' reactions to the stories or to ask story-related questions. This traditional whole-class read-aloud experience differs from parent–child storybook-reading interactions in a very important way: Most children can see only the pictures, not the print. To remedy this situation, Holdaway (1979) devised the shared-book experience, a strategy that uses enlarged print, repeated readings, and increased pupil participation to make whole-class storybook-reading sessions similar to parent–child reading experiences. Today the shared-book experience has become an important component of a quality early literacy program.

To use this strategy, the teacher first needs to select an appropriate book. Andrea Butler and Jan Turbill (1984) recommend stories that have (1) an absorbing, predictable story line; (2) a predictable structure, containing elements of rhyme, rhythm, and repetition; and (3) illustrations that enhance and support the text. These features make it easy for children to predict what is upcoming in the story and to read along with the teacher.

Once a book has been selected, an enlarged copy needs to be obtained. This can be done in several ways. The teacher can (1) rewrite the story on chart paper, using one-inch- or two-inch-tall letters and hand-drawn illustrations; (2) make color transparencies of the pages from the original picture book and use an overhead projector; or (3) acquire a commercially published big book (about twenty-four to twenty-six inches) version of the story. Commercial big books are

Dialogic Reading

Silvia Palenzuela

Dialogic Reading is a way to enhance emergent literacy with preschoolers. It's a conversation about books that focuses on teaching children new vocabulary and improving overall verbal fluency. Reading to children provides them with the opportunity to hear and learn new vocabulary, to hear the sound structure of words, and to see and understand the meaning of print and the structure of stories. It also provides them with firsthand experience of the pleasure of reading books.

The goal of Dialogic Reading is to develop the child's language skills through reading—to increase the child's number of words, length of sentences, complexity of responses, and ability to use decontextualized language.

HOW we read to children counts!

Children at the preschool age cannot read, and they need to "hear" the story before they can "say" anything about it. While reading the picture book, the adult has a conversation, a dialogue, with the child. In the context of reading the storybook, the adult models oral language and encourages the children to express their thoughts in words.

In Dialogic Reading, books are selected based on quality and richness of illustrations. Rhyme books and wordbooks are not proper choices for Dialogic Reading.

It is an active method. The child is highly engaged in the storytelling and it is keyed to the child's interests, intrinsic motivation, curiosity, and motivation to explore and experiment with a variety of literacy materials. The adult allows the child to take the lead, and follows the child's lead.

With continued practice in the Dialogic Reading method, the children will increase and strengthen their language skills.

DIALOGIC READING LEVEL 1

Goal: To encourage the children to talk during story time in order to increase their language skills. This is done by having the children name the pictures and gradually say more about them. Do not use yes-no or pointing questions.

How to Do It

1. Ask "what" questions:
   What's this?
   What is he pulling?
2. Follow answers with questions.
   Ask questions about an aspect of the object.
   What shape is this?
   What color is this?
   What's this part?
   Ask questions about what the object is used for.
   What is it used for?
   Who is using it?

3. Repeat what the children say.
4. Scaffold the children by prompting and cueing.
   Have you seen something like this?
   Do you remember what it was called?
5. Praise and encourage.
6. Shadow the children's interests.
   When the children show an interest in something on one of the pages, get them to talk more about it. Then go back to the reading.
7. Have fun!

DIALOGIC READING LEVEL 2

Goals: To continue with "wh" questions as prompts and to add expansions and open-ended questions.

How to Do It

1. Add only one or two words to what the child says.
2. Be sure to repeat at least part of what the child says.
3. Give feedback...at least some of the time (e.g., "Right!")
4. Pause after an expansion to see if the child will repeat spontaneously.
5. Sometimes ask the child to repeat the expansion.
6. Stress the new word or words and speak slowly.
7. Ask open-ended questions.
   What's happening here?
   What do you see in this?
   Tell me more.
   What else do you see?

Examples

A. *Child:* "a mouse"
   Adult: "a mouse hiding"
B. *Child:* "boat"
   Adult: "big boat"
C. *Child:* "It on that."
   Adult: "Right, it's on the couch."
D. *Child:* "I sawed it."
   Adult: "You saw it, did you?"
E. *Child:* "It eating."
   Adult: "Good, the ladybug is eating."
F. *Child:* "turtle up there"
   Adult: "The turtle is hiding."

Other Ways to Get Children to Talk

1. Model what you want the children to say (e.g., make comments about the pictures using sentences at about the same level as the children's and then pause).

TRADE SECRETS **4.1** (*continued*)

2. Say something that is incorrect and pause to see if the children correct you.

3. Say part of a sentence and have the children (or a child) fill in the last word.

DIALOGIC READING LEVEL 3

Goal: To focus on the use of new vocabulary while talking about the story plot or the children's personal experiences in order to:

■ reinforce vocabulary;
■ link the vocabulary with the story plot;
■ link the vocabulary with personal experience;
■ gain verbal fluency with new vocabulary.

Make sure the children can easily answer Level 1 and Level 2 questions before moving on to Level 3.

Use a book that is very familiar to the children. Always start a new book at Level 1.

How to Do It

1. Continue to repeat and expand what the children say.

2. Continue to use Level 1 and Level 2 questions as needed.

3. Continue to provide models, taking turns with the children.

Examples

A. Take turns with the child *telling the story*. The teacher can hold the book or the children can, whichever is easier. Provide help when needed with vocabulary words, but let the children direct the activity. Don't overcorrect and don't be too concerned with the children getting the story "right." The focus is verbal fluency and use of new vocabulary. Variation: Have the children ask the questions.

B. Ask *recall questions* (refers to story plot or narrative).
Why was he sad?
Where are they?
What happened at the end?

C. Ask questions that refer to *personal experiences*.
Have you ever been to a farm?
Tell me about it.

D. Ask questions that relate to *sequence of events*.
What happened first?
What happened next?
What happened last?

E. Ask questions that relate to prediction.
What do you think will happen next?
What would you do?

F. Have the children act out the story. They can describe what they are doing as they do it or simply speak the lines. The children also can describe who they are, what they are wearing, etc.

Here is an easy way to remember what to do. Just remember the word CAR!

Comment and wait.
Ask questions and wait.
Respond by adding a little more.

This is the storybook-reading strategy the teachers in the Miami/Dade Early Learning Coalition Early Reading First project are using. The Dialogic Reading strategy is a component of the project's chosen curriculum, *Literacy Express*. This curriculum was developed by Beth Phillips and Chris Lonigan. It is not yet available from a publisher.

---

becoming increasingly available. Scholastic and McGraw-Hill/The Wright Group, for example, publish enlarged versions of a number of high-quality picture books. Initially, only picture storybooks were available in the big book size. Today informational books also can be located in big book size. These ready-made big books have the advantage of saving teachers time by eliminating the need to make enlarged texts. Understandably, they are expensive since they include large versions of the original illustrations.

Unlike when regular-size books are shared with children, big books permit all children to see the print. Teachers may take advantage of the enlarged print by drawing young children's attention to the print in the same ways that an adult draws a child's attention to the print in a regular-size book during a read-aloud. Typically, teachers use a pointer to point to the words as they read big books and invite the children to read along, particularly to the words in a familiar text or to the refrain in a book. As children "read" along with the teacher, they internalize the language of the story. They also learn about directionality (reading from left to right with return sweeps), one important convention of print.

Through the use of big books, teachers can introduce children to other conventions of print: to the sequence of letter sounds in words; to the difference between letters, words, and sentences; to the spaces between words; to where to start reading on the page; to reading left to

TRADE SECRETS 4.2

Getting Children to Talk about a Story

Cory Hansen and Chris Boyd

I had the opportunity to observe in Chris Boyd's kindergarten classroom on the day she read De Paola's (1975) *Strega Nona,* a wonderful story of what happens when Big Anthony ignores good advice and overruns his town with pasta from the magic pasta pot. As Chris was reading the book, the carpet in front of her was scattered with children. Some were lying flat on their backs looking up at the ceiling; others were on their sides, only a finger wiggle away from good friends; and others were sitting up, cross-legged, their eyes never leaving the pages of the story. The last page of the story is wordless. Big Anthony's expression tells it all as he sits outside the house, his stomach swollen almost to bursting, with one last strand of pasta lingering on his fork. The children burst into laughter, and as Chris motioned with her index finger, they regrouped, calling out, "I think . . . , I think . . ." on their way to forming a large circle. And for the next half hour, that was what was talked about: what the children thought about the story.

The conversation began with what the children thought was going to happen and comparing it to what really did. Chris asked the children why they thought the way they did, and then the serious business of making meaning together began. (She gradually lowered herself down from the reading chair and joined in as one participant in this group talk about the story: the one with a copy of the text and the one writing comments into a notebook.) The kindergartners called on her only when they needed someone to reread part of the text to settle disputes. Chris did not enter the conversation unless the children lost sight of her one rule for talk about the story or unless an opportunity to seize a literary teachable moment emerged.

After the group examined Big Anthony's motives and explored connections from this story to their own lives, Chris and I had an opportunity to talk about how she structured and scaffolded meaningful talk about the story with young children. My first question was why the children were all over the room as she read. She explained that she offered the children the opportunity to "go to wherever they could do their best listening." In this way she felt she respected the children's choices and could hold them accountable if they acted in ways that did not show good listening by moving them to a different part of the room. By respecting their choices, focus was on listening and thinking rather than sitting or being still.

"So why," I was quick to ask, "do they form a sitting circle after the story?"

"Well, first, it is easier to hear what is being said if they are in a circle. I teach them to look at the person who is talking. I think it encourages them to listen carefully and think through what others are saying. As well, when they are all in a circle they begin to watch for nonverbal cues that show that another person has something to add or introduce to the conversation."

I noticed that the kinds of questions Chris asked her kindergartners during the talk were different than those I had heard in other classrooms. When the children were arguing about why Big Anthony didn't know to blow the three kisses, Chris's question to the group was, "Was there any clue that that might have been a problem for him?" Matthew was quick to suggest that Chris should read the part when Strega Nona was singing to the pot again. The children listened very carefully as Chris reread that part of the story and used the information from the book to settle their disagreement. While that particular part of the conversation was going on, Chris was writing hurriedly in her notebook. I asked her why she recorded what the children were saying as they talked about story.

"When I write down what they say, they see and feel the importance of their words. They know I value what they say and what they think is special enough to write down. It makes them realize how important talk about story really is. Also, I can bring the conversation back around to something a child said when everyone gets talking at once or if a soft-spoken or shy child makes a comment that may otherwise go unnoticed. Like when they were arguing about Big Anthony, Sara made a really smart comment about how the pot needed someone to be nice to it. Her comment was lost in the discussion but later on, after the issue was settled, I could bring it up again and then the conversation started anew."

I wondered why Chris didn't just have the children raise their hands when they had something to say. She told me that even though it takes a long time and lots of patience to teach children to follow her one rule for talk about story—talk one at a time and talk to the whole group—they eventually learn more than just being polite. Chris found that if she had children raise their hands to talk, they just sat there, waving their arms, waiting to say what they wanted without listening to and considering what other people were saying or connecting their ideas to the book or the opinions of others. Even though it is loud and messy at times, the results are worth the effort.

The kindergartners in Chris Boyd's classroom obviously loved the chance to talk about the story with each other. They used talk about the story to learn more about how things worked in the world and, in the process, learned more about the world of story.

When teachers follow the preceding guidelines, they can help ensure that their story reading has the maximum impact on children's language and literacy learning.

right; to return sweeps; to punctuation. In addition, through the use of big books, teachers are able to further children's development of important concepts about books (e.g., the front and back of a book, the difference between print and pictures, that pictures on a page are related to what the print says, that readers read the print, where to begin reading, where the title is and what it is, what an author is, what an illustrator is). In essence, teachers can use big books to teach skills in context.

While teachers can use big books to teach a broad range of language and literacy skills, they cannot introduce all of the skills to their students during a single reading. Therefore, big books should be read to children multiple times, like daily for a week. Various educators have designed daily procedures to guide teachers' big book reading. In Special Feature 4.2, we provide our version of a five-day big book–reading strategy based on our reading of the literature on shared big-book reading.

Many of the new packaged early childhood language and literacy programs (e.g., *Doors to Discovery,* published by McGraw-Hill/The Wright Group in 2002) not only include big books for shared-reading experiences but also include poems and songs on large colorful poster boards. The teachers guide suggests that each poem be shared with the children, pointing to each word as the poem is read, several times over several days. After several readings, the children can "read" the poems themselves. Of course, teachers can use the posters in the same way they used the big books, to introduce the children to the conventions of print; to the sequence of letter sounds in words; to the difference between letters, words, and sentences; and so forth. Of course, teachers also can make large posters using chart paper, magic markers, and their best manuscript penmanship. All of the children's favorite songs, poems, and fingerplays can be written in large print.

Extending Literature

Interactive storybook readings and postreading discussions are not the only way children can respond to books. They can use dramatizations, drawing, cooking, puppetry, and more to extend stories' content. In this section, we provide an overview of several possible literature extension activities.

CREATIVE DRAMATICS. Creative dramatics is informal dramatizing with no printed script or memorized lines. Stories that are good for dramatizing need dialogue and action—characters who say and do something. Sometimes props are used; sometimes the children use their imaginations. For example, they can imagine the bears' bowls, chairs, and beds when acting out *The Three Bears* (Galdone, 1979) or the Troll's bridge when dramatizing *The Three Billy Goats Gruff* (Galdone, 1973). Sometimes the teacher reads the story, pausing for the players to pantomime and fill in the dialogue. For example, student teacher Syma reads *Caps for Sale* (Slobodkina, 1947) to her young students. One child is the peddler; the other children, seated in their spots on the rug, are the monkeys. She reads: "Once there was a peddler who sold caps. He walked up the street and he walked down the street [Syma pauses while the child playing role of the peddler walks up the street and down the street] calling [Syma waits for the child to speak], 'Caps! Caps! Who wants a cap?'" The "peddler" does not say exactly what the peddler says in the book; this is acceptable. Syma moves on to the next page. Later, the children delight at shaking their fingers and then their hands at the "peddler" who wants his caps back from the "monkeys." Occasionally the teacher and children or the children alone decide on the scenes to play, and the dialogue and action develop.

Karen Valentine has props stored in large see-through plastic bags in her classroom's library center for various old favorites. During free-choice, Doug coerces three friends into playing *The Three Bears* with him. He puts on the yellow crepe-paper wig and assumes the role of Goldilocks and the narrator. One child puts on the Daddy Bear headgear (made of poster board), another child puts on the Momma Bear headgear, and a third child puts on the Baby Bear headgear. Doug lines up three chairs and gathers three bowls from the dramatic play center. He tells the story while his friends pantomime and speak. Doug often corrects their language since they are not saying exactly what he thinks they should say.

SPECIAL FEATURE 4.2

Shared Big-Book Reading

DAY 1

Before Shared Reading

- Read title, author, and illustrator. Point to each word as you read. Tell the children that the author is the person who wrote the book and the illustrator is the person who drew the pictures.
- Show the children the book's cover. Ask them to tell you what they think the story will be about. On chart paper, write a few words for each suggestion to help you and the children remember the predictions. Ask the children to explain their rationale for each prediction.
- Do a picture walk through the book. That is, show each page to the children. Point to the characters and ask, "Who might this be?" Point to the key objects on each page and ask, "What is this? What might it be used for?" Ask the children to describe what they see happening on each page.
- Make connections to the children's prior knowledge or experiences. "Remember when we . . . . ? Have you ever . . . ?"
- Introduce the children to vocabulary words that are key to their understanding the story.
- Build any necessary background knowledge.

DAY 2

Before Shared Reading

- Show the children the cover. "Does anyone remember the title of the book? the author? the illustrator?" Point as you read.
- Read the list of predictions the children made about the story.

During Shared Reading

- Show the children where you will begin reading, the direction you will read, and where you will go after you have read the first line. "Now, I'll begin reading right here. I'll read this line (draw your finger under the line) and then I'll return to here" (draw your finger back to the next line at the left-hand side of the page).
- Read the story. Pause on each page to ask questions like: "So what is happening so far in the story? Why do you think [insert character] said [insert what character said]? How do you think [insert character] is feeling now? What do you think is going to happen next? Why?" Encourage the children to ask questions and contribute their ideas about what is happening or is going to happen in the story.

After Shared Reading

- Compare what happened in the story with what the children thought would happen. Were any of their predictions accurate? Why or why not?
- Connect the story's content to their experiences. Ask questions like: "Has anything like that ever happened to you?" Focus on the story's problem. Would they have solved the problem the way the main character did?

DAYS 3,4, AND 5

Before Shared Reading

- Read the title of the story. Ask: "How many words are in the title? Count them with me." Read the author's name. Ask: "And what does the author of a story do?" Read the illustrator's name. Ask: "And what does the illustrator of a story do?"
- Prompt the children to retell the story by looking at the pictures. Ask questions to guide their retelling. [This should be a quick retelling.]

During Shared Reading

- Ask the children where you should begin reading.
- Invite the children to read the lines they know with you. Point to the words while you read. [Initially, the words they remember likely will be the repetitious words or sentences.] Compliment them on what fine readers they are!
- You might want to echo read. You read a line, and then the children read the same line. Point while you and they read, and compliment them on their reading.
- If this book's sentences end in rhyming words, focus on these words. Pause before you read the second word, allowing the children to fill in the missing word. Tell the children that ___ and ___ rhyme. Later, ask them what they just made.

After Shared Reading (*Do one of the following, a different one each day*)

- Return to the page or pages with a pair of rhyming words. Read the sentence or sentences again. Write the two words on chart paper. Can the children think of other rhyming words? Add these words to the words on the chart paper. [Nonsense words are acceptable; the focus is on rhyming.]
- Look for words that begin with the same letter. Read those two words, without pointing. Ask the children what they notice about those two words. Ask: "What letter makes that sound?" Say the sound slowly. Write the two words on chart paper. Can the children think of other words that begin with the same letter? Add their words to the chart paper.

- Hunt for a letter. Can the children, for example, find all of the letter *T*'s in the story? Mark each letter with a Post-it note so that all of the *T*'s can be counted. [Initially the children will need a model, a *T* on a card that can be moved under the letters on the page. Later they may be able to find the *T*'s without a model, and still later they may be able to find the *T*'s and the *t*'s.]
- Hunt for a particular word using a procedure like that above.
- Count the number of words in two of the sentences. Which sentence was longer?
- Select a sentence. Using a Post-it note, cover all of a word but the first letter. Read the sentence. Can the children guess what the covered word is? How do they know? Can they think of any other word that would "fit" in the sentence? Write their word on a Post-it. Read the sentence with the new word.
- When the story includes several dialogues and action, provide props to support the children's dramatization of the story.
- Plan an art activity that connects with the book (e.g., a collage activity after reading a Leo Lionni book, a watercolor activity after reading *Dawn* by Uri Shulevitz [1987]).

FOLLOW-UP

Place the book in a prominent location in the Library Corner. Invite the children to read it to you, another adult, or a peer during center time. Perhaps they would like to play teacher with a group of friends?

Such experiences promote many aspects of development by offering children an opportunity to take on the behaviors of others, to try out vocabulary and sentence structure perhaps unfamiliar to them, to play cooperatively with others, and to accept and give criticism.

PUPPETS. Many young children, particularly shy children, can speak through the mouth of a puppet in ways they can not speak on their own. Puppets provide children with another means—for some children, a safer means—of dramatizing a good story. Again, stories with strong dialogue and distinctive characters who do something are best suited for dramatization with puppets. Betty Coody (1997) recommends old favorite stories, like "The Three Little Pigs," "The Three Bears," "The Three Billy Goats Gruff," "Little Red Riding Hood," and so forth.

Manufactured puppets are available from many sources; for example, most early childhood equipment catalogs and teacher stores include puppets for retelling children's old favorites. Typically these are hand puppets (the kind that fit over the hand of the puppeteer). However, teachers can also construct their own puppets (Figure 4.3).

COOKING. Teachers of young children have long recognized the value of cooking activities as a component of their total program for young learners. In cooking, children experience math (e.g., measurement, counting, determining how much is needed so that everyone in the class gets a piece), reading (e.g., the recipe), social skills (e.g., following the recipe together, eating), health and safety habits (e.g., nutrition and preparing food), and eating the food they enjoyed making. As Betty Coody (1997, p. 141) notes, "Cooking makes the book memorable, and in turn, the story serves to make cooking in the classroom even more important."

Some books include a recipe for readers to test. For example, Tomie dePaola's (1978) *The Popcorn Book* suggests two ways popcorn might be made. What better incentive to try two approaches to making popcorn? The content of other books suggests appropriate cooking activities. For example, after hearing Russell Hoban's (1964) *Bread and Jam for Francis,* a natural response is for the children to try their hands at making jam sandwiches, and after hearing Ed Arno's (1970) *The Gingerbread Man,* a natural response is to make a gingerbread man. A rainy day presents a reason for reading at least two books followed by cooking: Listening to Maurice Sendak's (1962) *Chicken Soup with Rice* and making chicken soup with rice or listening to Julian Scheer's (1964) *Rain Makes Applesauce* and making applesauce. Many books can be stretched to connect with a related cooking activity. For example, an extension of Robert McCloskey's (1963) *Blueberries for Sal* might be the making of blueberry pancakes or blueberry muffins, and an extension of Ruth Krauss's (1945) *The Carrot Seed* might be the making of buttered carrots, carrot cake, or carrot bread.

FIGURE 4.3 Puppets

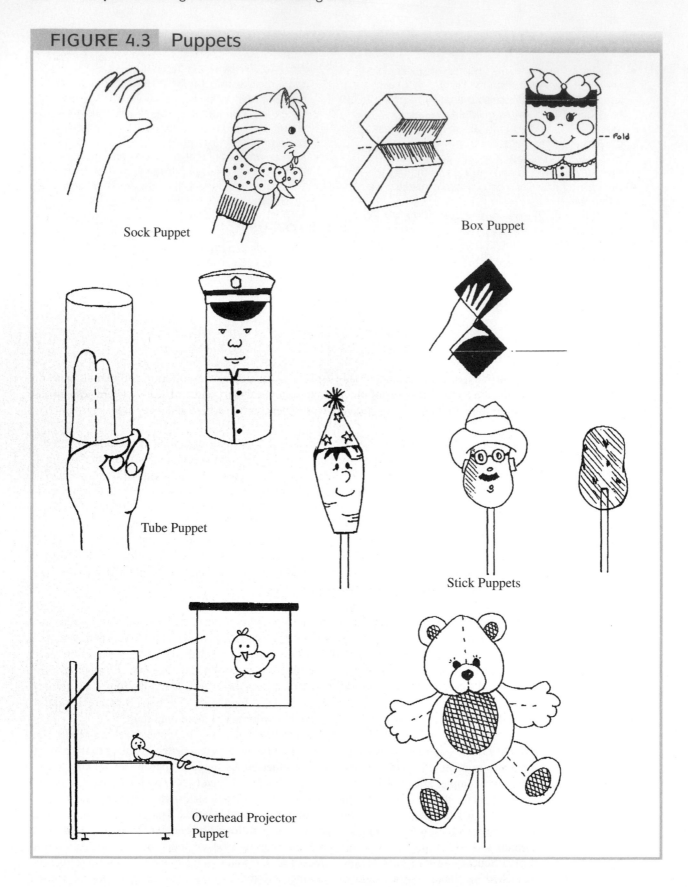

Sock Puppet

Box Puppet

Fold

Tube Puppet

Stick Puppets

Overhead Projector
Puppet

FELT OR FLANNEL BOARDS AND CHARACTERS.   In Chapter 3, we share information about the importance of providing opportunities for children to tell stories in the early childhood classroom. Our focus here is literature that stimulates storytelling. Typically, this literature is a folktale or a fairy tale. Children are nudged to retell these stories by teachers who tell them first. Sadly, many teachers have yet to be converted to the art of storytelling. Their children are missing much, for a good story can take children into a different world, into another place, and perhaps into another time.

Janet Towell (1998) provides several suggestions for teachers new to selecting stories for telling, instead of reading:

◆ Choose stories that are simple and relatively short, with a minimum number of characters and events and with no lengthy descriptive passages.

◆ Look for stories with dialogue and action. This permits the reader to take on the voices of the characters—to sound like a scoundrel or a villain, to sound like the dog or the cat—and to use gestures (though not too many of them) to draw listeners into the story.

◆ Choose stories with a problem that is resolved in a satisfying way.

◆ Substitute names in the stories with listeners' names. This makes the story even more memorable for young children, especially those whose names were used, and helps hold their attention.

◆ Use scribbles or notes to help you remember the structure and sequence of the story. A single word or a symbol will help jog a teller's memory in a momentary lapse.

To this list, Betty Coody would add:

◆ Do not memorize the whole story; only memorize certain portions, like the opening or introduction, the regularly recurring phrase or verse, and the conclusion.

Teachers can use several different kinds of visual aids to illustrate stories. Some might use stick puppets; some might draw with chalk while telling the story; others prefer to use a felt or flannel board with paper or cutouts made of interfacing fabric, for this is the most popular visual aid used in early childhood classrooms. (Interfacing fabric can be purchased in a store that sells materials for sewing. It is typically used to interface garments, to add stiffness to collars and cuffs.)

Books are available to reduce the time it takes for teachers to locate stories appropriate for telling and to make Pellon or paper characters. One of the authors' favorites is Doris Hicks and Sandy Mahaffey's (1997) *Flannelboard Classic Tales,* published by the American Library Association. This book contains the script for stories to tell and the patterns for the characters to accompany each story. For teachers with modest artistic talent, they are a must. Several commercial companies also provide "felt sets" of favorite preschool stories.

ART PROJECTS.   The central purpose of an art program for young children should be free expression. Teachers should offer children opportunities to be creative, to use their imaginations, to produce something original, and to be inventive. How the children do (the process) is far more important than what the children produce. Therefore, teachers of young children do not want to produce models that all children must copy or to tell children to "Draw a picture of your favorite part of the story." Instead, teachers of young children should put materials out for children's exploration and creation. Within these boundaries, literature can serve as a stimulus for many creative art projects.

◆ *Artist's media*—Many illustrators (e.g., Leo Lionni, Eric Carle, Ezra Jack Keats) use collage to illustrate children's books. Shirley Rigby, a collage artist and a teacher of four-year-olds, follows the reading of *Inch by Inch* (Lionni, 1962) with a brief discussion of Lionni's choice of medium—collage. She tells her young learners, "Lionni used collage to make the pictures in the book." She writes *collage* on large chart paper behind her. "Collage means to make pictures by cutting or tearing shapes from different kinds of materials—newspaper, wallpaper, fabric, aluminum foil, and so forth. I thought you might like to be collage artists, just like Leo Lionni, today. In the art center, you'll find all kinds of different materials. Try cutting or tearing these materials and pasting them on a sheet of colored construction paper."

Teachers can invite children to experience the media used by many different picture book artists. What better way for them to understand artists' techniques?

◆ *Papier-mâché*—Perhaps the children have a favorite literary character: Curious George? Francis? By inflating a balloon or balloons, the teacher can craft a form for the children's creation of a replica of their literary favorite. By dipping newspaper strips into a bowl of wallpaper paste thinned to about the consistency of cream and applying the strips to the balloons until the balloons have about four layers of paper on them, the children can create the literary animal shape. When the paper is dry, the children can paint the figure with tempera paint. The teacher can add distinguishing features (e.g., eyes, mouth).

◆ *Paint-on shapes*—Nadine Herman's three-year-olds love Eric Carle's books, especially *The Very Hungry Caterpillar*. One day, Nadine cut butterfly shapes for the children to paint on at the easel, instead of using the regular-size easel paper. More children than ever chose to easel paint. The following day the children attached pipe cleaners to the painted butterfly shapes for antennae. Nadine made a paper replica of a *Buddleia* plant (the plant that attracts butterflies) in one corner of the room, and the children hung their butterflies on the plant. Later, when Nadine read *The Very Busy Spider* (Carle, 1984), the children wondered: Could they paint on spider paper? Nadine answered, "How about using chalk on black spider shapes?"

WRITING.   Karen Carey-Wilkerson's children often write their own version of books they have read, particularly cumulative tales. For example, after reading *The Great Enormous Turnip* (Tolstoy, 1968), Karen's children wrote *The Great Big Cabbage*. First Tymone tried to pull up the cabbage, but it would not come out. Tymone drew the picture to accompany this text. Then Tymone and William tried to pull up the carrot, but it would not come out. William drew the picture to accompany this page of text. The story proceeded until all the interested children's names were included in the book. Karen photocopied the pages so that all the children could have a complete copy of the book to take home to read to their families.

Tabby Tiger is very popular with the Lambson Head Start Center children in New Castle, Delaware. He is the central character in several books the teachers read to the children. Because of the children's attachment to this storybook character, the Center's family liaison purchased a small stuffed animal that looks like Tabby Tiger and a spiral-bound journal notebook for each classroom. Each night a different child takes Tabby and the journal home. The child's "homework" assignment is to have fun with Tabby and to write about Tabby's adventure in the journal. As the center serves three- and four-year-old children, the children's parents or older siblings do most of the writing, though often the children add a few words in their personal script. In six months, no classroom has lost a Tabby Tiger. No child has failed to return the center the following day without Tabby Tiger. He has had a few memorable adventures that concerned him, like a few swishes in the washing machine and a ride on the back of a family's dog.

AUTHOR STUDY.   Ellen Booth-Church (1998) suggests that an author study is a great way to invite children to take an insider's look at the art and craft of writing and illustrating children's books. Each week or month, a different author holds center stage. Through discussion and careful analysis, the children come to understand the themes, characters, rhythm, story patterns, and structure used by different authors. Invite children to discuss and compare the books written by Ezra Jack Keats or Denise Fleming or Leo Lionni. Church describes how a group of kindergarten children discovered that Denise Fleming usually writes about animals and that there are rhythmic similarities between the text and the title of *In the Small, Small Pond* (1993) and *In the Tall, Tall Grass* (1991). Inspired, the children wrote their own book—*In the Big, Big Kindergarten*. Soon they moved on to comparing two authors. They learned that Leo Lionni usually uses collage (tearing paper into small pieces) and Denise Fleming does not. Both authors usually write about animals. Fleming uses short rhymes and phrases, and Lionni uses detailed stories.

Assessment: Discovering What Children Know and Can Do

In earlier chapters, we suggested that the best, most authentic opportunities for assessing young children's emergent literacy knowledge occurs during normal classroom activities. While children engage in storybook reading and story retelling and while teachers share books—regular-size and big books—with children, teachers can learn much about what their young students know about the concepts of print, the conventions of print, and about their young learners' comprehension of the story. Watching and recording (primarily using anecdotal notes and checklists), teachers can gather important information about children's literacy knowledge and learning.

Knowing what literacy accomplishments are important to note is critically important. Checklists help make teachers' observations of children's accomplishments more systematic. Some years ago the teachers at St. Michael's Early Childhood Center in Wilmington, Delaware worked together to construct a literacy checklist. They knew that children's book-reading behaviors were important for them to understand, but they were not certain just which book-reading behaviors were important to track as their young learners moved through their center. They agreed to form a study group to read and discuss professional literature on young children's literacy development in order to understand better how they should conduct their read-aloud and shared-reading sessions and what they should focus on during their observations of their young learners.

One outcome of their study was a checklist. They used the ideas presented in the literature to ensure that they had identified the "right" book-reading skills for their young children. But as described in Chapter 1, now nearly every state has prepared a set of standards (or guidelines or foundations) to guide the state's preschool children's learning and teachers' teaching. St. Michael's Early Childhood Center teachers had to reconsider their list in light of their state's preschool language and early reading standards.

We reproduce their revised checklist in Figure 4.4 to guide our readers' consideration of their young learners' literacy accomplishments. Each St. Michael's teacher has a notebook with a checklist for every child in the classroom. On the day that a child is the star, the teacher puts the star's checklist on the top of the notebook. Over the day, she marks those accomplishments she sees the child demonstrating. When the checklist is filled, she removes it, places it in the child's portfolio (more on using portfolios in early childhood classrooms in Chapter 9), and replaces it with a clean checklist.

Certainly, observing a behavior once is insufficient to justify drawing the conclusion that the behavior is a part of the child's permanent repertoire. Teachers will want to look for repeated evidence that the child is habitually exhibiting these accomplishments. We recommend

---

FIGURE 4.4   Checklist for Assessing Young Children's Book-Related Understandings

_____ can
(Child's name)

Concepts about Books	Date	Comments
look at the picture of an object in a book and realize it is a symbol for the real object	_____	_____
handle a book without attempting to eat or chew it	_____	_____
identify the front, back, top, and bottom of a book	_____	_____
turn the pages of a book correctly, holding the book upright	_____	_____
point to the print when asked, "What do people look at when they read?"	_____	_____
show how picture and print connect	_____	_____
point to where a reader begins reading on a page	_____	_____
point to a book's title on cover	_____	_____
point to a book's author on cover	_____	_____
point to a book's illustrator on cover	_____	_____
recognize specific books by their covers	_____	_____

(continued on next page)

FIGURE 4.4 *(continued)*

Concepts about Books	Date	Comments

Conventions of Print

show that a reader reads left to right with return sweeps

find a requested letter or provide the letter's name

ask questions or make comments about letters

ask questions or make comments about words

read words or phrases

read sentences

read along while adult reads familiar stories

Comprehension of Stories

answer and ask literal questions about story
(provide example)

answer and ask interpretive questions about story
(provide example)

answer and ask critical questions about story
(provide example)

ask questions about story

say new words and dialogue from story

retell stories

by relying on pictures and with help to recall details

without book and with knowledge of the details

without book and with knowledge of key story elements

   setting

   characters

   theme (what main character wanted or needed)

   episodes or events (___/___)

   ending

   climax ending resolution

   sequence

   from beginning to middle

   from middle to end

connect information in stories to events in his/her life

use own experiences to understand character's feelings and
motivation

Attitude Toward Books

participate in book-sharing routine with caregiver

listen attentively to a variety of genres

voluntarily look at books

show excitement about books and reading

ask adults to read to him/her

use books as resource for answers to questions

that teachers indicate the dates of their observations on the checklist and make quick notes of the specific behaviors the child exhibited. At St. Michael's, the checklist follows the child from year to year as a part of the child's portfolio. Knowing when each child demonstrated each literacy accomplishment helps teachers and parents understand individual children's patterns of development. Reading each child's checklist informs the teacher of the child's strengths and the instructional program for that child. Collectively reading all children's checklists informs the teacher of the instructional needs of all the children in the class.

Summary

We hope that readers will set up well-stocked, well-designed library corners in their classrooms, read to their children on a daily basis, and provide children with a wide variety of means to respond to the literature that they listen to during storybook-reading time.

To summarize the key points about selecting and sharing literature with young children, we return to the guiding questions at the beginning of this chapter:

■ *How can teachers set up a well-designed library center?*

A well-stocked and managed classroom library should be a key feature of every early childhood classroom. To encourage young children to engage in book reading in this area, the classroom library must be well-designed with partitions, ample space, comfortable furnishings, open-face and traditional bookshelves, and book-related props and displays. Teachers will know quickly if their classroom library meets the well-designed criteria; inviting classroom libraries are heavily used by the children.

■ *What are the characteristics of effective adult storybook reading?*

What adults say—the verbal interaction between adult (parent or teacher) and child—during story readings has a major influence on children's literacy development. During storybook readings, children learn about the turn-taking inherent in all conversation. The adult helps the child negotiate the meaning of the text, assisting by relating the content to personal experiences, providing information, asking questions, and setting expectations. Who talks the most and the content of the talk varies with the age of the child.

Specific read-aloud strategies have been recommended for use in early childhood classrooms. These include read aloud every day, select high-quality literature, show and discuss the cover of the book before reading, ask children to make predictions about the story, provide a brief introduction, identify where and what you will read, read with expression at a moderate rate, read stories interactively, read some stories repeatedly, and allow time for discussion during and after reading.

Shared reading, the reading of big books, is also recognized as a critically important practice in quality early childhood literacy programs because big books permit all children to see the print, something not possible when teachers read aloud a regular-size book. By using big books, teachers can introduce children to the conventions of print and the concepts about books.

■ *What are some of the ways children can respond to and extend the stories that they have been read?*

Interactive storybook readings and postreading discussions are not the only ways that children can respond to books. Children can also engage in dramatizing a story, in retelling the story using puppets and a felt or flannel board and characters, in participating in a cooking experience, in creating an art project, in writing, or in studying an author's art and craft of writing.

■ *How can teachers use storybook-reading sessions to assess children's literacy development?*

When children engage in storybook reading and shared reading, teachers can closely and systematically observe children's book-related behaviors and gather important information about children's literacy knowledge and learning. Teachers can learn about children's understandings of the concepts about books and of the conventions of print, and they can learn about children's comprehension of the stories. To provide a record of children's developing book-related knowledge, many early childhood teachers use checklists such as the one used at St. Michael's.

LINKING KNOWLEDGE TO PRACTICE

1. Visit an early childhood classroom and observe a storybook-reading or shared-reading activity. What type of book was being read? How did the teacher introduce the book? Did the teacher read with expression and at a moderate rate? What kinds of questions did the teacher and the children ask during the reading? After reading, was there a thoughtful discussion of the book? Did the children have an opportunity to respond to the story through art activities, drama, or writing?

2. Observe a library center in an early childhood classroom and evaluate its book holdings and design features. Are there a large number and wide variety of books available for the children to read? Are any basic types of books missing? Does the library center contain partitions, ample space, comfortable furnishings, open-face and traditional bookshelves, and book-related props and displays? Is there a writing center nearby?

3. Go with a friend or two to a library or bookstore. Plan to treat yourselves to a whole day of reading children's literature. Take your computers or four- to six-inch note cards with you. Record the bibliographic information and a brief description of the books you read. Be sure to read books for all age groups, infancy through kindergarten, and all kinds. What a wonderful day you will have! End the day browsing the various Web sites suggested in this chapter.

4. Tape yourself during a read-aloud with a small group of children. Analyze your read-aloud for the strategies suggested in this chapter. What goals would you set for yourself? Do a shared reading of a big book with a group of children. Audio- or videotape yourself reading. (Be sure to gain permission from the children's parents before you do the videotaping. Some parents do not want their children's face to be visible in a videotape. If so, position the camera so it is focused on you and not the children.) Analyze this big-book shared reading using the recommendations in Special Feature 4.2 as the lens through which you view your sharing of this big book.

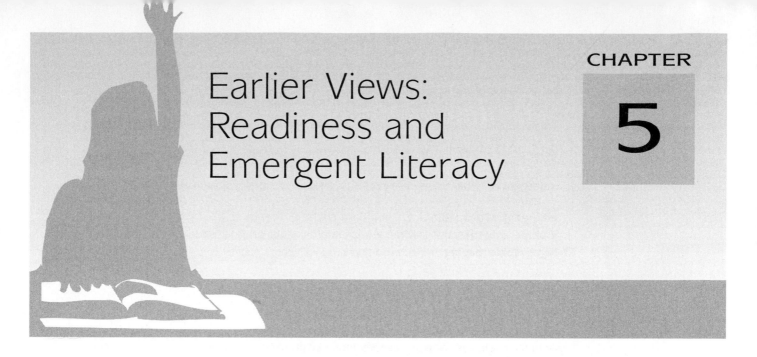

Earlier Views: Readiness and Emergent Literacy

Snuggled next to her mother, one-year-old Tiffany is listening to one of her best-loved bedtime stories, Goodnight Moon, *by Margaret Wise Brown (1947). Her mother reads:*

And two little kittens And a pair of mittens And a little toy house And a young mouse.

> *Pointing to the picture, Tiffany says, "Mamma, da mousey."*
> *"That's right, Tiffany," says her mother, who resumes reading:*

And a comb and a brush and a bowl full of mush And a quiet old lady who was whispering Hush.

> *Tiffany, touching the pictures of the bunny mother sitting in the rocking chair, says, "Dat's like Nane Gammaw."*
> *Her mother replies, "Yes, Tiffany, she looks like Grandma."*
> *Throughout the story, Tiffany comments on the illustrations. As her mother finishes the last line,*

Goodnight stars, goodnight air, goodnight noises everywhere.

a very sleepy Tiffany yawns, "Ganight, Mamma."

This chapter provides a historical overview of two perspectives that helped to shape early literacy instruction during the second half of the past century: the traditional readiness view that was popular in the 1950s, '60s, and '70s, and the emergent literacy perspective that took hold in the 1980s and '90s.

The traditional readiness view highlighted that certain areas of skill and knowledge are prerequisite for successfully learning to read and write. Unfortunately, this view emphasized the *wrong* prerequisites—perceptual motor skills that had little direct relationship with literacy acquisition. Much valuable instruction time was wasted having children walk on balance beams and listen to film canisters filled with different types of objects—activities that did not prepare them to learn to read and write. We present this view so that we will not repeat mistakes from the past!

The emergent literacy view, on the other hand, greatly enhanced our understanding of the beginnings of reading and writing. According to this view, the literacy learning process shares much in common with oral language development. Literacy acquisition, like oral language learning, begins early. For many children, like Tiffany in the example above, literacy development begins in infancy when caregivers read storybooks to children and children begin to notice print in the environment. According to the emergent view, literacy learning is an active, constructive process. By observing print and having stories read to them, young children discover patterns and create their own early versions of reading and writing that initially have

BOX 5.1	**conventions of print:** social rules (left-to-right/top-to-bottom sequence, words have spaces between them), and terminology (letter, word, page) of written language
Definitions of Terms	**early literacy:** a broad term that refers to the reading and writing behaviors that children engage in from birth to age 5
	emergent literacy: a view of literacy development suggesting children learn literacy by constructing, testing, and refining their own hypotheses about print
	emergent reading: forms of reading children use as they move toward conventional reading
	emergent writing: forms of writing children use as they move toward conventional writing
	graphic awareness: visually recognizing environmental print, letters, and words
	logographic reading: using environmental print's entire context to read words

little resemblance to conventional forms—the story they "read" may be quite different from the one in the book, and their writing may look like drawing or scribbles. As children have opportunities to use these early forms of literacy in meaningful social situations and as they interact with adults who draw their attention to the features and functions of print, their constructions become increasingly similar to conventional reading and writing. At the end of the chapter, we present a case study of Alicia, a Spanish-speaking kindergartner, to illustrate literacy development from an emergent perspective.

Many of the instructional strategies that grew out of emergent literacy—environmental and functional print, literacy-enriched play settings, shared writing—are very effective and should be a part of every early literacy program. We will describe these strategies in detail in Chapter 6.

BEFORE READING THIS CHAPTER, THINK ABOUT . . .

■ Your early experiences with storybooks. Do you recall snuggling into an adult's lap and sharing a storybook? Did this happen regularly, at bedtime? In line at the supermarket? On the bus? What were your favorite books as a young child?

■ How you learned to read and write. Do you remember reading and writing at home before going to school? Do you remember having lots of books in your home? Do you remember having access to paper and pencils? Were you an early reader—that is, did you learn to read without any formal instruction from an adult?

FOCUS QUESTIONS

■ How does the emergent literacy view of young children's literacy development compare with the traditional readiness view?

■ What knowledge about written language do young children exhibit when adults watch them closely?

■ What are emergent writing and emergent reading?

■ What home factors affect young children's literacy development?

■ What does emergent literacy look like in a language other than English?

The Traditional Readiness View

Some years ago, it was assumed that written language is acquired in a totally different manner than is speech. According to this view, literacy development starts much later than oral-language acquisition, and it involves totally different learning processes. Children were not considered to be ready to begin learning to read and write until about age six, and this

FIGURE 5.1

Visual Discrimination Worksheet

learning was not believed to occur naturally (Durkin, 1987). Children needed to be taught, using basal readers, worksheets, handwriting practice, spelling workbooks, and grammar exercises. Literacy instruction was serious business, best left in the hands of specially trained teachers. Parents were cautioned not to try to encourage early reading or writing for fear that children might learn incorrect concepts and skills, which would later have to be untaught by teachers.

This readiness view of literacy development can be traced to the maturational theories of the mid-1920s (Gesell, 1928). It was believed that children had to reach a certain level of intelligence and physical maturity before they could learn to read and write. During this same period, the concept of readiness skills took hold. According to this view, children needed to master a number of visual, auditory, and motor skills before they could learn to read. Reading readiness tests were developed to measure children's mastery of these skills, and readiness workbooks designed to promote perceptual-motor growth soon became a standard component of the beginning levels of basal reading programs (Stallman & Pearson, 1990).

The merger of the maturation and readiness orientations led to the persistent belief that early childhood was a time during which readiness skills should be taught as a prelude to real reading and writing (Teale & Sulzby, 1986). As a result, kindergarten and beginning first-grade students did lots of readiness activities that had little to do with actual reading. Figure 5.1 illustrates a typical reading readiness worksheet item. This visual discrimination exercise requires students to find the house that matches the one on the far left. Children usually did not have access to books until the middle part of first grade. Writing instruction was postponed even later, after handwriting, spelling, and phonics skills had been mastered.

Children's author Tomie dePaola's (1987, p. v) account of his own personal experience in kindergarten points out the major drawback of the readiness approach to early literacy instruction:

The day I had been waiting for a year and a half had arrived.

I was finally old enough to go to school. I was so happy and insisted on walking the last block by myself and going alone into the school building . . . . I went directly to the lady standing there (who I found out shortly was the principal) and asked where the kindergarten room was. Poor Miss Imick, the kindergarten teacher. After introducing myself to her, I immediately confronted her with "When do we learn to READ?" "Oh," she replied, "we don't learn how to read in kindergarten, we learn how to read next year." "All right," I announced, "I'll be back next year," and promptly walked out the forbidden front door and trudged all the way home. The school telephoned my mother. The police were called, my father rushed home from the barbershop where he worked. I was calmly sitting up in the attic reading one of my mother's slightly racy novels—upside down . . . .

My mother and father knew that threats of punishment wouldn't budge me from my resolve not to get back to school until the "next year" when I would learn to read, so the logical approach was used. "You know," my mother said, "if you don't *pass* kindergarten you can't go to first grade." So reluctantly I went to kindergarten where we "played," which was a waste of time as far as I was concerned.

The traditional approach withheld reading and writing activities from many children, like Tomie dePaola, who were ready and eager to begin mastering written language.

Emergent Literacy

Fortunately, at the same time that the earlier-is-better movement was taking hold, several new areas of research emerged, which were eventually to lead to a radically different conception of early literacy development. According to this new perspective, which has come to be commonly known as emergent literacy (Clay, 1966), written language acquisition has much in common with oral language development. Children begin learning about reading and writing at a very early age by observing and interacting with readers and writers and through their attempts to read and write (Sulzby & Teale, 1991). Each reading and writing attempt teaches children, as they test out what they believe about how written language works. Based on others' responses, their beliefs are modified. The next time they read or write, they test out their new knowledge. The term *emergent* conveys the evolving nature of children's concepts as they move from personalized, idiosyncratic notions about the function, structure, and conventions of print toward conventional reading and writing. As Catherine Snow and her colleagues (1998, p. 45) note, "growing up to be a reader [and writer] is a lengthy process . . . ."

Susan Neuman and Kathy Roskos (1998) point out several problems associated with the terms *emergent* and *conventional*. *Emergent* implies that there is a distinct point at which literacy acquisition begins, and *conventional* implies that there is a point at which acquisition suddenly ends with the appearance of fully mature reading and writing. Neuman and Roskos (1998, p. 2) argue, to the contrary:

> It is now recognized that there is no beginning point. Even at a young age, children are legitimate writers and readers. Similarly, there can be no end point, no single boundary denoting conventionalized practices. Rather, literacy development begins early, is ongoing, and is continuous throughout a lifetime.

Interest in emergent literacy began with studies of early readers, children who learned to read before they entered kindergarten. This research led to investigations of what preschool-age children typically learn about print. At the same time, researchers began to investigate children's home literacy experiences, seeking to discover the factors that promote early literacy acquisition.

The following sections review major findings of three strands of research on emergent literacy: children's concepts about print, early forms of reading and writing, and home literacy experiences. Many of these research studies link acquisition of knowledge or skills with specific ages. It is important to note that there are large individual differences in literacy development and that the ages at which particular knowledge or skills appear will vary widely for specific children. In fact, it is not unusual to find up to a five-year range in children's literacy development within a kindergarten classroom (IRA/NAEYC, 1998).

Part of this variation in the rate of literacy acquisition is due to differences in children's innate intelligence and aptitude. Considerable diversity also exists in children's experiences with oral and written language during the early years (IRA/NAEYC, 1998). That is, some children live in homes with adults who provide the kind of resources and support that optimize literacy acquisition, and others do not. In addition, variations exist in how essential written language is for communicating in different cultures (Neuman & Roskos, 1993). In cultures with a strong oral tradition, the motivation for acquiring literacy may not be as strong as in cultures emphasizing the importance of written language.

Concepts about Print

Research on early readers stimulated interest in what typical children were learning about literacy during the preschool years. The earliest studies on this topic were conducted in laboratory settings and had rather negative results, reporting that preschool-age children had only vague conceptions about reading and writing (Downing & Oliver, 1973–1974). In these studies, children were typically taken out of their classrooms and interviewed by a researcher; the adult, the setting, and the situation were not familiar to the children. Emergent literacy researchers shifted the focus to the knowledge about literacy that young children exhibit in everyday situations at home or in school classrooms. This shift in perspective resulted in a much more positive picture of preschool-age children's knowledge about print.

PURPOSE AND FUNCTIONS OF PRINT. One of the earliest discoveries that children make about written language is that print has meaning. Jerry Harste, Virginia Woodward, and Carolyn Burke (1984) found that many three-year-olds expect print to be meaningful. This understanding becomes evident when children point to words on signs, cereal boxes, or menus and ask, "What does that say?" Alternatively, after making marks on a piece of paper, children make comments such as, "What did I write?" or "This says . . . ."

Children also quickly learn the distinction between print and pictures, usually by age three. Ask three-year-olds to draw a picture and to write their names. Their markings when asked to draw a picture likely will be quite different from those made when asked to write their names. This distinction is important because it establishes a separate identity for print and allows children to begin learning about its functions and structure.

A third early discovery is that print is functional and can be used to "get things done" in daily life. Children's knowledge of the practical uses of print grows substantially during the preschool years. Elfrieda Heibert (1981) found that three-year-olds demonstrated limited knowledge of the purposes of several types of print, such as labels on Christmas presents, street signs, and store signs, but five-year-olds showed much greater knowledge of these functions.

GRAPHIC AWARENESS. Children begin to recognize environmental print—print that occurs in real-life contexts—at a very early age. Several researchers (e.g., Goodman, 1986; Lomax & McGee, 1987; Mason, 1980) have shown that many three- and four-year-olds can recognize and know the meanings of product labels (Colgate, Cheerios, Pepsi), restaurant signs (McDonald's, Pizza Hut), and street signs (STOP). Even if children do not say the correct word when attempting to read such print, they usually will come up with a related term. For example, when presented with a Coke can, the child might say "Pepsi."

In recognizing environmental print, children attend to the entire context rather than just the print (Masonheimer, Drum, & Ehri, 1984). This *logographic reading* begins quite early. Yetta Goodman (1986) found that 80 percent of the four-year-olds in her study could recognize environmental print in full context—they knew that a can of Pepsi Cola said *Pepsi.* Typically, by mid-kindergarten, many children learn to recognize a limited set of whole words without environmental context clues, using incidental cues such as shape, length, and pictures (Ehri, 1991).

Children often begin to recognize the letters of the alphabet at about the same time as they "read" environmental print. Interest appears to be a key factor in determining the specific letters that children learn first (McGee & Richgels, 1989). Children's own names and highly salient environmental print are often the source of initial letter learning. Marcia Baghban (1984), for example, describes how K (K-Mart), M (McDonald's), and G (Giti) were among the first letters recognized by her two-year-old daughter Giti.

CONVENTIONS OF PRINT. Conventions of print refer to the social rules (left-to-right and top-to-bottom sequence, spaces between words, capitalizing the first letter of each sentence) and terminology (letter, word, page) that surround written language. Knowledge of these conventions tends to grow slowly. For example, knowledge of the left-to-right and top-to-bottom sequence of print is often not acquired until age five or six, and metalinguistic terms such as *letter* and *word* continue to confuse many children during the primary grades (Clay, 1972).

Early Forms of Reading and Writing

Traditionally, strict criteria have been used to define the onset of reading and writing. Children were not considered to be reading until they could correctly recognize numerous printed words, and they were not considered to be writing until they had mastered correct letter formation and could spell words conventionally. Children's early attempts at reading (labeling illustrations or making up a story to go along with the pictures in a book) and their early tries at writing (scribbles or random groups of letters) were dismissed as insignificant and inconsequential.

As interest in emergent literacy increased during the 1970s, some researchers began focusing attention on these initial attempts at reading and writing (Clay, 1975; Read, 1971). It soon became clear that these early forms appeared to be purposeful and rule governed. Children appeared to construct, test, and perfect hypotheses about written language. Research began to reveal general developmental sequences, with the emergent forms of reading and writing gradually becoming more conventional with age and experience (Ferreiro & Teberosky, 1982; Sulzby, Barnhart, & Hieshima, 1989).

EMERGENT WRITING. Building on the earlier work of Marie Clay (1975) and of Emilia Ferreiro and Ana Teberosky (1982), Elizabeth Sulzby asked preschool children to write stories and to read what they had written (Sulzby, 1985b, 1990). Based on this research, Sulzby (1990) has identified seven broad categories of early writing: drawing as writing, scribble writing, letterlike units, nonphonetic letter strings, copying from environmental print, invented spelling, and conventional writing (see Figure 5.2).

FIGURE 5.2

Sulzby's Categories of Emergent Writing

Drawing as writing—Pictures represent writing.

Context: Angela (age 4), who is playing in the housekeeping center, makes a shopping list for a trip to the supermarket.
Text: "Hamburgers [the two bottom circles] and chocolate chip cookies [the two top circles]"

Scribble writing—Continuous lines represent writing.

Context: Rimmert Jr. (age 6) writes a thank-you letter to a family friend.
Text: "Thank you for your letter from America."

Letter-like units—The child makes a series of separate marks that have some letter-like characteristics

Context: Lauren (age 4) writes a story about a recent experience.
Text: "I buy the food at the store. I baked it, and I washed it and ate it."

FIGURE 5.2

(continued)

Nonphonetic letter strings—The child writes strings of letters that show no evidence of letter–sound relationships. These can be random groups of letters or repeated clusters of letters.

SI°°T|SDEMWHFTTT1SSSS++D

Context: Debbie (age 4) writes in her journal about a recent school experience.
Text: "We play together, and Bobby fought with us. We fight with him, then we play again."

Copying from environmental print—The child copies print found in the environment.

PHOUHS
APPLEJU
ICE

Context: Pierce (age 4), in the role of a veterinarian, writes a prescription for a sick teddy bear. He copies the words *apple juice* from a can he has retrieved from a nearby garbage can.
Text: "Penicillin" [invented spelling]
"Apple juice" [copying]

Invented spelling—The child creates his own spelling using letter–sound relationships. This can range from using one letter per word to using a letter for every sound in each word (as in the example below).

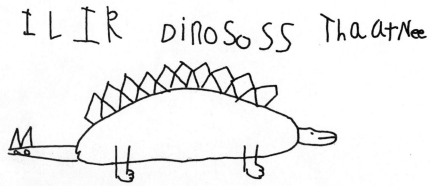

Context: Chris (age 5) writes in his journal.
Text: "I like dinosaurs. They are neat."

FIGURE 5.2

(continued)

Conventional—The child uses correct spelling for most of the words.

Context: Johnny (age 5) writes in his journal.
Text: "This is a dog jumping over a box.

Sulzby believes that these categories do not form a strict developmental hierarchy. While there is a general movement from less mature forms toward conventional forms, children move back and forth across these forms when composing texts, and they often combine several different types in the same composition. Several of the examples in Figure 5.2 show this type of form mixing. Angela's shopping list contains drawings to represent cookies and a hamburger, while a scribble stands for the word *and*. Pierce used both invented spelling and copying from environmental print to write his prescription for the sick teddy bear. Children also appear to adjust their form of writing to the task at hand. Kindergartners tend to use invented or conventional spellings when writing single words. When writing longer pieces of text, they often shift to less mature forms, such as nonphonetic letter strings or scribbles, which require less time and effort (Sulzby & Teale, 1991).

Sulzby cautions teachers against having unrealistic expectations of children's emergent writing capabilities. Case studies of early readers (Baghban, 1984; Bissex, 1980) might lead teachers to expect that invented spelling is a common occurrence among four- and five-year-olds. However, Sulzby's longitudinal research has revealed that children's writing development

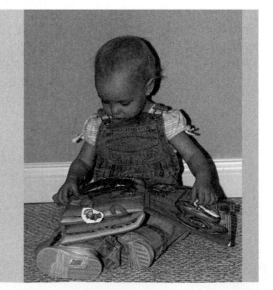

Emergent reading of familiar storybooks has an important role in early literacy development.

SPECIAL FEATURE 5.1

Allison's Emergent Reading of "The Hare and The Tortoise"

TEXT

Once upon a time, a hare and a tortoise lived near a large . . . . They lived in a large open field.

Every day, the hare went zigzagging across the field, with a *hippity-hop, hoppity-hop.* His long hind legs made it easy for him to move quickly. If danger was near, off he would scamper, quick as a flash.

The tortoise, on the other hand, was not very fast. He plodded along slowly, without a care in the world.

It so happened that the hare loved to make fun of how slowly the tortoise moved. The tortoise tried not to let it bother him, but he did not like it. One day the hare began teasing the tortoise in front of other animals.

"You are so slow." said the hare, "that I get tired just watching you! Why, if you were any slower, you would be standing still."

EMERGENT READING

Once upon a time there lived a hare and a tortoise.

Every day the hare goes zigzagging across the field, with a *hippity-hop, hoppity-hop.* When danger was near, he would scamper off in the quick of the night.

The tortoise and the hare were slow. He didn't care if the tortoise—the hare made fun of him. He plodded along slowly, without a care in the world.

One day the hare decided to tease the tortoise. When the tortoise passed by the hare started teasing the tortoise. You are so slow, I'll bet I could even beat you in a race.

You are so slow, so slow. You are like a statue.

---

is typically much slower, with invented spelling not arriving until late kindergarten for some and not until the end of first grade for others (Sulzby & Teale, 1991). Both groups of children (the early and the late spellers) are normal.

EMERGENT READING. Sulzby has also investigated the patterns in children's early attempts at reading familiar storybooks (Sulzby, 1985a). She found that children's storybook-reading behaviors appeared to follow a developmental pattern, with their attention gradually shifting from the pictures to the text and their vocalizations changing from sounding like oral storytelling to sounding like reading. The following is a condensed list of Sulzby's storybook-reading categories (Sulzby & Barnhart, 1990):

(1) *Attending to pictures, not forming stories*—The child looks at the pictures in the book, labeling or making comments about them.
(2) *Attending to pictures, forming oral stories*—The child looks at the book's pictures and weaves a story across the pages. However, the child's intonation sounds like she or he is telling an oral story. The listener must be able to see the pictures to follow the story.
(3) *Attending to pictures, forming written stories*—The child reads by looking at the book's pictures, and the child's wording and intonation sound like reading. The listener does not usually have to see the pictures to follow the story.
(4) *Attending to print*—The child attends to the print rather than to the pictures when attempting to read the story. The child may refuse to read because of print awareness, may use only selected aspects of print (e.g., letter–sound relationships), or may read conventionally.

Allison's (age five) emergent reading of "The Hare and the Tortoise" is illustrated in Special Feature 5.1. Her reading is representative of Sulzby's category "attending to pictures, forming written stories." Notice how Allison has memorized parts of the story and paraphrases the rest of the text, using her own words to reconstruct its meaning.

Research has shown that young children's emergent readings can be influenced by the number of times a child has heard a book read (Pappas & Brown, 1987) and how many times the child has read the book independently (Pappas, 1993). Repeated readings of a book, either by the child or an adult, increases the degree to which children's subsequent emergent reading approximates the actual text of the book. In addition, text features such as pictures and grammatical subordination and narrative structure have been found to affect children's emergent reading, as measured by the Sulzby scale (Elster, 1998). Thus, children's emergent reading levels should be expected to vary, depending on the features and familiarity of the texts being read.

Interestingly, children's level of early reading does not always correspond to their early writing (Sulzby, Barnhart, & Hieshima, 1989). For example, a child might be able to write with invented spelling, using letter–sound relationships to encode words. However, the same child might not use letter–sound relationships when decoding words during reading. So children who begin to use invented spelling are not automatically able to read their own writing. The pattern of relationships between the emergent forms of literacy is far from simple!

Home Literacy Experiences

The third and final strand of this research has focused on young children's home environments in an attempt to discover factors that promote emergent literacy development. Whereas the first two groups of studies focus on what children learn about written language, home literacy research is concerned with how this learning takes place.

Early studies in this area focused on umbrella characteristics such as family income and parents' levels of education (Sulzby & Teale, 1991). Results revealed positive relationships between these variables and reading achievement in the early grades. For example, children from middle-income families tend to be better readers than those from low-income families. Unfortunately, such findings do little to explain how these variables directly affect children's literacy growth.

Later studies have narrowed their focus and attempted to describe the actual literacy-related experiences that children have at home. These home literacy studies have identified several factors that appear to have important roles in emergent literacy acquisition. These factors are described in the sections that follow.

ACCESS TO PRINT AND BOOKS. In order to learn about literacy, young children must have opportunities to see lots of print and must have easy access to books. Plentiful home supplies of children's books have been found to be associated with early reading (Durkin, 1966), interest in literature (Morrow, 1983), and positive orientation toward schooling (Feitelson & Goldstein, 1986).

Because of the literate nature of our society, all children are surrounded by large amounts of environmental print. For example, they see print on product containers (Cheerios, Pepsi) street signs (STOP), and store signs (McDonald's, Pizza Hut). Differences do occur, however, in children's exposure to books and other forms of reading materials. Bill Teale's (1986) descriptive study of the home environments of twenty-four low-income preschoolers revealed that while some of the homes had ample supplies of children's books, other homes contained none. This is not to suggest that all children from low-income families lack exposure to reading materials at home. Purcell-Gates's study of twenty low-income families of differing ethnic backgrounds revealed great variability in the literacy experiences of children. The total number of literacy events in the low-income homes ranged from .17 to 5.07 per hour, meaning that some children had opportunities to experience more than twenty-five times the amount of literacy than other children! While on average the home literacy experiences of low-income children may not be as rich as those of average middle-class children, some nonmainstream children do have frequent interactions with print. Unfortunately, those children who do not have access to books at home are at a great disadvantage in acquiring literacy.

Larger societal factors, such as community access to literacy, also enter the picture. Neuman and Celano (2001), for example, found that low-income families had much more restricted access to public libraries and places to buy books. In addition, the school libraries in low-income neighborhoods had fewer books per child, lower-quality books, less-qualified librarians, and fewer computers. So limited access to literacy materials and good places to read, caused by societal inequities, may be contributing factors to many low-income children's "at-risk" status.

FIGURE 5.3

Ben's Post-it Note Message: "My Sister and Dad Took Me to Soccer Practice. Be Back at 4"

ADULT DEMONSTRATIONS OF LITERACY BEHAVIOR.   Children also need to observe their parents, other adults, or older siblings using literacy in everyday situations (Smith, 1988). When children see their family members use print for various purposes—writing shopping lists, paying bills, looking up programs in the television listings, and writing notes to each other—they begin to learn about the practical uses of written language and to understand why reading and writing are activities worth doing. If their parents happen to model reading for pleasure, so much the better. These children see literature as a source of entertainment. Children's exposure to these types of functional and recreational literacy demonstrations has been found to vary greatly.

SUPPORTIVE ADULTS.   Early readers tend to have parents who are very supportive of their early attempts at literacy (Morrow, 1983). While these parents rarely attempt to directly teach their children how to read and write, they do support literacy growth by doing such things as (1) answering their children's questions about print; (2) pointing out letters and words in the environment; (3) reading storybooks frequently; (4) making regular visits to the local library; (5) providing children with a wide variety of experiences such as trips to stores, parks, and museums; and (6) initiating functional literacy activities (such as suggesting that a child write a letter to grandmother or help make a shopping list).

The amount of such support that children receive during the preschool years varies greatly from family to family, and these differences have been found to have a considerable effect on children's literacy learning during kindergarten and the elementary grades (Christian, Morrison, & Bryant, 1998; Leseman & de Jong, 1998).

INDEPENDENT ENGAGEMENTS WITH LITERACY.   Young children need to get their hands on literacy materials and to have opportunities to engage in early forms of reading and writing. This exploration and experimentation allows children to try out and perfect their growing concepts about the functions, forms, and conventions of written language.

Independent engagements with literacy often take place in connection with play. Don Holdaway (1979) has described how, as soon as young children become familiar with a storybook through repetitive read-aloud experiences, they will begin to play with the books and pretend to read them. He believes that this type of reading-like play is one of the most important factors promoting early literacy acquisition.

Young children also incorporate writing into their play. Sometimes this play writing is exploratory in nature, with children experimenting with different letter forms and shapes. At other times, emergent writing occurs in the context of make-believe play. Figure 5.3 is an example of this type of play-related writing. Four-year-old Ben was engaging in dramatic play in the housekeeping center. He wrote a Post-it note message to another child, who was acting out the role of his mother, informing her that he was at soccer practice.

Young children also use literacy in functional, nonplay situations. An excellent example is Glenda Bissex's (1980) account of how her four-year-old son Paul, after failing to get her attention by verbal means, used a stamp set to write "RUDF" (Are you deaf?). He also attempted to secure his privacy by putting the sign "DO NOT DSTRB GNYS AT WRK" (Do not disturb . . . Genius at work) on his door.

Opportunities for these types of independent engagements with literacy depend on access to books and writing materials. As mentioned previously, research on children's home environments indicates that there are wide discrepancies in the availability of children's books and other reading materials. Similar differences also exist in the availability of writing materials. Teale's (1986) descriptive study of the home environments of low-income preschoolers revealed that only four of twenty-four children had easy access to paper and writing instruments. He noted that these particular children engaged in far more emergent writing than did the other subjects in the study.

STORYBOOK READING. Storybook reading is undoubtedly the most studied aspect of home literacy. Quantitative studies have attempted to establish the importance and value of parents' reading to their children. A meta-analysis of twenty-nine studies spanning more than three decades indicated that parent–preschooler storybook reading was positively related to outcomes such as language growth, early literacy, and reading achievement (Bus, van IJzendoorn, & Pellegrini, 1995).

Other studies have attempted to describe and analyze what actually takes place during storybook-reading episodes and to identify the mechanisms through which storybook reading facilitates literacy growth (e.g., Altwerger, Diehl-Faxon, & Dockstader-Anderson, 1985; Heath, 1982; Holdaway, 1979; Snow & Ninio, 1986; Taylor, 1986; Yaden, Smolkin, & Conlon, 1989). These studies have shown that parent–child storybook reading is an ideal context for children to receive all of the previously mentioned factors that promote literacy acquisition:

(1) Storybook reading provides children with access to enjoyable children's books, building positive attitudes about books and reading.
(2) During storybook reading, parents present children with a model of skilled reading. Children see how books are handled, and they hear the distinctive intonation patterns that are used in oral reading.
(3) Parents provide support that enables young children to take an active part in storybook reading. Early storybook-reading sessions tend to be routinized, with the parent first focusing the child's attention on a picture and then asking the child to label the picture. If the child does so, the parent gives positive or negative feedback about the accuracy of the label. If the child does not volunteer a label, the parent provides the correct label (Snow & Ninio, 1986). As children's abilities grow, parents up the ante, shifting more of the responsibility to the children and expecting them to participate in more advanced ways.
(4) Storybook reading encourages independent engagements with literacy by familiarizing children with stories and encouraging them to attempt to read the stories on their own (Holdaway, 1979; Sulzby, 1985a).

Other researchers have studied how cultural factors affect the manner in which parents mediate storybook reading for their children. Shirley Brice Heath (1982) found that middle-class parents tended to help their children link book information with other experiences. For example, John Langstaff's popular predictable book *Oh, A-Hunting We Will Go* (1974, Macmillan) contains the following lines:

> *Oh, a-hunting we will go.*
> *A-hunting we will go.*
> *We'll catch a lamb*
> *And put him in a pram*
> *And then we'll let him go.*

To help the child understand the term *pram,* a middle-class parent might say, "The pram looks just like your sister's baby carriage." Working-class parents, on the other hand, had a tendency

SPECIAL FEATURE 5.2

Alicia's Early Literacy Development in Spanish

Irene Serna and Sarah Hudelson

Native English-speaking children begin to read and write by engaging in daily literacy activities with family members and teachers. These adults support early literacy by creating opportunities for reading and writing and by responding to children's requests for assistance. What does early literacy look like in a language other than English? Alicia, a Spanish-speaking kindergartner we came to know through our research, provides a good example of how children construct their literacy in Spanish (Serna & Hudelson, 1993).

ALICIA'S HOME LANGUAGE AND LITERACY

Spanish was the dominant language in Alicia's home. Her mother reported that Alicia had requested that books be read to her since she was four years old. In addition, Alicia had been eager to engage in writing within family activities. At home, Alicia helped produce shopping lists, notes, and cards sent to family members. Of course, these were written in Spanish. Clearly, Alicia came from a very literate home environment that featured frequent storybook reading, many opportunities to write in connection with daily activities, and adults who supported her early attempts at reading and writing. In this regard, Alicia's early literacy development was quite similar to Tiffany's and that of other English-speaking children who come from supportive home environments. There was one significant difference—Alicia reported that her mother and grandmother frequently told her *cuentos* (folktales) and family stories. Thus, storytelling (oral literacy) was also a strong part of Alicia's home literacy experiences.

ALICIA'S LITERACY DEVELOPMENT IN KINDERGARTEN

Though Alicia participated in a bilingual Head Start program as a four-year-old, when she entered kindergarten, her score on an oral language proficiency test identified her as limited English proficient. Two-thirds of the children in her bilingual kindergarten program spoke English, and one-third spoke Spanish. Alicia used both languages to socialize with her peers. However, she primarily used Spanish to explain her thinking, to narrate stories, and to express herself personally. At the beginning of kindergarten, Alicia only discussed books that were read aloud in Spanish. By the latter half of the year, she was discussing books read in both languages. This was particularly helpful to the monolingual children because Alicia could interpret books and communications in English or Spanish. Alicia's role in the classroom became that of translator. Thus, while her one year of Head Start was not sufficient time for

Alicia to develop oral proficiency in English, the second year of bilingual programming in kindergarten did allow her to develop bilingual abilities.

Writing

Beginning in October of her kindergarten year, Alicia was asked to write in a journal for forty-five minutes daily. Throughout the year, she also drew and wrote in learning logs to record information from study in thematic units. She contributed to group language experience charts, which summarized findings from the children's thematic studies. In her earliest journal entries, Alicia wrote a patterned and familiar phrase in English, "I love my mom." A November entry demonstrated that Alicia had moved from producing a patterned phrase to creating a label for her picture: *"Mi papalote"* (my kite). In November, Alicia also wrote her first sentence describing a picture, *"Yo ciro mi babe Martinsito"* (I love my baby Martincito), using both invented (*ciro* for *quiero*) and conventional spelling. She also wrote additional patterned sentences, *"Mi Nana bonita come sopa Mi mami bonita come sopa"* (My pretty grandmother eats soup. My pretty mother eats soup.) In December, Alicia repeated phrases to write two lines of text describing her picture, *"Los colores del arco iris son bonitos Colores del arco ids"* (The colors of the rainbow are pretty. The colors of the rainbow.) Her writing did not become more expressive until February when she wrote about playing in the pile of snow that had been trucked to the school (see Figure 5.4).

This February sample demonstrates that Alicia's invented spellings included most sounds in each syllable, that the vowels were standardized, and that she confused some of the consonants. Though she put spaces between most words, conventional word separation was not used consistently.

In April, Alicia wrote a personal narrative about her little cousin Martincito, primarily describing how she cared for and played with him. Figure 5.5 contains two of the ten sentences she wrote in this personal narrative. Written over a three-week period, Alicia's personal narrative illustrates that her invented spellings were very close approximations of standard Spanish spellings. Alicia also separated words more consistently. Syntactically, all of her sentences were complete, and all grammatical inflections were correct. By the end of kindergarten, Alicia was the classroom's most fluent writer in Spanish. As a result, other children often asked her to write their personal narratives.

Reading

From September through February, Alicia retold stories from familiar, predictable picture books using some of the story language in Spanish and some in English. In March, her first story was typed for publication (in Spanish). Alicia read this text for the first time using letter–sound cues and a phonetic decoding strategy (i.e., she tried to sound out the words). While this initial reading was not very smooth, Alicia

(continued on next page)

SPECIAL FEATURE 5.2 *(continued)*

practiced reading the words until she could reread her own story fluently. From March to the end of the year, Alicia used this same strategy with familiar, predictable books in Spanish. Initially, each book was read utilizing the phonetic decoding strategy, focusing on sounding out unfamiliar words. Subsequently, she reread the text until she could read it fluently. Alicia chose to read books that had plain print, with only one or two lines of text per page. She rejected books with too many words or italic print. By the end of May, Alicia read the Spanish versions of Maurice Sendak's *Where the Wild Things Are* (1963, Harper & Row) and Robert Kraus's *Herman the Helper* (1974, Windmill), familiar and unfamiliar texts, respectively. She made a few mistakes, primarily grammatical. She did not correct

FIGURE 5.4

Alicia's February Writing Sample

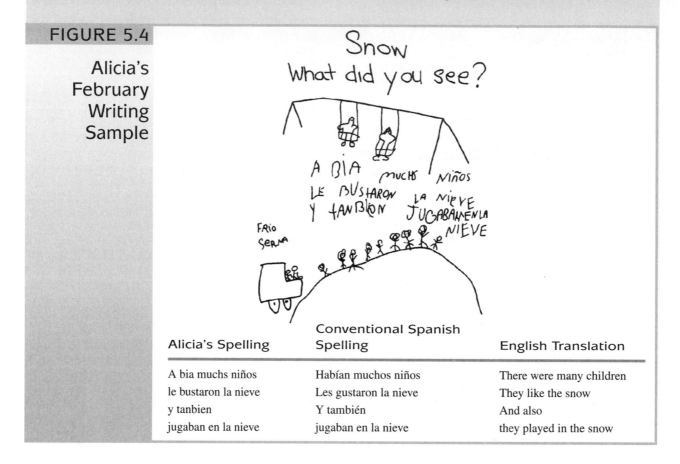

Alicia's Spelling	Conventional Spanish Spelling	English Translation
A bia muchs niños	Habían muchos niños	There were many children
le bustaron la nieve	Les gustaron la nieve	They like the snow
y tanbien	Y también	And also
jugaban en la nieve	jugaban en la nieve	they played in the snow

to not extend book information beyond its original context and would simply define the word *pram* for the child. Sulzby and Teale (1991) speculate that these differences in story-reading style may have a considerable effect on children's emergent literacy acquisition.

Learning Literacy in a Second Language

Children learn the dominant language of their home. Whatever the language—English, Spanish, Chinese, or Arabic—children are provided models of both oral and written language. Young children are eager to engage in talking, writing, and reading in the home's dominant language. So early literacy across languages looks quite similar. Some cultures and families place emphasis on oral storytelling in addition to reading and writing. Adults in these homes share stories with their young literacy learners and with each other. Of course, children from families whose dominant language is a language other than English will enter school using the language that works for them in their home environment. A quality program that supports these children's emergence as readers and writers is important.

Special Feature 5.2 presents a case study of Alicia, who is from a home in which Spanish was the primary language. When she entered kindergarten, Alicia was speaking perfect Span-

SPECIAL FEATURE 5.2 *(continued)*

these mistakes, but they were rather minor and did not change the meaning of the story. Alicia read more effectively, using multiple cues (letter–sound, meaning, and grammatical) as well as illustrations to decode unfamiliar words. Alicia also demonstrated that she was reading to construct the meaning of each text because she was able to retell each story accurately. By the end of kindergarten, Alicia had become a fluent writer and reader in Spanish. She was able to use sophisticated invented spellings that were very close approximations of standard Spanish spellings, and she could compose coherent narrative stories. Alicia learned to read in Spanish through reading both her own writing and familiar, predictable books. By April, Alicia was reading picture books fluently and independently. She was able to use multiple cueing systems and reading strategies in Spanish.

FIGURE 5.5

Alicia's April Writing Sample

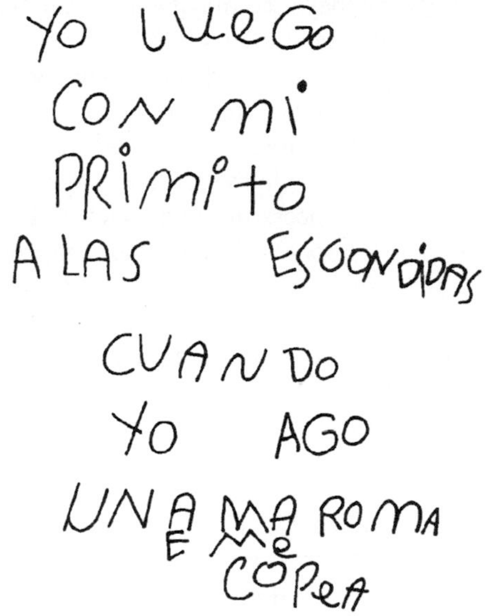

Yo lueGo
con mi
PRimito
A LAS   ESGoNDiDAS
                CUANDO
        Yo   AGO
UNA MA RoMA
        E me
        CoPeA

Alicia's Spelling	Conventional Spanish Spelling	English Translation
Yo juego	Yo juego	I play
con mi	con mi	with my
primito	primita	little cousin
alas escondidas	a las escondidas	hide-and-seek
Cuando	Cuando	When
Yo ago	yo hago	I make
una ma roma	una moroma	a somersault
e me copea	el me copea	he copies me

ish but was only partially proficient in oral English. She was fortunate to attend a bilingual kindergarten in which she was allowed to learn to read and write in Spanish and then transfer what she had learned to English literacy. As you will see, Alicia's emergent literacy learning follows the same developmental patterns of native English speakers.

Summary

The three research strands reviewed in this chapter have joined to provide a picture of the emergent literacy perspective. How does what you read in this chapter compare with how you learned to read and write? Were the supportive factors described in the section "Home Literacy Experiences" present in your home?

Here, we return to the questions posed at the beginning of the chapter and briefly summarize the information presented.

■ *How does the emergent literacy view of young children's literacy development compare with the traditional readiness view?*

According to the emergent literacy view, the literacy learning process shares much in common with the oral language development process. Literacy acquisition, like oral language development, begins early. For many children, literacy development begins in infancy when caregivers read storybooks to children and children begin to notice print in the environment. Literacy learning is an active, constructive process. By observing print and having stories read to them, young children discover patterns and create their own early versions of reading and writing that initially have little resemblance to conventional forms; the story they read may be quite different from the one in the book, and their writing may look like drawing or scribbles. As children have opportunities to use these early forms of literacy in meaningful social situations and as they interact with adults who draw their attention to the features and functions of print, their constructions become increasingly similar to conventional reading and writing.

According to the readiness view, literacy development begins much later (at about age six). The process through which children acquire literacy is unlike the oral language acquisition process. Rather than constructing knowledge about literacy by experimenting with forms of literacy in supportive environments, supporters of this view believed that children must be directly taught by specially trained teachers who guided children's acquisition of literacy concepts and skills, known as reading readiness skills, which had little to do with actual reading. Children did not meet real reading materials, like books, until the middle of first grade. Children did not write to communicate until much later, after they knew how to form letters and spell words.

■ *What knowledge about written language do young children exhibit when adults watch them closely?*

Watch children and you will see the following:

- Children as young as three years of age know the difference between drawing and writing, expect print to be meaningful (to say something), and know something about the purposes of print.
- Two- and three-year-olds play with sounds, thus exhibiting their phonological awareness knowledge.
- Three- and four-year-olds read product labels, restaurant signs, and street signs.
- Three-year-olds can name about one-third of the letters of the alphabet.
- Five- and six-year-olds identify words that begin with the same phoneme, thus exhibiting their phonemic awareness knowledge.
- Young children write /m/ for man, thus exhibiting their knowledge of phonics.
- Young children show that they know such concepts as print moves from left to right and top to bottom across the page and that words have spaces between them.
- Young children use early forms of writing and of reading, becoming more conventional with age and experience.

■ *What are emergent writing and emergent reading?*

On their way toward reading and writing conventionally, young children construct, test, and perfect hypotheses about written language. Research has shown general developmental sequences, with children's early forms of reading and writing gradually becoming more conventional with age and experience. These early reading and writing forms are known as emergent. Children using all forms of reading and writing are legitimate writers and readers.

■ *What home factors affect young children's literacy development?*

Several factors have been identified as having important roles in early literacy acquisition. These include

- opportunities to see lots of print and have easy access to books;
- opportunities to observe adults using literacy in everyday situations;

- adults who support children's literacy development by answering children's questions, pointing to letters, taking the children to the library, providing children with a wide variety of experiences, and initiating functional literacy activities;
- literacy materials that support children's engagement in early forms of reading and writing; and
- experiences with adults who share books with children.

■ *What does emergent literacy look like in a language other than English?*

Children learn the dominant language of their home. When these homes—be they English speaking, Spanish speaking, or Arabic speaking—provide a literate model, typically the young children who live in them are eager to engage in talking, writing, and reading in the home's dominant language. So emergent literacy across languages looks quite similar. Some cultures and families place emphasis on oral storytelling in addition to reading and writing. Adults in these homes share stories with their young literacy learners and with each other. Of course, children from families whose dominant language is a language other than English will enter school using the language that works for them in their home environment. A quality program that supports these children's emergence as readers and writers is important.

LINKING KNOWLEDGE TO PRACTICE

1. With a group of colleagues, talk about an early childhood classroom you have seen. Which view of literacy was evidenced in this classroom? Provide specific descriptions of what you observed (like the vignette at the beginning of this chapter) to support your decision of the view evidenced.

2. Read a storybook with a child of three years or older. Ask the child to point to where you should begin reading. Does the child know that you will read the print, not the pictures? After you have read the story to the child, ask the child to read the story to you. What form does the child use to read the story (e.g., attending to pictures, forming oral stories; attending to pictures, forming written stories; attending to print)? When you have finished reading the book, select an important word from the story. Can the child tell you the name of the letters in this word? Say a word that rhymes with this word. Now it's the child's turn. Can the child say another word that rhymes with this word? Say a word that begins with the same sound. Can the child say a word that begins with the same sound? Point to each letter. Can the child say the sound of each letter? Can the child blend the letter sounds to form the word? Compare your findings with those gathered by your colleagues.

3. Observe young children at play in a literacy-enriched dramatic play setting (for example, a home center equipped with paper, pencils, telephone books, television guides, cookbooks, junk mail, cereal boxes, etc.) Watch two or three children while they play in this setting. What do they talk about? What do they write? For example, do they make grocery lists? What does their writing tell you about what they know about the kinds of written language (lists, letter writing, check writing) and forms of written language (scribbles, nonphonetic letter strings, invented spellings)? Do they expect their writing to say something? How do they use the reading materials in the setting? Can they read the cereal boxes? What form of reading do they use to construct meaning from the print? What does your observation tell you about these children's development as readers and writers? If possible, complete this activity with a colleague who watches other children in the play setting. Compare the children's literacy behaviors in the same play setting.

4. Mem Fox (1993, p. 29) describes how she brings buckets of water into her college classroom and plunges naked dolls into the water saying, "If the water is Italian, will this child learn English? . . . If the water is a home without books, will this child be an avid reader? . . . If the water is a classroom in which the teacher bathes this child in good literature by reading aloud everyday, will the child's reading and writing develop in leaps and bounds?" Explain the point Mem Fox is making with this demonstration. Add three similar ideas to her "crassly obvious" points.

Emergent Literacy Strategies

As Isaac enters his kindergarten classroom, he and his classmates collect laminated helper necklaces from their name pockets on the attendance chart. Each necklace has a tag listing a classroom task. Isaac "reads" his tag—Errand Runner. He checks the nearby Helper Board where all the duties for each task have been described in both words and pictures. Today he will run any errands his teacher may have, such as taking the attendance count to the center's office. Yesterday, Isaac was Pencil Sharpener, which involved gathering and sharpening pencils. He hopes to be Pet Feeder tomorrow.

In Chapter 5, we described the emergent literacy perspective. According to this view, children begin to learn about reading and writing at an early age by engaging in everyday activities with their family and peers. Emergent literacy research has revealed that several types of home experiences stimulate early literacy learning: (1) easy access to print and books; (2) supportive parents or other caregivers who read stories aloud, demonstrate different types of literacy behaviors, answer children's questions about print, and scaffold children's literacy efforts; and (3) opportunities for children to engage in emergent forms of reading and writing. These home literacy experiences help children develop an awareness of the forms and functions of print.

Proponents of emergent literacy believe that early childhood programs should feature literacy activities that mirror the types of literacy experiences found in enriched home environments, such as print-rich settings, storybook reading, demonstrations of various forms of literacy, and lots of opportunities for children to engage in meaningful reading and writing activities. These types of experiences build on what children have already learned about written language, provide a smooth transition between home and school, and help ensure initial success with language arts instruction.

As stated in Chapter 1, we believe that effective early literacy programs should blend the best emergent literacy strategies with the best strategies from the scientifically based reading research (SBRR) approach. This chapter describes three key emergent literacy strategies: functional literacy activities, literacy play, and the language experience approach (also known as shared writing). These strategies are particularly valuable because they provide a broad spectrum of learning opportunities that are appropriate for children at different ages and with different prior experience with print. When used with large groups of children, opportunities exist for *all* children to gain valuable knowledge about literacy. We firmly believe that these emergent literacy strategies should be major components in every early literacy curriculum.

BEFORE READING THIS CHAPTER, THINK ABOUT . . .

■ How you used print as a child. Did you write notes to your family? Did you pretend to write checks? Send a letter to Santa? Write a thank-you card to Grandma?

■ Advertisement logos you remember from your childhood. Could you spot a McDonald's a mile away? Did your favorite toy or snack food have a special logo or trademark?

■ How print controls your actions on a daily basis. How old were you when you first recognized that the red octagonal sign with white letters meant stop the car?

■ How you played house as a child. Did you have real cereal boxes and egg cartons for your pretend kitchen?

FOCUS QUESTIONS

■ What are functional literacy activities, and how can teachers use these activities in a preschool or kindergarten classroom?

■ How can dramatic play centers be used to encourage young children's literacy development?

■ How can teachers help link literacy and play?

■ How does the language experience approach (or shared writing) increase a child's understanding of print and facilitate reading development?

Functional Literacy Activities

As we explained in Chapter 5, children's home literacy experiences are usually functional in nature. Children watch their parents and older siblings use reading and writing to accomplish real-life purposes. They often join in these activities (e.g., reading food labels and signs in the environment). It is important for teachers to provide opportunities for children to continue to learn about functional qualities of reading and writing.

In the vignette at the opening of this chapter, note how the helper necklaces in Isaac's classroom provide the same type of functional literacy experiences that children have at home. The print on the helper necklaces serves a real purpose and assists with everyday activities (classroom chores). The surrounding context—the chores that are done on a daily basis in the classroom—makes the print on the necklaces easy to recognize and understand.

Functional literacy activity is a broad-spectrum strategy that provides opportunities for children at different stages in their literacy development to learn new skills and concepts. For example, if Isaac is just beginning to learn about the meaning and functions of print, the helper necklaces provide an opportunity to learn that print can inform him about his assigned chores and help him remember these chores. If he has already acquired this basic concept, the necklaces provide opportunities to learn about the structure of print. For example, he may eventually learn to recognize some of the printed words on the necklaces (*runner, pencil, pet*), or to figure out some related letter-sound relationships (the letter *p* represents the sound that *pencil* and *pet* begin with).

BOX 6.1	**broad-spectrum instructional strategy:** strategies that are effective and appropriate for a wide range of learner abilities
Definition of Terms	**environmental print (EP):** the real-life print children see in the home or community, including print on food containers and other kinds of product boxes, store signs, road signs, advertisements, and the like. Because the situation gives clues to the print's meaning, EP is often the first type of print young children can recognize and understand
	functional literacy activities: reading and writing activities that accomplish real-life purposes, such as writing lists and reading directions
	functional print: print that guides everyday classroom activity (e.g., labels, lists, directions, sign-up sheets)
	language experience approach/shared writing: the teacher works with whole groups, small groups, or individual children to write down the children's oral language stories. These highly contextualized stories are easy for children to read
	literacy-enriched play centers: play centers that are enhanced with appropriate theme-related literacy materials

In the sections that follow, we describe two types of print that can provide children with functional literacy activities: (1) environmental print that exists in everyday life outside of school and (2) functional print that is connected with classroom activities.

Environmental Print

At home and in their neighborhoods, young children are surrounded by print that serves real-life functions: labels on cereal boxes and soft drink cans, road signs, billboards, and restaurant menus. This type of print is referred to as environmental print (EP). Because the situation gives clues to the print's meaning, EP is often the first type of print that young children can recognize and understand.

The educational benefits of EP are very controversial. On the one hand, proponents of emergent literacy believe that EP is a valuable instructional resource. For example, Prior and Gerard (2004, p. 9) state:

> We believe . . . that with the assistance of an adult, a child is easily able to recognize the letters in environmental print. Furthermore, we believe that using these highly motivating and visually appealing materials creates a meaningful foundation for learning about the alphabetic principle. In addition, we have found that when teachers use environmental print as an instructional tool to teach letters and sounds, the print in the actual environment serves as a constant reinforcement of the reading skills children are learning in school.

Other researchers with a bent toward the SBR point of view have argued that EP is of little instructional importance. For example, Ehri and Roberts (2006) found evidence that children did not focus on the alphabet letters in EP. Rather, children tended to focus on more visually salient cues such as color and logo designs. This led Ehri and Roberts (2006, p. 121) to conclude that "even though children may be able to read environmental print, this capability does not appear to promote letter learning."

Our position is that, because EP is so meaningful and easy to read, it should be available in all preschool and kindergarten classrooms. In order for this print to promote alphabet knowledge and phonics, teachers need to draw children's attention to letters that occur in EP. We recommend the following EP strategies:

◆ *EP board*—The teacher asks children to bring from home examples of EP that they can read. Selected pieces are displayed on a bulletin board titled "Print I Can Read." For example, the board might contain empty, clean product containers (cereal boxes, milk cartons, candy wrappers, toy boxes), menus for local fast-food restaurants, shopping bags with store logos, illustrated store coupons, and so on. Children work in small groups to try to figure out the meaning of all the pieces of EP on the board.

◆ *EP alphabet chart*—The teacher places pieces of chart paper around the room for every letter of the alphabet. Each day, children bring to class product labels they can "read." During circle time, these labels are read and attached to the correct chart. For example, the Kix (cereal) label would go on the *K k* page. Then the group reads the labels on all the charts, starting with the *A a* page. After several months, when most of the chart pages are full, the teacher can use the product labels from the charts to make books such as *I Can Read Cereals*.

◆ *EP folders*—Selected pieces of EP can be attached to file folders to make EP books (Anderson & Markle, 1985). For example, a pizza book could be made by pasting or laminating the product logos from pizza advertisements, coupons, and delivery containers onto the inside surfaces of a file folder (see Figure 6.1). Children can decorate the front cover with pizza-related illustrations. Other book possibilities include toothpaste, cookies, milk, cereal, and soft drinks. These EP folders should be placed in the classroom library so that children can show off to their friends how well they can read this type of contextualized print.

◆ *EP walks*—This strategy involves taking a class for a walk in the neighborhood surrounding the school (Orellana & Hernández, 1999). Before leaving, the children are told to be on the lookout for EP. As examples of EP are encountered during the walk, they are

FIGURE 6.1

EP Folder

Source: The DP board and EP walk strategies are based on ideas in the September 1994 issue of *Reading between the Lines,* published by the reading and writing specialists of the Paradise Valley School District, Paradise Valley, Arizona.

pointed out by the teacher or by the children. After the children return to the classroom, they draw pictures of the print they could read on the walk. The pictures are put into a group book, which the teacher reads aloud to the class, focusing their attention on the letters in this print. The children can then take turns reading EP items in the book.

◆ *Individual EP booklets*—This approach involves using magazine coupons or advertisements that feature products children are familiar with to make personalized "I Can Read" books. Children sort through the ads or coupons, select the products they recognize, and then use glue sticks to secure the coupons to premade construction paper booklets. The children can share their booklets with each other and take them home to read to family members.

◆ *Sociodramatic play*—As will be explained later in this chapter, environmental print can be used as props in children's dramatic play. For example, empty product boxes such as cereal containers and milk cartons can be used in the kitchen area of housekeeping or home centers. As children act out home-related themes such as making dinner, they will have opportunities to attempt to read the print on the containers. Teachers should draw children's attention to the letters in this play-related print.

Functional Print

Unlike environmental print that is found in the world outside of school, functional classroom print is connected with everyday school activities. This print is practical as well as educational. The helper necklace in the opening vignette helps children remember their assigned chores, making the classroom run more smoothly. Simultaneously, the necklaces offer opportunities for children to learn about the functions and structure of print. As with all functional print, the context helps children discover the meaning of the print and learn concepts about print (Strickland & Schickedanz, 2004).

In the sections that follow, we describe the major types of functional print that are commonly found in preschool and kindergarten classrooms: labels, lists, directions, schedules, calendars, messages, sign-in and sign-up lists, and inventory lists.

LABELS. As illustrated by the helper necklaces in the vignette at the beginning of this chapter, labels may be used to delineate tasks that students are assigned to complete, such as line leader, pencil sharpener, pet feeder, or paper passer. Labels can also be used to help organize the classroom. For example, cubbies can be labeled with children's names so that students know where their belongings are stored. Containers can be labeled to designate their contents, and labels can be used on shelves to indicate where materials are to be stored. Labels can also be used for designating different areas of the classroom (library, home center, blocks, games, art), informing children about the types of activities that are supposed to take place in each location. Finally, labels can be used to convey information. For example, teachers often use labels to identify objects in displays (e.g., types of sea shells) and pictures ("This is a . . ."). Trade Secrets 6.1 describes how one teacher uses labels with children's names for two purposes: to organize their backpacks and to provide a record of their progress in learning to write their names.

LISTS. Lists have a variety of practical classroom uses. Attendance charts can be constructed by placing each child's picture and name above a pocket. The children sign in by finding their name card in a box and by matching it with their name on the chart. After the children become familiar with their printed names, the pictures can be removed.

The teacher can use a second set of name tags to post jobs on a helper chart. This chart, which is an alternative to the helper necklaces described at the beginning of this chapter, contains a description of jobs needing to be done and display pockets that hold the children's name cards (see Figure 6.2). When attendance and helper charts are used on a daily basis, children quickly learn to recognize their own names and the names of their classmates.

DIRECTIONS. Instructions can be posted for using equipment such as tape recorders and computers. Classroom rules (e.g., "We walk in our classroom") can be displayed to remind children of appropriate behavior. In addition, children can create their own personal directives. For example, a child may place a "Look, don't touch!" sign on a newly completed art project or block structure. At first, children will need help from the teacher or from peers in reading these types of directions. Soon, however, they will learn to use the surrounding context to help them remember what the directions say. Teachers can help this process by constantly referring children

---

TRADE SECRETS 6.1

Head Start teachers Gloria Cortez and Mayela Daniels use labels with children's names to designate where children hang their backpacks. They have placed labels with each child's name (in large computer font) and their pictures above the pegs where backpacks are stored. To get some educational mileage out of this functional print, Mrs. Cortez and Mrs. Daniels decided to turn this display into a timeline of children's progress in learning to write their names. Every two months, the children write their name on a small piece of paper, and the teacher dates it. These samples of name writing are placed above their typed name and picture, in chronological order. This provides a concrete record of each child's writing development. It is quite motivating for the children to see their progress. Because the hooks are right next to the front door, the children's parents also get to enjoy this "portfolio on a wall."

FIGURE 6.2

Helper Chart

HELPERS

Susy	Joe	Carol
Pledge Leader	*Snack Helper*	*Line Leader*

Andre	Lupita	Jimmy
Messenger	*Hamster Feeder*	*Door Holder*

to these posted directions. For example, if a child is running in the classroom, the teacher could direct the child's attention to the "We walk in our classroom" sign and ask, "What does that sign say?"

Directions can also include recipes for cooking or directions for art activities. The directions can be put on wall charts. Even very young children can follow simple directions that use both words and pictures.

SCHEDULES.   A daily schedule can be presented at the beginning of class to prepare children for upcoming activities. Pictures can be used to help children remember the different segments of the day (see Figure 6.3). If children ask what is going to happen next, the teacher can help them use the chart to figure it out.

CALENDARS.   A monthly calendar can be set up at the beginning of each month and used for marking children's birthdays, parties, and other special events (field trips, classroom visitors, when a student's dog had puppies, etc.). The teacher can encourage the children to use the calendar to determine how many more days until a special event takes place and to record events of importance to them.

MESSAGES.   Often, unforeseen events change the day's plans. It's raining, so there can be no outdoor playtime. Instead of just telling children, some teachers write a message. For example:

FIGURE 6.3

Daily
Schedule

SCHEDULE

9:00	Opening	
9:10	Free-Choice Time	
10:00	Circle Time	
10:30	Snack	
10:45	Outdoor Play	
11:30	Go Home	

Circle time will be first thing this morning.
We have a special visitor!
She will share her cookies with us.

Because these messages inform children about activities that directly affect their day, even the youngest children quickly learn to pay close attention to these notices.

SIGN-IN AND SIGN-UP LISTS.   Children can write their names on lists for a variety of functional purposes. For example, kindergarten teacher Bobbi Fisher (1995) writes the date and day at the top of a large nine- by eighteen-inch piece of drawing paper and has her children write their names on the paper each morning when they first arrive in the classroom. Ms. Fisher and her assistant teacher sign the list also. During circle time, the list is read to the class as a means of taking attendance and to build a sense of community. As the children become familiar with each other's printed names, they take over the activity. She periodically uses this sign-in procedure to assess the children's emerging writing abilities.

Lists can also be used to sign up for popular classroom centers and playground equipment. Judith Schickedanz (1986) describes how teachers at the Boston University laboratory preschool had children sign up on lists to use popular centers such as the block and dramatic play areas. If children do not get a chance to use the area on a given day, they are first in line to use it the next day. Sign-up sheets are also used to get turns using tricycles on the playground.

Children should be encouraged to use emergent forms of writing. If a child's writing is completely illegible, the teacher may need to write the child's name conventionally next to the child's personal script. The teacher can explain, "This is how I write your name." Once the child's name is recognizable, this scaffold can be discontinued.

INVENTORY LISTS. Lists can also be used to create inventories of the supplies in different classroom areas. Susan Neuman and Kathy Roskos (1993) give an example of a chart that contains an inventory of the supplies in the art area. The list contains a picture and the name of each item, as well as the quantity of each item available. The sign informs children that there are eight paintbrushes, twelve pairs of scissors, lots of paper, and so on. During cleanup, children can use this information to make sure the center is ready for future use.

Linking Literacy and Play

In Chapter 3, dramatic play is described as an ideal context for developing young children's oral language. Dramatic play can also offer a context in which children can have meaningful, authentic interactions with reading and writing in early childhood classrooms (Roskos & Christie, 2000; Roskos & Christie, 2004; Yaden, Rowe, & MacGillivary, 2000). The following vignette, which involves four-year-old preschoolers, illustrates some of the advantages of integrating play and literacy:

> With some teacher assistance, Noah and several friends are getting ready to take a make-believe plane trip to France. The elevated loft in the classroom has been equipped with chairs and has become the plane, and a nearby theme center has been turned into a ticket office. Noah goes into the ticket office, picks up a marker, and begins making scribbles on several small pieces of paper. The teacher passes by with some luggage for the trip. Noah says, "Here Kurt . . . Here are some tickets." The teacher responds, "Oh great. Frequent flyer plan!" Noah then makes one more ticket for himself, using the same scribble-like script. The teacher distributes the tickets to several children, explaining that they will need these tickets to get on board the plane. As Noah leaves the center, he scribbles on a wall sign. When asked what he has written, Noah explains that he wanted to let people know that he would be gone for a while.

The most obvious benefit of linking literacy and play is that play is fun. When children incorporate literacy into their play, they begin to view reading and writing as enjoyable skills that are desirable to master. This is in marked contrast to the negative attitudes that can be perpetuated by dull skill-and-drill lessons and worksheets found in classrooms.

The airplane trip vignette illustrates how the nonliteral nature of play makes literacy activities significant to children. The pieces of paper that Noah produced would be meaningless in most situations. However, within the context of a make-believe plane trip, Noah's scribbles represent writing, and the pieces of paper signify tickets—not just to Noah, but also to the teacher and the other children. This make-believe orientation enabled Noah to demonstrate his growing awareness of the practical functions of print. He showed that he knew that printed tickets can grant access to experiences such as trips and that signs can be used to leave messages for other people.

The low-risk atmosphere of play encourages children to experiment with emergent forms of reading and writing. When children play, their attention is focused on the activity itself rather than on the goals or outcome of the activity. This means-over-ends orientation promotes risk taking. If outcomes are not critical, mistakes are inconsequential. There is little to lose by taking a chance and trying something new or difficult. Noah felt safe using scribble writing to construct tickets and signs. In nonplay situations, the tickets and signs themselves would assume more importance, decreasing the likelihood that Noah would risk using a personal form of script to construct them.

Like functional literacy, linking literacy and play is a broad-spectrum instructional strategy that offers children many opportunities to learn a variety of different skills and concepts. In order to illustrate this feature, we will use literacy-enriched play centers, a strategy described in detail later in this chapter. This strategy involves adding theme-related reading and writing materials to sociodramatic play areas. For example, the following literacy props could be used in the pizza parlor play center:

- Cardboard pizza crusts (large circles)
- Felt pizza ingredients (tomato sauce [large red circles the same size as the cardboard crusts], pepperoni, black olives, onions, etc.)
- Pencils, pens, markers
- Note pads for taking orders
- Menus
- Wall signs ("Place Your Order Here")
- Employee name tags
- Pizza boxes with company name and logo
- Cookbooks
- Bank checks
- Newspaper ads and discount coupons

This literacy-enriched pizza parlor setting provides children with opportunities to learn important concepts about print. At the most basic level, the literacy props illustrate that print has meaning. Children demonstrate this awareness when they point to a menu or wall sign and ask the teacher or peer, "What does that say?" These print props also provide opportunities for children to learn more advanced concepts such as the difference between a letter and a word. Literacy terms, such as *letter* and *word,* are often used by children and adults during play in print-enriched centers.

The pizza parlor setting contains many examples of the functional uses of print. Print is used to convey information on menus and pizza boxes. Signs such as "Place Your Order Here" and "The Line Starts Here" illustrate the regulatory function of print. Pizza parlors also are associated with literacy routines—sets of reading and writing actions that are ordinary practices of a culture (Neuman & Roskos, 1997). These routines demonstrate the instrumental functions of print and present opportunities for children to use emergent forms of writing and reading. Customers can read or pretend to read menus while placing orders. Waiters and counter clerks can use note pads to write down orders that will later be used by the chefs to determine which types of pizzas to bake. Chefs can consult cookbooks for information on how to prepare pizzas. Once the pizzas are baked, customers can use discount coupons from the newspaper to reduce the cost of their meals and pay their bill by writing checks. Not surprisingly, research has shown that adding print-related props to play areas results in significant increases in the amount of literacy activity during play (Roskos & Christie, 2004).

As young children have repeated exposure to print props, opportunities arise for developing alphabet and sight word recognition. Some children may learn to recognize the letter *p* because it is the first letter in *pizza.* Others may learn to recognize entire words such as *pepperoni, menu,* and *cheese.* Research has shown that children learn to recognize environmental print in play settings (Neuman & Roskos, 1993; Vukelich, 1994).

Opportunities also exist to learn comprehension skills. Neuman and Roskos (1997) have detailed how playing in print-enriched settings can lead children to develop several types of strategic knowledge that have a role in comprehending text. In a pizza parlor setting, children have opportunities to:

- *Seek information*—A child might ask a playmate about the identity of a word on the pizza menu.
- *Check to see if guesses and hypotheses are correct*—A child might ask the teacher, "Is this how you spell *pizza?*"
- *Self-correct errors*—While writing the word *pizza* on a sign, a child might exclaim, "Oops, *pizza* has two *z's!*"

Checking and correcting are self-regulatory mechanisms that build a base for cognitive monitoring during reading.

When children play in literacy-enriched settings, they are presented with opportunities to learn a variety of different literacy concepts and skills. In addition, children can learn these skills in a variety of ways, including observation, experimentation, collaboration, and instruction. As a result, children have greater opportunities at different levels of development to learn new skills and to consolidate newly acquired skills that are only partially mastered. Unlike narrowly focused skill-and-drill activities, opportunities exist for every child in the classroom to advance his or her literacy development. Table 6.1 presents examples of theme-related literacy materials that can be added to a number of different dramatic play centers.

Teacher Involvement in Play

Lev Vygotsky (1978) has described how adult interaction can facilitate children's development within the children's zone of proximal development. Play offers many opportunities for adults to scaffold children's early attempts at reading and writing. Teachers can encourage children to incorporate literacy activities into ongoing play episodes and can help children with reading and writing activities that the children cannot do independently. This, in turn, can promote literacy growth. Carol Vukelich (1994) found that when adults assumed the role of a more knowledgeable play partner with kindergartners in print-rich play settings, the children's ability to read environmental print was enhanced.

The benefits of adult involvement in play are not limited to literacy alone. The play itself can also be enriched. Berk, Mann, and Ogan (2006, p. 88) point out that "adult scaffolding makes make-believe more interesting, surprising, and absorbing."

The following vignette illustrates how one teacher used literacy scaffolding to enrich her four-year-olds' pizza parlor dramatization:

> Channing and several friends ask their teacher if they may play pizza parlor. The teacher says yes and brings out a prop box containing felt pizza pieces, pizza boxes, menus, tablecloths, and so on. The children spend about ten minutes separating the pizza ingredients (olives, pepperoni slices, onions, and cheese shavings made out of felt) into bins. When they have finished, the teacher asks which pizza shop they would like to be today. They respond, "Pizza Hut." While the children watch, the teacher makes a sign with the Pizza Hut name and logo. Channing requests, "Make a 'closed for business' sign on the back." The teacher turns over the paper and writes CLOSED FOR BUSINESS. She then hangs the CLOSED sign on the front of the play center. The children spend another ten minutes rearranging furniture and setting up the eating and kitchen areas in their pretend restaurant. When the children have finished their preparations, the teacher asks, "Is it time to open?" Channing responds, "Yeah. Switch the sign now." The teacher turns the CLOSED sign over so that the Pizza Hut logo is showing. The teacher then pretends to be a customer, reads a menu, and orders a pizza with pepperoni, green peppers, onions, and lots of cheese. Once the cooks have piled the appropriate ingredients onto the pizza, the teacher carries it over to a table and pretends to eat it. When she finishes eating, she writes a make-believe check to pay for her meal.

The teacher played several important roles in this episode. First, she served as stage manager, supplying the props that made the pizza play possible. She also provided scaffolding, making signs that the children could not make on their own. The *Pizza Hut* and CLOSED signs provided environmental print for the children to read and also created an opportunity for the children to demonstrate their growing awareness of the regulatory power of print. The pizza shop could not be open for business until the CLOSED sign was taken down.

The teacher also served as a coplayer, taking on a role and becoming a play partner with the children. Note that she took the minor role of customer, leaving the more important roles (pizza cooks) to the children. While in the role of customer, the teacher modeled several literacy activities—menu reading and check writing. Several children noticed these behaviors and imitated them in future play episodes.

The key to successful play involvement is for teachers to observe carefully and to choose an interaction style that fits with children's ongoing play interests and activities. Kathy Roskos and Susan Neuman (1993) observed six experienced preschool teachers and found that they used a repertoire of interaction styles to encourage literacy-related play. These veteran teachers switched styles frequently, depending on the children who were playing and the nature of the play. The teachers' ability to switch styles to fit the children's play agenda appeared to be as important as the specific interaction styles the teachers used.

TABLE 6.1

Literacy
Props for
Dramatic Play
Centers

Home Center	Business Office
Pencils, pens, markers	Pencils, pens, markers
Note pads	Note pads
Post-it® notes	Telephone message forms
Baby-sitter instruction forms	Calendar
Telephone book	Typewriter
Telephone message pads	Order forms
Message board	Stationery, envelopes, stamps
Children's books	File folders
Magazines, newspapers	Wall signs
Cookbooks, recipe box	
Product containers from children's homes	
Junk mail	

Restaurant	Post Office
Pencils	Pencils, pens, markers
Note pads	Stationery and envelopes
Menus	Stamps
Wall signs ("Pay Here")	Mailboxes
Bank checks	Address labels
Cookbooks	Wall signs ("Line Starts Here")
Product containers	

Grocery Store	Veterinarian's Office
Pencils, pens, markers	Pencils, pens, markers
Note pads	Appointment book
Bank checks	Wall signs ("Receptionist")
Wall signs ("Supermarket")	Labels with pets' names
Shelf labels for store areas ("Meat")	Patient charts
Product containers	Prescription forms
	Magazines (in waiting room)

Airport/Airplane	Library
Pencils, pens, markers	Pencils
Tickets	Books
Bank checks	Shelf labels for books
Luggage tags	("ABCs," "Animals")
Magazines (on-board plane)	Wall signs ("Quiet!")
Air sickness bags with printed instructions	Library cards
Maps	Checkout cards for books
Signs ("Baggage Claim Area")	

Curriculum Connections

Roskos and Christie (in press) have argued that in the era of accountability and early childhood standards, it is crucial that literacy-enriched play activities be linked with science-based early literacy outcomes and the academic curriculum (i.e., the "new basics"):

> In the past, classroom play has tended to be a stand-alone activity. We believe that a considerable amount, but not all, of play must be networked with instructional goals of the new basics. Play, in and of itself, is a network of interactions characterized by elements of non-literality, intrinsic motivation, self-initiation, and means over ends. But this highly motivating network must be joined with other activity settings in the preschool classroom in clear and consistent ways to support the learning progression of difficult ideas, such as the alphabetic principle (i.e., that the sounds of oral language are represented by letters). In large and small groups children can be taught how speech maps to print, but it is in play that they can put such concepts to practical use (from the child's point of view), and thus practice the transfer of new ideas to real situations.

This means that teachers need to do more than simply set up inviting play centers stocked with literacy props. The centers need to be connected to the content and skills that are being taught in other parts of the curriculum.

The Arizona Centers for Excellence in Early Education project, described in Special Feature 1.1(p. 11–12), provides a good example of how play can be networked with the "new basics." This box contains an example of a unit on building and construction in which instruction on theme-related vocabulary was linked across singing of a rhyme, shared reading of a big book, and dramatic play. The play area was set up so that children would have opportunities to use words that were introduced in academic instruction. This enabled play to have a clear instructional purpose—providing vocabulary practice with the names of tools. With this type of curriculum integration, both literacy and play are enhanced. Children have opportunities to learn literacy connected with their play, and the play becomes enriched with content from the academic curriculum.

Shared Enactments

In sociodramatic play, children make up their own stories as the play progresses. In shared enactments, on the other hand, the players enact a written story. This story can be composed by the children in the classroom or by an adult author.

Vivian Paley (1981) has developed a strategy that combines storytelling and play. Children first dictate stories that are tape recorded and later written down by the teacher. The teacher reads the stories aloud to the class, and then the children work together as a group to act out the stories. This strategy promotes children's narrative skills—over time, their stories become better organized and increasingly more complex—and makes contributions to many aspects of their social, oral language, and cognitive development.

In her book, *Boys and Girls: Superheroes in the Doll Corner,* Paley (1984, pp. 50–51) gives an example of a story written by one of her kindergarten boys:

> Superman, Batman, Spiderman, and Wonderwoman went into the woods and they saw a wicked witch. She gave them poisoned food. Then they died. Then Wonderwoman had magic and they woke up. Everybody didn't wake up. Then they woke up from Wonderwoman's magic. They saw a chimney and the wolf opened his mouth. Superman exploded him.

Note how this story has a rudimentary narrative plot: the main characters encounter a problem (dying as a result of eating poison); an attempt is made to solve the problem (magic); and there is a resolution (waking up). Then a new problem comes along (the wolf), and the narrative cycle continues. Also, notice that this child has incorporated superheroes from popular media with elements from classic fairy tales to build his story: finding a cottage in the woods (*Hansel and Gretel*), a witch who gives poison food (*Snow White*), and a wolf and a chimney (*The Three Little Pigs*).

Greta Fein, Alicia Ardila-Rey, and Lois Groth (2000) have developed a version of Paley's strategy that they call *shared enactment*. During free-choice activity time, the teacher sits in the classroom writing center (see Chapter 8), and children are encouraged to tell the teacher stories. The teacher writes down the children's words verbatim. When a child finishes with his or her story, the teacher asks if there is anything else he or she wishes to add. Then the teacher reads the story back to the child to make sure that it matches the child's intentions. The child decides whether to share the story with the group. If the child does, it is put in a special container called the story box.

Later, during shared enactment time, the teacher reads the story to the class, and the story is dramatized. Fein, Ardila-Rey, and Groth (2000, p. 31) describe a typical shared enactment session:

> The children gathered along two sides of a large space used for circle time and the teacher sits among them. The empty space before them became the stage. The teacher summoned the author to sit by her side and read the story out loud to the group. The teacher then asked the author what characters were needed for the enactment. The author identified the characters (often with the eager help of other children) and chose a peer to portray each one. When the actors had been assembled, the teacher read the story slowly as a narrator would, stopping to allow for action and omitting dialogue so that the actors could improvise. The players dramatized the story, following the lead of the author who acts as director. At the completion of the enactment and the applause, another story was selected for dramatization.

Fein and her colleagues used the shared enactment procedure with a class of kindergartners twice a week for twelve weeks and found that it resulted in a substantial increase in narrative activity (story enactment and storytelling) during free play. The investigators noted that this brief intervention appeared to penetrate the daily life of the classroom and promised to make important contributions to the children's narrative development.

Language Experience Approach or Shared Writing

The language experience approach (LEA), which became popular in the 1970s (Allen, 1976; Veatch et al., 1979), has children read texts composed of their own oral language. Children first dictate a story about a personal experience, and the teacher writes it down. The teacher reads the story back to the children and then gives them the opportunity to read it themselves. Sometimes the children illustrate their dictated sentences. In recent years, this strategy has become known as shared writing.

The LEA or shared writing strategy is an excellent means for teachers to demonstrate the relationship between speaking, writing, and reading. It can help children realize that (1) what is said can be written down in print, and (2) print can be read back as oral language.

Like functional print and play-based literacy, the language experience or shared writing strategy presents children with a broad array of learning opportunities. At the most basic level, LEA/shared writing helps children learn that the purpose of written language is the same as that of oral language: to communicate meaning. For other children, the strategy enables teachers to demonstrate explicitly the structure and conventions of written language. The children watch as the teacher spells words conventionally, leaves spaces between words, uses left-to-right and top-to-bottom sequences, starts sentences and names with capital letters, ends sentences with periods or other terminal punctuation marks, and so on. This is an ideal means to show children how the mechanical aspects of writing work.

LEA/shared writing has the additional advantage of making conventional writing and reading easier for children. By acting as scribe, the teacher removes mechanical barriers to written composition. The children's compositions are limited only by their experiential backgrounds and oral language. Reading is also made easier because the stories are composed of the children's own oral language and are based on their personal experiences. This close personal connection with the story makes it easy for children to predict the identity of unknown words in the text.

A number of variations of LEA/shared writing have been developed. In the sections that follow, two that are particularly appropriate for use with young children are described: group experience stories and individual experience stories.

Group Experience Stories

This strategy begins with the class having some type of shared experience: The class takes a field trip to a farm, to a zoo, across the street to the supermarket, to see a play; the class guinea pig has babies; the class completes a special cooking activity or other project. As described in Trade Secrets 6.2, shared reading of literature can also lead to a shared writing experience. Whatever the event, the experience should be shared by all members of the group so that everyone can contribute to the story.

The following is a description of how a kindergarten teacher might engage children in a group shared story-writing experience:

Step 1   The teacher begins by gathering the children on the rug in the whole-group area to record their thoughts about the experiences—to preserve what they recall in print. Teachers often begin with a request to "tell me what you remember about. . .?"

Step 2   As children share their memories, the teacher records exactly what the children say. The teacher does not rephrase or correct what a child says. The teacher records the children's language, just as they use it. The sentence structure, or syntax, is the child's. The spellings, however, are correct. As the teacher writes the child's comments on a large sheet of chart paper with a felt-tip marker in print large enough for all the children to see, the teacher verbalizes the process used to construct the text. (The teacher might choose to write on the chalkboard, overhead transparency, or chart paper.)

TRADE SECRETS 6.2

San Luis preschool teacher Mrs. Lisa Lemos links shared reading with shared writing activities. Today she has just finished reading the big book *There Was an Old Lady Who Swallowed a Fly,* by Simms Taback (Scholastic, 2000). It is one of the children's favorite books. Mrs. Lemos has decided to use the children's enthusiasm for the story as a stimulus for a group experience story, with a twist—it will be a group letter. Lemos starts the lesson by saying, "Maybe today we can write a letter to the Old Lady Who Swallowed the Fly. Who would like to help me write the letter?" Almost all of the children raise their hand and shout out, "Me! Me!" Lemos has already written the beginning of the letter at the top of a large piece of chart paper. She reads this to the children: "Dear Old Lady . . . ." Then she says, "Okay, what do we want to say next?" She picks Dileanna, who says, "Don't eat a fly and don't eat lots of candy." Mrs. Lemos writes down Dileanna's words, repeating them as they are written. Once she has written the words, Mrs. Lemos rereads Dileanna's sentence. Then she asks, "Why shouldn't she eat lots of candy?" and a child responds, "Because it's not good for us!" Mrs. Lemos then says, "What else can we say?" Keetsia volunteers, "Don't eat all of the animals," and Mrs. Lemos writes this down and reads it back to the class. As Mrs. Lemos writes *eat,* Nubia shouts out, "No, Mrs. Lemos, *eat* starts with a *t!*" Mrs. Lemos sounds out the word (/ē-t/) and says, "Yes, *eat* does have a *t,* but it comes at the end of the

word. Eat starts with the /ē/ sound. What letter makes that sound?" Several children respond *E.* The children continue contributing things that the Old Lady shouldn't eat: a cow and a spider. Then Mrs. Lemos asks, "Should we put anything else?" and several children mention healthy food. So Mrs. Lemos concludes the story with, "She should eat healthy foods." Nubia again helps with the spelling, pointing out that *healthy* starts with an *h.* Mrs. Lemos then rereads the story:

Dear Old Lady,
Don't eat a fly and don't eat lots of candy.
Don't eat all of the animals.
Don't eat a cow.
Don't eat a spider.
You should eat healthy foods.

Then Mrs. Lemos writes, "From your friend," and reads it to the class. Dileanna says, "And our names so she knows." Mrs. Lemos responds, "That's a good idea. Each of you can come up and write your name so she knows who wrote this letter. Roberto, would you like to come first?" All of the children then take turns writing their names at the end of the letter. Finally, Mrs. Lemos says, "We're going to read our letter one more time" and reads it again with class. The children have figured out what the print says by this point and are able to read along fluently with Mrs. Lemos.

Shared writing is an excellent way to teach the structure and conventions of writing

When doing group experience stories, the teacher takes sentences from only a small number of students. Taking sentences from all the children would make the sitting time too long for the young learners. If a student's contribution is vague or unclear, the teacher might have to ask the child to clarify the point or may have to do some *minor* editing to make the sentence comprehensible to the rest of the class. The teacher must exercise caution when a student's contribution is in a divergent dialect (e.g., "He be funny."). Changing this utterance to so-called standard English may be interpreted as a rejection of the child's language. This, in turn, might cause the child to cease to participate in future experience stories. In such cases it is usually better to accept the child's language and not change it.

Step 3 When the whole story is created, the teacher rereads it from beginning to end, carefully pointing to each word and emphasizing the left-to-right and return-sweep progression. Then the class reads the story as a group (a practice called choral reading). Often a child points to the words with a pointer as the class reads.

Step 4 The teacher hangs the story in the writing center, low enough so interested children can copy the story. Because the teacher wrote the story on chart paper (teachers' preferred medium for group stories), the story can be stored on the chart stand and reviewed periodically by the class. Sometimes the teacher rewrites each child's sentence on a piece of paper and asks the originator to illustrate his or her sentence. The pages are then collected into a book, complete with a title page listing a title and the authors' names, and placed in the library corner. These books are very popular with the children. Other times, the teacher makes individual copies of the story—via photocopying or word processing—for each child.

Individual Experience Stories

In an individual experience story, each student meets individually with the teacher and dictates her or his own story. As the child dictates, the teacher writes the story. Because the story is not intended for use with a group audience, editing can be kept to a minimum, and the child's language can be left largely intact. Once the dictation is completed, the teacher reads the story back to the child. This rereading provides a model of fluent oral reading and gives the child an opportunity to revise the story ("Is there anything you would like to change in your story?"). Finally, the child reads the story.

A variety of media can be used to record individual experience stories, each with its own advantages. Lined writing paper makes it easier for teachers to model neat handwriting and proper letter formation. Story paper and unlined drawing paper provide opportunities for children to draw illustrations to go with their stories. Teachers can also use the classroom computer to make individual experience stories. Children enjoy watching the text appear on the monitor as the teacher keys in their story. Word processing programs make it easy for the teacher to make any changes the children want in their stories. Stories can then be printed to produce a professional-looking text.

Individual experience stories can be used to make child-generated books. One approach is to write children's stories directly into blank books. Blank books are made of sheets of paper stapled between heavy construction paper or bound in hard covers. An alternative approach is to staple completed experience stories between pieces of heavy construction paper. For example, books can be made up of one student's stories ("Joey's Book") or of a compilation of different children's stories ("Our Favorite Stories" or "Our Trip to the Fire Station"). Child-authored texts can be placed in the classroom library for others to read. These books tend to be very popular because children like to read what their friends have written.

Individual experience stories have several important advantages over group stories. The direct personal involvement produces high interest and motivation to read the story. There is a perfect match between the child's experiences and the text, making the story very easy to read. Children also feel a sense of ownership of their stories and begin to think of themselves as authors.

The one drawback to this strategy is that the one-to-one dictation requires a considerable amount of teacher time. Many teachers make use of parent volunteers or older students (buddy writers) to overcome this obstacle. Another strategy is to have a tape recorder available for children to dictate their stories. Teachers can then transcribe the children's compositions when time allows. Of course, children miss out on valuable teacher modeling when tape recordings are used.

Summary

When most children enter preschool or kindergarten, they already possess considerable knowledge about reading and writing. Teachers can capitalize on this prior learning by using a number of effective yet remarkably simple broad-spectrum instructional strategies that link home and school literacy learning. In this chapter, we discussed three strategies that, along with storybook reading (Chapter 4), form a solid foundation for an effective, developmentally appropriate early childhood language arts program: functional literacy activities, play-based literacy, and the language experience or shared writing approach.

■ *What are functional literacy activities, and how can teachers use these activities in a preschool or kindergarten classroom?*

Functional print (labels, lists, directions, and schedules) is ideal for beginning readers because the surrounding context helps explain its meaning. This contextualized print is easy for young children to read and helps them view themselves as real readers. In addition, functional literacy activities help develop the concept that reading and writing have practical significance and can be used to get things done in everyday life. This realization makes print more salient to children and provides important motivation for learning to read and write. Functional print also presents opportunities for children to learn to recognize letters and words in a highly meaningful context.

■ *How can dramatic play centers be used to encourage young children's literacy development?*

Dramatic play provides an ideal context for children to have meaningful, authentic interactions with print. Dramatic play offers children of all ages and abilities multiple low-risk opportunities to explore and experiment with reading and writing.

■ *How can teachers help link literacy and play?*

Teachers can encourage such play by
1. stocking dramatic play centers with literacy props that invite children to engage in theme-related reading and writing activities;
2. providing preparatory experiences relating to play themes; and

3. assuming the stage-manager role and supplying resources, and by becoming a coplayer in the children's play. They can also use the play leader strategy to introduce theme-related problems for children to solve.

■ *How does the language experience approach (or shared writing) increase a child's understanding of print and facilitate reading development?*

The language experience approach/shared writing strategy involves having the teacher write stories that children dictate. The resulting experience stories are a dynamic means to demonstrate the connections among talking, reading, and writing. As the teacher writes the children's speech, the children immediately see the one-to-one correspondence between spoken and written words. Because the children are the authors of these highly contextualized stories, they can easily read the stories. Experience stories can be composed by either a single child or a group of children. Group stories are more time efficient, but individual stories are more personalized and ensure a perfect match between reader and text.

LINKING KNOWLEDGE TO PRACTICE

1. Visit a preschool or kindergarten classroom and record the different types of functional literacy activities and the ways they are used in the classroom. How did the children respond to or use functional print within the classroom? Did the teacher refer to the functional print?

2. Visit a preschool or kindergarten classroom and observe children playing in a dramatic play center. Note the types of literacy props available to children in this center. Record how the children use these materials in their dramatic play.

3. With a partner, design plans for a literacy-enriched play center. Select a setting appropriate for a group of children. Describe how this center might be created in a classroom. What literacy props could be placed in the play center? What functional uses of print might be used to convey information? What literacy routines might children use in this center? What roles might children and teacher play? How might you scaffold children's play and literacy knowledge in this play center?

4. Observe a LEA/shared writing activity. Describe how the teacher used this opportunity to teach children about the forms and functions of print.

The New View: Scientifically Based Reading Research Strategies

Martha Vasquez, teacher in a "reverse mainstream" preschool classroom in the Somerton school district in southwestern Arizona, is in the middle of a thematic unit on water and sea creatures. Today she has decided to center her instruction on syllable segmenting, a phonological awareness skill that is part of her state's Early Learning Standards. She begins by holding up cards with children's first names written on them. She asks the children first to recognize whose name is on the card and then clap and count the number of syllables in the name. The children have become quite good at this, quickly shouting out the names (e.g., "Christopher") and number of syllables ("three"). The children enjoy the activity and are very engaged. Next up is the Poster part of the lesson. Mrs. Vasquez first asks children how many syllables are in the word poster, *and the children shout out "two!" Then she reads the rhyme poster, which is about a submarine. While the main purpose of the poster is to teach rhyme recognition, Mrs. Vasquez focuses on vocabulary and syllable segmenting. She reads the poster with the children, encouraging them to make motions that go with rhyme (e.g., putting their fingers together to make pretend glasses for the word periscope). Then she asks individual children to count the syllables in several words from the story (e.g., sub-mar-ine). Finally, she moves onto the Vocabulary phase of the lesson. As before, she asks the children how many syllables are in the word* vocabulary. *She says the word in syllable segments and holds up a finger for each syllable. The children clap each syllable. Four children quickly shout out "five!" Being able to count the syllables in a five-syllable word is quite an accomplishment for four-year-olds! Next, Mrs. Vasquez holds up picture/word cards that contain words related to the unit theme. She asks the children to say the word and then asks them a question about it. For example, after the children identify the picture of a whale, she asks, "Where would you find a whale?" Several children respond, "In the ocean!" She also has them make motions for the words when appropriate (as with* wave). *When words contain more than one syllable (e.g.,* rainbow), *Mrs. Vasquez asks the children to clap and count syllables. The academic level of these activities is quite high for preschool, especially since two-thirds of the children in this reverse mainstreamed classroom have identified special needs. But all students seem able to successfully participate (two assistant teachers are there to help), and they appear to enjoy showing off their rapidly growing literacy skills.*

Mrs. Vasquez's instruction exemplifies the scientifically based reading research (SBRR) approach to early literacy instruction. She is directly teaching her students skills that will prepare them to learn to read in kindergarten and the primary grades. When she has children recognize their classmates' written names, she is teaching them print awareness. When she has them count the number of syllables in words, she is teaching a phonological awareness skill. When she has children identify, use, and discuss the words on the picture/word cards, she is directly teaching them new vocabulary. Since many of her children are English Language Learners, this latter skill is particularly important.

It is important to note that this type of direct, focused instruction is only part of the literacy instruction that the children in Mrs. Vasquez's classroom receive. She also reads them several books every day. In addition, the children have an hour-long center time in which they choose what to do. On the day described above, Mrs. Vasquez read the book *Rainbow Fish* by Marcus Pfister (North-South Books, 1992) to the class, and children had the following choices: (a) engage in dramatic play in an ocean-theme center, complete with a cardboard boat; (b) play with miniature replicas of sea creatures; (c) play a game where they would "catch" letters with a fishing pole with a string and magnet on the end; and (d) make a cut-and-paste picture of the Rainbow Fish with multicolored scales, and (e) read books in the library with the teacher.

Mrs. Vasquez's literacy program is an example of what we refer to as a blended curriculum. It combines emergent literacy strategies (described in Chapter 6) with science-based instructional strategies. Mrs. Vasquez directly teaches skills contained in the Arizona Early Learning Standards. The syllable segmenting activities described above help her children master the following standard: *Strand 2 Prereading Processes, Concept 3—Sounds and Rhythms of Spoken Language: c. Identifies syllables in words by snapping, clapping, or other rhythmic movement.* We believe that such a combination is the most effective way to help young children learn to read and write.

In the section that follows, we discuss strategies for teaching the following SBRR skills: phonological and phonemic awareness, alphabet knowledge, phonics, and print awareness.

BEFORE READING THIS CHAPTER, THINK ABOUT . . .

■ How you learned the names of the letters of the alphabet. Did you learn by singing the alphabet song?

■ How you learned the sounds letters make. Do you remember phonics workbooks or learning phonics rules (e.g., when two vowels go walking, the first one does the talking)?

■ Your own experiences with standardized tests. Were you required to take a test, like the Scholastic Aptitude Test or the Graduate Record Examination, and score above a minimum level to gain admission to your undergraduate or graduate program?

FOCUS QUESTIONS

■ What is the difference between phonological awareness, phonemic awareness, and phonics? In what sequence do young children typically acquire these skills? What does this sequence suggest about classroom instructional strategies?

■ How might early childhood teachers introduce young children to the letters of the alphabet?

■ How can early childhood teachers reassure the public that they are teaching phonics?

■ Why are standardized tests heavily used in the scientifically based reading research approach?

Scientifically Based Reading Research

As discussed in Chapter 1, scientifically based reading research (SBRR) came into prominence in the late 1990s, along with the movement to establish early childhood academic standards and skill-oriented policy initiatives such as No Child Left Behind and Good Start, Grow Smart. Whereas emergent literacy has relied primarily on qualitative forms for research, the SBRR perspective uses well-designed correlational studies and tightly controlled, quantitative experiments. Proponents of SBRR believe that these types of rigorous "scientific" research can reveal: (a) the skills and concepts that young children need to master to become proficient readers and writers and (b) the most effective strategies for teaching this content.

BOX 7.1

Definition
of Terms

alphabetic principle: the idea that letters, or groups of letters, represent phonemes

criterion-referenced test: a test used to compare a student's progress toward mastery of specified content, typically content the student had been taught. The performance criterion is referenced to some criterion level such as a cutoff score (e.g., a score of 60 is required for mastery)

norm-referenced test: a test that is designed to compare one group of students with another group

onsets: the beginning parts of words

phonemes: the individual sounds that make up spoken words

phonemic awareness: the awareness that spoken words are composed of individual sounds or phonemes

phonics: the relationship between sounds and letters in written language

phonological awareness: awareness of the sound structure of oral language

print awareness: children's ability to recognize print and their knowledge of concepts of print

rimes: the ending parts of words

standardized test: the teacher reads verbatim the scripted procedures to the students. The conditions and directions are the same whenever the test is administered. Standardized tests are one form of on-demand testing

Perhaps the SBRR movement's most valuable contribution to early literacy education has been the identification of "core" knowledge and skills that young children must have to become successful readers. Longitudinal studies have shown that preschool-age children's oral language (expressive and receptive language, including vocabulary development), phonological awareness, and alphabet knowledge are predictive of reading achievement in the elementary grades (Snow, Burns, & Griffin, 1998). Print awareness, which includes concepts of print (e.g., understanding how print can be used) and conventions of print (e.g., left-to-right, top-to-bottom sequence), has also been found to be positively correlated with reading ability in the primary grades (Snow et al., 1998).

SBRR investigators have also focused on identifying effective strategies for teaching this core literacy content to young children. One of the most consistent research findings is that young children's phonological awareness and alphabet knowledge can be increased via direct, systematic instruction (National Reading Panel, 2000). This instruction can often take the form of games and other engaging activities, but it also contains the elements of direct instruction: teacher modeling, guided practice, and independent practice.

In the sections that follow, we provide examples of how "core" early reading skills are taught in the SBRR approach: phonological awareness, alphabet knowledge, phonics, and print awareness. Examples of teaching the other core skill—oral language—are presented in Chapter 3.

Phonological and Phonemic Awareness Instruction

A "massive body of work has established that phonological awareness is a critical precursor, correlate, and predictor of reading achievement" (Dickinson, McCabe, Anastaspoulos, Peisner-Feinberg, & Poe, 2003, p. 467), and discriminating units of language (i.e., words, segments, phonemes) is linked to successful reading (National Reading Panel, 2000; Carnine, Silbert, & Kameenui, 2004). Clearly, phonological and phonemic awareness are two important, closely related skills that have an important role in early literacy development. Phonological awareness is a broader term, referring to awareness of the sound structure of speech. Phonemic awareness is an advanced subset of phonological awareness that involves awareness that spoken words are composed of individual sounds or phonemes (Yopp & Yopp, 2000). Both are important for all young children to possess if they are to become successful readers. These phonological processing skills lay the foundation for learning phonics, the relationships between letters and the sounds that they represent.

Marilyn Adams (1990) suggests that if children are to succeed at reading, especially if the reading program they meet in the primary grades relies heavily on phonics, phonemic awareness is the most crucial component of an early literacy program. Early childhood teachers must look for ways to help their young children attend to the sounds in the language. This is a new challenge for early childhood teachers. In the past, children have been denied phonological and phonemic awareness instruction because teachers did not realize the importance of this skill. Children were first taught to recognize letters and then taught the sounds associated with the letters (i.e., phonics). Now we know that before phonics instruction can be fully useful to young children, they need phonemic awareness. They must be aware of the individual sounds in words before they can begin to match these sounds up with letters. By not teaching phonological and phonemic awareness, teachers were making it difficult for many children to learn phonics!

Growth in phonological awareness begins in infancy, so even the teacher of the youngest child is a phonological awareness instructor. Initially, babies hear language "as one big piece of 'BLAH BLAH BLAH.' " However, as discussed in Chapter 2, babies quickly learn to hear the unique phonemes that make up their native language. These early speech lessons occur naturally as most adults use "parentese" to communicate with infants (parentese is an exaggerated, slowed, and highly articulated form of speech that allows infants to see and hear their native language; see Chapter 2). Phonological awareness begins when young children are able to hear the boundaries of words (for example, *Seethekitty* becomes *See the kitty*). As sounds become words that are frequently used in context to label specific objects, the acquisition of word meaning begins.

The ability to hear distinct words and make meaningful associations usually emerges between nine and eighteen months (Cowley, 1997), and children quickly become specialists in their native tongue. However, as children begin to hear and consistently produce the discrete sounds that comprise their language, the ability to hear and accurately produce the phonemes of other languages rapidly diminishes. Robert Sylwester (1995) calls this process "neural selectivity." The networks for phonemes that are not in the local language may atrophy over time due to lack of use. This creates a challenge for children who do not speak the language of instruction when they enter school, as they often experience difficulty with hearing the phonemes and word boundaries of a second language.

Research has revealed a developmental trajectory in children's acquisition of phonological processing skills (see Figure 7.1). In general the movement is from larger units to smaller units. Marilyn Adams (1990) suggests that before young children can become aware of phonemes—the individual sounds that make up spoken words—they first must become aware of larger units of oral language. Thus, children must first realize that spoken language is composed of words, syllables, and sounds. They need to learn to recognize when words rhyme by ending with the same sound and instances where several words begin with the same sound (i.e., alliteration). They also need to be able to segment sentences into words, and words into syllables. As mentioned earlier, this broader understanding is referred to as phonological awareness. Once these skills are mastered, children can begin to focus on the individual sounds of language and develop phonemic awareness. When children have fully mastered phonemic awareness, they are able to take individual sounds and blend them into whole words, break words down into individual sounds, and even manipulate the sounds in words (e.g., replace the middle sound of a word with another sound, so that *cat* become *cut* and *fan* becomes *fun*).

Recall from Chapter 1 that most states have adopted preschool language and early reading standards. Phonological awareness skills receive lots of attention in these standards. For example, Virginia's *Literacy Foundation Blocks* identifies the following phonological and phonemic awareness skills as "appropriate" for their young citizens to demonstrate by the end of their preschool years:

■ Identify words that rhyme; successfully generate rhymes
■ Successfully detect the beginning sounds in words

FIGURE 7.1	**PHONOLOGICAL AWARENESS**

Phonological Processing Skills	(1) Rhyme—words that end with same sound
	(2) Alliteration—words that start with same sound
	(3) Word and syllable segmenting—divide sentences into individual words and divide words into syllables
	
	PHONEMIC AWARENESS
	
	(4) Phoneme isolation (/kan/, /kar/, & /kap/ begin with /k/ sound)
	(5) Blending phonemes (/k-a-t/ = /kat/)
	(6) Segmenting phonemes /kat/ = /k-a-t/
	(7) Manipulating phonemes
	
	  ■ deletion /Snapple/ - /Sn/ = /apple/
	  ■ addition /p/ + /art/ = /part/
	  ■ manipulation /kat/ - /a/ + /o/ = /kot/

■ Listen to two one-syllable words and successfully blend to form the compound word (e.g., *rain bow* to *rainbow*)

■ Listen to a sequence of separate sounds in words with three phonemes and correctly blend the sounds to form the whole word (e.g., /k/ /a/ /t/ = *cat*)
(Source: www.pen.k12.va.us/VDOE/Instruction/Elem_M/FoundationBlocks.pdf)

Research is clear that phonological awareness and phonemic awareness are metalinguistic abilities (Adams, 1990). As such, children must not only be able to recite and play with sound units, but also must understand that sound units map onto parts of language. While children's initial entry into phonological awareness might be through recitations and playing with sound units, such activities appear to be insufficient. Explicit instruction is required (Snow et al., 1998). In addition, teachers are cautioned against focusing too much attention on rhyming. While rhyme is a good starting point for building awareness of the sounds of language, rhyming has not been found to be a significant predictor of children's reading skills (e.g., Muter & Diethelm, 2001; Mann & Foy, 2003).

In the sections that follow, we describe a number of strategies that teachers can use to increase children's phonological and phonemic awareness. We have ordered these to match the general development sequence of phonological processing.

Phonological Awareness

Phonological awareness activities focus children's attention on the sounds of words. In rhyming activities, children learn to recognize when words end with the same sound. In alliteration activities, the focus shifts to the beginning sounds of words. Segmenting activities help children learn to break oral sentences up into individual words and take individual words and break them up into syllables. Onset and rime activities involve segmenting initial sounds from ending syllables in selected groups of words. These activities make children aware of the sounds of language and lay the foundation for phonemic awareness.

RHYME. Rhyme activities focus children's attention on the ending sounds of words (e.g., *bee, flea, we*). There are two levels of rhyme awareness: rhyme identification, in which children can indicate which words rhyme, and rhyme production, in which children can, when given examples of rhyming words (*fat, cat, mat*), come up with other words that fit the rhyme pattern (*rat, sat, Laundromat*). Identification is the easier of the two. Research by Fernandez-Fein and Baker (1997) showed that children's knowledge of nursery rhymes and the frequency that they engage in word play were both strong predictors of children's phonological awareness. It is not surprising, therefore, that many research-based strategies for promoting phonological awareness in preschool and kindergarten use playful activities such as singing songs, reciting nursery rhymes, reading books that play with the sounds of language, and gamelike activities (e.g., Adams, Foorman, Lundberg, & Beeler, 1998).

Rhyme identification instruction often begins by inviting children to recite or sing well-known nursery rhymes such as "Jack and Jill," "Humpty Dumpty," or "Hickory Dickory Dock." After children become familiar with the rhyme, the teachers can go back and highlight the rhyming words, pointing out that these special words end with the same sound. Then teachers can help children identify the rhyming words. Once children are able to identify these words, teachers can repeat a rhyme, pausing before the words that rhyme, giving children time to predict the upcoming word ("Humpty Dumpty sat on a wall. Humpty Dumpty had a big _____.") (Ericson & Juliebö, 1998). This is the first step toward rhyme production. Ultimately, teachers can present the rhyming words from a story and ask children to supply more words that fit the rhyme pattern ("In this story, *wall* and *fall* rhyme—they end with the same sound. Can you think of other words that rhyme with *wall* and *fall*?").

Games are a fun, enjoyable way for children to consolidate their knowledge of rhyme. Brenda Casillas, a Head Start teacher in San Luis, Arizona, plays a "rhyming basket" game with her children. She begins by showing the children a basket full of pairs of objects that rhyme (e.g., rock and sock). Next, she takes out one object from each rhyming pair (e.g., the rock) and places it in front of her. She also asks the children to identify these objects. Almost all of the children in her class are English Language Learners, so this step helps build vocabulary as well as set the stage for the game. Finally, Mrs. Casillas passes the basket to the children and asks them to find an object that rhymes with whatever object she points to in front of her. For example, if she points to the rock, then the child is supposed to find the sock and say its name. By the middle of the school year, the four-year-olds in Mrs. Casillas's class have become quite skilled at this rhyme identification task. This helps the children meet an Arizona Early Learning Standard (*Strand 2 Prereading Processes—Concept 3 Sounds and Rhythms of Spoken Language: a. Recognizes words that rhyme in familiar games, songs, and stories*).

Trade Secrets 7.1 illustrates how kindergarten teacher Grant Clark uses the popular song, *Down by the Bay*, to help children learn to go a step beyond rhyme identification and produce their own rhymes.

ALLITERATION. Alliteration occurs when two or more words begin with the same sound (e.g., *Bibbity bobbity bumble bee*). As with rhyme, there are two levels of alliteration awareness: (a) identification—recognizing that several words start with the same sound and (b) production—after hearing several words that begin with the same sound (*sand, sailboat, seal, sun*), children can produce other words that start with the same sound (*sing, snake*). As with

---

TRADE SECRETS 7.1

A Rhyme Production Activity

In a video published by Allyn and Bacon (2000), kindergarten teacher Grant Clark demonstrates how a song/book, *Down by the Bay* by Raffi (Crown, 1987), can be used to help children learn to produce rhyming words that fit a pattern. *Down by the Bay* is a predictable song that has the refrain "Did you ever see a goose kissing a moose, Down by the bay?" "Did you ever see a whale with a polka-dot tail, Down by the

bay?" Two words always rhyme: fly-tie, bear-hair. When Mr. Clark reads the book to the class, he pauses slightly before reading the second word. This enables the children to use their knowledge of rhyme and the clues given by the book illustrations to come up with the second part of the rhyme. After he has finished reading the book, he continues to sing the song with the children, letting the children come up with their own pairs of rhyming words, some which are quite amusing. For example, one girl came up with "Did you ever see a book kissing a hook, Down by the bay?"

rhyme, instruction begins by reading or singing songs and stories that contain examples of alliteration (e.g., "My baby brother Bobby bounced his favorite ball.") As with rhyme, the teacher should first point out and explain the examples of alliteration ("*Baby, brother, Bobby,* and *ball* all start with the same sound, /b/."). Then children can be asked to identify the words that "start alike." Once children can recognize alliteration, they can be helped to come up with other words that start with the same sound.

San Luis Preschool teacher Lisa Lemos systematically introduces her children to a letter and its sound every two weeks using a published program, *Sound, Rhyme and Letter Time* (Wright Group/McGraw-Hill, 2002). For example, she introduced the sound of the letter *S* by showing children a chart that contains pictures of objects that start with this sound (*sun, seal, sailboat, sandwich, sand, sunglasses, seashell*). She began by having the children identify the objects on the poster. As was the case in Brenda Casillas's classroom, most of Mrs. Lemos's children are English Language Learners, so this helped to build vocabulary as well as phonological awareness. Next, she pointed out the names of all the objects that begin with the same sound: /s/. She then had the children take turns identifying and saying the names of the objects. She then asked if the children know any other words that start with this sound. At the beginning of the school year this was a challenge for the children. On the day that author Jim Christie observed in Mrs. Lemos's classroom, one child was able to come up with a Spanish word, *sol*, that starts with the /s/ sound. Mrs. Lemos praised the child for coming up with such an excellent example, commenting that both *sol* and its English counterpart *sun* start with the /s/ sound. Later that day, she sent a note home with the children, telling their families that the class is studying the letter *S* and requesting objects from home that begin with the /s/ sound. The next day, about half of the children brought objects to share. The children took turns sharing their objects with the class. For example, Alexis showed a small replica of a star and said its name. Mrs. Lemos said, "Yes, *star* begins with the /s/ sound." Then Mrs. Lemos wrote the word *star* on the white board and drew a small picture of a star. Next, Izac shared his stuffed snake (which was a big hit with his classmates), and Mrs. Lemos added *snake* and a drawing of a snake to the white board. After adding the names and drawings of all the objects that the children have brought to share, Mrs. Lemos puts a big sun in the middle of the *S* web. This web remained up for the remainder of the two weeks that the /s/ sound was studied. Through these activities, Mrs. Lemos was helping her children master the Arizona Early Learning Standard *Strand 2 Prereading Processes—Concept 3 Sounds and Rhythms of Spoken Language: d. Recognizes when different words begin or end with the same sound.*

Trade Secrets 7.2 describes how preschool teacher Brenda Casillas teaches alliteration and also helps children to learn letter-sound correspondences (i.e., phonics).

WORD AND SYLLABLE SEGMENTING.   Activities that help children learn how to segment sentences into words and words into syllables help set the stage for full phonemic segmentation—the ability to divide words up into individual sounds.

TRADE SECRETS 7.2

An Advanced Alliteration and Alphabet Recognition Activity

Toward the end of the school year, Head Start teacher Brenda Casillas uses an alliteration production strategy to review the letter recognition, letter sounds, and beginning sounds that the class has studied during the year. Today she is reviewing the letter *M*, its sound, and words that begin with the /m/ sound. She begins by asking, "Who remembers what the letter *M* looks like?" Most of the children hold up their hand, and Mrs. Casillas asks Jasmine to come up and write the letter *M* in the middle of a piece of chart paper. Jasmine writes a big capital *M*,

and Mrs. Casillas says, "Good job! Jasmine wrote an uppercase *M*. Now I'm going to write a lowercase *m* beside it." Next Mrs. Casillas asks, "Can you find the letter *M* in the classroom? Point to an *M*." The children all respond affirmatively, and Mrs. Casillas asks several children to find the letter in the room. For example, Deidre says, "I know . . . Monday," and points to the word on the wall calendar. [This is the alphabet recognition component of the lesson.] Finally Mrs. Casillas asks, "Can you think of words that begin with the /m/ sound?" The children are very good at this, coming up with the following /m/ words: *McDonald's, moon, Macias* (the child's last name), *monkey, map, many, money, mailbox, mouse,* and *mommy.* [This is the phonological awareness/alliteration component of the lesson.]

◆ *Word segmenting*—The goal is to develop children's awareness that oral language is made up of strings of individual words. Children initially have difficulty with word boundaries. For example, young children often think that *before* is actually two words (because of syllable segmentation) and that *once upon a time* is one word (because the words are often blended together with little pause in between). Teachers can help children divide speech up into separate words by reciting familiar nursery rhymes (e.g., "Jack and Jill") and inviting the children to join in. The teacher then explains that rhymes are made up of individual words. She recites the rhyme again, clapping as each word is spoken. Children then join in, clapping the words along with the teacher. This is continued until the children can clap the words accurately. Finally, the teacher reconstructs the rhyme by inviting each child to say one word of the rhyme in sequence (The Wright Group, 1998). Activities in which children track print, such as the shared reading of big books described in Chapter 4, are also effective ways to help children discover the concept of word.

◆ *Syllable segmenting*—Activities that develop the ability to analyze words into separate syllables take segmenting to the next stage. Syllables are a unit of spoken language larger than a phoneme but smaller than a word. Once children can divide words up into syllables (*begin* can be divided into *be-gin*), full phonemic awareness is just a step away (*begin* can be segmented into *b-e-g-i-n*). The vignette at the beginning of this chapter describes how Martha Vasquez teaches this important skill. She begins by having children clap and count the syllables in their classmates' last names. She then has children clap and count syllables in a rhyme poster and in vocabulary words on picture/word cards. What we like best about Mrs. Vasquez's approach is that she keeps returning to this skill throughout the day, giving children many brief but focused opportunities to practice and perfect it.

ONSET AND RIME SUBSTITUTION. Onset and rimes are often used as an instructional bridge between phonological and phonemic awareness. Onset and rimes are "families" of words that end with the same vowel and consonant cluster (e.g., *-at: bat, cat, fat, hat, mat, rat, sat*). The beginning consonant is referred to as the onset and the medial vowel and ending consonant are called the rime. Onset and rime substitution activities, in which the child substitutes different onsets with a set rime (*c-ake, b-ake, sh-ake, m-ake*) are easier than phonemic awareness activities because the word is only broken into a beginning and ending part (*f-ake*) rather than into individual phonemes (*f-a-k*). Onsets and rimes also build a foundation for learning the sounds represented by vowels. In the primary grades, onsets and rimes are often used as a way to teach long and short vowel sounds because rimes have consistent letter-sound relationships. The vowel *a* can represent many different sounds but when it is paired with *ke*, forming the *ake* rime, it almost always represent the long *a* sound. In primary-grade phonics instruction, rimes are often referred to as phonograms or word families. Trade Secrets 7.3 presents an example of a preschool onset and rime lesson.

TRADE SECRETS 7.3

An Onset and Rime Activity

New Castle County, Delaware, Head Start teacher Debby Helman uses an onset and rime activity as a transition from circle time to getting-ready-for-lunch time. Ms. Helman begins by telling the children that to leave the circle today they are going to play a game with rhymes. She begins, "Listen to this word: *hop*. Now if I take the /h/ away from *hop* and I put a /p/ on /op/, what new word did I make? /p/-/op/." The children are quiet. Just as she is about to speak, Jemelda shouts, "Pop!" Ms. Helman compliments her and invites her to go wash her hands for lunch. She asks, "Who can put a different letter sound on /op/ and make a different rhyming word? [pause] When you see a red light you ___." A child shouts, "Stop!" Ms. Helman says, "Right! /St/ on /op/ makes /st/-/op/. She invites the child who provided the word *stop* to go wash his hands. She says, "We wash up spills with a ___op." Kathryn says, "Mop!" Ms. Helman says, "Kathryn took the /p/ off /op/, put on an /m/, and made *mop*. Kathryn goes to wash her hands. These examples have helped the children understand how to play this game. Soon the children produce *shop, cop, top, bop, nop,* and more /-op/ words. [Notice that *nop* is a nonsense word. It is acceptable to play this game with nonsense words.]

Phonemic Awareness

The phonological awareness exercises described above build a base in which children become aware that the words in speech are composed of sequences of individual sounds or phonemes. This conscious awareness of phonemes sets the stage for children to discover the alphabetic principle that there is a relationship between letters and sounds. Learning these letter-sound relationships, in turn, facilitates "sounding out" written words that are in children's oral vocabulary but are not familiar in print (Stanovich, 1986).

On entering school, children's level of phonemic awareness is one of the strongest predictors of success in learning to read (Adams, 1990). In fact, phonemic awareness has been shown to account for 50 percent of the variance in children's reading proficiency at the end of first grade (Adams, Foorman, Lundberg, & Beeler, 1998).

Unfortunately, phonemic awareness is difficult for many young children to acquire. Marilyn Adams and her colleagues (1998, p. 19) report that

> Phonemic awareness eludes roughly 25 percent of middle-class first graders and substantially more of those who come from less literacy-rich backgrounds. Furthermore, these children evidence serious difficulty in learning to read and write.

One reason that phonemic awareness is difficult to learn is that there are few clues in speech to signal the separate phonemes that make up words (Ehri, 1997). Instead, phonemes overlap with each other and fuse together into syllabic units. Adams and her colleagues (1998) give the example of *bark*. They point out that this word is not pronounced /b/, /a/, /r/, /k/. Instead, the pronunciation of the medial vowel *a* is influenced by the consonants that precede and follow it. Because phonemes are not discrete units of sound, they are very abstract and are difficult for children to recognize and manipulate (Yopp, 1992). This is why most children need direct instruction on phonemic awareness. The challenge is to make this instruction appropriate for young children. We believe that strategies presented below meet this important criterion.

PHONEME ISOLATION. Phoneme isolation activities focus children's attention on the individual phonemes, the smallest units of sound, that make up words. This is the beginning of true phonemic awareness.

- ◆ *Sound matching*—children decide which of several words begins with a specific sound (Yopp & Yopp, 2000). For example, the teacher can show children pictures of familiar objects (*cat, bird, monkey*), and ask which begins with the /b/ sound.

- ◆ *Sound isolation*—children are given words and asked to tell what sound occurs at the beginning, middle, or ending (Yopp, 1992). For example, the teacher can ask, "What's the sound that starts these words: *time, turtle, top*?" Or she can ask children to "Say the first little bit of *snap*" (Snow et al., 1998).

PHONEME BLENDING. In blending activities, children combine individual sounds to form words. The game "What am I thinking of?" is a good way to introduce blending to preschoolers (Yopp, 1992). The teacher tells the class that she is thinking of an animal. Then she says the name of the animal in separate phonemes: "/k/-/a/-/t/." Children are then asked to blend the sounds together and come up with the name of the animal.

PHONEME SEGMENTING. Segmenting is the flip side of blending. Here, teachers ask children to break words up into individual sounds (Stahl et al., 1998). Lucy Calkins (1994) calls the ability to segment words "rubber-banding," stretching words out to hear the individual phonemes. For example, the teacher can provide each child with counters and Elkonin boxes, a diagram of three blank squares representing the beginning, middle, and ending sounds in a word (e.g., ☐☐☐). Children are asked to place counters in the boxes to represent each sound in a word. For the word *cat*, a marker would be placed in the left-hand square for /k/, another in the center square for /a/, and a third in the right-hand square for /t/. The concrete props are designed make this abstract task more concrete for children.

PHONEME MANIPULATION. Phoneme manipulation is the most advanced form of phonemic awareness. These activities require children to add or substitute phonemes in words:

■ *Phoneme addition*—say a word and then say it again with a phoneme added at the beginning (*an > fan*) or end (*an > ant*);
■ *Phoneme deletion*—say a word and then say it again without the initial (*farm > arm*) or ending (*farm > far*) sound; and
■ *Phoneme substitution*—substitute initial sounds in lyrics of familiar songs (*Fe-Fi-Fiddly-i-o > De-Di-Diddly-i-o*) (Yopp, 1992).

In a video published by Allyn and Bacon (2000), kindergarten teacher Grant Clark demonstrates how the book *The Hungry Thing* by Jan Slepian and Ann Seidler (Scholastic, 1971) can be used to teach phoneme manipulation. In the book, a large creature comes into town with a sign saying "Feed me." When asked what it would like to eat, the creature mispronounces the name of a series of foods. For example, if it wants pancakes, it says "shmancakes." The adults try to come up with complicated interpretations (e.g., schmancakes are a strange kind of chicken), but a little boy figures out that one just needs to substitute a different beginning sound to make sense of what the creature is saying (*schmancakes > fancakes > pancakes*). Once the children in his class catch on to the pattern, Mr. Clark pauses and sees if the children can figure out what food the creatures wants (*tickles > pickles*). The children soon are shouting out the correct names of the food as soon as the creature mispronounces the words. After reading the story, Mr. Clark follows up by playing a game. He reaches into a bag, which he says is his lunch bag, and describes a food item, mispronouncing the initial sound like the creature in the story. For example, when he grabs the replica of a clump of grapes, he says, "Oh, these must be napes!" Then he asks the children what they think *napes* are. They quickly catch on and say "grapes!" He then pulls out a simple cardboard replica of a cluster of grapes. Next is *phitza*, etc.

How can you tell phonological awareness instruction from phonics instruction? Kindergarten teacher Patty Buchanan provided us with the following easy-to-remember response: Phonological awareness instruction can be provided in the dark. Why? Phonological awareness instruction is helping children *hear* the sounds in the language; phonics instruction is helping children associate sounds with letters. Therefore, for phonics instruction the lights must be on so that the children can see the print. Phonics instruction is a form of alphabet instruction. We discuss alphabet instruction next.

Alphabet Instruction

Alphabet identification in kindergarten is a strong predictor of later reading achievement (Chall, 1996), and the National Early Literacy Panel has identified alphabetic knowledge as a core component of early literacy instruction (Strickland & Shanahan, 2004). In addition, research indicates that the phonemic awareness instruction is more effective when it is taught along with alphabet knowledge (Ehri, Nunes, Willows, Schuster, Yaghoub-Zadeh, & Shanahan, 2001). As discussed above, phonemes are not discrete units in speech (Adams, Foorman, Lundberg, & Beeler, 1998). Instead, phonemes are influenced by adjacent sounds in words. Alphabet letters provide a concrete representation for the "elusive" phonemes that make up words.

What do children seem to be learning when they begin to name and write alphabet letters? By the time young children say the alphabet letter names, they have begun to make discoveries about the alphabet. Children who have had experiences with print come to understand that the squiggles on the paper are special; they can be named. Toddler Jed, for example, called all letters in his alphabet books or in environmental print signs either *B* or *D* (Lass, 1982). At this very young age, he had already learned that letters were a special form of graphics with names. Three-year-old Frank associated letters with things that were meaningful to him. He argued with his mother to buy him the *Fire truck* (not just the car) because "It's like me!" He pointed to the *F*. (Incidentally, his argument was successful.) Giti pointed to the *z* on her blocks and said, "Look, like in the zoo!" (Baghban, 1984, p. 30). These three young children have learned to associate letters with things important to them.

Alphabet knowledge can be divided into two subskills: identification and naming. Alphabet identification involves being able to point out a letter that someone else names. For example, a teacher might ask a child to point to the letter *c* on an alphabet frieze (a chart that lists all of the letters in alphabetical order). Alphabet naming requires naming a letter that someone else points to. For example, the teacher could point to the letter *c* on the alphabet chart and ask, "What's the name of this letter?" Of the two skills, naming is the more difficult.

We have also included phonics—the study of letter-sound relationships—in this section. Once children have developed phonemic awareness and have begun learn to identify the letters of the alphabet, they can begin to learn the sounds that are associated with those letters. So we have categorized phonics as the most advanced aspect of alphabet learning. Many pre-K and K teachers make phonics the capstone of their teaching of each letter. What often happens in large group phonics instruction with four-year-olds is that children with good phonemic awareness learn letter-sound relationships as a result of this teaching, whereas children who are slower in developing phonological processing skills will receive extra exposure to letters and their names. This is not necessarily bad, as long as the teacher understands what each child is expected to get out of the instruction. Of course, a preferable alternative is to use small group instructions tailored to needs of individual children.

Should early childhood teachers expect all children to identify and name all letters of the alphabet by the time the children are five? Certainly not! However, state early childhood academic standards always include alphabet knowledge as a key instructional outcome. For example, the Arizona Early Learning Standards and the 1999 reauthorization of Head Start (*Good Start, Grow Smart,* 2002, p. 8) both specify that by the end of preschool, children should be able to *name* at least ten letters of the alphabet. So building alphabet knowledge does need to be a key component of early literacy programs.

While it is generally accepted that alphabet knowledge should be an instructional objective, there is some controversy over which specific letters to teach and the order in which to teach them. Some argue that different letters should be taught to each child. For example, Lea McGee and Don Richgels (1989) believe that it is preferable to teach letters that match children's current interests and activities. In order to deliver this type of individualized alphabet instruction, teachers need to observe closely to learn about the types of contexts in which children notice letters (e.g., environmental print, computer keyboards, books, friends' T-shirts). These contexts provide wonderful opportunities for informal talk and instruction about the alphabet.

Examples of "informal" alphabet learning activities include:

◆ *Environmental print*—Bring environmental print items to class (empty cereal boxes, cookie bags, etc.) and encourage children to read the print's message and discuss prominent letters (e.g., the letter *C* on a box of corn flakes).

◆ *Reading and writing children's names*—As discussed in Chapter 6, printed versions of children's names can be used for a variety of functional purposes, including attendance charts, helper charts, sign-up lists, and so on. Names of classmates have inherent high interest. Take advantage of every opportunity to read these names and to call attention to letters in the names ("Look, Jenny's and Jerry's names both start with the same letter. What letter is it?").

◆ *Traditional manipulatives*—Many traditional early childhood manipulatives can be used to support children's alphabet letter name learning. These manipulatives include alphabet puzzles, magnetic uppercase and lowercase letters, felt letters, letter stencils, and chalk and chalkboards.

◆ *Writing*—Whenever children engage in writing, on their own or with a teacher (e.g., shared writing), their attention can be drawn to the letters of the alphabet. Remember that even if children are using scribbles or another personalized form of script, they are attempting to represent the letters of alphabet and thus are learning about letters.

◆ *Alphabet books*—Many types of alphabet books are available. For young children who are just learning the alphabet, books with simple letter–object associations (e.g., illustrations that show a letter and objects that begin with the sound associated with the letter) are most appropriate (Raines & Isbell, 1994). Alphabet books offer an enjoyable way to introduce children to letters and the sounds they represent. Research has shown that repeated reading of ABC books can promote young children's letter recognition (Greenewald & Kulig, 1995).

It is also beneficial for children to make their own alphabet books. These child-made ABC books typically have a letter at the top of each page. Children then draw pictures and/or cut and paste illustrations of objects that begin with the sound of each letter. They can also write any words they know that contain the target letter. An adult can label the pictures.

◆ *Making letters*—Young children enjoy finger painting letters; painting letters on the easel or on the sidewalk on a hot day with a brush dipped in water; rolling and folding clay or Play-Doh to make letters; and making and eating alphabet soup, puzzles, or pretzels. All of these activities provide meaningful, playful contexts within which young children can learn alphabet names.

Other researchers recommend that the alphabet be taught in a systematic order to all children, using more direct forms of instruction. Two basic assumptions underlie this position. First, it is assumed that it is difficult for teachers to individualize alphabet instruction for all the children in their classroom. If this individualization is not done effectively, some children will "fall through the cracks" and not learn much about the alphabet. Second, it is assumed that there is a logical sequence for alphabet instruction. Some letters should be taught before others. For example, Treiman and Kessler (2003) discovered that young children learn letters in about the same order. For example, *O* is one of the easiest letters for children between the ages of three and seven to recognize. Letters such as *D, G, K, L, V,* and *Y* are more difficult for children and typically are among the last children recognize. Hence, Bowman and Treiman (2004) suggest that teachers should expose children to the printed letters in the order of difficulty, introducing the easiest letters first to build the foundation, followed by the more difficult letters.

We strongly recommend a blended approach, providing children with the individualized, informal forms of alphabet learning described above plus systematic instruction on selected letters. The order of the letters can be based on ease of learning or on other curriculum factors. For example, teachers may wish to focus on letters that fit with the stories and experiences highlighted in the curriculum. If the class is going to take a field trip to the fire station, for example, it might be an ideal time for them to learn the letter *F*. This letter will be encountered on the field trip, in shared reading of books about fires and fire fighters, in play activities connected with the theme, and in shared writing.

The following are some of the strategies that we recommend for direct instruction on the alphabet.

Direct, systematic instruction on selected letters promotes alphabet knowledge.

Songs

The alphabet song is the way children are most often introduced to letters at home (Adams, 1990). While there are some advantages to learning the names of letters in this fashion (e.g., the names give children a peg on which to attach perceptual information about letters), the song can also lead to misconceptions (e.g., that *lmnop* is one letter). In addition, Schickedanz (1998) argues that learning to recite the alphabet from memory is a trivial accomplishment that contributes little to children's learning to read. Yet the recent report by the National Research Council (Burns, Griffin, & Snow, 1998) suggests singing the alphabet song as one of many activities early childhood teachers should use to support children's literacy learning.

Other songs can also be used to help children learn the alphabet. For example, Marla Chamberlain, who teaches at the San Luis Preschool in Arizona, uses a song with the lyrics

> *Can you find the letter _?*
> *The letter _?*
> *The letter _?*
> *Can you find the letter _,*
> *Somewhere in this room?*

She writes the lyrics on five large pieces of tagboard with slots to hold different letters. The class currently is studying the letter *M,* so she has written this letter on four cards that can be placed in these slots. The song now becomes:

> *Can you find the letter M?*
> *The letter M?*
> *The letter M?*
> *Can you find the letter M,*
> *Somewhere in this room?*

Mrs. Chamberlain sings the song with the children and then waits for them to answer the question posed by the song. Most of the children hold up their hands. One child says "monkey," pointing to a picture of a monkey on a poster that has an upper- and lowercase *M* on it. Another child points to the class calendar and says "Monday." Because of the slots, this song chart can be used for practice in identifying all of the letters that the class studies.

Letter Charts

Letter charts contain a letter (usually its upper- and lowercase forms) and pictures of objects that start with the letter. Teachers can purchase or make these, using pictures from magazines, environmental print, etc. As described above in the section on teaching alliteration, San Luis Preschool teacher Lisa Lemos systematically introduces her children to a letter and its sound every two weeks, using a published program, *Sound, Rhyme and Letter Time* (Wright Group/McGraw-Hill, 2002). This program provides a letter poster showing pictures of objects that begin with a "target" letter. For example, the letter *S* poster has pictures of a sun, seal, sailboat, sandwich, sand, sunglasses, and a seashell. During the first week, Mrs. Lemos focuses on the sound of the letter, helping children realize that all of the objects on the chart start with the same sound, /s/. She also helps children come up with other words that start with the /s/ sound. During the second week, Mrs. Lemos teaches children about the letter *S*. She begins by reviewing the words represented on the poster, reminding the children that all these words begin with the /s/ sound. Next she writes a label for each picture on a Post-it note, with the first letter in a different color, and places the labels on the pictures. She points out that all of the words start with the same letter, S. Next Mrs. Lemos removes the labels from the poster and has the children put the labels back on the chart next to the corresponding object. When they do this, Mrs. Lemos asks them to say letter name, letter sound, and whole word. This is repeated over several days so that all of the children get several turns. By using this two-week routine with each letter, Mrs. Lemos is helping her children develop phonemic awareness, letter recognition, and phonics.

Alphabet Word Walls

A word wall is a collection of words displayed on a classroom wall that is used for instructional purposes. In an alphabet word wall, large upper- and lowercase letters are arranged on the wall in alphabetical order, and words that begin with each letter are posted below. Each day, one or two special words are selected for placement on the word wall. These words can come from the stories, rhymes, songs, and poems that the class is reading. They can also include children's names, familiar environmental print, and words from thematic units, and they are placed under the letters that they start with. At the pre-K level, teachers often include a picture to go along with each printed word. Picture supports tends to get phased out in kindergarten. The teacher can use the words on the word wall to reinforce letter identification and letter naming. Lisa Lemos uses her word wall during transitions from large group to small group instruction. She asks each child to point to a letter that she says (letter identification), or she will say the name of a letter, hand the pointer to a child, and ask the child to point to the letter (letter naming). Each child gets a turn before going to the next activity, and Mrs. Lemos helps those who have difficulty. Usually children can quickly point to or name the letters because the pictures that go with the words and the familiar environmental print give helpful clues. Trade Secrets 7.4 describes how a kindergarten teacher makes use of an alphabet word wall to teach letters and their sounds.

Games

Games are frequently used in SBRR instruction to provide children with the practice needed to consolidate and retain the skills that are being taught through direct instruction. When practice activities are put into a game format, skill practice can become fun and enjoyable for children. They will persist at games much longer than activities such as worksheets and workbook exercises. On the day that author Jim Christie was observing Martha Vasquez's syllable segmenting instruction described at the beginning of this chapter, Ms. Vasquez had also planned an alphabet game for her preschoolers to play during center time. The game involved fishing for letters that were on little replicas of fish. The children would catch the fish with magnets on strings suspended from small poles. One of Mrs. Vasquez's assistant teachers, Christian Garibay, stationed himself in the dramatic play area so that he could scaffold the children's play with the letters. When children caught a letter, he would ask them to name it. What was remarkable is that a group of five boys spent more than thirty minutes engaging in this letter naming practice.

At the San Luis Preschool, teacher Lisa Lemos has her children play a game that combines alphabet practice with the traditional "A tisket, a tasket, a red and yellow basket" song. A small group of children sits on the floor, and Mrs. Lemos gives one of them a letter carrier hat and a small basket that contains large pieces of poster paper, each with a letter written on it. While the children sing the "tisket, tasket" song, the "mail carrier" walks around the group and gives one child a letter from the bag. The child who receives the letter then must say the name of the letter. Then this child becomes the mail carrier. Again, the game format and make-believe role-playing ensure high levels of child engagement.

Researcher Judy Schickedanz (1998) recommends two alphabet games that are particularly useful in reinforcing young children's growing alphabet knowledge:

- *alphabet-matching puzzles,* in which the children match loose letter tiles with letters printed on a background board;
- *alphabet clue game,* in which the teacher draws part of a letter and then asks children to guess which letter he or she is thinking of. After children make their guesses, the teacher adds another piece to the letter and has the children guess again.

Phonics Instruction

Phonics involves using the alphabetic principle (letters have a relationship with the sounds of oral language) to decode printed words. Young children differ greatly in their need for instruction in this important decoding skill. Stahl (1992, p. 620) explains: "Some will learn to decode on their own, without any instruction. Others will need some degree of instruction, ranging from pointing out of common spelling patterns to intense and systematic instruction." Thus, as

TRADE SECRETS
7.4

Word Walls

At the beginning of the kindergarten year, Mrs. Burl begins each school day by asking her class to share any print items they brought from home. These items are usually packages or wrappers from products the children's families use at home. She asks each child who brought an item to read the name of the item to the rest of the class. After the children have read their environmental print, Mrs. Burl selects one of the products, Aim toothpaste, and asks the children where they think the Aim toothpaste container should go on their ABC word wall. The children think for just a moment when Anissa suggests cutting the wrapper into two parts—one part for *Aim* to go under the letter *Aa* on the word wall and the second for *toothpaste* to go under the letter *Tt*. Mrs. Burl asks the class for a thumbs-up (for yes) or thumbs-down (for no) vote. The children give her a unanimous thumbs-up. Mrs. Burl quickly cuts the package, circles the appropriate words, and asks the child who brought the wrapper to pin each word under the correct letter on the word wall.

The word wall concept allows teachers to stimulate children's awareness of words and knowledge of letters and sounds (Hedrick & Pearish, 1999; Morrow, Tracey, Gee-Woo, & Pressley, 1999; Wagstaff, 1998). Teachers may use a range of word wall activities to reinforce and support young children's growing phonemic abilities and reading skills. Mrs. Burl begins the kindergarten year with an ABC word wall that focuses on the initial letter sounds. Later, when the children's awareness of the sound–symbol relationship grows, she will add blends and consonant digraphs to the ABC word wall (see Figure 7.2).

Mrs. Burl found the word wall concept to be useful for teaching a variety of minilessons and stimulating the children's interest in words and reading. She also found that parents are interested in the word walls because they provide an ongoing visual record of the many lessons Mrs. Burl uses to teach alphabet knowledge and phonemic awareness to her students.

Figure 7.2 A Kindergarten ABC Word Wall

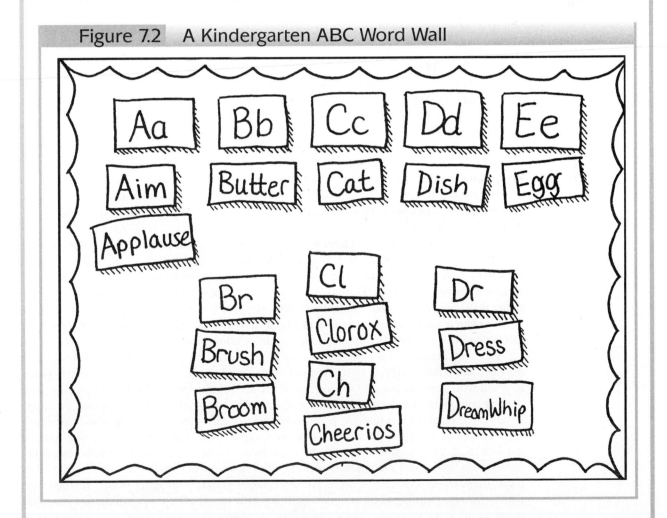

in all other aspects of literacy instruction, it is important for phonics teaching to match the needs of individual students.

The children who learn phonics more or less on their own simply need to be provided with the types of meaningful reading and writing activities described in Chapters 4 and 6—shared reading and writing, literacy-enriched play, and functional literacy activities. As these children engage in these purposeful literacy activities, they gradually discover the relationship between letters and sounds.

Those who need a moderate amount of assistance profit from what Morrow and Tracey (1997) term "contextual instruction." This type of instruction occurs in conjunction with the same types of activities described in the preceding paragraph—shared reading and writing, literacy-enriched play, and functional literacy activities. The only difference is that while children are engaging in these activities, the teacher draws children's attention to letter–sound relationships that are present.

Morrow and Tracey (1997, p. 647) give an example of how one teacher, Mrs. M., drew her students' attention to the letter *M* and its sound during an activity that involved both shared writing and functional writing:

> Because her class had finished putting on a show for their grandparents, Mrs. M. thought it would be a good idea if they wrote a thank-you note to the music teacher who assisted them with the performance. The note was composed by the students with the teacher's help. She wrote the note on the board and sounded out each word to help the students with spelling. After they finished writing, Mrs. M. read the entire note and had the students read the note aloud:

> *Mrs. M.:* How should we start this letter?
>
> *Student:* Dear Mr. Miller.
>
> *Mrs. M.:* Very good. [as she writes] "Dear Mr. Miller" has three words. *Dear* is the first word, *Mr.* is the second word, and *Miller* is the third word. I just realized that my name and Mr. Miller's name both begin with the same letter, *M*. Let's say these words together, "Mr. Miller, Mrs. Martinez."

This type of spontaneous teaching can occur in connection with all the literacy learning activities described in Chapters 5 and 6. Of course, such teaching requires a teacher who is on the lookout for teachable moments involving letter–sound relationships. Because most, if not all, preschool and kindergarten classes contain some children who need moderate assistance, we recommend that teachers make an effort to take advantage of these types of teaching opportunities when they arise.

Another way to help children acquire knowledge about phonics is through writing (IRA/NAEYC, 1998; Stahl, 1992). Once children have reached the invented spelling stage in their writing development, they begin to use their knowledge of letter names and letter–sound relationships to spell words. During this stage, children spell words the way that they sound rather than how they are conventionally spelled. For example, a child may spell the word *leave* with the letters *lev* because this is how the word sounds. When children use invented spelling, their attention is naturally focused on letter–sound relationships.

Research indicates that temporary use of invented spelling can promote children's reading development (IRA/NAEYC, 1998). For example, a study by Clarke (1988) found that young children who were encouraged to write with invented spelling scored higher on decoding and reading comprehension tests than children who were encouraged to use conventional spelling.

Finally, teachers can provide preplanned phonics activities to children who have developed an awareness of the sounds that make up spoken words and who can recognize some of the letters of the alphabet. This can be done by adapting the phonemic awareness, letter recognition, and word recognition activities discussed earlier in this chapter so that they focus on letter–sound relationships. We recommend selection of letter–sound relationships that fit in with ongoing class activities or that fit the needs of specific children, rather than using an arbitrary sequence (consonants first, short vowels second, long vowels third, etc.). Trade Secrets 7.5 describes how preschool teacher Lisa Lemos provides this type of phonics instruction.

<table>
<tr><td>

TRADE SECRETS 7.5

Blending Letter–Sound Relationship Instruction with Phonological Awareness Instruction

San Luis Preschool teacher Lisa Lemos combines an onset and rime substitution activity with one of her children's favorite nursery rhymes, *Pop Goes the Weasel*. Lisa has written the rhyme on a large piece of chart paper so that the children can follow the print as they recite and sing the rhyme. After the children have sung the rhyme several times, Mrs. Lemos tells them that today they are going to play a game with the rhyme. The children come up, one at a time, and draw letters out of a bag. They use these letters to change the word *pop* by replacing its first letter.

</td><td>

Bianca is first and draws the letter *H*. She names the letter. Then Mrs. Lemos asks her what sound *H* makes. When she hesitates, several other children make the /h/ sound. (Here the preschoolers are actually engaging in phonics, making connections between letters and sounds.) Then one of the children catches on and says, "It's going to be *hop*. It's going to be *hop*!" Mrs. Lemos writes the letter *h* on several small cards and tapes them over the *p* at the beginning of the word *pop* in the song lyrics on the chart. Then Mrs. Lemos and class sing the rhyme again, this time substituting *hop* for *pop*. This is repeated with the letters *b* (*pop* > *bop*), *c* (*pop* > *cop*), *t* (*pop* > *top*), and *s* (*pop* > *sop*). The children quickly catch on to the pattern, and many shout out the new word as soon as the new onset is drawn out of the bag.

</td></tr>
</table>

Several of the phonemic awareness activities described earlier in this chapter can easily be modified to teach phonics by having children identify which letters represents the various sounds and then writing words so that children can see the letter–sound relationships:

- *Letter–sound matching*—Show pictures of familiar objects (cat, bird, and monkey) and ask children which begins with the /m/ sound. Then ask which letter *monkey* starts with. Write the word on the chalkboard. Ask the children for other words that start with the /m/ sound, and write these words on the board.

- *Letter–sound isolation*—Pronounce words and ask children what sounds are heard at the beginning, middle, or end. For example, ask the children, "What sound is in the middle of *man, cat,* and *Sam*?" Once the sound is identified, ask the children what letter represents the sound. The words can then be written on the chalkboard, along with other short-*a* words.

In a similar fashion, letter recognition activities can be modified to teach phonics by shifting the focus from letters to their sounds.

- *Environmental print*—Discuss letter–sound relationships that occur in environmental print. For example, if children have brought in cereal boxes from home, the teacher could ask questions such as "What letters make the /ch/ sound in Cheerios?" Children could then be asked to identify other words that start with the /ch/ sound, and these words could be written on the chalkboard.

- *Reading and writing children's names*—When referring to children's names in attendance charts, helper charts, and other places, call children's attention to letter–sound correspondences in their names. For example, the teacher might say, "Jenny's and Jerry's names start with the same sound. What letter do both their names start with?"

- *Games*—Create games that enable children to reinforce their growing knowledge of letter–sound relationships in an enjoyable manner. A popular type of phonics game requires children to match letters with pictures that begin with letter sounds. For example, the letter *b* might be matched with a picture of a bird. If you use this type of phonics matching game, be sure to tell the children the word that each picture represents to avoid confusion with other words that the picture could represent. In the example of the *b/bird* item, a child might justifiably believe that the picture of bird represented the word *robin* or *sparrow* rather than *bird*.

Word walls, discussed above in the section on alphabet knowledge, can also be invaluable aids in helping children learn phonics. The words displayed on a word wall are familiar to children and often have strong personal significance and meaning. These high-meaning words can serve as pegs on which children can attach letter–sound relationships. Teachers should routinely take advantage of these words by linking them with phonics activities and lessons. For example, if children already can identify and name the letter *r*, a teacher may decide to help them learn the *r* letter–sound correspondence by asking them to find words that start with /r/ sound on the word wall (as opposed to finding words that begin with the letter *r*).

Many children will need more direct instruction on letter–sound relationships, but not during the preschool years. Preschool and kindergarten children who need extensive help learning phonics really need more experience with phonemic awareness, letter recognition, and informal types of phonic instruction described in this chapter. These activities will build a foundation that will help these children benefit from more systematic approaches to learning phonics later.

Print Awareness Instruction

Print awareness is a broad term that refers to children's ability to recognize print, ranging from contextualized environmental print (e.g., the word *Pepsi* on a soda can) to decontextualized written words (e.g., the word *dog* in a children's book). Print awareness also encompasses concepts about print, including book concepts (author, illustrator, title, front, back) and conventions of print (directionality, capitalization, punctuation).

In Chapters 4 and 6, we described a number of emergent literacy strategies that can be used to promote print awareness, such as functional print, shared reading, shared writing, and literacy-enriched play. In the sections that follow, we describe how print awareness can be taught through more direct forms of instruction.

Teaching Concepts about Print

Although concepts about print instruction are strongly associated with the emergent literacy approach, print concepts also receive attention in SBRR programs. For example, Early Reading First projects are required to teach "print awareness" by providing print-rich classroom environments and teaching book concepts during shared reading. So even though Early Reading First has its roots in the SBRR approach, it also makes use of effective emergent literacy strategies.

Some teachers in Early Reading First projects who are firm believers in the SBRR philosophy also use more direct forms of instruction to teach concepts about print. Head Start teacher Connie Felix uses this approach to help her children in San Luis, Arizona, learn the distinction between pictures, words, and alphabet letters. Mrs. Felix has prepared a large chart with three columns labeled Picture, Word, and Letter. An example of each is pasted next to the label (e.g., there is photograph next to the label *Picture* and a written word next to the label *Word*). She has put a number of cards into a bag. Each card contains an example of a picture, word, or letter. She begins by explaining each of these concepts. The children are very interested, and several quickly recognize the examples that Mrs. Felix has provided ("That's an *A*" and "It's *cat*"). Children take turns drawing a card out of the basket. When they have drawn a card, they tell the class what is on the card, say to which category it belongs, and tape it to the correct column on the chart. If a child struggles, classmates help out. For example, Angela picks a card with a classmate's name on it. She recognizes the name and says "Elian." Mrs. Felix prompts her with the question, "Which type is it? A picture, word, or letter?" When Angela does not respond, several classmates chime in, "It's a word." Angela then places the card in the correct column and feels proud that she has done this correctly.

Key Words

The key word strategy, developed by Sylvia Ashton-Warner (1963), is another excellent way to build young children's ability to recognize words. It is a very simple and elegant strategy: children choose words that are personally meaningful and that they would like to learn to read. Real-life experiences, favorite children's books, writing workshop, and language experience stories are primary sources for these key words. Children learn to recognize these words quickly because of their high meaning and personal significance.

The key word strategy is often associated with emergent literacy because of its focus on personal meaning, learning by doing, and social interaction. However, key words also meets the specifications for a SBRR strategy because it involves direct instruction. It features teacher modeling, guided practice, and independent practice. We have included key words in this section because we believe that it is one of the most effective way to directly teach pre-K and kindergarten children to recognize whole words.

Here is how the key word strategy works: The teacher asks each child in the class to pick a favorite word that he or she would like to learn to read. This word is written on a large card while the child watches. (This is sometimes done in circle time so that the whole class learns about each child's key word.) The children then write their key words plus any other words that they remember. Finally, they engage in various games and practice activities with their key words.

The following are some of the key word games and practice activities recommended by Jeanette Veatch and her associates (Veatch, Sawicki, Elliot, Flake, & Blakey, 1979, pp. 30–32):

- *Retrieving words from the floor*—The children's words (with young children this will be the words of a partner or a small group) are placed facedown on the floor. On the signal, each child is to find one of her or his own words, hold it up, and read it aloud.

- *Claiming the cards*—The teacher selects many words from the class, holds them up, and the child who "owns" each word claims it.

- *Classifying words*—The teacher selects categories that encompass all of the words selected by the children. The categories are introduced, and labels are placed on the floor for each category. The children must then decide in which category their words belong. For example, the children who have animal words would stand next to the sheet of paper that says *animals*.

- *Making alphabet books*—Children record their words in the correct section of an alphabet book that is divided by initial letters. This is a good example of how children can learn about words and letters simultaneously.

- *Illustrating*—The child can draw a picture about the key word, dictate the word to a teacher to write on a card, and then copy the word into a picture dictionary word book.

- *Finding words*—Children might find their key words in books, magazines, and newspapers.

Veatch and her colleagues recommend that children collect key words and keep them in a box or on a ring file known as a "word bank." Another possibility is to have children keep their key words in a word book. In this variation, the teacher writes a word on a card for the child, then the child copies the word into his or her word book. Periodically, the teacher can have children review their words in their word banks or word books. Besides providing opportunities for children to practice recognizing key words, word banks and word books serve other valuable functions. They provide children with a concrete record of their reading vocabulary growth. It is very motivating for children to see their collections of words grow larger and larger. In addition, the words can be used to help children learn about letters and the sounds they are associated with. For example, if children are learning the sound associated with *b,* the teacher can have children find all the words in their collections that begin with that letter.

Trade Secrets 7.6 describes a variation of the word bank strategy in which children write their key words in a *Word Book*. Notice how the teacher, Bernadette Watson, prompts Amanda to use letter–sound relationships when she writes Amanda's key word, *elephant,* on the card.

Assessment: Finding Out What Children Know and Can Do

The No Child Left Behind Act specifies that "scientifically based research" relies on measurements and observational methods that provide reliable and valid data. Reliability refers to the consistency of the data—if same test is administered to the same child on consecutive days, the child's scores should be very similar. And if two different teachers administer an assessment to

TRADE SECRETS 7.6	My Word Book

Bernadette Watson

As the children entered the classroom, Ms. Watson greeted them, gave them a three- by five-inch card, and asked them, "What is your word for today?" Children answered. Amanda said, "elephant." Ms. Watson positioned her hand to write *elephant* on the card. Before she wrote the word, she asked Amanda how she decided on this word as her word for the day. Amanda had seen a program on television about elephants the night before and had decided, right then and there, that *elephant* would be her word today.

"So," asked Ms. Watson, "what letter do you think *elephant* begins with?"

"I don't know," responded Amanda.

"It's an *E*," said Ms. Watson. "What letter is next?" She stretched the sound, "L-l-l-l-l."

Amanda responded, "*L!*"

"You're right," exclaimed Ms. Watson, "and then it's another *e*, and a *p-h-a-n*. And what do you think the last letter is? T-t-t-t-t."

Amanda said, "*T!*"

"Absolutely," said Ms. Watson.

Amanda took her card with *elephant* written on it with her and set off to locate her word book. Having found it, she sat at a table to copy her word into her book. First she drew a picture of an elephant. Above it, she copied the word *elephant*. At the beginning of the year, that is all she would have done. Now, she also wrote a sentence under the picture: "isnt.v" (I saw on TV).

When she was done, Amanda took her book to the library center. Here she might read her words to herself or to a friend. The pictures she had drawn greatly help her remember her word for the day.

the same child, again the scores should be very similar if the assessment is reliable. Validity refers to the extent to which an assessment really measures what it claims to measure.

Standardized assessments use carefully scripted procedures so that the conditions and directions are always the same whenever the test is administered. Each student taking the test hears the same directions, is given the same test items, and has the same amount of time. This "standardization" helps to increase the reliability of the assessment. It is not surprising, therefore, that the SBRR approach makes heavy use of standardized types of assessments.

In Table 7.1, we provide a description of several of the standardized assessments in reading currently in use in early literacy programs. For example, the Peabody Picture Vocabulary Test (PPVT) is required to be used in all Early Reading First programs across the United States.

There are two types of standardized tests:

(1) **Criterion-referenced tests** are developed with a specific set of objectives that reflect district, state, or federal learning standards. For instance, the Department of Health and Human Services, under the National Reporting on Child Outcomes plan, requires that all Head Start children be tested twice annually on such skills as their ability to recognize a word as a unit of print, identify letters of the alphabet, associate sounds with written words, and so on. In the fall and spring, each child is individually administered a test to assess their Head Start entry and exit reading skills. In Special Feature 7.1, we describe a criterion-referenced ongoing assessment procedure used by an Early Reading First project in Yuma, Arizona. The goal in criterion-referenced tests is for all students to demonstrate mastery of the information and skills they have been taught.

(2) **Norm-referenced tests** are designed to measure the accomplishment of one student relative to the whole class, or to compare one classroom of pre-K students to another classroom within the same school or center, or to compare all the classrooms in a district, or to compare all children across the country. Norm-referenced standardized tests can be used to determine whether a school's curriculum reflects national expectations of what children should know at a specific grade level and to compare students to one another.

As readers know, it is now common practice for states to mandate that children take a standards-based standardized test, typically in the spring of the academic year. The state's aim is to gather information on how a school and the school district are achieving with respect to all standards.

Table 7.1 Standardized Reading Measures

Title/Publisher	Purpose	Description	When to Use It
Dynamic Indicators of Basic Early Literacy Skills (DIBELS)–Letter-Naming Fluency	To assess fluency with which children identify letter names. To identify children at risk of reading difficulty early before a low reading trajectory is established.	Individually administered, timed phonemic awareness task. Randomly ordered lower- and upper-case letters are presented to children for 1 minute: children are instructed to name as many letters as they can	Beginning kindergarten through fall of first grade or until children are proficient at accurately producing 40–60 letter names per minute
Phonemic Segmentation Fluency Publisher: CBM Network, School Psychology Program, College of Education, University of Oregon http://dibels.uoregon.edu/	To assess children's ability to segment orally presented words into phonemes. To identify children who may be at risk of reading difficulty.	Individually administered, timed phonological awareness task. Words are orally presented to children for 1 minute; children are instructed to segment each word into individual phonemes (i.e., sounds)	Winter of kindergarten through first grade or until children are proficient at accurately producing 35–45 phonemes per minute
Gates MacGinite Reading Tests, Third Edition Publisher: Riverside Publishing Company	Commercially published test designed to identify specific strengths and weaknesses in reading comprehension	Achievement test designed to assess a child's knowledge of important background concepts of reading, identify strengths and weaknesses in the area of beginning reading, and serve as a measure of reading skills for children who make less than average progress in reading by the end of first grade	Level "PRE" and "R" for use with beginning kindergartners to assess background concepts; Level "R" for measuring reading skills of students who are not making adequate progress; other seven levels used to provide a general assessment of reading achievement
IDEA Proficiency Test (IPT) Publisher: Ballard & Tigh	To determine the English language skills of students who have a non–English language background	Children are assessed on oral language abilities, writing, and reading. Asked to write their own stories and respond to a story.	Administered to children K–12
Individual Growth and Developmental Indicators (IGDI) www.getgotgo.net	To identify children's phonological awareness strengths and weaknesses	Three components to the test: picture naming, rhyming, and alliteration. Takes approximately 5 minutes to administer.	Used for ages 3–5
PALS Pre-K http://pals.virginia.edu/PALS-Instruments/PALS-PreK.asp	To provide information on children's strengths and weaknesses	Measures name-writing ability, upper- and lowercase alphabet recognition, letter sound and beginning sound production, print and word awareness, rhyme awareness, and nursery rhyme awareness	Used in fall of pre-K and can be used as a measurement of progress in the spring
Peabody Picture Vocabulary Test-III (PPVT-III) Publisher: American Guidance Service	To measure receptive vocabulary acquisition and serve as a screening test of verbal ability	Student points to the picture that best represents the stimulus word	Beginning at age 2.5 years to 90+ years
The Phonological Awareness Test (PAT) Publisher: LinguiSystems	To assess students' phonological awareness skills	Five different measures of phonemic awareness (segmentation of phonemes, phoneme isolation, phoneme deletion, phoneme substitution, and phoneme blending) and a measure of sensitivity to rhyme	Beginning the second semester of kindergarten through second grade

Curriculum Based Measurement

Tanis Bryan and Cevriye Ergul

An important part of teaching early literacy skills is continuous monitoring of children's learning. Although teachers "take in" thousands of bits of information about their students' learning every day, preschool teachers need reliable and valid measures to help them evaluate young children's development of the early literacy skills being taught in their classrooms. Over the past thirty years, as curriculum-based measurement (CBM) has been developed to help teachers monitor children's progress. The intent is for teachers to collect technically sound but simple data in a meaningful fashion to document students' growth and determine the necessity for modifying instructional programs.

Critical early literacy skills assessed with preschool CBMs are phonological awareness, alphabet letter naming, and oral vocabulary. CBM test stimuli are drawn from the curriculum. Teachers administer CBMs weekly across the school year and use the data for instructional planning. Teachers find CBM a feasible addition to their schedules because it is fast (two minutes per child weekly), inexpensive, and easy to administer. Because CBM is directly connected to daily instruction, the information is useful to teachers. Teachers use CBM to continuously measure their students' gains, determine if their students are learning at the expected rate, and evaluate their instructional strategies. Ideally, a team of teachers collaborate in each step of doing CBM.

Here is a step-by-step description of how teachers use CBM.

Step 1 Select children. Teachers can select two to four children who are monitored weekly or rotate two to four children each week so that all children in the classroom are monitored monthly. It's important that each cohort includes a child with learning delays or problems, such as a child who has developmental delays or disabilities, and/or a child at risk for disabilities. Include a child with typical achievement and/or a child with high achievement to help figure out if a particular child is having a problem or if all the children are making errors, and the instruction is missing its mark (e.g., the material is too difficult for everyone).

Step 2 Develop CBMs. Teachers take a close look at the curriculum and weekly lesson plans and decide which vocabulary, sounds, and letters will be emphasized each week. Each CBM should assess: Receptive Vocabulary ("Show Me"), Expressive Vocabulary ("Tell Me"), Letter Identification, and Alliteration (identification of initial sounds). The CBM should include six to eight words, two to four alphabet letters, and two sounds for alliteration from each week's lesson plan. It is important to use the same number of words, sounds, and letters each week because this allows teachers to evaluate the children's development across time.

A score sheet is prepared for each child (see Figure 7.3). The score sheet lists the sources for the items, such as the book/page or poster that shows the words in the item, as well as space for comments and descriptions of the types of errors (e.g., okay with initial sounds but unable to pronounce the rest of the word, mispronunciation of the whole word, certain types of mispronunciations of words or letters) or any other event that influenced the child's responses (e.g., off-task behavior, sick, weather too hot).

Step 3 Administer CBMs. CBMs are administered at the same time each week, following the same procedures and wait time for each child. On Receptive Vocabulary, the child is shown a poster or page that has several pictures from the lesson and asked to "Show me _____". On Expressive Vocabulary and Letter Identification, the child is shown a poster or book page and asked to name the object or letter pointed to. On Alliteration, the child is shown a card with the target word illustrated at the top of the card and three other illustrations in a row at the bottom of the card. One of the illustrations should have the same initial sound as the target word. Two sample items should be provided. The teacher displays each card and sounds out the words. The child is asked to point to one of the three pictures at the bottom with the same initial sound as the target picture.

Step 4 Analysis. At the end of each week or monthly, each child's scores on each test are summed and a graph is prepared (see Figure 7.4). The horizontal axis indicates the week of the unit and the vertical axis presents the number of correct responses on each CBM subtest. Graphs give teachers an overview of each child's mastery of the curriculum. Teachers compare the performance of children with special needs, at risk, typical achieving, and high achieving.

Step 5 Using the results. First, teachers establish expectations for students. Should every child get every item on every CBM? Should every

SPECIAL FEATURE 7.1 *(continued)*

FIGURE 7.3 CBM Score Sheet

ACE3 CBM SCORE SHEET – UNIT [VROOM VROOM / WEEK [One]

Child's Name _____ School _____

Date of Test _____ Examiner _____

Purpose: Track how well the child is learning the vocabulary words and letters you are teaching using DOORS.

Directions: Read the script in the box below. Enter the scores in the box below. Enter the scores on the left side column.

Letter Identification
Letter Card (card with all letters):

D d _____ L l _____ M m _____ J j _____

correct _____

Show Me
Our Big Book of Driving: Pages 2-3.

Van _____
Bicycle _____
Motorcycle _____
Fire Truck _____

correct _____

Tell Me
Picture Word Cards: Pull the word cards for the following items:

Taxi _____   Bus _____
Tire _____   Stop sign _____

correct _____

Comments:
_____
_____
_____

LETTER IDENTIFICATION:
Present the letter card to the child, and "Say, "We are going to look at this card with all these letters. Tell me the name of letter I point to."

SCORE:
1 Point = correct answer or self-correction within approximately 3 seconds.
0 Point = incorrect answer.
NA (No Answer) = Asked twice and no answer at the end of three seconds.

SHOW ME (Identification):
Open the lap book version of "Our Big Book of Driving" to pages 2-3. Place the book in front of the child and Say, "We are going to look at these pictures. Point to the picture that I tell you. "
"Show me the _____."

SCORE:
1 Point = correct answer or self-correction within approximately 3 seconds.
0 Point = incorrect answer.
NA (No Answer) = Asked twice and no answer at the end of three seconds.

TELL ME (Production):
Place the word cards in front of the child and "Say, "We are going to look at these pictures. Tell me the name of the picture I point to."
"Point to each picture and say, "Tell the name of this ."

SCORE:
1 Point = correct answer or self-correction within approximately 3 seconds.
0 Point = incorrect answer.
NA (No Answer) = Asked twice and no answer at the end of three seconds.

ACE3 CBM SCORE SHEET (ALLITERATION)
'VROOM VROOM / WEEK 1

Alliteration (Picture cards)

Toy _____   Toilet _____

Toaster _____   Toes _____

correct _____

Comments: _____
_____

ALLITERATION (Identification of initial sounds):
Use alliteration picture cards.
1. Sample item 1
"Say, **"Here is a picture of bread. It starts with the 'b' sound."** Repeat the word and say **"Now look at these pictures. Which one starts with "b."** Name each bottom picture. If child does not get correct answer, say the top picture's name and correct answer emphasizing initial sounds.
2. Sample item 2
Repeat the instructions of sample item 1 using the pictures' names in this sample.
3. Test items 1 and 2
"Say, **"Here is a picture of a (picture name). Now which one of these pictures starts with the same sound."** Name the top picture and then point to each picture in the bottom and say out loud.

SCORE:
1 Point for each correct answer or self-correction within approximately 3 seconds.
0 Point = incorrect answer.
NA (No Answer) = Asked twice and no answer at the end of three seconds.
Sample responses are not scored.

(continued on next page)

child get three of the four items? Teachers reviewing the data should ask: a) are one or two children not meeting expectations, b) are all children not meeting expectations, or c) are all the children exceeding expectations? We recommend that teachers use the performance of the typical or average achieving student to establish an Expectation Line. Then teachers can evaluate whether the child with disabilities or at risk for disabilities is learning at about the same rate as typical children or needs additional instruction.

Teachers are encouraged to include parents in the process by sending parents (or discussing) an explanation of CBM, the words and letters being focused on in each exploration or week, and the child's graph. The teacher should explain the graph, noting positive changes in the child's progress. Parents also should be provided activities to do at home that support classroom learning.

FIGURE 7.4 Sample CBM Graph

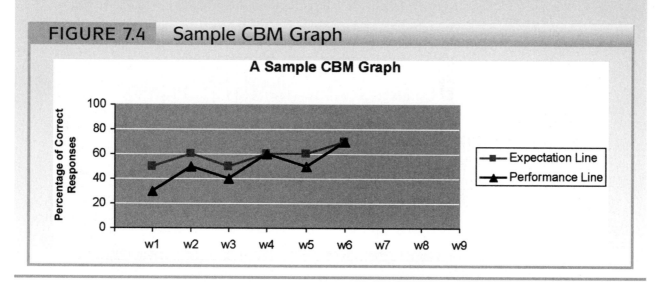

Special Feature 7.2 by Karen Burstein, an evaluation expert, provides useful information about both types of standardized assessments. In addition, Dr. Burstein describes the assessments used in the Arizona Centers of Excellence in Early Education Early Reading First project.

Summary

Whereas Chapters 6 and 8 describe activities that can implicitly teach children how to write and read, this chapter deals with explicit literacy instruction. It describes a variety of developmentally appropriate strategies that teachers can use to directly teach children how to read. Each skill has been found to be important to children's success as readers. What have you learned?

■ *What is the difference between phonological awareness, phonemic awareness, and phonics? In what sequence do young children typically acquire these skills? What does this sequence suggest about classroom instructional strategies?*

Phonological awareness (realization that spoken language is composed of words, syllables, and sounds) is broader than phonemic awareness (realization that words are composed of phonemes). Both are important for all young children to possess if they are to become successful readers. Whereas phonological and phonemic awareness just involve sound, phonics involves learning the relationship between letters and the sounds they represent. The instructional sequence now recommended by research is to begin by helping children build the basic concepts of phonological awareness, then to move toward helping children develop awareness that words are composed of phonemes, and

SPECIAL FEATURE 7.2

Standardized Assessment of Young Children

Karen Burstein

During the past twenty years, assessment of young children has assumed increased prominence, as seen in No Child Left Behind's emphasis on yearly testing. Today early childhood teachers are frequently expected to administer and interpret multiple standardized tests as well as conduct informal evaluations of children across the year. The notion of testing young children evokes passionate debate among teachers and scholars. To some it provides reliable measures for examining programs and attainment of standards; to others it conjures up negative images of subjecting children to trying experiences of questionable value. That said, there continues to be a push to test children in order to track their progress in preschool. What are early childhood educators to do?

Because early childhood educators are being asked to systematically observe, record, and conduct standardized assessments in their classrooms, a basic understanding of the types of tests and their limitations is important, as is familiarity with the language of assessment. The Early Childhood Education Assessment section of the Council of Chief State Schools Officers coordinated the aggregation of a Web-based glossary of common language around assessment and standards (www.ccsso.org/projects). This is a useful resource for teachers trying to navigate the maze of federal and state testing requirements.

REASONS FOR TESTING

As assessments of young children are increasing, teachers and scholars ask why. The driving force behind assessment lies in the results: what information does the assessment yield? Who can use it? What is the benefit to the child? There are four primary reasons for assessment (Shepard, Kagan, & Wurtz, 1998):

1. *Accountability*—Districts/schools are compared across communities, and the question posed is whether they are achieving state standards or benchmarks. For this purpose, early childhood programs are likely to be using Dynamic Indicators of Basic Early Literacy Skills (DIBELS), its preschool counterpart *Get It Got It Go* (Individual Growth and Development Indicators) and AIMS Web. These are standardized, individually teacher-administered measures of early reading skills that are responsive to the implementation of teaching methods consistent with scientifically based reading research. These tests provide districts and schools with benchmark information and teachers with child-specific skills attainment.

The instruments are administered approximately three times annually and yield results on children's acquisition of skills in sound (phonemic awareness), alphabet, letter, vocabulary, and oral reading fluency

2. *Identify children who are not benefiting from instruction and refer for special education or additional services*—Since the implementation of IDEA (formerly P.L. 94-142) in 1975, the most common reason for administering standardized assessments to young children is to assist in determining children's eligibility for special services. These tests include standardized measures of IQ, such as the Wechsler Preschool and Primary Scale of Intelligence (WPPSI) or the Stanford-Binet Intelligence Scales for Early Childhood (Early SB5), and measures of different areas of child development such as the Vineland Social-Emotional Early Childhood Scales and Peabody Picture Vocabulary Test-III. All of these tests are individually administered and some require special training or advanced credentials to administer and interpret. Students' raw scores are usually converted into standard scores that fall along a continuum that allows for comparisons of individuals to a "normal" distribution of same-age children. They typically do not indicate academic strengths or weaknesses and generally do not help teachers develop instructional plans. The advantage of standardized assessments is that they expedite the process of determining eligibility for special services. However, important educational decisions should be based on multiple sources of information including observations, work samples, and family interviews.

3. *Program evaluation and progress monitoring*—One of the most prevalent and high-profile models of program evaluation is the Head Start National Reporting System (NRS). Early in 2003, the Bush administration announced its intention to require all four- and five-year-olds in the federal Head Start program to be assessed at the beginning and end of each program year. The NRS assessments are standardized and measure a limited set of skills that include expressive and receptive English vocabulary, uppercase letter naming, early math skills such as number identity and simple addition and subtraction. Teachers administer the NRS, but it is scored by an external organization that sends reports of overall program outcomes to Head Start and local administrations. It is important to understand that the primary focus of the NRS is the overall progress that groups of children make in each Head Start program. The NRS is not designed to assess the school readiness of individual children (Head Start In Focus, April 2003).

(continued on next page)

SPECIAL FEATURE 7.2 *(continued)*

Programs can also be evaluated at the local level. For example, all Early Reading First projects are required to have an evaluation plan to measure their effectiveness in boosting pre-K children's school readiness. The Arizona Centers of Excellence in Early Education (ACE[3]), discussed earlier in this book, developed an evaluation model that included semiannual administration of a battery of standardized assessments, semi-monthly systematic classroom observations, and weekly curriculum-based measurements. Many adequate "skills-specific" measures exist, so assessments were selected based on reliability and validity reported by test publishers and the test "fit" with the population of children being assessed (i.e., the populations were represented in the norming samples). A team of local substitute teachers were trained to be the examiners. The ACE[3] assessment battery provided the following information about each child: an English Language Fluency level, a baseline of initial sounds and rhymes, areas of competence in print awareness, a measure of receptive vocabulary, and the number and names of the letters recognized. Upon completion of the battery, teachers received the ACE Preschool Continuum of Progress (see Figure 7.5), an easy-to-understand summary of each child's assessment results and a set of graphs of overall class results. Parents were provided with similar information and, at the end of the year, an exit summary of their child's skills in each area.

4. *Inform teachers of students' instructional needs—* From the teacher's perspective, the most important reason for assessment is to obtain accurate information about the instructional needs of their students. The assess-plan-teach model of instruction directs teachers to:

■ know the content of the Early Childhood Education Standards in their community;
■ align their classroom curriculum to these standards;
■ assess each child's skill attainment on these standards;
■ plan instruction that is responsive to children's assessed needs and skills;
■ deliver instruction that explicitly targets needs; and
■ reassess to ensure that children are learning the content that was delivered.

Within this model, assessment is a critical step in good instruction. As the call for assessment has increased, there are now a plethora of measures covering a myriad of skills. Even curriculum developers have begun to develop standardized measures aligned with their materials. However, the vast majority of standardized assessments are limited in their scope and number of items. Couple this limitation with the dramatic developmental variations in young children and one can begin to understand the consequences of trying to use standardized assessments to fully inform teachers of the needs of their students. Teachers need specific information from multiple models of assessment in order to develop effective plans and activities for their classes. Each teacher's skill repertoire should include not only standardized assessment but knowledge about child development and strong skills in observation techniques, work sampling, parent interviewing and collaboration, curriculum alignment, and curriculum-based measurement (see Special Feature 7.1).

finally to help children develop awareness of letter–sound associations. Therefore, the **instructional sequence is from broad concepts to smaller and smaller units of sound.**

■ *How might early childhood teachers introduce young children to the letters of the alphabet?*
We recommend that early childhood teachers use a combination approach to alphabet instruction. They should used "personalized" instruction to teach their young learners the names of the letters that match specific children's current interests and activities. For example, children can be taught to **recognize letters in their names, friends' names, familiar environmental print, and print used in play settings.** In order to deliver this type of individualized alphabet instruction, teachers need to observe closely to learn about the types of contexts in which children notice letters. Teachers should also teach the alphabet to the whole class in a systematic way, using songs, letter charts, ABC word walls, and games. This combination of **personalized** instruction and **direct, systematic** instruction will ensure that all children have an opportunity to learn to identify and name the letters of the alphabet.

■ *How can early childhood teachers reassure the public that they are teaching phonics?*
Some children seem to learn phonics on their own; teachers need to provide them with numerous meaningful reading and writing activities that will allow them to discover

SPECIAL FEATURE 7.2 *(continued)*

FIGURE 7.5	ACE Preschool Continuum of Progress

ACE Preschool Continuum of Progress: Niño at a glance!

Child Name _____   Program Year _____

Teacher: _____   Center/Site: _____

The purpose of this form is to assist parents and teachers to make appropriate educational goals for children enrolled in the ACE program and to track progress across the school year. It concludes with a summary and end of the year report to families.

Curriculum Based Assessment Results (initial, midyear, end of year)

Letter Identification   1) _____ 2) _____ 3) _____

Initial Sounds (alliteration)   1) _____ 2) _____ 3) _____

Rhyming   1) _____ 2) _____ 3) _____

Get Ready to Read   1) _____ 2) _____ 3) _____

CBM Quarterly   1- Letter name) _____ Show Me) _____ Tell Me) _____ Alliteration) _____

                2- Letter name) _____ Show Me) _____ Tell Me) _____ Alliteration) _____

                3- Letter name) _____ Show Me) _____ Tell Me) _____ Alliteration) _____

                4- Letter name) _____ Show Me) _____ Tell Me) _____ Alliteration) _____

Developmental Assessment (name) _____ Brief Summary _____

_____

_____

Summary of teacher observations and anecdotal records _____

_____

_____

_____

Parent Goals (What the parent wants the child to work on during the program year): _____

_____

_____

_____

IEG Individual Education Goals: _____

    1) _____

    2) _____

Goals from IEP to be supported in the classroom: _____

_____

Monthly Explorations/Theme:

September _____

Circle each of the letter names that the child has learned. Letter names learned: F   M

Instructional Modifications: 0) no modification necessary   1) modify classroom   2) more instruction

        3) more practice   4) more structured play   5) more parent involvement   6) other _____

Social development activities:

Activities sent home:

[Note: Page 2 contains reports on the remaining monthly explorations and themes, and Page 3 contains reports of the parent conferences that are conducted in the fall and spring.]

how our language works. Other children need some phonics instruction; teachers need to offer them the same kind of meaningful reading and writing activities and also need to draw children's attention to letter–sound relationships present in these activities—not once, but often. Teachers need to be alert to teachable moments for drawing children's attention to letter–sound relationships in many reading and writing activities. Remember, phonics instruction is appropriate only when children exhibit phonological and phonemic awareness.

■ *Why are standardized tests heavily used in the SBRR approach?*

The SBRR approach places heavy emphasis on using reliable and valid assessment procedures. Conditions and directions are always the same whenever a standardized test is administered. Each student taking the test hears the same directions, is given same test items, and has the same amount of time. This "standardization" helps to increase the reliability of the assessment.

LINKING KNOWLEDGE TO PRACTICE

1. Create descriptions of several developmentally appropriate phonological awareness activities, from the most basic concepts to the more advanced, that might be used with young children. Make copies of your activities for others in your class.
2. Create descriptions of several developmentally appropriate phonemic awareness activities for use with young children. Make copies of your activities for others in your class.
3. Create a description of several developmentally appropriate alphabet recognition activities for use with young children. Make copies of your activities for others in your class.
4. The use of standardized tests has increased dramatically in recent years. Search your state's Web site or contact a school district for information on required state reading assessments. Contact a local Head Start for information on the mandatory twice-yearly testing of Head Start children.

Teaching Early Writing

When Carol was three and four, she lived in California, and her beloved Grammy lived in Minnesota. Whenever her mother wrote home, Carol wrote to her grandmother. When she had completed her letter, her mother always asked, "And what did you tell Grammy?" Carol pointed to the scribbles on the page, every scribble, and eagerly told her mother exactly what the letter said. Her mother listened intently, always ending with, "And you wrote all that?" Later, her clever mother inserted a slip of paper into the envelope telling Grammy the gist of Carol's message. Grammy's response to Carol's letter always arrived within a week or two. Carol and her mother snuggled together on the overstuffed green sofa to read Grammy's letter, over and over. When her daddy came home from work, Carol met him with "It's a Grammy letter day!" Then, she'd "read" Grammy's letter to her daddy.

Proponents of emergent literacy contend that children learn written language just like oral language. That is, children learn to read and write simply by having opportunities to see print in use and by engaging in activities where literacy is embedded in the task, just like Carol did in the vignette above. These people believe that children learn without ever knowing they are learning. This view supports the implicit teaching of literacy. Other educators believe that children need instruction to help them focus on the abstract features of our written language, like on letter names and sounds. This perspective supports the explicit teaching of literacy and is consistent with the newer view of literacy learning, the scientifically based reading research (SBRR) view. We believe both views hold merit. Children do need opportunities to see writing in use and to experience the purposes of literacy. Children also need to be directly taught about the functions and features of print. The key is that the activities and experiences that early childhood teachers offer young children must be appropriate for the children's age and stage.

In Chapters 3 through 7 we present the core components of a blended early childhood language and literacy program:

- multiple language opportunities for children in various classroom contexts (e.g., circle time, learning centers, dramatic play, and language-centered activities) (Chapter 3);
- response to teachers' questions (Chapter 3);
- sharing of ideas in daily storybook reading by the teacher (Chapter 4);
- opportunities for children to attempt to read books on their own in the library center (Chapter 4);
- opportunities to respond to books that are read (Chapter 4);
- functional reading and writing activities (Chapter 6);
- literacy activities linked to play (Chapter 6);
- language experience or shared writing activities (Chapter 6); and
- activities designed to explicitly teach early reading skills (e.g., phonological awareness, alphabet letter and sound knowledge) (Chapter 7).

Though some children seem to learn to write simply by engaging in meaningful writing activities, all children profit from some explicit instruction.

This chapter focuses on one other key component of a high-quality early literacy program: writing instruction. In this chapter we describe several effective means for teaching children about writing: the writing center, writing workshop, and publication.

BEFORE READING THIS CHAPTER, THINK ABOUT . . .

■ How you learned to write. Not handwrite, but write. Do you remember writing messages to special people, maybe messages that were lines and lines of scribble? Do you remember writing on walls, much to someone's dismay?

FOCUS QUESTIONS

■ What are the key features of children's development as writers?
■ Why is a writing center an important area in the preschool classroom? How might an adult teach in the writing center?
■ How does a teacher teach during a writing workshop?
■ Why is it important to publish children's writing?
■ What writing skills do states suggest young children should demonstrate by the end of the preschool years? How might teachers gather information on their children's acquisition of these skills?

Children's Development as Writers

How do children become writers? Lesley Morrow (2005, pp. 206–207) reviewed the early writing development literature and summarized her findings in seven key features:

◆ *"Children's early literacy experiences are embedded in the familiar situations and real-life experiences of family and community."*
Reread this chapter's opening vignette. Carol learned about letter writing by watching her mother write to Carol's grandmother. In everyday family activity, Carol's mother wrote for other purposes: grocery lists, reminder notes, telephone messages, invitations, and more. Carol watched, learned about the purposes of writing, and occasionally wrote her own lists, notes, messages, and invitations.

BOX 8.1	**functions of writing:** writing for different purposes (e.g., writing to remember by preparing a list or a phone message; writing to control by writing a traffic ticket)
Definition of Terms	**focus lesson:** whole-class lessons on writing that typically occur at the beginning of writing workshop
	writing center: special area in the classroom stocked with writing materials and tools
	writing workshop: scheduled time for writing, with the explicit teaching of something about writing in a focus lesson, writing time, and a group share time

◆ *"Early writing development is characterized by children's moving from playfully making marks on paper, to communicating messages on paper, to creating text."*

Karen and Marika are playing in the restaurant play setting in the dramatic play center. Marika is the waitress, with writing pad in hand. Karen, reading the menu, points and says that she wants a hamburger. Marika writes a line of linear scribble. Dashing to the chef, she shouts, "That customer wants a hangaburger, and she wants it right now." She tears the writing from the pad and tosses it aside. Her oral language carried the message, not the marks on the paper. Later in the choice time, Marika works at writing a message to her mother. Karen has invited her for a "play date." The teacher had prepared a "dictionary" of all the children in the class. Each page has a picture of a classmate with his or her name beneath it. Marika uses this resource to copy Karen's name. She asks her teacher, "How do you spell *house*?" The teacher helps her stretch the word to hear the sounds. Marika writes HS. Satisfied that her mother will know what this means, she carefully folds the paper and puts it in her backpack. Clearly, this writing is meant to communicate a message. Note how the context affects Marika's writing.

◆ *"Children learn the uses of written language before they learn the forms."*

The form of the writing refers to letter formation, spelling, and so forth. Carol wrote in an early form (linear scribble) to tell her grandmother what she had been doing in California. Marika wrote in an early form in the play context (linear scribble) and a more advanced form (invented or phonics-based spelling) in the writing center to tell her mother about a play date with Karen. Carol and Marika demonstrated that they are learning about the functions of written language, even though they cannot yet produce the form conventionally.

◆ *"Children's writing develops through constant invention and reinvention of the forms of written language."*

Children's early experimentations with print are mindful of their babblings in oral language. Listen closely and a mother is certain she hears her baby say "Mama." Look closely and a teacher will be sure she sees a correctly formed letter in a child's letterlike writing. When the adult, mother or teacher, responds enthusiastically to the child's invention, the child responds enthusiastically—and begins to try again. The rich context around the children in a print- and language-rich society and adults' positive response both work to shape the children's inventions, oral or written, toward speaking and writing in the language of the society in which they live.

◆ *"Children learn about writing through explicit instruction from teachers, and by observing others more skilled than themselves."*

The opening vignette shows how Carol learned about sending written messages by observing her mother. Marika learned how to write her message to her mother with explicit instruction from her teacher, who sat beside her in the writing center and helped her match sounds with the correct symbols. Both kinds of instruction are needed: the explicit instruction of teaching a writing skill and the implicit instruction of observing others who know more engage in a writing event.

◆ *"Children need to write independently."*

Quality early-childhood writing programs provide many opportunities for children to write independently. Inserting writing tools (paper and writing implements) into all classroom centers, not just the writing center, provides children with many opportunities to use what they know about the forms of written language to create a message.

◆ *"Children need to write in social settings."*

But writing independently does not mean writing alone. Writing is a social act. Through interactions with others, children come to understand the needs of their audience. Through interactions with others, children learn how to spell words, what to write about, the purposes writing might serve, where to look in the classroom for help spelling a word. They copy what their peers or teachers are doing. So early childhood teachers need to arrange the classroom environment in ways that support each child writing independently but writing with the support of more knowledgeable others, teachers and peers.

These seven research-based features guide our recommendations on the design of a high-quality writing program in early childhood classrooms.

Even the youngest of children like to write—not only on paper, but also on walls and floors. Early childhood teachers, then, must take advantage of this natural urge by providing a variety of writing materials to their young writers, learning to ask the right question at the right time and providing the right instruction at the right time to nudge their young writers' development. Early childhood teachers need to provide children with many opportunities to experiment with creating their text for many different purposes. In the following section, we explore the what and the how of writing instruction in an early childhood classroom.

The Context for Writing: The Writing Center

A writing center is a special area in the classroom that is stocked with materials that invite children to write. When setting up such a center, teachers need to remember that writing is a social act. Children want to share their writing with peers, to know what their peers are writing, to ask for assistance with the construction of their text. "Morning. How do you spell 'morororornnn-nnninggg'?" Knowing children's need for talk while writing, teachers typically provide a table and chairs in the writing center.

Gather the Needed Materials

In addition to a table and chairs, teachers stock the writing center with materials that invite children to write, to play with writing materials. Such materials include but are not limited to the following:

■ many different kinds of paper (e.g., lined theme paper, typical story paper, discarded computer or office letterhead paper with one side clean, lots of unlined paper, paper cut into different shapes to suggest writing about particular topics, paper folded and made into blank books, stationery and envelopes, cards);

■ various writing tools (e.g., pencils, markers—be certain to purchase the kind that can withstand the kind of pressure young children exert as they write—crayons, felt-tip pens, a computer or computers with a word-processing program);

■ writing folders for storage of each child's writing efforts;

■ an alphabet chart at the children's eye level and in easy view from all chairs; and

■ a box or file drawer in which to store the file folders.

Notice that oversized (fat) pencils and special primary-lined paper were not recommended as the only paper and pencils to be provided. For young children, Miriam Martinez and Bill Teale (1987) recommend unlined paper because it does not signal how writing is supposed to be done. Children are freer to use the emergent forms of writing—pictures used as writing, scribble writing, letterlike forms, and so on—that do not fit on the lines of traditional lined writing paper or story paper (e.g., top half blank, bottom half lined).

In addition to these required items, many teachers include the following items in their classroom writing center:

■ a bulletin board for displaying such items as samples of the children's writing, examples of different forms of writing (e.g., thank you notes, letters, postcards, stories), writing-related messages (e.g., "Here's our grocery list"), messages about writing (e.g., "Look at this! Shawn's sister published a story in the newspaper"), and the children's writing;

■ posters showing people engaged in writing;

■ clipboards for children who want to write someplace other than at the table;

■ mailboxes (one for each child, the teacher, the principal or center director, and other appropriate persons, as determined by the children) to encourage note and letter writing;

■ alphabet strips on the writing table so that the children have a model readily available when they begin to attempt to link their knowledge of letter sounds with their knowledge of letter formations;

■ blank books made by placing two or three pieces of blank paper between two sheets of colored construction paper and stapled on one side, often cut in a shape that corresponds with the topic being studied (e.g., butterflies or tree when studying the environment, heart when studying the body);

■ card sets of special words (e.g., words relating to the topic being studied, classmate names, common words) made by writing a word on an index card and (when possible) attaching a picture of the word, punching a hole in the corner, and using a silver ring to hold the card set together;

■ dry-erase boards or magic slates;

■ letter stamps and letter pads; and

■ plastic, wooden, and/or magnetic letters and letter templates.

Mailboxes can be made in various ways. For example, they might be made from the large tin food cans available from the cafeteria. Kindergarten teacher Debbie Czapiga, a clever seamstress, made mailboxes for each child by sewing pockets of discarded jeans onto a colorful, stiff piece of fabric. She then attached the strip of fabric to the bottom of the chalkboard and labeled each pocket with a child's name.

Most teachers introduce the materials to the children gradually; that is, they do not place all these materials in the writing center on the first day of school, which young children would find overwhelming. They make the writing center new and exciting over the year by regularly adding new materials and tools.

Arrange the Materials

With so many different materials in the writing center, keeping the supplies orderly and replenishing them can be time consuming. Some teachers label the places where the various tools and paper belong in the writing center; this helps all the children know where to return used materials and it helps a child "clerk" know how to straighten the center at cleanup time. Further, labeling the places where the items belong permits a quick inventory of missing and needed items. Figure 8.1 provides an illustration of a well-equipped, well-arranged writing center.

Computers and Word Processing

A growing number of early childhood classrooms have computers in the writing center. Teachers in these classrooms are indeed fortunate! So are the children in these classrooms. Doug Clemets and Julie Sarama (2003) summarized the research on young children and technology. In the language and reading area, they report that computers facilitate increased language use (children talk more to peers when they are at the computer than at other activities). Software programs can help children develop prereading skills also. In writing, children "using word processors write more, have fewer fine motor control problems, [and] worry less about making mistakes. Young children cooperatively plan, revise, and discuss spelling, punctuation, spacing, and text meaning and style" (pp. 36–37). Notice the two chairs in front of each computer. This arrangement encourages increased talk between peers. Technology expert Patricia Scott highly recommends the following software packages for their user-friendly qualities; that is, young children can easily use them to write: *Orly's Draw-a-Story, Claris for Kids,* and *The Writing Center* (the new and improved version). Some older favorites include *Kid Works 2* (Davidson), *Storybook Weaver* (MECC), *Wiggins in Storybook Land,* and *The Incredible Writing Machine* (The Learning Company).

FIGURE 8.1 A Well-Equipped Writing Center

Marilyn Cochran-Smith, Jessica Kahn, and Cynthia Paris (1986) point out that all writers, regardless of age, require time at the computer when their attention is focused on learning word-processing skills. For example, Bev Winston, a kindergarten teacher, introduced her young students to word processing during the school's orientation days, those days that precede the first full day of school. Then she watched her children as they played with word processing during their free-play time and provided instruction as each child needed it. Word processing is a tool to preserve children's important first writings. It is important for teachers to keep this in mind. Young children need time to experiment with this tool just as children need time to experiment with pencils, pens, markers, and so forth.

Writing in Other Centers

Earlier we suggested that every center in the classroom should be literacy enriched. Every center should have print materials (e.g., books, magazines, pamphlets) connected with the topic under investigation available for the children's use. In addition, every center should include props to support the children's writing explorations (e.g., paper and writing implements). Miriam Smith's and David Dickinson's (2002) Literacy Environment Checklist asks "Are there writing tools in the dramatic play and block area? Are there props that prompt children to write in the dramatic play and block area?" When classrooms are assessed with the Early Language and Literacy Classroom Observation Toolkit, they earn points when the rater responds with a yes to these questions.

When every center has writing tools, children can use writing to achieve a variety of purposes and practice using the form of writing (linear scribble, phonics-based spellings) that serves their need at the moment. In the science center, for example, teachers should provide forms to encourage children's recording of their scientific observations. Addie, a delightful four-year-old, was studying the life cycle of the butterfly when we met her. Because paper and writing tools were available, she recorded her discovery (see Figure 8.2). (After we requested a copy of her writing for publication in this book, she made poster copies of her discovery for

FIGURE 8.2   Life Cycle of a Butterfly by Addie

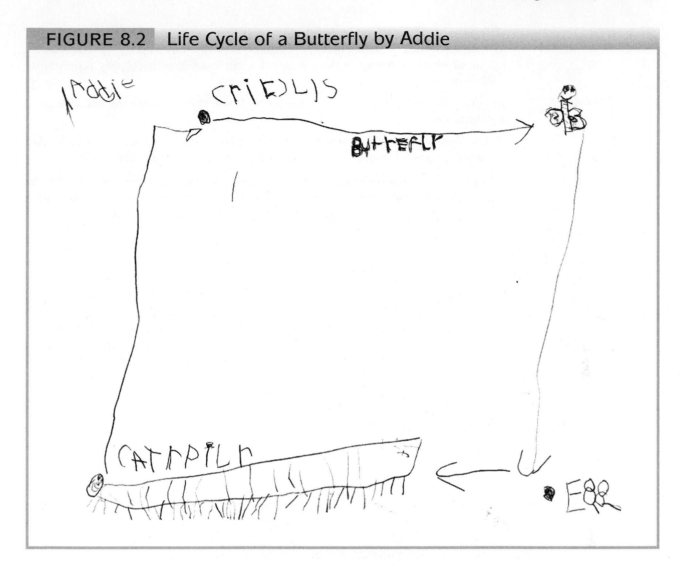

every person in her neighborhood.) Writing tools in the library center encourage children to use books as models for their writing. See, for example, Allen's story in Figure 4.1, modeled on Eric Carle's *The Very Hungry Caterpillar*. When blue paper and writing tools were available in the block center, children made "blueprints" of the building they intended to construct, labeling the rooms. The blueprints that lined the walls of the block center during the construction unit provided a model for the children's drawing and writing. Using paper in the math center, children in Eileen Feldgus and Isabel Cardonick's (1999, p. 72) classrooms made bar graphs to illustrate their classmates' answer to a question (e.g., "Have you ever had a cast?"), wrote their observations of different objects' weight, and recorded their guesses of how many objects were in a jar. (Chapter 6 in their book contains numerous suggestions for engaging children in writing across the curriculum.) Clearly, putting writing tools at children's fingertips allowed them to use those tools for multiple purposes.

The Writing Workshop

The writing workshop was first described by Donald Graves (1983) in his book *Writing: Teachers and Children at Work*. All members of the writing workshop meet to intensively study the art and craft of writing. The workshop typically has the following components:

◆ *Focus lesson*—A five-minute lesson to teach children about the writing process ("I want to make a change in my writing. I'm going to *revise*. Here's how I'll do it."); a procedural aspect of the writing program ("We help our friends while they write. We say things like,

'Tell me more about your dog. What color is he?'"); a quality of good writing ("I can tell more about my dog by adding his color, black. So I'll write 'I hv a blk dg.'"); a mechanical feature of writing ("Always make *I* a capital, a big letter."); or about why people write ("We need to make a list.").

♦ *Writing*—A ten- to fifteen-minute period during which children write and talk with peers and the teacher.

♦ *Group share*—A ten-minute period during which one or two children read their writing pieces to the group and receive positive feedback and content-related questions.

While the writing workshop was originally designed for the elementary grades, it can be easily adapted for use with younger children. Here is an example of how one kindergarten teacher has used the workshop approach to help her students develop as writers.

Focus Lessons

Focus lessons are short lessons that explicitly teach the children about an aspect of writing. Kindergarten teacher Bernadette Watson uses focus lessons to teach her students how to match letter sounds with the correct letter symbols. In one lesson, she helped the children sound out the spellings of the words in the sentence "I went to New York." She stretched the words out (e.g., w-e-n-t) and focused the children's attention on the sound of each letter ("What letter makes the /w/ sound?) or letter cluster ("How about /ent/?). See Trade Secrets 8.1 for a description of this focus lesson. Because she knows that her students would not fully understand the relationship between sounds and symbols as a result of one lesson, Ms. Watson weaves the content of this lesson into many lessons and reinforces this understanding when she talks with her young writers about their writing.

Writing Time

The focus lesson is followed by a time for the children to write. While the children write, the teacher meets with the young writers about their writing. The opportunity to talk while writing is a critical component of writing workshop. The talk is about the content and the mechanics (usually the letter–sound relationships) of the piece. Through conferences, teachers can give one-on-one instruction, providing the child with just the right help needed at that minute.

TRADE SECRETS 8.1

Teaching about Sound–Symbol Relationships: An Invented Phonics-based Spelling Focus Lesson

Bernadette Watson

Teacher: I didn't tell you this before. I went on a trip to New York this weekend. The New York Marathon (the running race) was on this weekend, so there was a lot of traffic! It took us a long time to get to New York. That's what I'm going to write about today. I'm going to start by drawing a picture. I'll just draw a road. That will help me remember what I'm going to write about. [Teacher draws a road.]

I'm going to write "I went to New York City." Will you help me write the words? "I" Oh, that's an easy one. [Writes "I"] W-e-n-t [stretches word]. "w"-"w"-"w."

Child: "Y."

Teacher: It does sound like a "Y." We'll use "Y" for that sound. E-N-T.

Children: "N!" "N!" [Teacher writes *N*.]

Teacher: W-E-N-T-T-T

Children: "T!" [Teacher writes "T."]

Teacher: to

Child: I know how to spell to—"t" "o."

Teacher: How do you know that?

Child: I don't know. I just do. [Teacher writes to.]

Teacher: [Reads, I went "to."] New. "N"-"N"-"N."

Child: It's like my name. *N*

. . . and so on.

Group Share Time

The workshop is culminated by group share time. During the group share session, two or three children sit, one at a time, in the author's chair and share their pieces with the other writers in the class. Typically, the other children are gathered at the sharing writer's feet, listening attentively while the writer reads the piece, preparing to make comments or ask questions. The following describes one group share in Ms. Bernadette Watson's kindergarten classroom:

> *Demetri:* "I like your story."
>
> *Ms. Watson:* "Remember, Demetri, when we talked about how we tell the writer what we really liked about his or her story? Can you tell Aaron what you liked about his story?"
>
> *Demetri:* "I really liked the part where you thought you would get a dog, because I want a dog, too."
>
> *Aaron:* "Thanks."

The classroom rule is that the writer calls on three children for a question or a comment. The first response is a comment. The other two must be questions. Ms. Watson uses this time to help her children begin to understand the difference between a comment (statement or sentence) and a question. Learning the difference takes lots of practice.

Aaron calls on another child, Luisa, for a question.

> *Luisa:* "Did you draw your picture and write, or write and draw your picture?"
>
> *Aaron:* "I drew the pictures and then wrote." [Aaron calls on Bill.]
>
> *Bill:* "I know how to spell *to*. Do you?"

Aaron is unsure how to respond to Bill's question. He writes a string of letters with no match to letter sounds. According to Elizabeth Sulzby's categories of emergent writing, Aaron's writing is representative of the nonphonetic letter strings (see Chapter 5, pages 108–110, for a description).

Ms. Watson understands his confusion and comes to his rescue. She asks, "Bill, can you write *to* on the chart paper for us? [Bill eagerly displays what he knows.] Listen to Aaron's sentence. *I want to get a dog.* Count the number of words in Aaron's sentence." Ms. Watson says the sentence and raises a finger for each word. I want to get a dog. [Children respond correctly.] What Bill is saying is that Aaron's third word, I want *to,* is written *t-o*. Should we add that to our word wall? Then you can look at the word wall when you need to write the word *to* in your sentences. [She takes a three- by five-inch card, writes *to* on the card, and ceremoniously adds it to the classroom word wall.] Thanks so much, Aaron and Bill. We learned about Aaron's hope for a birthday present and how to write the word *to* today. Who else would like to share?"

Through group shares, young children learn that writing is meant to be shared with others. Writers write to communicate their thoughts and ideas with their readers. Young children also learn about the how of sharing with others (reading in a loud voice so others can hear, holding their writing so others can see) and about the difference between a question and a comment. Teachers use children's texts and questions and comments as a context to teach about writing.

Some teachers bring a chair unlike any other in the room into the classroom (e.g., a stool, a rocker, a stuffed chair) to serve as the author's chair. When the children or the teacher read to the group, the reader sits in this special chair.

Bernadette Watson's writing workshop is not unlike that described by Eileen Feldgus and Isabell Cardonick in their book, *Kid Writing: A Systematic Approach to Phonics, Journals, and Writing Workshop* (1999). Richard Allington wrote the introduction to their book. We quote from Allington's comments on the power of the writing workshop approach and the key literacy strategies embedded in it.

> . . . these exemplary teachers offered effective strategy teaching that developed children's understanding of the alphabetic principle. . . . First, the exemplary teachers typically worked to

develop phonemic segmentation, letter-sound associations, and onset-rime knowledge in the context of children's meaningful attempts to compose written messages. . . . Second, these exemplary teachers taught decoding skills and strategies contextually—drawing from the texts children had written or selected to read. . . . Third, these exemplary teachers taught directly and systematically.

(Feldgus and Cardonick, 1999, p. ix)

As Allington notes, the skills and strategies teachers explicitly teach in writing workshop not only help young children construct written texts, but also help them decode words. In Trade Secrets 8.2, we describe how one kindergarten teacher uses Kid Writing in her kindergarten classroom.

Ms. Emerson's students write, share, and publish. Ms. Emerson celebrates what they can do, verbalizing that they are doing ("Oh, you made a capital *B* there, didn't you?), and seems always to be telling the children what good writers they are. She claims that nothing she does is "original"; she borrowed all her ideas from Feldgus and Cardonick. She encourages every teacher of young children to use Kid Writing. Kindergarten students can write, and the children in her classroom prove the accuracy of her belief.

Journals and Interactive Forms of Writing

Teachers want to provide young children with opportunities to write for many different purposes and to use different forms (or modes) of writing. Maggie Murphy modeled writing a letter (a form or mode) to stay in contact with people (a purpose) in the writing center. Nancy Edwards demonstrated writing a list (a form or mode) to help her remember (a purpose) in a writing workshop group lesson. In this section, we describe three kinds of writing that are particularly beneficial for beginning writers: journals, dialogue writing, and pen pals.

TRADE SECRETS 8.2

Kid Writing

The children in Ginny Emerson's kindergarten classroom are writers. Several years ago Ms. Emerson "converted" to Eileen Feldgus and Isabell Cardonick's (1999) Kid Writing program. As Feldgus and Cardonick suggest, Ms. Emerson introduces her children to written language through journal writing in a writing workshop format.

This classroom is rich with functional print. Ms. Emerson pays particular attention to posting words that the children might need in their writing. For example, the light switches are labeled *Up* and *Down*. The attendance chart is labeled *Boys* and *Girls*, with space for the children to sign in each day. The inside of the classroom door is labeled *Inside*; the outside is labeled *Outside*. Ms. Emerson often reminds the children to use the classroom print as a resource, asking, for example, "Where can you find the word *outside* in our classroom?" There is a word wall. The categories are letters of the alphabet. The words listed are high-frequency words, arranged alphabetically. Words are added to the "Words We Use a Lot" word wall as Ms. Emerson introduces them during minilessons (what some people call focus lessons).

Ms. Emerson watches her young writers to learn what minilessons they need. When she noticed that the children often needed the /ing/ sound in their writing,

she followed the Kid Writing authors' suggestion and made a crown with /ing/ written on it. Each day during the writing workshop, a child is assigned to be the "King of /ing/." The child proudly wears the /ing/ crown. When the young writers want to write "shopping" or "going," they use the King of /ing/ to help them remember how to write /ing/. The "Star of are" wears a hat with a star and the word *are* written on it. There is also a "Wiz of is" moving about the classroom.

All this activity, of course, comes after Ms. Emerson gets her Kid Writing program going, shortly after the first day of school. To kick off the program, she follows the description of the first day of writing found in Kid Writing (p. 33). She demonstrates for the children different ways of writing, from wavy lines to zigzag writing to magic lines to letterlike forms that resemble alphabet letters to alphabet letters. The children "write" in the air. With every stroke they make, Ms. Emerson reinforces what they know with encouragement such as, "You are such great wavy-line writers!" She follows this lesson with a lesson on using a sound (the first, most prominent sound) to write a word. Many subsequent lessons help children stretch out words, listening to the sounds, much like Bernadette Watson's focus lesson. Other lessons, for example, teach children how to use a dash as a placeholder for a word they cannot spell or about using rime to help them spell.

Journals

Traditionally journals have been used to focus on personal expression and learning. Children write to themselves about what is happening in their lives in and out of school, the stories they are reading, and what they are learning in different subject areas. The writer is his or her own audience. The text might be pictures and writing, or just pictures, or just print.

Kindergarten teacher Phoebe Ingraham describes several kinds of journal writing that her kindergartners use for many different purposes.

- *Creative journals*—Children develop their ideas into pictures and words so that they can be kept forever on the pages of the journal.
- *Literature response journals*—Children write about their favorite books.
- *Literacy journals, theme journals, and learning logs*—Children record observations, questions, and insights to make important links between what they already know and what they are learning.

Dialogue Writing

By the time children are four or five years old, most have become quite proficient at oral dialogue. Teachers can capitalize on this strength by engaging children in written conversations (Watson, 1983). In written conversations, the teacher and child use shared writing paper or dialogue journals to take turns writing to each other and reading each other's comments. This strategy makes children's writing more spontaneous and natural by helping them see the link between written and oral language. In addition, the teacher serves as an authentic audience of children's writing, providing motivation for engaging in the writing process.

The teacher initiates these written conversations by writing brief messages to each student, who in turn reads what the teacher has written and writes a response back to the teacher. The teacher then reads these responses and writes additional comments, and this continues in a chainlike fashion.

Teachers usually begin by making declarative statements about personal experiences rather than by asking children questions. Questions have a tendency to result in brief, stilted replies from children (similar to their oral responses to verbal interrogation by a teacher). For example,

> *Teacher:*   Did you do anything nice over the weekend?
> *Child:*   No.

On the other hand, when teachers write personal statements to the children, they respond more spontaneously. Nigel Hall and Rose Duffy (1987, p. 527) give the following example:

> *Teacher:*   I am upset today.
> *Child:*   What is the matr with you?
> *Teacher:*   My dog is sick. I took her to the vet, and he gave her some medicine.
> *Child:*   I hop she get betr sun did the medsn wok?

Obviously, it is helpful if children can use legible forms of invented spelling to write their messages. However, this strategy can be used even with children who are at the scribble or well-learned unit (random streams of letters) stage of early literacy. With these children, a brief teacher–child conference is needed so that children can read their personal script messages to the teacher.

Pen Pals

Once children get used to engaging in written conversations with their teachers, they will naturally want to engage in written exchanges with their peers. Miriam Martinez and Bill Teale (1987) describe how a "postal system/pen pal" program was successfully implemented in several

Texas early childhood classrooms. Children in the morning half-day classes wrote weekly letters to pen pals in the afternoon classes; children in full-day programs were assigned pen pals in other full-day program classrooms. Children were purposely paired with partners who used different writing strategies. For example, a scribble writer was matched with an invented speller. Letters were exchanged once a week and placed in mailboxes located in the writing center. A teacher or aide was at the center to assist in cases where children received letters they could not read. Teachers reported that student response was overwhelmingly positive. Here, real audiences and real purposes for writing are provided.

Publishing Children's Writing : *make writing/drawing public*

Brenda Power (1998) suggests several reasons why teachers should help young children publish their writing in books. Making their own books helps children learn:

■ to hold the book right side up and to turn the pages correctly;
■ that books have covers, titles, and authors;
■ letters and sounds through their writing of the book and how to decode words by reading their own words;
■ about the importance of an author and an illustrator to a book.

To publish with young children is to take their written texts and do something special with them. To publish is to make the writing public, to present it for others to read. There are many different ways to publish young children's writing. For example:

◆ Ask each child to bring a clear, plastic eight- by eleven-inch frame to school. (Of course, frames must be purchased for those children whose parents can not provide them.) Have the children publish their work by mounting their selected pieces, one at a time, in their frames. Hang the frames on the back wall of the classroom on a Wall of Fame.
◆ String a clothesline across the classroom. Using clothespins, clip the children's writings to the clothesline.
◆ Punch a hole in the upper left corner of several pages. All pages may be construction paper pages. If not, include a piece of colored construction paper or poster board on the top and bottom of the pile of pages for the book's cover. Thread string, yarn, or a silver ring through the hole to hold the book together.
◆ Ask each child to bring a light-colored T-shirt to school. (Again, teachers will need to provide T-shirts for children whose parents can not provide them.) Invite the children to use laundry marking pens and markers to write and illustrate their stories on their T-shirts.

◆ Purchase a low-cost photo album with large, stick-on plastic sleeves. (These can be found at discount stores and occasionally at flea markets or rummage and garage sales.) Place one page of each child's writing in one of the plastic sleeves. The same photo album can be used over and over as one piece of writing can be substituted for another piece of writing. Occasionally, all children might write on the same topic, and a class book might be created on this topic (e.g., a field trip to the apple orchard). Preserve these special books for the children's reading and rereading.
◆ While engaging in a special experience, take photographs of the children. Glue the pictures to pieces of colored construction paper. Ask each child to select a photo. Ask the child to write about the chosen picture on a piece of white paper. Cut the white paper into an interesting shape, and mount it on the construction paper below the photo. Laminate each page and put the pages together with spiral binding. (Teachers might wish to type and mount the conventionally spelled version of the child's writing on the paper along with the child's personal script. Be sure to include both versions of the writing. If a child's script is not included, the child writer often does not recognize the writing and cannot read the print.)
◆ Cover a large bulletin board with bright paper or fabric. In large cut-out letters, label the bulletin board something like "Young Authors" or "Room 101 Authors." Divide the bulletin board evenly into rectangular-shaped sections, one section for each child in the class, using yarn or felt-tipped marker. Label each section with a child's name. Encourage the children to mount one of their pieces of writing in their special section each week. A staple or pushpin might be used to mount the writing.

These are but a few of the many ways that children's writing might be published. We repeat: Publishing with young children means making their writing public—available for others to read. It is important to note that it is developmentally inappropriate to require young children to revise or recopy their writing, though sometimes they are willing to add to their text. Most young children do not have the attention span or interest to make revisions or to recopy the text.

If the child's writing is a personal script—that is, if it is a form of emergent writing that needs the child's reading for meaning to be constructed—the teacher might elect to include a conventionally spelled version of the message with the child's personal script version. As noted above, it is important to include the child's personal script version on the page with the conventionally spelled version to avoid taking ownership from the child.

Handwriting

So far, we have focused on providing young children with opportunities to write. What about handwriting? Drilling young children on how to form the letters of the alphabet correctly is a developmentally inappropriate practice. Forming letters correctly requires a good bit of manual dexterity, something most young children are developing. Teachers should provide young children with numerous opportunities to engage in activities that help develop their dexterity, like puzzles, sewing cards, table games, cutting, and drawing. Models of appropriately formed letters should be available for the children's reference. This means that teachers should correctly form the uppercase and lowercase letters when writing for and with the children, and an alphabet chart of uppercase and lowercase letters should be available at eye level for the children's use in the writing center. When children have achieved some control, the teacher might work one-on-one with the children. Since the letters in a child's name are the most important, the teacher might choose to begin instruction by helping the child correctly form these letters. Do not expect perfection, and be sure to keep the instruction playful.

If teachers of young children are to correctly form the upper- and lowercase letters, some may need directions on how to form letters. See Figure 8.3 for this assistance.

FIGURE 8.3

Zaner-Bloser Manuscript Alphabet

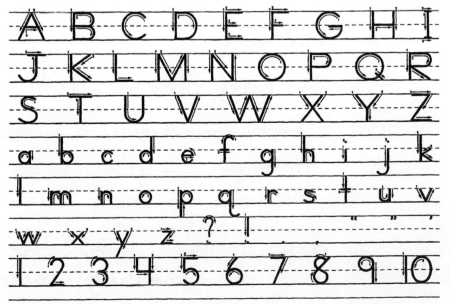

Zaner-Bloser Manuscript Alphabet

Assessment: Discovering What Children Know and Can Do

As we said in several earlier chapters, most states have established standards in literacy, indicators of what their young citizens need to know and be able to do when they enter kindergarten. These standards were developed through scientifically based research. In writing, states have identified a standard like that developed by early childhood educators in Virginia: Children will write using a variety of materials (www.pen.k12.va.us/VDOE/Instruction/Elem_M/Foundation Blocks.pdf). Following the statement of the standard, states identify the specific skills. See Figure 1.2 in Chapter 1 for Virginia's specific writing skills. Such state standards define the skills on which early childhood teachers should monitor their children's writing progress. Of course, the standards also guide early childhood educators' curriculum development and instruction.

We also said this before: The best, most authentic opportunities for assessing young children's literacy knowledge occur during normal classroom activities. When children write while they play in the literacy-enriched classroom centers or write during writing workshop, teachers can learn much about their children's written expression skills.

But watching while children engage in play in literacy-enriched classrooms or write during writing workshop is not enough; teachers also must make a record of their observations. What tools are available for teachers to gather information about their children's ongoing progress toward achieving the above skills and meeting the standard?

Anecdotal Notes

Head Start teachers in the Delaware Early Reading First project place four- by six-inch Post-it note paper in visible places around the room. As they (or other adults in the classroom) see a child engaged in writing, they write a quick description of the child's behavior. Figure 8.4 is an example of a Post-it note entry. After the children depart for the day, the teacher and assistants gather the Post-it notes and place them in the appropriate children's portfolio. (See Chapter 9 for information about portfolios.) Note how they label the note before placing it in the child's portfolio for the skill demonstrated.

Checklists

The most common writing checklist used in early childhood programs is a version of the early forms of writing scale readers read about in Figure 5.2. Several school districts and child care centers across the United States have transformed this continuum into a checklist for teachers

---

FIGURE 8.4

Sample Anecdotal Note

Antwon   5/17

Writing Center

Antwon drew a picture and wrote 'I lik Tabe Tigr. Where iz he?'

Copied 'where' from cards; used inventive spelling himself — no help.

FIGURE 8.5

Early Forms of Writing Developmental Checklist

Name _____

Forms of Writing	Date(s) Observed	In What Context (eg., dramatic play, writing center, science center)?
■ uses drawing (might be circular scribbles)	_____	_____
■ uses drawing and writing	_____	_____
■ uses linear scribble	_____	_____
■ uses letter-like shapes	_____	_____
■ uses random letters	_____	_____
■ uses invented spellings	_____	_____
■ uses conventional spellings	_____	_____

to use to track their children's progress toward conventional spelling. Figure 8.5 is an example of the checklist used by Delaware Early Reading First Head Start teachers. Each child has a checklist like this stored in his or her portfolio. In the lines to the right of the category, the teachers record the date on which they observed a child writing using one (or more) of the categories.

Summary

Whereas Chapters 5 and 6 describe activities that can implicitly teach children how to write and read, this chapter and Chapter 7 deal with explicit literacy instruction. This chapter described a variety of developmentally appropriate strategies that teachers can use to directly teach children how to write. What have you learned?

■ *What are the key features of children's development as writers?*

Lesley Morrow reviewed the early writing development literature and identified seven key features of children's development as writers: (a) Children's early literacy experiences are embedded in the familiar situation and real-life experiences of family and community; (b) Early writing development is characterized by children moving from playfully making marks on paper, to communicating messages on paper, to creating text; (c) Children learn the uses of written language before they learn the forms; (d) Children's writing develops through constant invention and reinvention of forms of written language; (e) Children learn about writing through explicit instruction from teachers and by observing others more skilled than themselves; (f) Children need to write independently; (g) Children need to write in social settings.

■ *Why is a writing center an important area in the preschool classroom? How might an adult teach in the writing center?*

A writing center is that area of the classroom where the teacher has stocked materials (different kinds of papers, various writing tools, alphabet strips, computers) that invite children to write. The teacher is an important other in the writing center. As a co-writer, the teacher writes alongside the children and models the writing process, informally teaching children about the forms (letters, thank-you notes) and features (spelling, letter formation) of print. As a skilled writer, the teacher can teach children as he or she writes by casually talking about letter–sound relationships, how to begin a letter, or what might be said in a letter.

■ *How does a teacher teach during a writing workshop?*

Each writing workshop begins with a focus lesson. The goal of these lessons is to teach children about some aspect of writing (e.g., how to make revisions; how to add describing words; how to spell words). The focus lesson is followed by writing time. During writing time, the teacher talks with individual children about their writing. Here, the teacher might help a child stretch words to hear sounds, add details to the child's drawing, or talk with the child about the topic of the piece. Through conferences, the teacher provides one-on-one instruction. After the writing time, two or three children share their work with their peers and the teacher. Now the teacher and the other children can ask questions about the writing.

■ *Why is it important to publish children's writing?*

Publishing helps young children understand that they write so others can read their thoughts. Making young children's writing efforts public is important. The publishing process need not be complicated.

■ *What writing skills do states suggest young children should demonstrate by the end of the preschool years? How might teachers gather information on their children's acquisition of these skills?*

Most states have established standards in literacy, indicators of what their young citizens need to know and be able to do when they enter kindergarten. Most states' standards include a written expression standard. Following the statement of the standard, states identify the specific skills young children must demonstrate, such as the following: Copy or write letters using various materials; print first name independently, in upper- and lowercase letters; print five to eight letters with a writing tool; copy three- to five-letter words; use inventive (phonics-based) spellings to convey messages or tell stories; and use writing for various purposes.

Teachers can use anecdotal notes, checklists, and performance sampling to gather information on their children's progress toward demonstrating these skills and meeting the standard.

LINKING KNOWLEDGE TO PRACTICE

1. Visit a classroom set up for three-year-olds and a classroom set up for five-year-olds in an early childhood center. Draw a diagram of each classroom's writing center and make a list of the writing materials the teacher has provided. Compare the materials in these classrooms' writing centers with the list of recommended materials on pages 168–169. Describe the differences between the writing center set up for three-year-olds and that set up for five-year-olds. Observe the classrooms' teachers as they interact with the children in the writing center. Describe what they talk about with the children.

2. Visit a kindergarten classroom during writing instruction time. How does what the teacher is doing compare with what you read in this chapter? Is the teacher implementing a writing workshop? What evidence is there that the children write regularly?

3. Visit your state's Department of Education Web site to obtain a copy of your state's pre-K language and literacy standards. You will need to search carefully because states label their standards using different terms (e.g., guidelines, foundations, building blocks). Do your state's standards for young children include an early writing standard? If so, what is it? How does the standard compare with what you have read in this chapter?

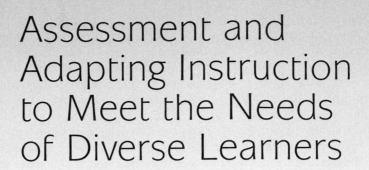

Assessment and Adapting Instruction to Meet the Needs of Diverse Learners

Mrs. Saenz is observing four-year-old Martine and Monique playing together in the post office center. The children are pretending to be post office people and are busy sorting letters into a mail sorter (a plastic office sorter that is divided into twenty-four slots, each labeled with an alphabet letter sticker). As she watches the children put the letters in the slots, Mrs. Saenz notices that Martine is accomplishing this task by recognizing the first letter of each name, then matching it to the appropriately labeled slot. She also notices that Monique, who is learning English, is simply putting the letters into the slots without paying any attention to the names on the envelopes. After a few moments, Martine stops Monique.

Martine: No, Monique. Look at the name. See the big letter? That letter tells you to put it in this mailbox.

Monique: What it say?

Martine: It says B. I think it is for Bobby. See? [He puts the letter in the B mailbox.]

Monique: Gimme. [She reaches for another letter.] What it say?

Martine: It says R.

Monique: [Thinking for a moment, she starts to sing the alphabet song. She puts her hand on each letter as she sings it.]

Martine: That helps find 'em fast, uh?

Mrs. Saenz carefully observes this interaction and makes brief anecdotal notes describing what Monique and Martine know and can do. This information will also help her to adjust instruction to better meet both children's learning needs.

In several of the preceding chapters we have presented strategies for implicit and explicit instruction in early literacy. While these instructional activities form the core of an effective language arts program, they cannot stand alone. Two other elements are needed to ensure that the instructional strategies meet the needs of every child in the class: assessment and adaptations of instruction for all children, particularly with linguistic diversity and special needs.

We begin this chapter by discussing the goals literacy professionals have identified as those that teachers should help their young learners meet. Then we consider the two general assessment approaches that teachers might use to gather information: ongoing or classroom assessment and on-demand or standardized assessment. We continue to believe in the power of ongoing classroom assessment and encourage teachers to use the various assessment strategies we have described in previous chapters. However, since the publication of the earlier edition of this book, standardized assessments have become increasingly prevalent across the country, even in early childhood education. Therefore, we also believe that teachers need to be familiar with standardized assessments. As the editors (Short, Schroeder, Kauffman, & Kaser, 2002, p. 1999) of *Language Arts* said in the issue focused on literacy testing, ". . . Educators can no longer afford to ignore these tests since the results are often used to make life-altering decisions about students and curriculum and to evaluate teachers and programs." In this chapter, we provide an overview of standardized assessment; details on the standardized assessments used to assess children's language and literacy learning can be found in Chapter 7. We end the chapter with two special features by colleagues. These authors present strategies for adapting instruction to meet the needs of second-language learners and children with special needs.

BEFORE READING THIS CHAPTER, THINK ABOUT . . .

- How your teachers assessed your literacy progress. Did you take spelling tests? Did you read stories and answer comprehension questions? Did you ever evaluate your own progress?
- How information about your literacy progress was shared with your parents. Did your parents read your report card? Did your parents attend conferences? Were you involved in sharing information about your progress with your peers or parents?
- How children with special learning needs were accommodated in your classes. Were there children who spoke other languages in your classes? Did your teacher adapt instruction for children with different learning needs?

FOCUS QUESTIONS

- What is important for teachers to know about children's literacy development?
- What are the two general approaches teachers might use to assess their children's literacy learning?
- What types of ongoing assessment tools are used to collect information about children's progress?
- How do teachers use the information they collect?
- How do ongoing assessment techniques help early childhood teachers meet the needs of diverse learners?

Determining What Children Know and Can Do

Instruction and assessment are intertwined in excellent literacy instruction. In the opening vignette, Ms. Saenz observed two children with differing levels of alphabet recognition. Ms. Saenz's careful observations are supported by developmental guidelines created by early childhood experts. She knows that though Martine and Monique differ in their ability to recognize alphabet letters, both are making remarkable progress. She also knows that as a second-language learner, Monique has made tremendous strides. Further, Ms. Saenz's observations provide her with a better understanding of the different strategies (alphabet song and one-to-one letter matching) Monique is using to learn the name of each of these symbols. The lessons Ms. Sanez will teach tomorrow are guided by the observations she made of what and how the children learned today.

Ms. Sanez is sensitive to the challenges of accurately assessing Monique's language and literacy learning. She knows that the results from the assessment process can be used to make many vital decisions. She wants the conclusions she reaches about her English language learner (ELL)

BOX 9.1	**individual education plan (IEP):** a written document developed by a multidisciplinary team that includes the student's parents, the student's regular and special education teachers, and other school administrative and support personnel. It describes the student's current level of functioning, his or her goals and objectives, the types of support the student needs, and the dates for the initiation and duration of that support
Definition of Terms	**individual family service plan (IFSP):** a written document developed by a multidisciplinary team that focuses on the child's needs and goals. The focus of this type of plan may also include direct support for the family of a child with disabilities. In addition, the IFSP may specify the type of support parents may offer to their child to help the child successfully transition to school
	on-demand assessment: a type of assessment that occurs during special time set aside for testing. In most cases, teaching and learning come to a complete stop while the teacher conducts the assessment
	ongoing assessment: a form of assessment that relies on the regular collection of children's work to illustrate children's knowledge and learning. The children's products are created as they engage in daily classroom activities. Thus, children are learning while they are being assessed
	showcase portfolio: exhibits samples of student work that illustrate the student's efforts, progress, and achievements. The showcase portfolio is shared with others, usually the child's parents
	working portfolio: where the student and teacher place work that is reflective of the student's achievement. Both the student and the teacher may place work in the working portfolio

children's development to be valid. She is sensitive to the recommendations for assessing ELL children Julia Park provides in Special Feature 9.1.

The primary purpose of early childhood assessment, then, is to improve instruction. As Lorrie Shepard, Sharon Kagan, and Emily Wurtz (1998, p. 52) note:

> When children are assessed as part of the teaching–learning process, then assessment information tells caregivers and teachers what each child can do and what he or she is ready to learn next. Finding out, on an ongoing basis, what a child knows and can do helps parents and teachers decide how to pose new challenges and provide help with what the child has not yet mastered. This type of assessment guides teachers' instruction. Teachers also use their assessment of children's learning to reflect on their own teaching practices so that they can adjust and modify curricula, instructional activities, and classroom routines that are ineffective.

However, increasingly administrators need to collect evidence to document the effectiveness of the instructional program and to assess the program's children's progress toward a set of learning goals. This is assessment for accountability purposes. Jacqueline Jones (2004) suggests that when this kind of documentation is needed, when individual data on each and every child in the program is not needed, teachers should consider assessing a sample of the program's children rather than all of the children.

What Is Important for Teachers to Know about Children's Literacy Development?

Sheila Valencia (1990) and Grant Wiggins (1993) agree on a primary principle of assessment: Teachers must begin assessment by determining what they value. Teachers must answer these questions: What is important for us to know about our children's development as readers, writers, speakers, and listeners? What do these young learners need to know and be able to do when they exit the preschool years?

Today early childhood educators have a new resource to help them answer these questions. Early childhood educators (sometimes with parents, administrators, and higher-education faculty) in nearly every state in the United States have worked together to create language and early literacy (and mathematics, social and emotional development, science, social studies) standards

SPECIAL FEATURE **9.1**

Assessing English Language Learners

Julia Park

Research suggests that assessment problems often stem from a lack of training, awareness, and sensitivity (Santos, 2004). To do a good job of assessing young children whose home language is not English, skill, sensitivity, and knowledge of the child's culture and language are required (Biggar, 2005). Deepening one's understanding of the impact of culture and language on the assessment process is the first step. Julia Park provides best practices recommendations for appropriate assessment of young children whose home language is not English below.

Recommendations for culturally appropriate assessment:

1. **Learn about ELL's literacy background.** Teachers should never assume that students who share the same language will observe the same cultural practices or understand the same types of texts. In understanding that ELLs differ in the literacy practices of their native language, teachers may be in a better position to determine whether those literacy practices are facilitating or interfering with the development of literacy in English.

2. **Use screening and assessment for appropriate purposes and determine the purpose of assessment beforehand.** Assessment strategies should help teachers find out what students know and can do; not what they do not know and cannot do. Also, when the purpose for assessment is determined beforehand, better decisions about what information should be gathered can be made.

3. **Decide how to assess children.** Multiple forms of evaluation through a variety of authentic assessment tools should be conducted to fairly assess the placement and progress of children and to plan instruction.

4. **Use culturally and linguistically appropriate assessment tools.** In assessing young ELLs, great emphasis should be given to the alignment of assessment tools and procedures with the specific cultural and linguistic characteristics of the children being assessed.

5. **Adopt a multidimensional approach including alternative assessments (observations, journals, conferring, questionnaires, and portfolios).** Alternative assessment tasks are more appropriate and fair ways to measure academic progress. They provide teachers with the ability to identify what students need.

6. **Assess in nontraditional ways.** Because ELLs are in the process of acquiring language as they acquire content, teachers need to ensure that their assessment addresses the linguistic component of the learning continuum. Therefore teachers should provide ELLs with opportunities to demonstrate knowledge in nontraditional ways such as the opportunity to show and practice knowledge in nonlanguage-dependent ways (drawing pictures, building structures).

7. **Consider modifications for ELLs who are in the process of acquiring English.** Allow a qualified bilingual professional to assist with the assessment.

8. **Begin assessment with several examples and simplify directions.** Giving the directions in the student's native language could also be a consideration.

9. **Allow students to use their language abilities to complete literacy tasks and to express their knowledge in the language they know best.** Oftentimes, knowledge of the first language means that students possess linguistic skills that can assist them in mastering literacy tasks in the second language.

10. **Involve families in the assessment process.** When conducting assessments, professionals should seek assistance from a family member or cultural guide to confirm their interpretations of the child's behavior during the assessment process.

11. **Include a qualified representative of the child's cultural and linguistic group to assist in the interpretation of the results when bilingual professionals are not available.**

12. **Always consider to what degree perceived developmental delays are related to cultural or childrearing practices, difficulties in translation, or other.**

(or *building blocks*, or *learning foundations*); various terms are used interchangeably. (See, for example, Figure 1.2 for a copy of one state's, Virginia's, language and early reading standards.)

In addition, some national groups have defined standards or outcomes. For example, Head Start has developed an outcomes framework, defining six framework domains (listening and understanding; speaking and communicating; phonological awareness; print awareness and concepts about book knowledge; early writing; and alphabet knowledge).

Standards are important because they express shared expectations for children. That is, the educators in each state or national group have agreed upon what they value. Further, once stated, all educators have a common language for assessing children's progress toward those goals or outcomes. Not only do standards guide teachers' assessment of children's progress, but also they guide what teachers teach. As Barbara Bowman (2006, p. 46) said in her keynote address at NAEYC's National Institute for Early Childhood Professional Development, "standards say clearly that teachers are responsible for organizing the learning environment so that children learn."

We begin this section by exploring the most appropriate ways teachers might gather information about their children's literacy development. We describe the tools for the ongoing gathering of information about children's language and literacy learning, how to store information, and issues involved in interpreting and sharing the information gathered. Readers should know that it is generally believed to be more difficult to determine what young children know and can do than what older children know and can do. Both the nature of early learning and young children's developing language skills provide teachers and caregivers with assessment challenges.

Two Kinds of Assessment

Once teachers have decided what is important for them to know about their children's literacy development, they must then decide how to gather this information. Teachers use two kinds of assessment to measure their children's progress toward the achievement of the state standards: ongoing and on demand. Charlene Cobb (2003, p. 386) uses an analogy to describe the difference between the two forms.

> A visit to the doctor's office is to [ongoing] assessment what an autopsy is to [on-demand assessment]. Let's say you see a doctor, for either a perceived need or a regular checkup. The doctor examines you, makes a diagnosis, and provides a treatment based on his or her discovery and your needs. This is a form of ongoing assessment. Suppose you come home from the doctor and find out that your neighbor has suddenly died. You're told that nobody knows what happened, but an autopsy is planned. An autopsy is [like an on-demand assessment.] [On-demand assessments] are done to determine what happened . . .

Why both kinds of assessments? Sandra Heidemann, Claire Chang, and Beth Menninga (2004, p. 87) describe the kinds of assessments the teachers in their very successful early childhood project in Minnesota use and why assessment is important to the success of their project:

> In effective assessment systems, teachers use multiple measures, such as informal observations, work sampling, and documentation along with more formal assessment, to guide their instruction.

Teachers assess, then, *to guide their decisions about what to teach.* Effective teachers engage in an assess-plan-teach model. These three elements are central to quality teaching.

We begin by considering ongoing assessment because this is the kind of assessment used most frequently by teachers of young children. Engaging in this kind of assessment demands that the teacher be a very careful observer of young children.

Ongoing Assessment

Ongoing assessment relies on regularly collecting artifacts to illustrate children's knowledge and learning. "It is the process of gathering information in the context of everyday class activities to obtain a representative picture of children's abilities and progress" (Dodge, Heroman, Charles, & Maiorca, 2004, p. 21). The artifacts (the children's products) are produced by the children while they engage in their daily classroom activities, such as those described in every chapter in this book. The products of these activities, then, serve the dual purposes of instruction and assessment. Because the children's artifacts are stored in portfolios, ongoing assessment often is called *portfolio assessment.* Because teachers are gathering *samples* of children's work to illustrate what the children know and can do, ongoing assessment sometimes is called *work sampling*. Ongoing assessment differs from on-demand assessment in several ways:

■ Children work on their products for varying amounts of time, and the procedures or directions often vary across the classroom or across classes in the building.

■ What each child and the teacher select as evidence of literacy learning may be different, not only across the children in the school or center but also across the children in a teacher's class.

■ The classroom teacher analyzes each child's performance on the tasks and makes judgments about each child's learning.

■ The classroom teacher's judgments are used immediately to define the child's next learning goal. The assessment, then, has an immediate effect on instruction for each child.

■ The assessment of the work produced over time in many different contexts permits the teacher and the child to gather more than a quick snapshot of what the child knows and is able to do at a given moment.

Ongoing assessment, then, permits both the teacher and the student to examine the child's knowledge and learning. Young learner Phyllis shares what this means as she uses her journal to describe her growth as a reader and writer:

I comed to this school a little bit nervous, you know. Nothin'. [She shakes her head for added emphasis.] I couldn't read or write nothin'. Look at this. [She turns to the first few pages of her writing journal.] Not a word! Not a word! [She taps the page and adds an aside.] And the drawin's not too good. Now, look at this. [She turns to the end of the journal.] One, two, three, four. Four pages! And I can read 'em. Listen. [She reads.] Words! [Nodding her head.] Yup! Now I can read and write a lotta words!

Ongoing Assessment Tools

Phyllis's journal is one of several tools her teacher uses to gather information about Phyllis's literacy learning. Like Phyllis, her teacher can compare the writing at the beginning and at the end of the journal to learn about Phyllis's literacy development over time. Each tool used permits teachers to gather information about their children's literacy learning while the children perform the kinds of activities described in this book. Readers were introduced to several of these tools in previous chapters.

◆ *Anecdotal notes*—These are teacher notes describing a child's behavior. In addition to the child's name, the date, and the classroom area, the specific event or product should be described exactly as it was seen and heard. The following is an example of one of kindergarten teacher Karen Valentine's anecdotal notes:

Martia 9/25
M./ in the library center "reading" a page in a big book. As she reads, she points to the words. She runs out of words before she is done reading (each syllable = pointed to word). She tries again, and again, and again, and again. She leaves, shaking her head.

Teachers use many different kinds of paper (e.g., computer address labels, note pads, paper in a loose-leaf binder, index cards, Post-it notes) to make anecdotal records of children's behavior.

Bobbi Fisher (1998) describes her anecdotal note system as an Anecdotal Class Grid. Here is how to make and use an Anecdotal Class Grid (pp. 128–129).

Take one piece of paper. Make 2" × 1½" boxes, as many as the one page will hold.

Put a child's name in each grid. Be sure there is a box for every child in the class.

Throughout the week, write short notes describing the children's behavior, much like Karen Valentine's note above.

Begin each week with a blank grid.

A benefit of a class grid is that at a glance teachers can see which children have been observed and which have been overlooked. As Fisher notes, "This week-by-week record

Teacher observations of children's work provide an important summary of what the teacher noticed over the year.

becomes an important summary of what [teachers] noticed over the year and provides a detailed record of the child's work" (p. 128).

Teachers use anecdotal notes to describe the strategies children use to decode words, the processes children use while they write, the functions of writing children use while they play, and characteristics of children's talk during a presentation to the class. Note that anecdotal notes describe exactly what occurred and what was said verbatim, with no judgment or interpretation applied. Kindergarten teacher Lynn Cohen (1999) reminds teachers to "get the basic story and most significant details, keeping the information as factual as possible" (p. 27).

◆ *Vignettes or teacher reflections*—Vignettes are recordings of recollections of significant events made after the fact, when the teacher is free of distractions. Because vignettes are like anecdotal notes, except that they are prepared some time after a behavior has occurred and are based on a teacher's memory of the event, vignettes are used for purposes such as those identified for anecdotal notes. These after-the-fact descriptions or vignettes can be more detailed than anecdotal notes and are particularly useful when recording literacy behavior that is significant or unique for a specific child.

For example, Ms. Valentine observed a student attempting to control his peers' behavior by writing a sign and posting it in an appropriate place. She did not have time to record a description of the student's behavior immediately. As soon as the children left for the day, she recorded her recollection of the event:

> For days Jamali had been complaining about the "mess" left by the children getting drinks at the classroom water fountain after recess. "Look at that mess! Water all over the floor!" At his insistence, the class discussed solutions to the problem. While the problem wasn't

solved, I thought there was less water on the floor. Evidently, Jamali did not. Today he used the "power of the pen" to attempt to solve the problem. He wrote a sign:

BEWR!! WTR SHUS UP
ONLE TRN A LITL
(Beware! Water shoots up. Only turn a little.)

He posted his sign over the water fountain. This was the first time I had observed him using writing in an attempt to control other children's behavior.

Vignettes, then, are recollections of significant events. Because teachers can write vignettes when they are free of distractions, they can be more descriptive about the child's concern that drove the literacy-oriented behavior, and they can connect this event to what is known about the child's previous literacy-oriented behaviors.

◆ *Checklists*—Checklists are observational aids that specify which behaviors to look for and provide a convenient system for keeping records. They can make observations more systematic and easier to conduct. The number of checklists available to describe children's literacy development seems almost endless! We have presented several for readers' use in previous chapters. For example, see St. Michael's Early Childhood Center's Assessing Young Children's Book-related Understandings (see Figure 4.4, pages 99–100, and the Early Forms of Writing Developmental Checklist in Chapter 8).

Checklists are useful because they provide information that teachers can see at a glance, showing what children can do. Teachers have learned that (1) children sometimes engage in a behavior today that does not reappear for several weeks, and (2) many different variables (e.g., a storybook being read, other children in the group) can affect the literacy behaviors children show. Hence, teachers are careful to record the date of each observation and to use the checklist many times over the year in an attempt to create an accurate picture of their children's literacy development.

◆ *Questioning or interviewing*—Teachers interview to obtain information they cannot uncover any other way. Sometimes it is difficult to determine the significance of a literacy behavior, particularly when early forms of emergent writing, such as scribbles or random letters, are being used.

Unfortunately, young children often find it difficult to answer adult questions. Often the information involves tacit knowledge; young children may not know that they know the answer to the question. The kinds of questions teachers ask are very important. Peter Johnston (1992) suggests that teachers ask three kinds of questions:

(1) descriptive questions (e.g., What happens during storybook reading time in our classroom? What do you usually do when you are reading a book?);

(2) structural questions (e.g., Do you read when you write? Can you tell me about how and when?); and

(3) contrast questions (e.g., Who are your two favorite authors? How are their stories the same? How are their stories different?).

To Johnston's list, we add Graves's (1983) process questions (e.g., I see you erased something here. Can you tell me why you made this change, this revision?).

Johnston noted that teachers might want to consider adding a pretend audience for the question. For example, a teacher might say, "Suppose a new child was added to our classroom. What things would you tell him or her about reading to help him or her know what to do and how to be good at reading?"

◆ *Video and audio recordings*—Teachers often use audiotaping to document children's reading progress. For example, teachers might record a child's reading of a favorite book to study the child's reading attempts, or children's retellings of stories read to them to study their comprehension of stories.

Teachers use videotape to capture children's literacy behaviors in a variety of contexts. Some teachers focus the camera lens on an area of the classroom, such as the dramatic play area or the writing center, to gather information about children's literacy-related social interactions during their play and work. Viewing the tapes provides valuable information, not only about the children's knowledge of context-appropriate oral language and their ability to engage in conversations with others, but also about the children's knowledge of the functions of writing.

♦ *Products or work samples*—Some products, such as samples of children's writing, can be gathered together in a folder. If the children's original works cannot be saved (e.g., a letter that is sent to its recipient), a photocopy can be made of the product. Other products, such as three-dimensional structures the children have created with labels written by them, might not be conveniently saved. In these cases, a photograph—still or video—can be made. Because memories are short, the teacher should record a brief description of the product or the activity that resulted in the product.

Addressing Storage Problems

Mrs. Saenz has developed an assessment notebook that helps organize information about children's literacy learning. Her notebook consists of several sections. One section contains a checklist she has developed to document children's emergent writing. Another section contains a checklist she created to document emergent reading behaviors, including information about concepts of print and alphabet recognition. Mrs. Saenz's notebook also has a section for writing vignettes. To prompt her memory of an event, Mrs. Saenz uses a digital camera that allows her to take pictures of the children engaging in specific literacy behaviors. Later in the day, she downloads the disk, prints the photo, and writes her interpretation of the event on the bottom margin of the photo. In addition, the camera automatically dates the picture, making it easier for Mrs. Saenz to document this information quickly. Using these various tools will result in the accumulation of many items that will need to be stored someplace.

For teachers to maintain this kind of assessment system, they must be very well organized! Typically, teachers maintain a folder on each child. Many teachers find that folders with pockets and center clasps for three-hole-punched paper serve as better storage containers than file folders. Interview forms, running-record sheets, and other similar papers can be three-hole-punched, thus permitting easy insertion into each child's folder. When anecdotal notes and vignettes are written on computer mailing labels, the labels can be attached to the inside covers of each child's folder. When these notes are written on index cards, the cards can be stored in one of the folder's pockets. Also, a plastic resealing sandwich bag might be stapled inside each child's folder to hold an audiotape. The self-sealing feature of the bag means that the tape can be securely held inside the folder. The class's folders might be housed in a plastic container or in hanging files in a file cabinet.

Creating a Portfolio

There are at least two kinds of portfolios. Gaye Gronlund (1998) calls the folders described above "working portfolios." She suggests that the working portfolio should provide "accurate documentation about how a child is growing and developing" (p. 5). The work samples, anecdotal notes, and so forth housed in working portfolios are not representative of the child's best work. Rather, the items housed in working portfolios evidence a child's typical, everyday performance. Teachers use these working portfolios to guide their instructional planning for each child. From the working portfolios, children and their teachers select specific pieces for inclusion in each child's "showcase portfolio." Here pieces that exhibit the best work the child produced are housed. For example, Ms. Gronlund describes how one "preschool program had children sign in each day by their names (in whichever way they could) in the special Sign-in Book. The teacher then cut out the best samples for the child's showcase portfolio" (p. 5).

WHAT IS A PORTFOLIO?   That question has been answered by F. Leon Paulson, Pearl Paulson, and Carol Meyer (1991, p. 60), who define a portfolio as "a purposeful collection of [a sample of] student work that exhibits the student's efforts, progress, and achievements . . . . The collection must include student participation in selecting [the] contents, the criteria for selection, the criteria for judging merit, and evidence of student self-reflection."

The purpose of portfolios, as defined by Frank Serafini (2001, p. 388), is for teachers "to uncover the possibilities for students to understand each child as a whole, and to attempt to provide a window into a student's conceptual framework and ways of seeing the world." What a working or a showcase portfolio actually looks like varies from teacher to teacher, school to school, and center to center. For example, a Colorado teacher used gallon-size zip-top bags bound together with large metal rings. This teacher's students decorated poster-board covers, which the teacher laminated (Wilcox, 1993). Some teachers use hanging files, each carefully labeled with a child's name, and the bottom drawer of a file cabinet (so young children can easily see into the drawer) as their children's portfolio. Other teachers use pizza boxes decorated by the children. One teacher used a handmade fabric wall-hanging with a pocket for each child. Still other teachers are beginning to create digital portfolios. For example, Minjie Paark's teacher pulled examples of Minjie's literacy behaviors as reflected using the ongoing assessment tools described above and digital photos from Minjie's working portfolio, scanned select items, and prepared an end-of-year digital showcase portfolio on a CD for Minjie's parents.

Deciding what to use is the practical starting point with portfolio assessment. As Gaye Gronlund (1998) notes, "Decisions in this area must be made, experiments tried, and a comfortable style selected." There is no one right storage scheme for children's portfolios. Teachers might use one kind of system for their children's working portfolios and another for their children's showcase portfolios.

HOW ARE ARTIFACTS SELECTED FOR INCLUSION? Maintaining a classroom portfolio system does not mean saving everything the child does and sending nothing home. Saving everything creates what Gaye Gronlund calls "a storage nightmare!" The pieces placed in a working portfolio are selected because they show children's everyday performance related to the literacy accomplishments the program has determined the children should know and be able to do. The pieces placed in the showcase portfolio are selected from the working portfolio because they show the child's best accomplishment relative to the literacy accomplishments.

Having a specific reason for selecting each artifact is critically important. What are the specific reasons? Please recall the discussion earlier in this chapter about state standards and national group outcomes. These might drive the teacher's and children's decisions about what should be selected for inclusion in each of the children's portfolios. For example, to demonstrate that Tyrone, a three-year-old, could identify labels and signs in the environment, Kristol Warren, his teacher, included the following piece of evidence in Tyrone's working portfolio. One day, the children were lining up for outdoor play. Tyrone looked at the sign above the door and said, "I know what that says." Surprised, Ms. Warren said, "Really? What does it say?" Tyrone responded, "It says *out*." It didn't; it said *exit*. However, Tyrone was using the context to attempt to decode the print above the door. Ms. Warren had no time to write an anecdotal note. When the children left for the day, she wrote a vignette of this event. She included this vignette in Tyrone's working portfolio and later in his showcase portfolio as an illustration of the same literacy accomplishment. When Ms. Warren wrote the vignette, she was careful to date it. Many teachers have discovered that it is helpful to have a date stamp readily available in the classroom in the area where the portfolios are stored. Dating each item selected for inclusion in working portfolios permits the teacher and the child to arrange the items in chronological order to show changes or learning over time.

WHO SELECTS THE PIECES FOR INCLUSION? With young children, the majority of the items chosen for inclusion in working and showcase portfolios are selected by teachers or are chosen jointly by the children and their teacher. Even the youngest children, however, should be permitted to select some pieces independently—particularly for their working portfolios. Teachers must remember that the portfolios belong to the children and that student ownership is critical. Hence, when teachers assist their students in selecting artifacts, they must do so in ways that maintain the students' ownership of their portfolios. As Frank Serafini (2001) points out, portfolios are something teachers do with children, not to children.

FIGURE 9.1 Portfolio Entry Slip

Portfolio Entry Slip

Name _____Tyrone_____   Date __3|11__

Child/Teacher chose to include this piece because it shows: __Tyrone using writing to control a peer's behavior.__

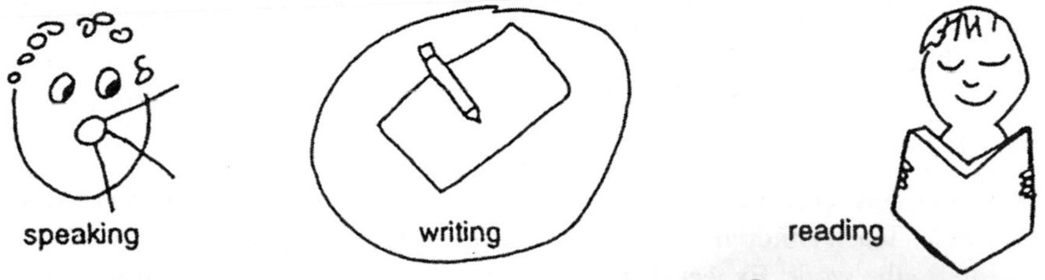

speaking   writing   reading

What does it show the child learned? __(1) a function of writing; we write to control others' behavior (2) exhibits knowledge learned from experiences in a play setting__

WHY WAS EACH ARTIFACT SELECTED FROM THE WORKING PORTFOLIO FOR INCLUSION IN THE SHOWCASE PORTFOLIO?   To encourage thoughtful selection of items for inclusion in the children's showcase portfolios, portfolio experts suggest that an entry slip should be attached to each artifact when it is moved from the children's working portfolio to their showcase portfolio. Entry slips require students to engage in a "dialogue with their inner, critical selves" (Wilcox, 1993, p. 20). An entry slip helps readers of children's showcase portfolios know the importance of the work selected for inclusion. "Why do I want this artifact in my (or this child's) showcase portfolio? What does it show about me (or this child) as a reader, a writer, a learner, a literate individual?"

Just what does an entry slip look like? See Figure 9.1 for an example of the entry slip used by Kristol with the vignette described above.

HOW OFTEN SHOULD ARTIFACTS BE SELECTED FROM THE WORKING PORTFOLIO FOR INCLUSION IN THE SHOWCASE PORTFOLIO?   Teachers differ in how often they select items for inclusion in the children's showcase portfolios. Teachers have discovered that too much accumulated work overwhelms children and their teachers, making it difficult for them to be selective, so it seems wise to follow this rule: The younger the child, the more frequently the artifacts should be selected from the working portfolio for the showcase portfolio. Perhaps once every four weeks would be a prudent guide. However, a key to the decision regarding frequency of selection will be the number of artifacts the children and their teachers have created and stored in their working portfolios. Having too few items also limits the children's and teacher's ability to select.

Another variable in determining when to select items will be the school's or center's identified times for reporting to parents through written reports and parent–teacher, parent–teacher–child, or parent–child conferences. The portfolios will serve as the information base for these reporting systems.

SHARING THE PORTFOLIOS WITH OTHERS. Carol Wilcox (1993, p. 33) reports teacher Karen Boettcher as saying, "The heart of portfolios is sharing." Following are some ways in which the information in portfolios can be shared with others:

◆ *Sharing with peers*—One important audience for portfolios is the children's classmates. By sharing, children learn unique things about their classmates. They learn about the learning strategies their peers have used successfully. They learn what peers are struggling to learn, and they learn to offer assistance in their peers' struggles. They learn about peers' special talents. They learn about new ways of writing. They learn about how their peers read books. They set new goals for themselves.

How children share their portfolios, of course, will be determined by the age of the children.

Ellen Booth-Church (1999) proposes the following guidelines to ensure successful portfolio sharing:

(1) Ask a different child to present once a week on a designated portfolio day.
(2) Teach children how to interact with each other, by asking the presenter questions about the work. Expect that initially the children's questions will be stilted. Later, through modeling, children will learn important social, observational, and interviewing skills.
(3) Teachers should show acceptance of the children's work.
(4) Teachers should share their work.

◆ *Sharing with parents*—The significant adults in each child's life are another important audience for portfolios. Of course, teachers will use the children's portfolios during parent-teacher conferences. Gaye Gronlund (1998) also recommends that the working portfolio be shared with parents during parent–teacher conferences. She believes parents might develop unrealistic expectations for their child if only the best examples of the child's literacy accomplishments are shared.

Sometimes children will join these conferences to provide their own perspective on their own development as readers, writers, and speakers. At other times, children will independently use their portfolios to explain their literacy development to their parents. Even Bernadette Watson's kindergartners ran their own portfolio conferences for their parents! Teachers not only need to teach children how to respond to their peers, but also to inform parents about how to respond to their children's portfolios. Carol Wilcox (1993) has detailed the story of Michael, a young learner who had a devastating experience when sharing his portfolio with his parents. Their response focused on his poor spelling and handwriting performances, rather than on his accomplishments and his literacy development. He was not, after all, spelling words conventionally!

How does a portfolio assessment system *really* work in a classroom? Please read Dehbra Handley's brief description of her portfolio system in her preschool classroom (see Trade Secrets 9.1).

On-Demand Assessment

Teachers use, or are required to use, another kind of assessment to understand their students' literacy learning. This kind of assessment is often referred to as the assessment of learning or on-demand assessment (Johnston & Costello, 2005). Think of on-demand assessments like an annual physical checkup. Periodically, we all need to stop what we are doing to take a formal measure of the state of our health. On-demand assessments occur at specific times, like once a year or every three months. For example, on Tuesday all kindergarten children in the school district may be asked to take a pencil-and-paper test. They might be asked to listen to several short stories composed of two or three sentences. Then the children would be asked to put an X on the picture that best matches each story. They may be asked to circle the letters said aloud by the teacher. They might be asked to listen to sounds said aloud by the teacher (e.g., *b*) and to circle the letter that makes that sound.

TRADE SECRETS 9.1

Portfolio and Assessment: Paying Attention to What Kids Do

Dehbra Handley

How does the portfolio system work in a preschool setting? The portfolio system I use is a two-part system that includes the actual portfolio work and an assessment process. The process enables me to get a better look at how each of my students is doing. It helps me identify where little nudges might be needed. Through my children's work samples, I am able to see and share with my students' parents their child's literacy development.

My students' portfolios are created from large thirty-six- by twenty-four-inch pocket folders. The children decorate these, and then the folders are laminated. They are kept in a designated special place near our computers within the reach of each little learner. Everything and anything can (and often does) go into the portfolio.

In the beginning of the year, I explain to the students that their work is important. Therefore, they have the choice of displaying it in the classroom, taking it home, or saving it in their portfolio. They know that all work saved in their portfolio is still theirs, and any work displayed in the classroom can be saved or taken home. Choosing what to do with their work has several positive effects on the child: it fosters decision-making skills, develops ownership and control over the portfolio, and validates that the child's

work is important without having to have the teacher place any extrinsic value on it.

The other half of the portfolio system is the assessment and parent-reporting part. The assessment section is based largely on my observations that I describe in anecdotal notes or checklists. I spend part of each day making observations based on three areas: socioemotional development, cognitive development, and physical development. These observations then are distilled into a descriptive review of the student; a section reflects each of the three developmental areas noted.

The descriptive review and the portfolio are then shared with the parents during a home visit with the family. The student is always a part of the home visit; the child is the narrator for the work and is given the opportunity to select the pieces he or she would like to keep. In this way we are able to reduce the number of portfolio pieces and begin the collection process again. I explain and show the parents the developmental areas that each piece of work or photo demonstrates. Much of what I tell the parents is included in the descriptive review. The parents are given a copy of the review to keep for their own records.

After our second and final home visit, the student work is then incorporated into a big book. This book contains all of the special pieces the parent and child have decided together (during the home visit process) should be saved for this purpose. With the completion and presentation of the big books to the families, our portfolio process comes to an end.

Standardized

Most readers likely would label these kinds of on-demand assessments as *tests*. On-demand assessments are administered, scored, and interpreted in the same way for all test takers. Each student taking the test hears the same passages and answers the same questions. When all variables are held constant, the assessment would be known as a "standardized" on-demand test.

Some early childhood teachers express concerns with the administration of these kinds of assessments to young children. Susan Andersen (1998), an early childhood consultant and former teacher, details several of these concerns. She objects to the "artificial situation" (p. 25)—children separated, each child working alone—in which children must be placed for such tests. There can be no responding to each other's questions, no cooperating with each other. Such tests place what Anderson calls unnecessary stress and unrealistic expectations on young children (and their teachers) when children's performance is used as the measure to compare teachers against teachers, schools against schools, districts against districts, or states against states or to make decisions about the school's eligibility for federal programs for the coming school year.

Often the purpose of standardized tests is accountability: How are the children in this classroom, school, school district, state, or nation doing compared to the children in other classrooms, schools, school districts, states, and nations? Often the focus is on group performance rather than on the performance of individual students. Samuel Meisels and Sally Atkins-Burnet (2004) argue that this is the case with the Head Start National Reporting System, for example. Initiated in the fall of 2003, the Head Start Bureau and Administration for Children and Families began requiring Head Start teachers across the country to administer a fifteen- to twenty-minute test twice a year (fall and end of the program year) to all children participating in Head Start programs across the country. (For information on Head Start's National Report System, see www.headstartinfo.org/nrs_i&r.htm.)

Classroom Based

Some early childhood programs administer other kinds of on-demand assessments. In these programs, teachers arrange to meet individually with each child three or four times a year to administer an on-demand assessment as one means of gathering specific information about each child's literacy development. For example, these teachers might ask children to show them the front of the book or how to turn the book's pages; to point to the title; to demonstrate their understandings of print by showing them where they should begin reading, where to go after reading a line of text, and what is read, the print or the pictures; to point to a letter, a word, a period, and a question mark; to listen to a story and read along, pointing while they read, when they can; or to retell the story.

In 2004, the National Association for the Education of Young Children and the National Association of Early Childhood Specialists in State Departments of Education prepared a joint position statement on curriculum, assessment, and program evaluation. These two major early childhood associations agreed that "reliable assessment [should be] a central part of all early childhood programs" (NAEYC/NAECS/SDE, 2004, p. 51). The purpose of assessment, these educators believe, should be to assess children's "strengths, progress and needs" (pp. 51 & 52). (A copy of the full position statement can be accessed at www.naeyc.org/resources/position_statements/pscape.asp.) This chapter provides early childhood teachers with the keys for implementing an assessment system consistent with this purpose.

Adapting Instruction to Meet the Needs of Special Populations

The main purpose of this book has been to describe how to set up and implement an effective, developmentally appropriate language arts program for pre-K and kindergarten children. Chapter 3 presented strategies for promoting children's oral language development, and Chapters 4 through 8 have detailed best practice in teaching reading and writing to young children.

Recall that one of the underlying themes of this book is respecting the tremendous diversity of children who are enrolled in today's early childhood programs. It is not surprising, therefore, that the general strategies we have recommended for pre-K and kindergarten-age children will sometimes need to be modified to meet the needs of specific children.

As explained earlier in this chapter, ongoing assessment is a key requirement for providing this type of individualized instruction. Another important requirement is for teachers to be aware of the needs of special populations—groups of children who face common problems and challenges.

This section contains information on adapting instruction to meet the needs of two groups of children—bilingual second-language learners and children with various types of disabilities. Early childhood educators will undoubtedly encounter many members of both groups of children during their teaching careers. Tailoring instruction to meet the needs of linguistically and developmentally diverse children is one of the hallmarks of excellent teaching. The special features that follow give practical tips to assist teachers in this challenging task.

English as Second Language Learners

Currently, more than one in seven students in U.S. schools speak English as a second language (Barone, 1998), and the proportion is much higher in some areas, such as California and other parts of the Southwest. In addition, the percentage of second-language learners tends to be higher in the earliest grades, forecasting even greater linguistic diversity in future classrooms. For example, one survey of Head Start programs reported that 22 percent of the students spoke Spanish at home and that 4 percent came from families who spoke one of 139 other languages (Tabors, 1998)! It is vitally important for early childhood educators to be prepared to help these children learn to speak, read, and write English. In Special Feature 9.2, Myae Han describes the current research and best practice strategies recommended for enhancing young English as a second language learners' language and early literacy skills.

SPECIAL FEATURE 9.2

Supporting English Language Learners' Language and Literacy Learning: How Should We Teach?

Myae Han

A large body of research on school-age immigrant children is available today; however, immigrant children under age six are largely ignored in bilingual and English as second language education (Tabors, 1997). Researchers attribute this to a number of myths and misconceptions about how young children learn a second language (L2) (Gonzalez, Yawkey, Minaya-Rowe, 2006). One of the myths is that children learn a second language quickly and easily with no special attention or instruction—if they learn the second language at an early age. Thus, the field has hardly considered ways to help preschool children learn English. In this feature, I describe the ways to support preschool English as second language (ESL) or English Language Learner (ELL) children.

As a former preschool teacher in the multilingual classroom and a mother of an ELL child, I have witnessed many struggling ELL children trying to adapt to a new language and culture. Because this has not been recorded in any literature, people have formed a misconception about learning a second language, namely that "earlier is easier." However, researchers agree that learning a second language is not as easy as what people think even when children are exposed to a second language environment before age six (Tabors, 1997).

A second myth is that teachers need to be bilingual to teach bilingual children. Research shows teachers do not have to be bilingual to teach bilingual children. Moreover, it is very difficult to find bilingual teachers. Further, even teachers who speak two languages may not be able to accommodate the language needs of the children in their classrooms. The children in a single classroom may speak many different languages. Multi-language classrooms are a common phenomenon today in America. For example, as a preschool teacher in Arizona, my classroom was a mix of children whose home language was Japanese, Korean, Turkish, Spanish and English. I speak two languages (Korean and English); I do not speak Japanese, Turkish, or Spanish. Even though I did not speak all of my students' native language, I still could support all the children's literacy learning. The authors of this book have included this special feature (and the other special features that focus on young native-language Spanish-speaking children's language and literacy development) to help early childhood teachers meet the language and literacy needs of all their young students.

Where might a teacher begin? The literature suggests that in order to ensure the success of ELL children, teachers need to begin by understanding the children's linguistic *and* cultural needs. An effective ESL language and literacy program should incorporate multicultural education strategies. Patton Tabors (1997) provides the following general strategies to support preschool ELL children's learning.

Begin by gathering information about the children's cultural and linguistic backgrounds. Obtain 1) basic demographic information, 2) information on the linguistic practices in and outside of the home, and 3) information on the relevant cultural beliefs regarding child rearing practices (e.g., discipline, toileting, and feeding). This information will give teachers ideas about how the culture expects children to behave. Teachers can collect such information from questionnaires, informal chats with parents, and home visits. If neither parent of a child speaks English, then it is imperative that the questionnaires (and other written materials sent to the home) are translated into the native language and a translator accompanies the teacher on the home visit. But where might a teacher turn for such assistance? Such help can be found in the international student office of a local university program, an English language institute, or a local international community organization. Representatives from such organizations might become volunteers or classroom visitors.

Second, learn a few key words in each child's home language. Knowing even a few words provides for at least low-level communication and an opportunity to develop rapport with each child. Learning simple words such as hello and good-bye is useful in making an initial contact. Making these simple words a part of classroom instruction also can benefit English-speaking children; they, too, can learn words in another language so they can communicate with their peers. One preschool teacher sings the following poem with children during morning greeting time:

Hello (poem)
Hello (Hola) is handy word to say,
At least a 100 times a day.
Without hello (Hola), what would I do
Whenever I bumped into you?
Without hello (Hola), where would you be
Whenever you bumped into me?
Hello (Hola) is a handy word to know.
Hello (Hola). Hello (Hola). Hello (Hola). Hello (Hola).

Children chant the poem together in all the languages spoken by their peers (*bonjour* in French, *pree veyet* in Russian, *an-yong* in Korean, *nee-how* in Chinese, *ohay O* in Japanese). This kind of activity helps to boost ELL children's self-esteem by showing appreciation of their native language in classroom.

(continued on next page)

SPECIAL FEATURE 9.2 (continued)

Third, in the learning of a second language, most children go through a nonverbal stage that may last from a couple of weeks to several months. During this stage, children may use gestures to communicate. When children use gestures, teachers should provide the words for the children's gesture (e.g., *"Milk. You want a glass of milk."*). Make sure to repeat the words or phrases in many different contexts (e.g., *"Block. You want the block from Antwon."*).

Fourth, do not expect young ELLs to use decontextualized talk, to talk about events removed from the immediate context. Early communication should be based on the immediate context, what Tabors calls the "here and now." For example, a teacher might say, "You're playing with blocks. It looks like you're building a tower. Are you building a tower?" Talk about what the child is doing right now. Such talk plays a role of positive reinforcement for the child's activity, as well as teaching a new vocabulary. Such running commentary provides young children with an opportunity to learn meaningful language in context. Children can learn about the words *block* and *tower* while they are playing

Fifth, take the ELL children's level of second language proficiency into account when planning instruction. Different kinds of questioning techniques should be thoughtfully used in consideration of a child's level of language proficiency. Many current theorists describe second language acquisition as sequential stages (Herrera & Murray, 2005): preproduction (nonverbal, silent stage), early production, speech emergence, intermediate fluency, and advanced fluency.

> *Preproduction Stage.* During the preproduction stage, the literature recommends that teachers use simple questions, such as *"Can you point to ___? Can you find ___?"* Children at this level may not be able to say the name of the object, but they are acquiring an understanding of the name of the object; the number of words in their expressive (speaking) language is smaller than the number of words in their receptive (hearing) language.
> *Early Production Stage.* During the early production stage, teachers might use yes/no and either/or questions.
> *Speech Emergence Stage.* For children in the speech emergence stage, teachers can use open-ended questions, such as *"Why did ___ happen? How does ___ work?"*
> *Intermediate Fluent Stage.* For children in this stage, teachers can use the questions that foster the children's conceptual development, such as *"What would you recommend or suggest?" "Can you describe ___?"* (Ventriglia, 1996).

CURRICULUM FOR ELLS: INSTRUCTIONAL STRATEGIES THAT WORK

Classroom Environment

Imagine yourself in a subway station trying to find a way to get to the other station. Add a little more imagination; you are in a foreign country, and everything is labeled in a language you cannot read. How would you find your way?

This may be how new immigrant children feel when they enter the classroom in the United States for the first time. Fortunately, most preschool classrooms are filled with hands-on materials and activities for the children's engagement. Teachers can modify their classroom environment to make easy access for ELLs. An environment that thoughtfully accommodates the cultural and linguistic needs of children helps smooth ELL children's adjustment and transition from home to school. Such environments also support ELL children's language and literacy development. Below are several suggested ways to make the classroom environment more welcoming for ELL children.

- Include pictures and words in each ELL child's first language when labeling classroom areas and objects.
- Display daily schedule with pictures, such as story time, snack time, cleanup, hand wash, etc. This gives a general sense of daily structure.
- Display children's names with pictures and verbalize them as often as possible. Have other English-speaking children say the names of ELL children. This supports positive peer relationship. Peer partners are very helpful in a classroom with a diverse population. Researchers have found that peer tutoring has a positive impact for both English-speaking and ELL children (Hirschler, 1994).
- Have ample play materials that children can play with without assistance. Teachers should ensure that they are providing places in the classroom where ELL children can feel comfortable, competent, and occupied.
- Early in the school year, it is desirable to stick with a strict routine to minimize the ELL children's confusion. This helps the ELL children to adjust in the classroom and feel more secure sooner.
- Include a picture dictionary in the classroom library.

Free-Play Time/Center Time/Choice Time

Most preschool classrooms provide a free-choice time during the day. Researchers found that lengthy play periods (at least forty-five to sixty minutes) can promote children's self-expression and self-direction (Isenberg & Jalongo, 1993). Children become self-directed learners when they know that they have enough time during

SPECIAL FEATURE 9.2 (continued)

the school day to complete the learning activities they have chosen. Free-play time is also less stressful than structured group time for ELL children. It also is a time when the classroom adults can provide individual support to the ELL children within the context of joyful activities.

What can teachers do to support ELLs during free-play time? Tabors (1997) recommends two strategies: running commentary and context-embedded language. Running commentary is a strategy called "talking while doing." When teachers use this strategy, they explain their actions or others' actions as an activity unfolds. For example, a teacher might say, *"I'm getting some writing paper from the shelf here and I'll need a Magic Marker from the writing tools box. I'm writing a note to myself to remember to get popcorn for the children tomorrow. I write 'p-o-p-c-o-r-n [saying each letter as she writes it]."* Context-embedded language is language related to the immediate situation, particularly in the course of sociodramatic play. In child-initiated activities, the child creates a context first, and then the teacher follows the child's action verbally so that the teacher's language is more meaningful to children. For example, Martinec and De'Zebbra are building in the block corner. The teacher says, *"De'Zebbra is putting one block down. Martinec is putting one block on top of De'Zebbra's block. De'Zebbra is putting one block on top of Martinec's block."* The teacher continues this description of the children's actions in this context until she says, *"Look! Martinec and De'Zebbra built a tall tower!"*

Storybook Time

Large-group story time is one of the most challenging times for teachers with ELL children. Teachers fear that these children may not understand the story but still need to listen to a book. The following are several suggestions for ways teachers might make storybook reading more successful:

- Start with patterned books or predictable books. These books are highly repetitive and have simplified texts that make it easy for ELL children to become engaged with them. Gradually expand beyond predictable books to books consistent with the children's interests. When choosing books, consider the vocabulary, length, and cultural sensitivity.
- When children are not following the book's words, talk the story rather than reading it. Also consider the use of puppets or storytelling props to assist children's understanding of story. For example, one of the popular children's books *There Was an Old Lady Who Swallowed a Fly* can be better understood with a prop of a big old lady. Before the story is read, say the names of the animals. As the story is read, attach the animal figures to the old lady's stomach.

- Keep storybook reading time short. Don't make storybook reading time a patience contest. If the book is too long, it is fine to stop in the middle and finish at a later time.
- Consider small-group book reading. Instead of having one large-group story time, teachers can have small-group story time with different groups of children during free-choice time or by splitting the group into two groups and having the teacher read to one group while the classroom assistant reads to the other group. When grouping children, flexible grouping (mixing ELL children with English-speaking children) is recommended. However, depending on the type of book, the content, and level of difficulty, the teachers may consider grouping only the ELL children together on some occasions.
- Repeated reading is important. Read the same book at least three or four times. Children get more information each time they listen to the story. It is also important to remember to focus on different aspects of the story each time the book is read. For example, during each reading, focus on different vocabulary words, predictions of what will happen next, comprehension questions, or alphabet letters.

EXPLICIT INSTRUCTION

Literacy involves the coordination of many different skills or abilities such as phonemic awareness, phonics, oral reading fluency, vocabulary, spelling, etc. A recent study (Lesaux & Siegel, 2003) found that phonological awareness instruction in the context of a blended early literacy program in kindergarten is as effective for ELL speakers as it is for English language speakers in the early grades. Phonological awareness instruction can begin before ELL children achieve oral language proficiency in English. Nonie Lesaux (2004) suggests the following phonological awareness instruction guide for pre-K ELL children:

- Initially select the words that include sounds common to both languages.
- Separate auditory similar sounds.
- Ask the children to repeat the word before attempting the task.
- Use small-group instruction so the children have multiple opportunities to hear models and to maximize participation.
- Use manipulatives and actions (clapping, stomping) to actively engage the children.
- Accompany words with pictures to provide context and/or use words from read-aloud selections.
- Accept oral approximations. Children often borrow from their native language when pronouncing words in English.
- Explicitly teach sounds in English that have no equivalent in the children's native language.

(continued on next page)

In addition, Lesaux recommends 1) when teaching vocabulary, focus on a small number of critical words and emphasize the words over time, 2) use cognates (a large number of words that have the same meaning in two languages), and 3) use visuals to represent relationships and to help with abstract language to support comprehension.

SUMMARY

While learning a second language is not as easy as people think, even for preschool children, it is clear that knowledgeable early childhood teachers can do much to support their young children's transition from their home language to understanding and speaking English—in addition to their native language.

Children with Special Needs

Recent legislation has mandated that children with disabilities be placed in the least restrictive environment. The goal is inclusion, allowing each child with special needs to have the maximum possible amount of integration into general education classrooms. The resulting mainstreaming of children with special needs into regular classrooms has radically changed the role of classroom teachers at all grade levels. Teachers are now expected to work as part of a multidisciplinary team (along with special education teachers, psychologists, and other specialists) to develop an individualized education plan (IEP) for each child with identified special needs.

While this movement toward full inclusion has generated new challenges and responsibilities for teachers, it has also created wonderful new opportunities for children with disabilities. Koppenhaver, Spadorcia, and Erickson (1998, p. 95) explain:

> The importance of inclusive instruction for children with disabilities is that they receive instruction from the school personnel who have the greatest knowledge of literacy theory and practice, the most training, and the greatest print-specific resources. They are surrounded by models of varied print use, purposeful reading and writing, frequent peer interaction and support, and the expectation that children can, should, and will learn to read and write.

These types of positive literacy experiences are especially important for children with disabilities. Marvin and Mirenda (1993) investigated the home literacy experiences of children enrolled in Head Start and special education programs. They found that the parents of children with special needs placed a much higher priority on oral communication than on learning to read and write. Parents of preschoolers with disabilities reported less adult-initiated literacy activity in the home, less exposure to nursery rhymes, and fewer trips to the library.

In Special Feature 9.3, Karen Burstein and Tanis Bryan describe how teachers can make accommodations to promote language and literacy learning for children with a variety of special needs. These adaptations, when combined with the activities described in this book, should enable teachers to get all students off to a good start in learning language and literacy.

On Your Mark, Get Set, Go: Strategies for Supporting Children with Special Needs in General Education Classrooms

Karen Burstein and Tanis Bryan

ON YOUR MARK

Teachers in preschools and kindergartens are increasingly likely to have children with special needs in their classrooms. Typically, the majority of these children have speech and/or language impairments, developmental delays, and learning disabilities. A smaller number of these children have mental and or emotional disturbances, sensory disabilities (hearing or visual impairments), and physical and health impairments. The latter reflects increases in the number of children surviving serious chronic conditions (e.g., spina bifida, cystic fibrosis) and attending school as well as increases in the number of children with less life-threatening but nonetheless serious health (e.g., asthma) and cognitive (e.g., autism) problems.

One of the primary goals of early education is to prepare all young children for general education classrooms. Making this a reality for children with

SPECIAL FEATURE 9.3 (*continued*)

special needs requires that teachers make accommodations and adaptations that take into account the individual child's special needs. Teachers' willingness to *include* children with disabilities and their skillfulness in making adaptations are critical determinants of effective instruction. This special feature outlines strategies and suggestions for teachers who have young children with special needs in their classrooms. Our purpose is to provide suggestions for making adaptations so that teachers feel comfortable, confident, and successful including these children in their classrooms.

GET SET

Cognitive, physical, sensory, developmental, physical, emotional—there are so many variations in development! It is not reasonable to expect general education teachers or special education teachers to be experts on every childhood malady. The primary lesson to remember is that children are far more alike than they are different from one another. Whatever their differences, children desire and need the company of other children. They are more likely to develop adaptive behaviors in the presence of peers. Children with special needs can succeed academically and socially in mainstreamed settings (Stainback & Stainback, 1992; Thousand & Villa, 1990).

Setting the stage for an inclusive classroom takes somewhat more planning. Effective planning includes input and support from the school administration, other teachers, parents of children with special needs, and possibly the school nurse. Early and frequent collaboration with your special education colleagues is particularly helpful. There are significant differences between general and special education teachers' perspectives on curriculum and methods of instruction. Sometimes they differ in expectations for children.

Collaboration works when teachers constructively build on these different points of view. Collaboration produces multiple strategies that can be tested for effectiveness (as in the proverbial "two heads are better than one"). For collaboration to work, teachers have to respect different points of view, have good listening skills, and be willing to try something new. It also requires systematic observation and evaluation of strategies that are tested. Teachers have to ask, "How well did the strategy/adaptation work? What effect did it have on the children in the class?" Here are some strategies for collaboration:

- Attend the student's multidisciplinary team meeting.
- Keep a copy of the individual family service plan (IFSP) or individualized education plan (IEP) and consult it periodically to ensure that short- and long-term goals are being achieved.
- Arrange to have some shared planning time each week with others who work with children with special needs.

- Brainstorm modifications/adaptations to regular instructional activities.
- Identify who will collect work samples of specific tasks.
- Assess the student's language, reading, and writing strengths, and give brief probes each week to check on progress and maintenance.
- Share copies of student work with your collaborators and add these artifacts to the child's portfolio.
- Collaborate with families. Parents are children's first and best teachers. Additionally, they possess personal knowledge of their children that far surpasses any assessment data we may collect.

GO

As previously mentioned, the majority of children with special needs have difficulties in language, reading, and written expression. Research indicates that these problems stem from deficits in short-term memory, lack of self-awareness and self-monitoring strategies, lack of mediational strategies, and inability to transfer and generalize learned material to new or novel situations. Hence, many children with special needs may have difficulty in classroom settings that utilize a high degree of implicit teaching of literacy. These children typically can benefit from explicit instruction. Here are some general teaching strategies that teachers can use to support children with special needs:

- Establish a daily routine on which the child with special needs can depend.
- Allocate more time for tasks to be completed by children with special needs.
- Structure transitions between activities, and provide supervision and guidance for quick changes in activities.
- Adapt the physical arrangement of the room to provide a quiet space free of visual and auditory distractions.
- Plan time for one-on-one instruction at some point in the day.
- Use task analysis to break learning tasks into components.
- Recognize the different learning styles of all students, and prepare materials in different ways—for example, as manipulatives, audio recordings, visual displays, and the like.
- Try cross-ability or reciprocal peer tutoring for practice of learned material.
- Begin teaching organization skills such as the use of a simple daily planner.
- Teach positive social behaviors to all children.
- Consistently implement behavior change programs.
- Recognize and help children with special needs deal with their feelings.

(*continued on next page*)

SPECIAL FEATURE 9.3 (continued)

- Encourage all children to respect and include children with special needs in their academic and play activities.
- Establish a routine means of communication with parents.
- Locate strategies that help parents to select materials that are developmentally and educationally appropriate for their children.

SPEECH DEVELOPMENT

When children come to school, they are expected to be able to communicate. Language is the ability to communicate using symbols; it includes comprehension of both oral and written expression. Speech is one component of oral expression. Many young children come to school with delays in speech and language (comprehension and expression). Speech problems such as misarticulations and dysfluencies are frequently seen in young children with and without special needs. Less obvious are problems understanding others' speech. Fortunately, the majority of children with language problems are able to successfully participate in all aspects of general education with a few modifications to the environment or curriculum.

Frequently, children with language problems receive special education services from a speech and language pathologist. However, the classroom teacher also has important roles to fulfill: (1) monitoring children's comprehension of instructions and classroom activities, and (2) providing opportunities for oral language practice and interaction with peers and adults.

The following are strategies that classroom teachers can use to help promote speech development in children with oral language delays:

- Collaborate with the speech and language pathologist in selecting activities, materials, and games that promote language development.
- Model appropriate grammar, rhythm, tone, and syntax.
- Keep directions simple, brief, and to the point.
- For students who have difficulty expressing themselves, do not rely solely on open-ended questions.
- Use yes or no questions that are easier to answer.
- When students with speech problems speak, give them your full attention and ensure that other students do the same.
- Errors should not be criticized. Pay attention to the content of the child's message. Do not call attention to misarticulations, especially dysfluencies, as the problem may become more serious if attention is called to it (Lewis & Doorlag, 1999).
- Children who stutter may have improved speech quality if alternate styles of communication are used, such as whispering, singing in a higher or lower pitch, or choral reading.
- Give children with special needs multiple opportunities across the day to converse with you.
- Encourage parents to routinely engage in conversations using children's new words, experiences, and relationships.

Special strategies are also needed to help language-delayed children learn the meanings of new words (receptive vocabulary) and be able to use these new words in their speech (expressive vocabulary):

- Teach vocabulary in all subjects: math, science, social studies, health, and so on.
- Assess the child's prior knowledge before introducing a new topic.
- Have the student develop a word book of new words for practice. Pair these words with pictures.
- Encourage children to ask about words they do not understand. Pair these new words with concepts already known.
- Have the students paraphrase new words they are acquiring.
- Use physical demonstrations of words, such as verbs and prepositions, that are difficult to explain. Show children the meanings of these words.
- Have the students physically demonstrate the meanings of words.
- Use manipulatives that children can handle to teach new words.
- Give multiple examples of word meanings.
- Teach students to use picture dictionaries to locate unfamiliar words.
- Keep parents informed of these special strategies and urge them to continue their use outside of school.

For children with more severe special needs, secure the services of a specialist in augmentative communication. These individuals have specific skills in communication boards, electronic communication devices, and computer voice synthesis. For more information about this special area, contact the Assistive Technology On-Line Web site at www. asel.udel.edu?at-online, sponsored by the DuPont Hospital for Children and the University of Delaware.

WRITING INSTRUCTION

Most young children with special needs do not have physical impairments. However, many may experience delays in both fine and gross motor development. These delays may affect a child's ability to effectively grasp a pencil or shape letters and numbers. Large or ball-shaped crayons are often effective writing tools for children who have not developed a pencil grip. Many commercial built-up pencils or pencil grips are

SPECIAL FEATURE 9.3 (continued)

also available. When using these grips, be sure to instruct the child in the proper finger and hand placement on the pencil. For very young children with special needs, tracing letters in sand is a good place to start. Practicing letter structure in fingerpaints or liquid soap is also effective. Paper used by young children can be brightly colored to produce a contrast between the writing and the background. Initially, plain paper without lines is preferable to that with lines, as printing is similar to drawing. Using successive approximation of the appropriate size and shape of letters can be accomplished with wide-lined paper with different-colored lines. These lines serve as cues for the child to stop or go. Young children with more severe special needs may require the support and services of occupational therapists. These therapists can provide you with expertise and specialized equipment to promote fine motor development.

Written expression by young children with special needs may present several problems for the teacher and the child, as writing is both a process and a product that requires physical and cognitive skills. The written product should be assessed using observable and measurable goals that correspond with the strengths and weaknesses of the child. Teachers need patience and repeated observations of children's written work in order to effectively evaluate and plan for writing instruction. The following are strategies for promoting written expression by young children with special needs:

- Allocate time for writing each day.
- Have children create simple stories from tangible objects that they can touch and manipulate, rather than asking for a memory or a concept. For example, give a ball to the child and ask the child to tell you about this ball. Have an adult serve as a scribe for the child and take dictation, writing down the story as it is composed. When the child is able, ask the child to copy the dictated copy and draw a picture of the ball.
- Compliment children on the content of their stories. Ask for more information about the topic and help them expand their stories.
- Develop a template for writing—for example, putting name and date on a specific area of the paper.
- Celebrate the child's successes!
- Exhibit examples of all children's work.

Including young children with special needs in the general education setting can be a rewarding experience for the children and their teachers. Assisting children to meet their potential is a teacher's responsibility. These strategies have proven to be effective for teachers supporting children with special needs in special and general education classrooms. However, the most effective tool for teachers is shared planning and collaboration. We urge teachers in all settings to share their skills, experience, and techniques with one another and celebrate the diversity of learners in the schools of this new century.

Summary

Chapters 4 through 7 presented the instructional strategies that create the framework for an effective early childhood language arts curriculum. However, these strategies by themselves are not sufficient to construct a program that ensures optimal language and literacy learning for all children. This chapter presents the other two key ingredients: assessment and adapting instruction to meet the needs of second-language learners and children with special needs.

■ *What is important for teachers to know about children's literacy development?*
Teachers need a thorough knowledge of language and literacy guidelines for young children. This information may be obtained from several sources, including state standards and nationally defined outcomes.

■ *What are the two general approaches teachers might use to assess their children's literacy learning?*
Teachers use two kinds of assessment to measure their children's progress toward the achievement of the state standards: ongoing and on demand.

■ *What types of ongoing assessment tools are used to collect information about children's progress?*
Changes in what we know about literacy learning have necessitated major changes in our ways of measuring young children's literacy accomplishments and progress. In addition to on-demand assessments that provide samples of student literacy behavior, teachers

rely on ongoing assessment procedures that are connected with the daily literacy activities that take place in the classroom. This ongoing assessment makes heavy use of systematic observation and the collection of samples of children's work. The classroom library, writing center, and dramatic play areas are ideal settings for this type of assessment, and anecdotal notes, vignettes, and checklists provide effective ways to record data.

■ *How do teachers use the information they collect?*

Teachers (and children) collect information and store it in working portfolios. The products and information contained in a working portfolio are analyzed by the teacher (and the student) to assess the student's progress over time. These types of authentic assessments provide just the type of information that teachers need to know to provide effective literacy learning experiences for children.

Teachers also use the information they collect in portfolios to share with parents. Parents need to know how their children are progressing, and most parents need to have concrete examples with explicit information provided by the teacher to see how their child's early literacy efforts will develop into conventional reading and writing. Most early childhood educators recommend showing parents examples from the working portfolio and the showcase portfolio.

■ *How do ongoing assessment techniques help early childhood teachers meet the needs of diverse learners?*

In order to make literacy learning experiences accessible to all children in the classroom, teachers also need to make accommodations for the tremendous diversity that is present in today's classrooms. Special features by Myae Han and by Karen Burstein and Tanis Bryan explain how instructional activities can be modified to meet the needs of children who are learning English as a second language and those who have language disabilities and other special needs.

LINKING KNOWLEDGE TO PRACTICE

1. One way teachers determine what they want and need to know about children's literacy development is by reviewing national, state, and local standards. Contact your state and a local school district to obtain a copy of the local standards for language arts at the pre-K and kindergarten levels. Given what you have learned about children's early literacy development in this textbook, do these standards appear to be reasonable goals for language arts instruction at these levels?
2. Interview a pre-K or kindergarten teacher about the information-gathering tools that he or she typically uses to collect information about children's literacy development. How does the teacher organize this information to share with parents?

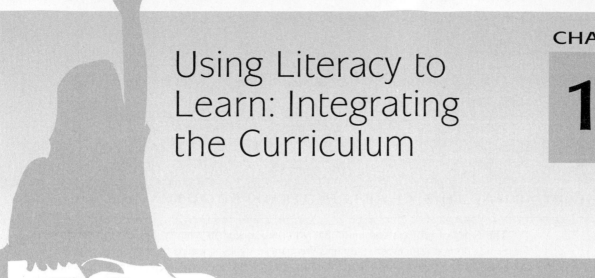

Using Literacy to Learn: Integrating the Curriculum

The four-year-olds in Ms. Flores's preschool class had been talking about their experiences at the grocery store. Ms. Flores decided to use a What do you KNOW? What do you WANT to know? and What did you LEARN? (KWL) chart to find out what the children already knew about grocery stores ("They have lots of food." "I like the cereal place.") and what they wanted to learn ("Where does the food come from?"). The class decided to study grocery stores to find the answers to their questions. During the weeks that followed, the class took several field trips to nearby grocery stores, invited store employees to visit their classroom, read books about grocery stores, and engaged in dramatic play in a grocery store play center stocked with store-related literacy (signs, empty product containers, note pads for grocery lists) and mathematics (scales, calculator) props. While engaging in their investigations and play, the children learned quite a lot about grocery stores (social studies concepts), and they also developed important literacy and mathematic skills.

For many years, early childhood teachers have connected, or integrated, the curriculum. This approach to curriculum planning and implementation has had a variety of labels. Some teachers use the term *interdisciplinary curriculum* (Jacobs, 1989), while others speak about immersing their children in the study of a theme (Manning, Manning, & Long, 1994). Other early childhood teachers suggest they are using the project approach (Katz & Chard, 1993).

When the language arts are woven into the very fabric of all subject matter areas, it is a classic win-win situation. Subject matter content and the language arts are both learned more effectively. As teacher Tarry Lindquist (1995, p. 1) points out:

> It is through the language arts that my students most often reveal their knowledge and apply their skills. Reading, writing, listening, and speaking are integral to all learning. Without language arts, the construction of meaning in specific topics is impossible.

An integrated approach to curriculum has three basic requirements: (1) a classroom environment rich with materials to support children's investigations, (2) a daily schedule that permits interweaving the various subject matter areas and focusing on a topic for sustained periods of time, and (3) teachers who view their role as a facilitator of learning rather than as a transmitter of knowledge.

In this chapter we describe how many teachers are connecting the language arts, helping children use literacy to learn, planning integrated curricula designed to meet their children's interests and needs, designing classroom environments that support their children's investigations, and arranging for the time that is needed for their children's study and play.

BOX 10.1	**integrated curriculum:** organizing the concepts, goals, content, and learning activities around a topic of interest and importance to children. Sometimes called thematic teaching
Definition of Terms	**KWL chart:** a strategy for facilitating comprehension. Prior to studying a topic, the teacher creates a chart with the children listing what they already know about the topic (the K) and what they want to learn (the W). After the topic has been studied, the teacher makes a list of new things that the children learned (the L of the chart)

BEFORE READING THIS CHAPTER, THINK ABOUT . . .

■ The types of projects and units that you participated in when you were in school. What topics do you remember studying? Were these topics selected by the teacher, by the students, or both? What sorts of activities were included in the projects or units? How did you share the findings or products?

FOCUS QUESTIONS

■ How can teachers plan and implement an integrated curriculum unit or project?
■ How can teachers arrange the classroom's physical environment and daily schedule to support the integrated curriculum?

The Integrated Approach to Curriculum Design

A group of teachers in Colorado chose the topic of dinosaurs and developed it into an integrated unit. Judith Gilbert (1989) described these teachers' unit. First, the teachers decided on the concepts they wanted to address and queried their young students about the questions they wanted answered during their study of dinosaurs. For example, one concept centered on one of the children's questions about the size of dinosaurs: How big were dinosaurs? The teachers designed an activity to help their young children understand dinosaurs' size and to answer their question. One of the teachers drew a full-size outline of a dinosaur on the school's parking lot. The number of children who could fit inside a dinosaur was estimated and calculated. Many children could fit inside the dinosaur outline! Then the teachers had the children lie flat on the parking-lot outline, with one child's feet touching the top of another child's head, extending from the bottom of the dinosaur drawing's feet to the tip of the dinosaur's nose. In this way, the children were able to determine that a dinosaur was about ten children tall. Did that mean a dinosaur could see over the school building? To help the children answer this question, ten children's silhouettes were traced vertically on a roll of butcher paper. The school's custodian kindly climbed to the roof of the building and hung the butcher paper from the top of the school building. The children discovered that the paper was longer than the school building was high! This helped the children understand that dinosaurs could see over their school building. Numerous other activities were implemented to help the children answer their questions and understand the major concepts about dinosaurs.

In the preceding example, concepts about dinosaurs and children's questions drove the teachers' creation of the educational activities. Subject-matter areas appropriate to the activities or projects were woven naturally into the children's investigations. The seams among the subject-matter areas were erased. The teachers had to be alert to the knowledge and skills the children were acquiring through the activities. In addition, the teachers had to consider new ways to legitimately weave subject areas and skill development into the activities.

Susan Neuman (2006, p. 35) suggests that through the integrated curriculum approach teachers can organize large amounts of content into meaningful concepts for their young learners. This approach

. . . helps children to build knowledge networks and provides more time and focus for repeated practice of familiar concepts. Further, children learn and apply skills in various contexts, increasing the likelihood of transfer and extending understanding . . . . Thematic teaching that works helps children understand a topic well, as opposed to skimming and covering many areas.

How do teachers make the right decisions and design quality curricula? What might their classroom schedules look like? How do they design their classroom environments? These questions are the focus of this chapter.

Erasing the Seams: Designing Integrated Curricula

Phase 1: Selecting a Topic

Lillian Katz and Sylvia Chard (1993) suggest that teachers use relevance to young children's daily lives to drive their identification of topics appropriate for children's study. They suggest topics like the children's homes, families, and food; the local community's people and businesses; important local events and current affairs; nearby landmarks, rivers, hills, or woods; and natural phenomena like the weather, water, wind and air, plants, and animals. Note how topics such as these, regardless of their breadth, help children "make sense of their own personal experience and of life around them" (Katz & Chard, p. 68). Gayle Mendes (2005, p. 12) agrees with Katz and Chard. She suggests that

> From birth, [children] begin exploring their world. At each stage of early development—infant, toddler, preschool, and primary—children look around and try to make sense of their social and physical environments. They gradually learn more about their expanding community and eventually come to see themselves as citizens.

It is clear that if children are to invest themselves in the study, the topics selected must be important to them. They must not be "intellectually trivial . . . , limited in content" (Neuman 2006, p. 34). Blending these experts' suggestions, the writers of this book advise early childhood teachers to consider broad topics relevant to the lives of their children and their community.

Phase 2: Determining What the Children Already Know and What They Want to Learn about the Topic

Once the topic or theme has been selected, it is important for the teacher to know what the children already know and what misconceptions the children possess about the topic before planning begins. Often teachers begin by constructing a KWL chart with their children—a chart with three columns, the first two of which show the answers to the questions: What do you already know? What do you want to learn? After the study of the topic is completed, the third column of the chart shows the answer to, What did you learn? (Ogle, 1986). The teacher serves as the recorder of the children's collective knowledge.

This is exactly how Melissa Scholl (2005) began her three- and young four-year-olds' study of babies. She and her coteacher (who was pregnant) asked, "What do you know about babies?" They discovered what their young learners knew and what they wanted to know. These young learners wanted to know such things as how to take care of babies and what they had been like when they were babies.

At this stage of information gathering, it is important to accept and record all comments made and questions generated by the children. Not only is knowing what children know important for their teachers, but knowing children's misconceptions also provides their teachers with insights into needed learning experiences.

With three-year-olds, this information-gathering stage likely will be one on one and rather informal, with the teacher quickly recording the children's comments and questions. With four- and five-year-olds, a group discussion might be more likely. During a group discussion, because teachers are members of the classroom learning community, the teacher might raise questions to extend the children's thinking about what they might learn. For example, as the children consider the topic of dinosaurs, a popular topic with many groups of children, if no child raises the question about how big they really were, the teacher might suggest that this is something she or he would like to learn. "Do we know how big dinosaurs really were? I've seen them on television, but I've always wondered: If a dinosaur stood beside me, how much taller than me would it be? I've also wondered: Could a dinosaur fit in this room? I don't think so, but how tall and long were they? I'm interested in answers to these questions." With that, the teacher's question (How big were dinosaurs?) could be added to the What do you want to learn? column on the KWL chart.

Carol Avery (1993) described another reason teachers need to understand what their children know about a topic before they plan activities. In a forty-five-minute discussion, her young students demonstrated their knowledge of all of the concepts about urban, suburban, and rural communities outlined in the Lancaster County, Pennsylvania, district curriculum guide. Her students had lived in the area for all their young lives and had attended to their environment. Life had provided her children with this knowledge. Had Avery not begun with a What do you already know? discussion, she would have wasted time presenting information and offering her children activities on concepts they already understood.

Phase 3: Determining Ways to Answer Children's Questions: The Activities or Projects

The concepts to be addressed, the questions generated, and the children's misconceptions drive the decisions about which activities these children will do during their study of the topic of interest. Since major concepts relative to each topic are embedded in children's and teachers' questions, teachers know their children will come away from their study with important understandings. In addition, teachers know that the various subject matter areas are embedded in the questions.

Teachers using the integrated approach do not set out at the beginning of their planning with the intention of ensuring that all subject matter areas are covered. They know that most, if not all, subject areas will be embedded in each topic's study using this approach. If activities are planned thoughtfully, the activities will draw heavily on a variety of disciplines for facts, skills, concepts, and understanding. In fact, it will be nearly impossible not to weave the language arts into nearly all of the activities. The children will be doing lots of listening, reading, writing, enacting, speaking, and observing.

Melissa Scholl's (2005) children learned about babies through the following activities:

- Studying displays of their baby pictures
- Listening to and "reading" fiction and nonfiction books on babies
- Playing with baby dolls, bathtubs, and washcloths in the water table
- "Babysitting" a classroom doll overnight and documenting the experience with a camera and journal
- Listening to presentations about babies from experts
- Studying the differences between a two-month-old and an eleven-month-old
- Watching as mothers bathe, diaper, and feed their babies
- Comparing what babies do with what they do at the "old ages" of three and four
- Interviewing their parents for answers to their questions (e.g., "How long was I?" "How much did I weigh?")

Judy Helm (1999) describes how a group of four-year-olds approached their study of photography. The children interviewed and worked with experts. That is, their teacher made arrangements for them to interact with adults who knew a lot about photography. Helm reminds teachers to talk with the experts before their visit to the classroom about the children's developmental level and to encourage the experts to consider leaving something with the children, perhaps something like "a small light table so that the children can view slides they've taken together" (p. 28).

Children might also go on field trips as a part of their investigation of the topic. They might bring clipboards, paper, and pencils with them to make sketches of what they see. An adaptation and extension of Elena Bodrova's and Cindy Leong's (2006) suggestions for helping children understand what the people at a field trip site do and say are detailed in Special Feature 10.1. Attention to the language and actions of the roles of the people at the site will

SPECIAL FEATURE 10.1

Making the Most of Field Trips

1. Identify the different roles the children will see at the field trip site. For example, on a field trip to a veterinarian's office, the children will see a doctor, nurse, and receptionist.
2. Prior to the field trip, visit and speak with each person the children will meet at the site. Ask each person to demonstrate what he or she does and says.
3. During the field trip, act out each role in front of the children. For example, in the receptionist area of the office, the teacher might explain that this is where people wait with their pets to see the doctor. The people must talk to the receptionist before seeing the doctor. The teacher might say, "This is Mrs. Johnson and she is the receptionist. Mrs. Johnson, please tell the children what you do and show us what you do and say when a sick pet comes into the office." Mrs. Johnson says, "I'm the receptionist. I say hello to the people as they come in. I make sure they sign in and then I get the chart—the nurse's and doctor's report of what happened the last time the pet was sick." Then, the teacher should play the sick pet's owner's role. The 'pet owner' walks up the counter. The receptionist says, "Hello, could you please sign in here?" She hands the sign-in chart to the 'pet owner', and the 'pet owner' signs in. The teacher shows the children the sign-in chart. The receptionist says, "Do you have an appointment?" The 'pet owner' says, "Yes, I have an appointment." The receptionist says, "What seems to be the problem?" The 'pet owner' says, "Lotus, my cat, keeps throwing up her food." The receptionist says, "Please have a seat in the waiting area. The nurse will come get you to take you and Lotus to the doctor in a minute. I am going to get Lotus's chart." The receptionist shows how she gets the chart and puts it where the nurse can collect it. She then tells the children that she will tell the nurse that the 'pet owner' and Lotus are waiting for her. The teacher says, "Now I sit down with Lotus and play with her while we wait for the nurse and the doctor." Repeat this process for each role.

4. While each role is being acted out, take a picture of each stage in the sequence. For example, take a picture of (a) the receptionist handing the 'pet owner' the sign-in form, (b) the 'pet owner' and receptionist talking, (c) the receptionist getting the chart, (d) the 'pet owner' sitting playing with the baby, and (e) the receptionist putting the chart where the nurse can retrieve it.
5. Back in the classroom at circle time, share the photos with the children. Talk about what each person did and said. Practice the language associated with each picture. (The children do not need to recall the exact words; the gist of the language linked with each photo is very acceptable.)
6. Create a literacy-enriched veterinary play setting in the dramatic play center. Set the center up so that it replicates the field trip site. For example, create a veterinary's office play setting with reception and examination room areas. Include materials in each area that the children can use as they do and say what they saw and heard during the field trip. Teachers should enter the play setting as the owner of a sick pet, modeling the language heard and doing what was seen on the field trip.

greatly enhance the quality of the children's play in the dramatic play area back in the classroom. Definitely teachers should bring digital and/or video cameras with them on class trips to record the significant aspects of the trip.

Finally, children can explore the topic using various resources in classroom learning centers. The teacher's task is to collect and organize materials related to the topic and then observe and listen to the children's interactions with these materials. These observations provide insight into what children are learning about the topic of study.

SHARING LEARNING WITH OTHERS. As teachers plan for and consider various ways for children to express their learning, they want to be cognizant that knowledge can be expressed in many different ways. The question is, what is the best way for children to share their learning with others? Several different kinds of products will be possibilities. Typically, the children will choose the product that seems most appropriate for them. Judy Helm suggests that sharing is a wonderful means of concluding the project. She suggests that children might make a large display, make a book about what they learned, produce a videotape that "tells the story of their project," or hold an open house for their families (1999, p. 31).

INTEGRATING LITERATURE INTO THE STUDY.   As young children engage in investigation activities, they will be "reading" many different materials (books, encyclopedias, pamphlets), or more likely having information read to them. The teacher's role is to gather trade books (fiction and nonfiction) that are correlated with the topic under study. For example, when Nancy Edwards's kindergartners studied the pond, her library corner was filled with books about water and the animals that live in it. In addition, books carefully selected to link to each day's activity were placed in other classroom centers. For example, nonfiction books on frogs were placed in the science area. Edwards placed a bookmark in the book showing the frog's life cycle. As the children watched the tadpoles develop, they used the book as a resource to help them answer their questions, e.g., "What do tadpoles eat?" "What will happen next?" She placed counting books with a water animal theme in the math area. The dramatic play center was transformed into a picnic and fishing area; she placed books about picnicking and fishing in the dramatic play area. In this way, Edwards helped her young learners see books as resources. (Of course, she also placed paper and writing tools in each center so that the children could record their thoughts.)

Phase 4: Assessment and Evaluation

As described in Chapter 9, assessment and evaluation are intricately woven into the learning process; teachers gather data about their children's study of topics (assessment), and they make judgments about what their children have learned and need to learn (evaluation) while their children are engaged in learning.

While children work, teachers gather evidence to document their children's learning, skill development, and dispositions toward learning. Using these data, teachers and the children themselves make judgments about the children's learning. Note that unlike in past years, it is not just the teacher making judgments about the children's learning. Child self-evaluation is a critical component of the new assessment and evaluation procedures.

Evidence, then, of the children's learning is demonstrated by the products created during the children's investigations, constructions, dramatic play, writing, and speaking while they study topics. Not only is the teacher gathering information about what the children are learning about the topic of study, but the teacher is also gathering information about each child's reading, writing, speaking, and listening learning. Every activity is an opportunity to gather data about the children.

Phase 5: Involving Parents

While "Involving Parents" is listed as the fifth phase of designing and implementing an integrated unit, parents can and should be involved throughout the study of a topic. If teachers want parents to be involved in what is going on in the classroom, then parents must be brought into each topic's study.

Lillian Katz and Sylvia Chard (1993) suggest that teachers can help parents become involved in their children's study by:

(1) Helping children share information about their study with their parents while the study is progressing. For example, newsletters, written by or with the children, detailing the classroom activities can provide information for conversations. Similarly, occasionally photocopying a page from the children's learning logs provides a record of what the children learned on a particular day. Some teachers bring parents together regularly as a group to speak to them about their curricular intentions. Knowing that some parents will be unable to attend such a meeting, a follow-up summary can be sent to those parents who were unable to attend. Perhaps a parent with secretarial skills would be willing to prepare minutes of the meeting. Many parents want to be involved and need teachers' assistance in the how of their involvement.

(2) Encouraging parents to ask questions of their children about their study and to become involved in their children's study. Some children are excellent at responding to the age-old parent question, "What did you learn in school today?" Many children, however, answer

"Nothing." Effective teachers look for ways to help parents structure their questions so that they generate a genuine parent–child conversation about children's learning. These teachers might include illustrations of possible kinds of questions (sometimes constructed with the children) at the end of a classroom newsletter. Other teachers hold a meeting to help parents ask the kinds of questions that generate more than a "yes," "no," or "nothing" answer.

(3) Involving parents "in providing information, pictures, books, and objects for the whole class in its pursuit of knowledge on the topic" (Katz & Chard, 1993, p. 106). Are there parents who hold jobs who are willing to speak to the children about their occupations? Could the children interview their parents to discover what they do?

These kinds of involvement activities help parents feel they are taking an active part in their children's education. Parents are important partners in their children's education.

Designing the Classroom's Physical Environment to Support the Integrated Curriculum

The classroom is the stage on which the drama will be played. The props it contains and how it is set up are critically important to the successful implementation of an integrated curriculum. Both the materials provided and the physical arrangement of these materials in the available space affect children's behaviors (Gump, 1989; Morrow & Weinstein, 1982, 1986). The classroom floor plan used by one teacher of young children, Sandra Lawing, is shown in Figure 10.1 as an illustration of several points teachers need to consider in arranging their classrooms.

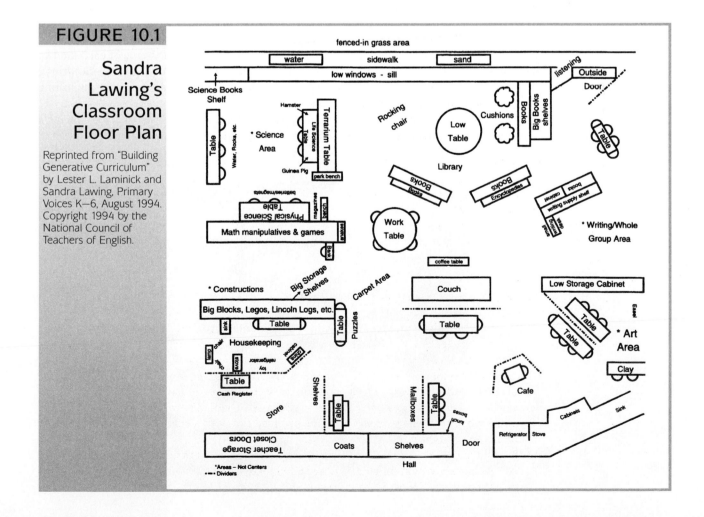

FIGURE 10.1

Sandra Lawing's Classroom Floor Plan

Reprinted from "Building Generative Curriculum" by Lester L. Laminick and Sandra Lawing, Primary Voices K–6, August 1994. Copyright 1994 by the National Council of Teachers of English.

Carve the Large Classroom Space into Small Areas

Notice how Sandra Lawing's classroom is divided into small, well-defined activity areas. Small, clearly defined areas encourage more interaction and sustained activity than do large areas. In addition, smaller areas accommodate fewer children, which leads to a quieter classroom and fewer behavior problems. Each area (or center, as it is often called) needs to be clearly evident to its users. Areas can be clearly defined with movable furniture (such as bookshelves, cupboards, tables, boxes), screens, and large plants (real, if possible, but if not, artificial will do).

Typically, these centers are designed around each content area. Hence, classrooms have a science center, a mathematics center, a library center, a writing center, a dramatic play center, and so forth. To assist children's understanding of the purposes of the areas, each area should be clearly labeled with a sign mounted near the children's eye level. With young children, an appropriate picture or symbol should accompany the written label.

Gather Appropriate Resources to Support the Children's Learning

Typically, the materials needed to support children's engagement in activities are housed in the various centers. Suggestions for materials for the writing center can be found in Chapter 8 and for the reading/library area in Chapter 4.

Each item should have a designated storage place. This designation helps children to find the materials with ease and to replace the materials for the next child's use. This means that each center needs shelves, tables, or boxes for the materials, with the designated spot for each material clearly labeled.

Within each center, the method of exhibiting the materials should be considered. For example, blocks of like sizes, like shapes, or like materials should be grouped together in the block center (sometimes called the construction site). The labels might read: *long, rectangular, wooden blocks*; or *small, square wooden blocks;* or *red Lego blocks*. Pictures of each kind of block by the words will support the youngest children's reading. Similarly, paper in the writing center can be grouped by color, kind, and size. Labels might include those for publishing paper, rough-draft paper, stationery, and cards.

Functional signs (e.g., "Make construction plans here!") can also be used to guide children's behavior in each center. Experiences with such signs encourage even the youngest children to

Placing items in labeled, designated places helps children find and return the materials they need.

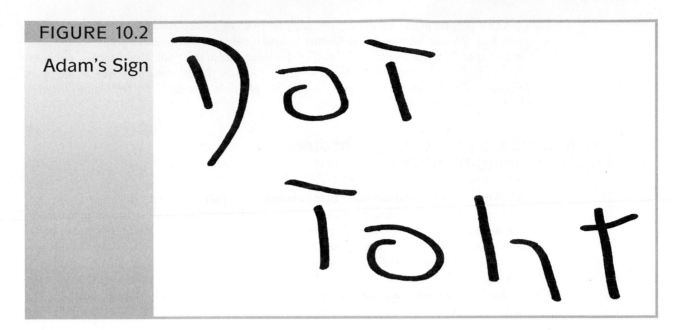

FIGURE 10.2

Adam's Sign

attend to the functional purposes of print and to begin to make use of signs to achieve their purposes. We present an example of a kindergartner named Adam's use of a functional sign, "Dot toht" (Don't touch), in Figure 10.2. (No one touched his paper while he was away from the writing center.)

Place Similar or Related Centers Near Each Other

Sandra Lawing placed the library center and the writing center close to each other. These two centers belong together because they both encourage children's development and use of literacy. In fact, some educators combine these centers into a literacy center because their focus is children's literacy development. The two centers occupy a major portion of the classroom space.

Make Literacy Materials a Part of the Fabric of Each Center

Sandra Lawing's classroom's science center has many science books in it. So does her block area. By including books, writing tools, posters with print, magazines, and other relevant materials in each center, each center's potential for developing children's literacy is enhanced. Putting literacy materials in the various centers supports children's literacy development and is an important way for teachers to enhance children's literacy learning. By enriching all centers, children read, write, speak, listen, and observe to learn.

In environments like those described above, children are immersed in literacy learning in every center. Such environments support children's natural literacy experimentation throughout the entire day. Because these environments are rich with print (e.g., books, magazines, posters, functional signs, writing paper and tools), young children can engage in meaningful explorations of speaking, listening, reading, and writing in real-life situations. They read the OPEN sign, and they know what it means. They record their observations in their learning log to help them remember what they saw. They are readers and writers because their teachers have provided them with multiple opportunities to interact with the written word.

How might teachers know that their classrooms are literacy-rich environments for young children? How might administrators know that all of the classrooms in their building are literacy-rich environments for young children? Many Early Reading First projects use the *Early Language and Literacy Classroom Observation* (ELLCO) form (Smith & Dickinson, 2002) to help them judge the quality of their classroom's literacy environment. The Literacy Environment

Checklist portion of the ELLCO is divided into five categories: Book Area, Book Selection, Book Use, Writing Materials, and Writing around the Room. Raters assign points for the presence of specific items within each category. For example, in the Book Use category, raters assign points for the number of books in the science area, in the dramatic play area, in the block area, in other areas of the classroom, and for the presence of a place for children to listen to recorded books or stories.

Organizing the Classroom's Daily Schedule: Creating a Rhythm to the Day

Recall that children need chunks of time to investigate topics alone, with small groups of other children, and with the whole group. On the one hand, flexibility in the schedule is needed to permit students to focus on flowers or insects for a block of time when their needs and interests dictate. On the other hand, some predictability to life in the classroom is necessary. In this section, we consider how to create a schedule that supports children's engagement in meaningful learning.

Sample classroom schedules are provided in Figure 10.3. In each of these schedules, the teachers followed several common principles. They have

---

FIGURE 10.3

Daily Schedules

A Toddler Schedule

9:00	Arrival
9:00–10:15	Activity Time
10:15–10:25	Clean-Up
10:25–10:40	Snack
10:40–10:50	Book Time (individual lap reading)
10:50–11:20	Outdoor Play
11:30	Dismissal

A Preschool Class Schedule—A.M.

9:00–10:30	Activity Time (snack is brought into the room at 10:05 A.M. to be one of the activities the child can choose)
10:30–10:35	Clean-Up (each child is given a specific job)
10:35–10:50	Gathering Time
10:50–11:20	Outdoor Play
11:20–11:45	Lunch (with clean-up and toothbrushing when each child finishes)
11:45–12:00	Storybook Reading

A Kindergarten Schedule—Half Day

8:45–9:00	Arival/Greeting Time
9:00–9:20	Circle Time
9:20–10:20	Activity or Free-Play Time
10:20–10:30	Clean-Up
10:30–10:45	Snack and Quiet Reading
10:45–11:10	Group Time
11:10–11:30	Outdoor Play
11:30–11:45	Literature Time
11:45	Dismissal

- balanced quiet times with noisier times, and sitting and listening time with movement time;
- provided large chunks of time for individual and small-group investigations and shorter amounts of time for whole-group activities;
- recognized their children's need for time to work together as a whole group, to work with peers in small groups, and to work independently;
- shown that they value having children choose and make decisions about how to structure their personal time.

A growing number of preschool children attend full-day programs, like Head Start and day care. In addition, a growing number of states are implementing full-day kindergarten programs; in some states full-day kindergarten is mandated while in others it is optional or being piloted in only some districts. Dixie Winters, Carol Saylor, and Carol Phillips (2003) investigated the benefits of full-day kindergarten and discovered that the research on the effects of full-day kindergarten on children's social development and academic achievement is positive, particularly for children from low-income backgrounds. Of course, the caveat is *when implemented with a high-quality curriculum and appropriate teaching practices*. Teachers respond positively to the full-day model. They report that the pace is more relaxed, less tiring, and less stressful for the children. They have a greater sense of accomplishment because they are able to accelerate all the children's language and literacy skills. Parents, too, respond positively. For working parents, a full-day program means that their children are ensured a level of quality care for a major portion of the day and they experience fewer day care issues. Also, they report that the teachers know their children better and that their children's early literacy skills are greatly enhanced. So what might a full-day schedule for young children look like? See Figure 10.4.

Through the use of these principles, these teachers demonstrate their recognition of children's need for diversity and variety in their daily activities. They also recognize children's need for predictability and a not-so-hidden structure to each day—a rhythm.

How firmly should teachers hold to a time schedule? Carol Wien and Susan Kirby-Smith (1998) suggest that teachers consider having an order of events but allowing the children to dictate the timing of the changes in activities. Kirby-Smith worked with two teachers of toddlers (age eighteen to thirty months) to test the idea of letting children's interests dictate the length of activities. After an initial period when the teachers experienced frustration and a period when the children were very happy, the teachers came to see that allowing the children's rhythm to control the timing allowed the children to focus. The teachers discovered that children preferred

FIGURE 10.4

Full-day Daily Kindergarten Schedule

8:45–9:00	Arrival/Greeting/Sign-in (each child signs in and collects a book to read on the rug)
9:00–9:20	Morning Meeting Time
9:20–10:20	Center Time (with snack at child's chosen time)
10:20–10:50	Morning Outdoor Play
10:50–11:20	Writing Workshop
11:20–11:30	Washing Up for Lunch
11:30–12:00	Lunch (family style, with conversation)
12:00–12:30	Storybook Reading Time
12:30–1:00	Quiet Time (nap, for those who need it, and independent book reading for others)
1:00–1:30	Afternoon Outdoor Play
1:30–1:50	Small Group Time (classroom adults each work with a small group of children)
1:50–2:50	Center Time
2:50–3:10	Afternoon Meeting Time (review of day's activities; writing of daily 'diary')
3:10–3:15	Ready for Dismissal

(1) being greeted on arrival and helped to make an activity choice; (2) having a long free-play period with snack and toileting naturally occurring without interrupting the whole group's play; (3) having a short circle time with music and action after the long free-play period; and (4) ending the morning with outdoor play time. Now the toddlers "co-own" the curriculum.

What Happens During Whole-Group Time?

Some teachers call whole-group sessions group time or circle time. Of course, it is during these times that the children and their teacher come together, typically in a carpeted area of the classroom. During the first group time of the day, teachers usually take attendance; make announcements; with kindergarten and older children, recite the pledge of allegiance to the flag; check the date on the calendar; report on the news of the day; and discuss plans for the day. Other whole-group sessions are used for introducing and discussing the integrated unit being studied; for the teacher to read literature aloud; for teacher presentation of a lesson on a writing or reading strategy; for singing songs; for the choral reading of poems; and for bringing closure to the day.

These group sessions typically last ten to thirty minutes, depending on the children's developmental needs and the teacher's intentions. Many of these whole-group times have been discussed in detail in other chapters. As Susan Neuman and Kathy Roskos (1993, p. 147) suggest, teachers' intent during whole-group sessions often is "to actively engage [all the children] in thinking and talking, reading and writing about ideas related to [the] topic of interest."

What Happens During Small-Group Activity Time?

Increasingly, early childhood teachers are recognizing the need to pull small groups of children together for explicit instruction on the language and literacy skills described in Chapter 7. For example, the teachers in the Miami/Dade County Early Learning Coalition Early Reading First project divided their children into three groups. For thirty minutes each day (ten minutes in each small-group activity), the children rotate among the three literacy activities. The classroom teacher engaged in a dialogic reading activity with six children; the classroom assistant engaged in a print awareness activity with another group of six children; and a third group of children played independently with literacy-related materials. Every ten minutes, the children moved to a new activity. In this way, the teachers were able to work with a small group of children explicitly using SBRR-supported strategies. Some days the children with similar literacy needs were grouped together. Other days, the teacher intentionally created small groups of children with differing literacy needs.

Early childhood teachers pull small groups of children together for explicit instruction.

What Happens During Center or Activity Time?

Typically, the children's curiosity will be aroused or their focus will be directed during the whole-group meetings. During the activity times, the children can act on their interests. During these times, the children might move freely about the classroom, selecting the area or center of interest to them. They might write in the writing center, read books in the cozy corner library, build structures in the block or construction center, or investigate and record their observations in the science center. It is important for teachers to provide children with time to engage in activities of their choice and to plan the use of their time.

It is also important for teachers to actively engage in learning with their children during these free-choice times. This is not the time for teachers to work at completing administrative tasks. It is the time to read a book with a child or two, take a child's dictation, happen upon a child at just that moment when she or he needs instruction, or play with the children in the dramatic play area.

During these free-choice times, the children might work with a small group of peers to answer questions of shared interest. In other instances, groups might form spontaneously; those five children who are interested in playing in the dramatic play area come together for play and stay until they are tired of playing in the center.

Integrated Units Alive in a Classroom

How do the parts of the day come together in the interdisciplinary study of a topic of interest to the children? How is it that children engage in purposeful activities that support the development of their abilities to speak, listen, read, and write? The following special feature provides an example of a developmentally appropriate integrated unit.

Special Feature 10.2 presents a unit on babies that Charlotte Woodward uses with her three-year-olds at the College of Education preschool at Arizona State University. As Woodward explains, the topic is of high interest to this age group because many three-year-olds have baby brothers and sisters. Notice how, even at this young age, children can use reading and writing as part of their investigation of babies and can even engage in some simple experimentation to learn more about babies' toy preferences.

SPECIAL FEATURE 10.2

The Baby Project

Charlotte Woodward

Integrated projects play an important role at the College of Education preschool at Arizona State University. These projects, or explorations, enable children to delve deeply into an area of special interest and to develop language and literacy skills at the same time. The interest and curiosity of the young preschool students initiate these projects. Although projects vary widely from year to year, one project that makes the exploration list frequently is the baby project. We think this is a popular subject for several reasons. The preschool's three-year-olds frequently have a baby brother or sister at home. And, of course, three-year-olds were babies themselves not long ago. They soon become the school's experts on the subject.

A baby project is usually initiated when a young student's mother gives birth to a baby. We begin the project with a special event, such as a visit of a mother and her baby. (It is sometimes not a good idea to have the baby belong to one of the three-year-olds, as sibling rivalry or sibling overprotectiveness can make it hard for the big brother or sister.) The mother brings along a baby bath, towels, powder, and so on, and gives the baby a bath. The children watch and talk about what they are seeing. Following the initial event, the children who wish can bathe doll babies at the water tables. We provide them with all the necessary supplies: towels, diapers, powder (cornstarch), baby soap, and the like.

As the project progresses, we have one or two more visits from mother and baby. If the mother has a scale, we might see how much the baby has grown and how it has changed. Things such as being able to turn over and sit up without being held are discussed. Another time the mother might come before snack time and feed the baby a bottle, baby food, cereal, or a teething cracker (depending on the age of the child). During snack time, the young students are offered a taste of the baby food or teething cracker.

(continued on next page)

SPECIAL FEATURE 10.2 *(continued)*

For a culminating visit, the class conducts its own experiment with the baby. Prior to the visit, the children look through selected toys from a baby catalog and decide on several toys that the baby might like to play with. Three toys are then purchased. When the mother and baby arrive, these toys are put on the baby's blanket, and the children watch closely to see which toy the baby goes to first. Last year it was a soft red ball with a bell inside. Later, when the children discussed why this toy was chosen they decided it was the red color and the noise the bell made.

Once the project is underway, books about babies are displayed in the class library and featured in the daily story-reading time. Here are some of the popular titles, many of which have a multicultural perspective, since the COE Preschool has a multicultural enrollment.

Bend's Baby by Michael Foreman (1987)
Tell Me a Story, Mommy by Angel Johnson (1989)
The Berenstain Bear's New Baby by Stan and Jan Berenstain (1974)
Eat Up Gamma by Sarah Hayes (1988)
In the Middle of the Night by Kathy Henderson and Jennifer Eachus (1992)

Geraldine's Baby Brother by Holly Keller (1994)
On Mother's Lap by Ann Scott (1972)
Mama, Do You Love Me by Barbara Joose (1991)
Peter's Chair by Ezra Jack Keats (1967)

We also stock our dramatic playroom with an extra supply of baby dolls and baby accessories. Taking care of baby develops into a very popular activity, as make-believe parents bathe, feed, and play with their "babies." This dramatic play provides an ideal context for children to work through and assimilate the knowledge about babies that they are gaining from other parts of the curriculum. This play also offers a wonderful opportunity for teachers to assess children's learning.

The project might end with construction of baby albums. Children bring to class several of their own baby pictures. Children mount them inside a blank book. A teacher assists by printing the child's name and "Baby Book" on the cover. The children can then dictate to the teacher words to go with the photos. Children are encouraged to draw in the books, perhaps a self-portrait. The books are taken home to share the results of the project with their parents.

Summary

Children learn best when they are engaged in inquiries that involve using their language to learn. For this to happen, the various content areas need to be naturally integrated. Through immersion in the study of a broad topic that is relevant to the lives of the students and their community, children read, write, speak, listen, and observe. How does this approach to an integrated curriculum match with your memories of projects and units when you were in school?

To summarize the key points about facilitating oral language learning, we return to the guiding questions at the beginning of this chapter:

■ *How can teachers plan and implement an integrated curriculum unit or project?*

The teacher begins by helping children select a topic for study and by determining what the children already know and want to learn about the topic. Next, the teacher engages the children in learning activities or projects. As children work on their investigations, the teacher engages in ongoing assessment and evaluation of children's learning. The teacher also involves parents in all phases of the unit.

■ *How can teachers arrange the classroom's physical environment and daily schedule to support the integrated curriculum?*

Teachers can create a classroom environment that supports an integrated curriculum by (1) carving classroom space into small, well-defined areas; (2) gathering appropriate resources to support the children's learning; (3) placing similar or related centers near each other; (4) making literacy materials part of the fabric of each center; and (5) creating an aesthetically pleasing environment.

The daily schedule should also support the integrated curriculum. A wonderful environment without blocks of time to use it is worthless. Large chunks of time are necessary for individual and small-group investigations and shorter amounts of time for whole-group activities. Quiet times during which children sit and listen should be balanced with active times. The schedule should also feature flexibility, so that children have the freedom to pursue their interests, and predictability, so that there is a rhythm to the day.

TABLE 10.1

Evaluating the Quality of Interdisciplinary Units

Kathy Roskos

	Yes	Somewhat	No

The topic is . . .

- child-centered
- broad in scope
- relevant to these children
- relevant to real-life in these children's community

During the study of the topic . . .

- the teacher begins by discovering what these children know (their prior knowledge) and what they want to learn
- children are given choices about which aspect of the topic they wish to investigate
- reading, writing, speaking, and listening are naturally woven into the activities
- activities are planned to help develop concepts and to answer the children's questions
- children share what they have learned with others
- the teacher provides information (e.g., how to take notes, how to write an informative report, how to make an oral presentation) the children need to successfully complete their projects and activities
- quality literature is woven into the study

Assessing students' learning . . .

- is ongoing, while the children complete the activities
- includes student self-evaluation

Teaching this unit, the teacher . . .

- involves the students' parents
- functions like an orchestra conductor, getting things started and moving them along, providing information and resources, and coordinating the buzz of activities
- conferences with the students

LINKING KNOWLEDGE TO PRACTICE

1. Kathy Roskos (1995) worked with a group of teachers to design a set of criteria and a scale that can be used to assess the quality of integrated units. An adaptation of these teachers' and Roskos's ideas is presented in Table 10.1. Visit a preschool or kindergarten classroom and use this scale to evaluate an ongoing unit or project.

2. While visiting the classroom, observe the physical environment. How does the classroom match up with the five criteria for a supportive physical environment presented in this chapter?

3. Obtain a copy of the ELLCO. Administer it in a classroom to rate the literacy-rich quality of this classroom.

4. What is the daily schedule in this classroom? Does this schedule support or hinder an integrated curriculum?

Helping Families Facilitate Language and Literacy Development

Nestling close on Grandma's big, soft, featherbed, Grandma reads Billie her favorite book,
The Little Engine That Could. *Grandma barely finishes the last word in the book when Billie*
asks her to read it again. As Grandma rereads, Billie echoes the refrain, "I think I can, I think
I can, I think I can!" After the story, Grandma always says, "If you think you can, you can do
anything." To this day, whenever Billie is challenged to learn new concepts or deal with
difficult situations, she remembers Grandma saying, "Just think you can, just think you can!"

If you share memories like Billie's, you are indeed fortunate. Research demonstrates that a
family's role in a child's language and literacy development is directly related to the child's
communicative competence (Hart & Risley, 1995), positive attitudes toward reading and writing, and literacy achievement (e.g., Christian, Morrison, & Bryant, 1998; Nord, Lennon, Liu,
& Chandler, 2000; Epstein, 1986).

When parents and teachers share information, the child benefits.

■ Your early literacy experiences. Do you remember precious moments snuggling with a special person and sharing a book? Do you remember talking with an adult who provided you with many experiences and the words to describe these experiences? Do you remember an adult helping you read words in your environment?

■ Your memories of a parent's report of a parent–teacher conference about your classroom behavior and learning. Do you remember if your parents always heard positive reports about your learning? Do you remember what happened if the teacher made suggestions for home learning activities?

■ News flashes, newsletters, and other written communication you carried home from school. Do you remember these being posted in your home, perhaps on the refrigerator door? Do you remember them helping you answer the question: What did you do in school today?

FOCUS QUESTIONS

■ What is known about the relationship between what parents do and children's literacy development?
■ In what ways might early childhood teachers communicate personally with parents?
■ How might teachers run a parent–teacher conference?
■ In what ways might teachers communicate with parents in writing?
■ What resources might an early childhood teacher provide to parents and parents provide to teachers to support young children's early literacy learning?

What Roles Do Families Play?

Collin (1992, p. 2) refers to the parents' nurturing role in their child's literacy development as "planting the seeds of literacy." Almost all parents want to plant these seeds, but many are unsure of the best way to begin. Similarly, most parents and other primary caregivers vastly underestimate the importance of their role in helping children become competent language users (McNeal, 1999). In this chapter, we discuss strategies teachers can use to inform parents of all cultures and other primary caregivers about the critical role they play in their child's language and literacy development, and how parents and teachers can work together to enhance language and reading and writing opportunities in the home. Special Feature 11.3 provides a multicultural perspective on this issue.

Parents play a critical role in helping children learn about print. Many children learn about literacy very early. This task is accomplished quite naturally as children sit on the laps of parents, other family members, or caregivers sharing a storybook. Surrounded by love, these children easily learn about the functions of print and the joys of reading. Being read to at home facilitates the onset of reading, reading fluency, and reading enjoyment. Unfortunately, a growing number of studies have documented a lack of parent–child reading opportunities, especially in low-income homes (Christian, Morrison, & Bryant, 1998; Griffin & Morrison, 1997). Lesley Morrow (1988) surveyed parents of children in three preschools serving poor families (incomes of less than $10,000, 40 percent minority, 75 percent single-parent headed). Ninety percent of these parents indicated that they read to their children only once a month or less! This lack of parental involvement

| BOX 11.1

Definition
of Terms | **bias:** a preference for or dislike of something; sometimes an unfair or unexamined feeling
developmental spelling: another name for invented spelling, where children use two or three letters to phonetically represent a word (e.g., *happy* might be spelled as *hape*)
family resource schools: schools with programs that reach out to families by providing parent education, adult education, health services, etc. |

Communicating with parents begins at the classroom door.

may have a significant effect on the children's learning throughout their schooling. For example, Billie Enz's (1992) study of 400 high school sophomores revealed that 70 percent of the remedial readers could not recall being read to by their parents as children, while 96 percent of the students in advanced placement courses reported that their parents had read to them regularly. In essence, it appears that a child's future literacy and subsequent success in school depend on parents' ability and willingness to provide the child with thousands of planned and spontaneous encounters with print (Enz & Searfoss, 1995).

Parental involvement also has an important effect on children's writing development. In the following example, notice how four-year-old Timeka's early attempts at writing are subtly supported by her mother:

> Sitting at a table with crayon in hand, Timeka is engrossed in making squiggly lines across a large paper. Timeka's mother, sitting across from her, is busy writing checks. After Timeka finishes her writing, she folds her paper and asks her mother for an envelope so she can "pay the bank, too." As mother smiles and gives Timeka the envelope, she remarks, "Good, our bank needs your money."

This brief example illustrates how Timeka is taking her first steps to becoming literate. While most children need formal instruction to learn to read and write conventionally, children who have parents who guide and support their beginning literacy efforts learn to read and write more quickly. As Timeka observes her parents and other adults writing, she discovers that these marks have purpose and meaning. Timeka then imitates, to the best of her ability, this process. Since the adults in Timeka's life also regard her efforts as meaningful, Timeka is encouraged to refine both her understanding of the functions of print and her writing skills. In that regard, Timeka's scribbles are to writing as her babbling was to talking. Because her parents approve and support her attempts instead of criticizing or correcting them, Timeka practices both talking and writing. This dual effort also simultaneously develops her understanding that words and thoughts can be expressed both orally and in print (Fields, Spangler, & Lee, 1991). Parents who value their children's growing literacy abilities also encourage their development.

Dilemmas Facing Modern Families

The "family in America—Black, White, Hispanic, and Asian—is actually in the throes of basic upheaval" (Carlson, 1990, p. xv). As evidence, Carlson cites the three factors most likely to affect school performance: the employment of both parents in more than 70 percent of nuclear families, the high divorce rate, and the increase in single-parent families. Recent research studies report that 40 percent of today's schoolchildren will have lived with a single parent by the time they reach the age of eighteen (Flaxman & Inger, 1991). The financial and psychological stresses many single-parent families face may not allow parents either the time or emotional energy to sustain conversation or read to their children on a regular basis.

Another significant factor is the cycle of poverty and undereducation. Research consistently reveals that a child whose parent has poor literacy skills is at great risk of repeating the illiteracy cycle (Nord, Lennon, Liu, & Chandler, 2000; Christian, Morrison, & Bryant, 1998; Lonigan & Whitehurst, 1998). Likewise, Betty Hart and Todd Risley's (1995) study clearly demonstrates that welfare parents often transmit their limited vocabulary and lower oral communicative competence to their children.

Two factors span socioeconomic and cultural differences. First, as educators we must help parents understand the crucial role they play in helping their children become successful communicators, readers, and writers (Epstein, 1995). Secondly, we must build parents' knowledge of how to support their child's language and literacy development. How else will parents be able to fulfill their role as their child's first and most important teachers? Table 11.1 presents Age-Appropriate Support Activities that parents may choose to use with their young children to help them to develop language and literacy skills.

Helping Parents and Primary Caregivers Become Effective First Teachers

Helping parents become successful language and literacy models is one of a teacher's most important tasks. To fulfill this responsibility, teachers at all grade levels must interact with parents constantly! However, this role may be more challenging than many teachers initially anticipate. In this chapter, we describe two categories of communication efforts: personal interactions and classroom instructional publications.

Personal Interactions

Personal interactions are opportunities for parents, other family members, and early childhood teachers or caregivers to share information about a child's individual needs in two-way conversations. Personal interactions also offer unique opportunities for modeling communication and literacy strategies. These personal interactions include home visits, family workshops, phone calls, parent–teacher conferences, progress review conferences, and specific problem conferences.

Today's teachers need to be aware that English may not be their children's parents' dominant language; therefore, a teacher may need to have a translator help with communication during personal interactions. Regardless of how teachers choose to communicate, observation shows that whatever the content, medium, or language, any message is enhanced if it is delivered warmly, respectfully, and with genuine concern.

HOME VISITS.   Perhaps the best way to reach parents prior to children's formal entry into preschool or kindergarten is through home visits. Teachers demonstrate how to bring stories to life for children and parents by modeling story-reading strategies, encouraging language interactions, and supporting beginning writing opportunities. Teachers also discuss age-appropriate language and literacy behavior.

Since the 1970s, home-visit programs have increased in number, especially as states and communities refocus attention and resources on young children. The programs can have long-term benefits by offering maternal and child health care, parenting education, school readiness skills, guidance on how to create a literate home environment, and a direct link to other social services (Jacobson, 1998).

FAMILY WORKSHOPS.   Another strategy for involving and directly informing parents of preschool and kindergarten students about how to support their children's language and literacy learning is through family workshops. The purpose of the workshops is to share explicit information about the children's development and the class curriculum, and to provide practical

TABLE 11.1　Age-Appropriate Support Activities: Birth to Age Five

Months		Language	Print Recognition	
		Speaking/Listening	Receptive/Reading	Expressive/Writing
0–6	CD	Babbling, extensive sound play.		
	PS	Talk to baby. Sing to baby. Make direct eye contact with baby when speaking. Use parentese.		
6–12	CD	Echolia, vocables, first words.	Is able to listen to short stories. Wants to handle books.	
	PS	Label objects. Scaffold child's language efforts.	Provide cloth and cardboard book. Read to your child.	
12–24	CD	Begins to use words and gestures. Responds to simple requests.	Begins to recognize environmental print/logos.	Begins to use writing implements to make marks.
	PS	Listen and actively respond. Read stories. Engage in frequent conversations.	Confirm print recognition, "Yes, that is Coke." Read to your child.	Offer chalk/chalkboard, paper, and crayons.
24–36	CD	Uses simple sentences, adds new words rapidly, and experiments with inflection.	Attends to pictures—describes pictures, then begins to form oral stories reflecting pictures.	Knows print has meaning and serves practical uses. Makes scribble marks.
	PS	Engage child in complex conversations frequently. Listen to child.	Read, read, read to your child. Ask child to label characters and objects.	Provide access to many types of writing implements/paper.
36–48	CD	Proficient language user. Engages in dramatic play. Likes to learn songs.	Attends to pictures. Repeats familiar story phrases.	Print recognition—may write letter-like units, and nonphonetic letter-like string.
	PS	Serve as co-player in dramas. Teach new songs. Ask child questions to encourage two-way dialogue.	Reread familiar stories. Ask open-ended questions. Begin home library.	Model writing process. Demonstrate your interest in your child's writing efforts.
48–60	CD	Uses language to obtain and share information.	May begin to recognize individual words.	Conventional writing emerges as letter–sound relationship develops.
	PS	Offer logical explanations. Listen and respond thoughtfully and thoroughly.	Shared reading. Frequent visits to library and expand home library. Demonstrate your enjoyment of reading.	Being writing notes to child. Read your child's writing.

CD: Child's development
PS: Parental support

suggestions that parents may use at home to support their child's learning (Brown, 1994; Rhodes, Enz, & LaCount, 2006).

Teachers must prepare for family workshops. They need adequate supplies. They may need to organize the room. They need to set up refreshments (parent–teacher organizations or center budgets can often reimburse teachers for refreshments). Teachers should remember several points when running a family workshop. First, the workshop should begin promptly. Second, start with a get-acquainted activity to put people at ease and begin the workshop on a relaxed, positive note. Third, remember that parents should not be lectured to; instead, they should experience hands-on, highly engaging activities. After the parents have engaged in the activity,

SPECIAL FEATURE 11.1

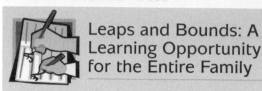

Leaps and Bounds: A Learning Opportunity for the Entire Family

Michelle Rhodes and Marilyn LaCount

The mission of the Leaps and Bounds program is to provide high-needs communities with a research-based program that provides generally Spanish-speaking parents and family members with practical knowledge necessary to prepare their children for kindergarten. The family-friendly activities use common, home-related items to promote logical mathematic knowledge, language-literacy development, and social competence.

WORLD AS A CLASSROOM WORKSHOP SERIES

Parents, family members, and their children attend four 75-minutes workshops in which they engage in activities demonstrated by program facilitators (often preschool or kindergarten teachers at the school site) and college student interns. The four workshops include:

Workshop #1 and #2—Learning around the House

Activities focus on learning in and around the house, including the kitchen, bathroom, and family room. Activities will also focus on learning with music, art, and play. Children also learn when they visit the grocery store, go to the doctor's office, go for a walk, ride the bus, etc. Learning opportunities are everywhere. In these workshops, parents will learn to teach their child through everyday activities in their environment.

Workshop #3 and #4—Learning in the Environment

Activities focus on family outings in the familiar environment (i.e., baseball game, grocery store, going out to eat, going to the park, etc.). Activities focus on learning in the environment as well as in the car or bus or in walks through their community.

One of the most important features of the workshops is the time parents; children, and facilitators spend together brainstorming about how families can extend these simple learning activities, for example, using environmental print the child recognizes to make an alphabet book, or My Favorite Food list, at home. Through active participation and open social interaction, this program provides parents and family members with the support and confidence necessary to be their child's first teachers. By simply providing parents and family members with knowledge and support in utilizing inexpensive and immediately accessible resources, the program encourages parents to spend more time with their children. Thus, they are better able to fulfill their role as their child's first teacher. Programs like Leaps and Bounds can increase parental involvement at home and increase learning and performance in school.

provide brief, specific information about the theory underlying the process. Most importantly, remember to smile. When the teacher has a good time, the families will also!

PHONE CALLS. Another powerful tool for communicating with parents is the telephone. Unfortunately, phone calls have traditionally been reserved for bad news. However, successful teachers have found that brief, positive, frequent telephone conversations help establish a strong partnership with parents (Fredericks & Rasinski, 1990). When parents receive a phone call about something exciting at school, they immediately sense the teacher's enthusiasm for teaching their child and are more likely to become involved in classroom activities. Thus, whenever possible, the phone should be used as an instrument of good news. Whenever a call is made and for whatever reason, it is important to have the parents' correct surname; there are many step-families in today's schools. All calls to parents should be documented. A phone log can be effective for managing and maintaining a record of phone conversations (see Figure 11.1). This log should contain a separate page or section for each child in the class, making it easy to trace the contacts with specific parents (Enz, Kortman, & Honaker, 2002).

PARENT–TEACHER CONFERENCES. Children are complex, social individuals who must function appropriately in two very different cultures—school and home. Parents need to understand how a child uses his or her social skills to become a productive member of the school community. Likewise, experienced teachers appreciate the child's home life and recognize its significant influence on a child's behavior and ability to learn. Partnerships reach their full potential when parents and teachers share information about the child from their unique perspectives, value the child's individual needs and strengths, and work together for the benefit of the child.

FIGURE 11.1

Phone Call Log

Child: Robert Romero   Parent's name: Mrs. Rodriguez

Phone #: 555-7272

Date: *Feb. 2*   Regarding: *Robert has been absent for 3 days*

Action: *Robert has chicken pox, he will be out at least 4 more days.
Older brother will pick up get well card from class and bring home
storybooks for entertainment.*

Date: *March 3*   Regarding: *Academic Progress*

Action: *Robert having great success with reading, especially paired-reading.
Is hesitant to write during writer's workshop. Teacher will send
home writing briefcase and have parents write stories with him.*

Date: *April 12*   Regarding: *Writing progress*

Action: *Robert showing more confidence and comfort with his writing. He
shared a story he wrote with parents to the class today.*

Date: Regarding:

Action:

Date: Regarding:

Action:

Date: Regarding:

Action:

Date: Regarding:

Action:

The best opportunity teachers have for engaging parents in this type of discussion is during parent–teacher conferences. Conferences should feature a two-way exchange of information. There are generally two types of parent–teacher conferences: preestablished conferences that review the child's classroom progress and spontaneous conferences that deal with a range of specific concerns occurring throughout the year.

PROGRESS REVIEW CONFERENCES.   The progress review conference is an opportunity for parents and teachers to share information about children's social interactions, emotional maturity, and cognitive development. One way to help a parent and teacher prepare to share information during the conference is a preconference questionnaire. The teacher sends the questionnaire home to the parent to complete and return prior to the conference. In Figure 11.2, we present the notes made by Manuel's mother as she prepared for her conference with Ms. Jones, her son's kindergarten teacher. The information Mrs. Rodriguez provides also tells Ms. Jones what concerns she has; therefore, Ms. Jones has a better idea about how to focus the conference. Remember, it may be necessary to have this letter and questionnaire translated into the language spoken in the home.

During the progress review conference, the teacher, of course, will share information about the child's academic progress. In Chapter 9, we discussed how to develop and maintain assessment portfolios and document observational data for each child. The portfolio allows the teacher to document the child's development over time. In addition to academic progress, most parents want to know about their children's social interactions and classroom behavior. The observational data that the teacher has recorded helps provide a more complete picture of the child in the classroom context.

FIGURE 11.2

Preconference Questionnaire

Dear Parent,

To help us make the most of our time, I am sending this questionnaire to help facilitate our progress review conference. Please read and complete the questions. If you have any other concerns, simply write them down on the questionnaire and we will discuss any of your inquiries during our time together. I look forward to getting to know both you and your child better.

1. How is your child's overall health?
   Good, but Manuel gets colds alot.

2. Are there specific health concerns that the teacher should know about? (include allergies)
   Colds and sometimes ear infections.

3. How many hours of sleep does your child typically get?
   About 9

4. Does your child take any medication on a regular basis? If so, what type?
   He takes penicillin when he has ear infections.

5. What are the names and ages of other children who live in your home?
   Maria, 9; Rosalina, 7; Carlos, 3.

6. How would you describe your child's attitude toward school?
   He likes school.

7. What school activity does your child enjoy most?
   P.E. and art

8. What school activity does your child enjoy least?
   Math

9. What are your child's favorite TV shows?
   Power Rangers, Ninja Turtles

   How many hours of TV will your child generally watch each night?
   Three

10. What is the title of your child's favorite storybook?
    Where the Wild Things Are.

11. How often do you read to your child?
    His sisters read to him most nights.

12. What other activities does your child enjoy?
    Playing soccer.

Other concerns:
I can't read his writing. His sisters' was good in Kindergarten.

When working with parents, teachers are encouraged to use a structured format during the progress review conference. The structure keeps the conference focused and increases the chance of both teachers' and parents' concerns being adequately discussed (Enz, Kortman, & Honaker, 2002).

The success of the parent–teacher relationship depends on the teacher's ability to highlight the child's academic and social strengths and progress. When areas of concern are discussed, it is important to provide examples of the child's work or review the observational data to illustrate the point. Often, the issues the parents reveal are directly related to the concerns the teacher has. Whenever possible, connect these concerns, as this reinforces the feeling that the teacher and the parents have the same goals for helping the child learn. It is essential to solicit the parents' views and suggestions for helping the child and also to provide concrete examples about how they might help the child learn.

To make sure both teacher and parents reach a common understanding, briefly review the main ideas and suggestions for improvement that were discussed during the conference. Allow parents to orally discuss their views of the main ideas of the conference. Check the parents' perceptions. Finally, briefly record the parents' oral summary on the conference form. Figure 11.3 is a progress review conference form from Manuel's conference.

SPECIFIC PROBLEM CONFERENCES. Occasionally, concerns will emerge that require the teacher to work with the family immediately. The following case studies illustrate how teacher and parents worked together to help identify and resolve a specific problem in the home that was creating tension in the child's school life.

Four-year-old Sibby started preschool as a happy, confident child. She loved story time and had memorized several stories that her family had read to her over and over again. Sibby had

FIGURE 11.3

Progress Review Conference Form

Student's name: *Manuel Romero*   Parent's name: *Mary Romero*

Conference date: *Nov. 1*   Time: *4:30 p.m.*

Positive Statement: *Manuel is so eager to learn*

Review Conference steps:

Our conference today will consist of three parts. First, I will ask you to review your child's progress, sharing with me both academic/social strengths and areas of concern. Next, I'll review Manuel's work with you and discuss his academic/social strengths and areas in which we will want to help him grow. Finally, we will discuss the main points we discussed today, and review the strategies we decided would help Manuel continue to make progress.

1. **Ask for Parent Input:** What have you observed about Manuel this year that makes you feel good about his learning? (Take notes as parent is sharing)

Manuel likes school, drawing, friends, stories.

What are your main concerns?

His writing looks like scribbles. He's not reading yet but he likes stories read to him.

2. **Teacher Input:** I would like to share some observations about Manuel's work and review both areas of strengths and skills that need to be refined. *Manuel interest in reading is wonderful. He is eager to write in class journal. Though his printing is still developing, he is beginning to use "invented" spelling. Look at this example in his portfolio.*

> MT MpN PR RG2
>
> Mighty Morphin Power Rangers

Notice how he is separating the words. Ask him to read his work for you if you are having difficulty decoding or deciphering it. His printing skills will improve naturally with time and encouragement. He is really progressing well. Sometimes young girls develop finger muscles sooner. We need to support his efforts. Manuel enjoys sharing his writing in class with his friends and his art work is full of detail. Manuel has many friends and gets along easily with others.

3. **Closure:** Let's review those things we talked about that will facilitate continued success. (Teacher needs to write down this information as the parent talks)

a. *Manuel's printing is "okay" for him.*

b. *Manuel is writing. I am surprised to see that he really is writing. I just need to have him read for me. Then it's easier for me to figure out what his*

c. *letters say.*

learned to print her name and was excited about writing her own letters and stories (scribble writing and some letterlike streams). Sibby was interested in environmental print and often brought empty product boxes and wrappers to preschool because she was proud that she recognized words and specific letters. She loved playing in the dramatic play center and frequently demonstrated her understanding of the many practical functions of print. After winter break, Sibby's behavior changed abruptly. She said she didn't know how to read when she went to the library center, and she refused to write during journal time. Her teacher, Mrs. Role, quickly called Sibby's parents.

Mr. and Mrs. Jacobs came to preschool the following day. Mrs. Role described the dramatic change in Sibby's behavior and asked the Jacobses if they had any ideas about what may have caused the change. The Jacobses had also noticed a change in Sibby's confidence. After discussing her behavior, they mentioned that Sibby's grandmother, a retired high school English teacher, visited their home over winter break. They were surprised that Sibby's grandmother had been critical of their display of Sibby's stories on the refrigerator. Grandmother stated, "That youngster needs to know the correct way to write!" She felt that "praising Sibby's scribbles kept her from wanting to learn the right way to form letters," but they were sure Sibby had not overheard any of these comments. However, they remembered that Grandmother babysat Sibby one afternoon just before her visit was over. Mrs. Jacobs promised she would talk to Grandmother about the babysitting episode.

The following week, Mrs. Jacobs reported that Grandmother had decided "it was time someone taught Sibby how to print her letters properly." During the afternoon Grandmother and Sibby were together, Sibby had spent most of the time practicing making letters correctly. In addition, Grandmother required Sibby to say the letter sounds as she repeatedly wrote each letter. Grandmother told Sibby that she "would not be able to read and write until she knew all her letters and their sounds."

The Jacobses and Mrs. Role attributed Sibby's reluctance to read and write to her grandmother's inappropriate instructional efforts. Sibby was going to need a great deal of encouragement and support from her parents and her teacher to regain her confidence.

Classroom Instructional Publications

Classroom instructional publications are designed to describe the children's learning activities or directly inform parents about specific literacy concepts. They may include informal news flashes, weekly notes, and a more formal monthly newsletter that features regular columns, such as Dear Teacher, Family Focus, and Center Highlights. With the growing number of homes with computers and Internet access, some teachers may be able to publish their classroom instructional publications on a classroom Web site or Listserv. Of course, teachers must check with their children's parents to learn which homes have access to these services. Sadly, those teachers who work with young children from low-socioeconomic families likely will find few families with Internet access. The digital divide is widening, rather than narrowing, in the United States. Communities are struggling to learn how to increase Internet access to families of modest financial means.

INFORMAL WEEKLY NOTES. Because consistent communication helps create a sense of community, the authors strongly recommend weekly or, at minimum, bimonthly notes. Frequent communications allow teachers the opportunity to

- provide a bond between school and home experiences;
- extend parents' understanding of developmentally appropriate curricula;
- involve parents in assessing the child's growth and development;
- encourage parents to reinforce and enrich children's learning; and
- strengthen the working partnership between parents and teacher.

Weekly notes are typically one page long and generally include (1) information about upcoming events; (2) items about children's achievements; (3) explanations about the curriculum that help parents understand how children learn to read and write; (4) practical and developmentally appropriate suggestions for working with children; and (5) recognition of parents

FIGURE 11.4

Informal Weekly Note

Dear Parents:

Last week our field trip to the hospital was exciting and we learned even more about how doctors and nurses serve our community. Have your child read you the story they wrote and illustrated about what we learned on our hospital journey. One of the most exciting stops in the hospital was the baby nursery. All of the children were interested in their own first stay at the hospital. Perhaps you will be able to share your memories about that event. A great big thank you to Mrs. Delgato and Cecille Ortiz for helping to chaperon. They also helped our students write their stories.

This week we will discuss fire safety at home and school. Our first lesson is called "Stop, Drop, and Roll," which teaches us what to do if our clothes catch on fire. Next, we will discuss the proper use and storage of matches and lighters. We will also map a safe exit from our room in case of fire and review appropriate behavior during an emergency (no talking, listen to teacher's directions, leave all possessions, walk the planned escape route). We will actually have a schoolwide fire drill to practice these skills. Because you and your child's safety is so important, I am asking that you work with your child to draw and label a map of your house and design the best fire escape route. Drawing the map and labeling the rooms of your house teach your child vocabulary words and reinforce the fire safety concepts I am teaching in school. On Friday we will go to our local Fire Station. Attached to this note is a permission slip. Since this is a walking field trip, I will need at least four parent volunteers. I hope you can join us. To help all of us learn more about fire safety, the Fire Marshall will provide the children and their families with a booklet called "Learn Not To Burn." The book is available in Spanish also. If you would like additional copies, let me know. Please review this informative and entertaining booklet with your child.

To learn even more about fire safety and fire fighters, you might wish to read the following books to your child. These books are available in the classroom, school, and local public library.

EL Fuego, by Maria Ruis and Josep McParramon, Harron's.
Pumpers, Boilers, Hooks and Ladders: A Book of Fire Engines,
by Leonard Everett Fisher, Dail Press.
Fire Fighters, by Ray Brockel, Children's Press.
Curious George at the Fire Station, by Margret and H.A. Rey, Houghton Mifflin.
Puedo Ser Bombero, by Rebecca Hankin, Children's Press.
The Whole Works: Careers in a Fire Department, by Margaret Reuter, Children's Press.

If you have any personal experiences in the area of fire safety, please let me know and you can be an Expert Speaker for our classroom.

Sincerely, Mrs. Jones

---

who have helped support classroom learning—for example, parents who accompanied the class on a field trip (Gelfer, 1991).

It is important for informal weekly notes to be reader friendly and brief and to suggest successful activities for parents and children to do together. These suggestions typically are well received if they are stated in a positive, proactive manner—for example, "Reading to your child just ten minutes a day helps your child become a better reader," not, "Your child will not learn to read unless you read to her or him."

Figure 11.4 is a sample of an informal weekly note. Observe how Ms. Jones reviews the previous week's activities, taking the opportunity to thank parents who have provided supplies or support. Next she describes the focus of this week's curriculum and provides suggestions that will help parents reinforce this information at home. Notice how Ms. Jones uses friendly, everyday language to introduce and explain new concepts and suggests realistic, content-appropriate literacy activities that encourage parents to become involved in classroom learning.

NEWS FLASHES. Occasionally events require immediate publication, or an upcoming activity warrants attention (e.g., parents need to be reminded that their children will attend school for only a half day because of parent–teacher conferences or alerted that their children will be on the TV news tonight). Teachers may use news flashes to inform parents about TV programming that is relevant to curriculum the class is currently studying or provide supplemental information about an author study (see Figure 11.5). News flashes might also be used to tell a parent about a noteworthy event in the child's life that day (e.g., Zack wrote his first letter today!).

FIGURE 11.5

News Flash

Ms. Jones' class will be studying the writings of Mercer Mayer! Some of his books include

Little Monster's Neighborhood
Little Monster At School
Little Monster At Home
Little Monster's Alphabet Book
Little Monster's Bedtime Book
Just For You
Just Me and My Dad
Just Grandma and Me
Just Me In the Tub
Just Go To Bed
I Just Forgot
Just Me and My Friend
Just Me and My Mom
Just Shopping With Mom
The New Baby

All of these books are published by Western Publishing Company, Inc. Racine, Wisconsin. Look for these and other Mercer Mayer books in your public library!

MONTHLY NEWSLETTERS. Like weekly notes, monthly newsletters create a sense of community. The goal of monthly newsletters should be to provide parents with specific information about children's literacy development. In addition, monthly newsletters offer parents an opportunity to preview the curriculum and classroom projects for the upcoming month. As most parents have extremely busy schedules, monthly newsletters help them plan ahead and thus increase the likelihood that they will be able to participate in school activities. Monthly newsletters are generally two or three pages long and typically use a two- or three-column format. Regular features, such as Dear Teacher, Family Focus, Curriculum Overview, Center Highlights, and Monthly Calendar inform parents in a direct, but fun and interesting, manner. In Figure 11.6, we provide a sample kindergarten newsletter written for the month of October. Notice the regularly featured columns.

DEAR TEACHER LETTERS. As the sample newsletter demonstrates, parents frequently have questions about reading to their children. An effective way to address these inquires is through Dear Abby–type letters. The teacher frames the questions based on common concerns she hears from the parents. The following are examples of typical parent questions, answered by advice based on Jim Trelease's (1989) work.

Dear Teacher: My three-year-old often becomes restless when I read stories to him. What can I do to keep his interest? *Signed, Wiggle-Worm's Mom*

Dear Wiggle-Worm's Mom: While most children enjoy having stories read to them, most young children also have a short attention span. Hence, younger children need to be actively involved in the reading. Asking your son to predict what he thinks will happen next or asking him to point to a character or discuss some aspect of the illustration is an excellent way to keep his attention.

Dear Teacher: I have three children, and our evenings are hectic to say the least! I also work, so the time I have is limited. When is the best time and for how long should I read to my kids? *Signed, Watching the Clock*

Dear Watching: Excellent question! Many parents have multiple responsibilities, and time is always an issue. The best time is whenever you can consistently schedule about fifteen to twenty minutes alone. For most parents, that time appears to be just

FIGURE 11.6

Mrs. Jones'
October
Newsletter

Ms. Jones' October Newsletter

Kindergarten Curriculum

 It's October and the Kinder-gartners in Ms. Jones' class are learning about our 5 senses—Halloween style! During this month we will learn about sight: how our eyes work, and eye health and safety. We will also have our vision tested. We will study the super sense of smell: How the nose and olfactory nerves work, and how smell and memory are related. We will learn how the ear hears and discover how hearing aids work. We will test our tongues to determine how the sense of taste works to detect sweet, salty, sour, and bitter. Finally, we will learn about the largest organ on our bodies—our skin! The sense of touch can teach us many things about our world.

Dear Teacher: Questions about Reading.

Dear Teacher,
Hola! Both my husband and I speak and read Spanish. Though our son speaks both languages, would it confuse him if we read him storybooks in Spanish?
Signed, Bilingual/Biliterate

Dear Bi-double L,
How wonderful it is that your son is already speaking two languages! It is perfectly fine to read books written in Spanish to him in Spanish—just as you would read books written in English to him in English. While he is learning to read in both languages, he will also begin to write in English and Spanish.

Parent Partnership: Your Child Learns to Write.

DR TUTH FRE ILS MI TUTH
PLS HEL ME FD et

Can you read this? This is a note to the tooth fairy. It was written by a child who lost her first baby tooth. Let's decode this note together.

DR TUTH FRE ILS MI TUTH

Dear Tooth Fairy, I lost my tooth.

PLS HEL ME FD et

Please help me find it.

As adults, we have been conditioned to read only conventional spelling. On first glance, this note may resemble only a string of letters. On closer inspection, we detect that its writer is trying to convey an important message. When young children begin to use print, their parents and teachers should encourage all attempts. Treating a child's scribbles or letter streams as important and meaningful encourages the child to continue her efforts. As she experiments with reading and writing, her understanding of the rules of our language increases. Eventually, developmental or invented spelling matures into more conventional spelling. To read more about this process you might want to read *Spell. . . is a four letter word* by J. Richard Gentry, (1987) from Heinemann Publishing Company in Portsmouth, New Hampshire.

(cont.)

before bed. However, some parents report that they find time right after the evening meal. Whenever you feel rested and can give your children fifteen to twenty minutes of undivided time is the best time to read to them.

Dear Teacher: My four-year-old son wants to hear the same story over, and over, and over. Is this normal? Shouldn't I read a new book each night? *Signed, Repeating Myself*

Dear Repeating: As adults we tend to like variety, but most young children between the ages of two and seven have a favorite story, and this storybook may be as comforting to them as their best-loved stuffed toy. So the question becomes how to have both variety and comfort. At this age, favorite books tend to be short, so one suggestion is to read two or three books at story time. Try reading the new books first and the favorite book last. When your child begins to read along with you, this is the perfect time to have him read this favorite book to you or to another child in your household. Frequently a child's favorite book becomes the first one he will read independently.

Dear Teacher: When I read my five-year-old daughter a book at story time, I worry about her comprehension skills. Should I ask questions? *Signed, Just the Facts*

Dear Facts: I'm so glad you asked that question. The stories you read will frequently inspire your child to share many of her thoughts, hopes, and fears. These discussions are

FIGURE 11.6

(continued)

Preparing for Parent/Student/Teacher Conferences

Conferences are wonderful opportunities for parents, student, and teacher to sit beside one another to share the students' work and review their progress. In our class each student will share the contents of his/her portfolio with both parents and teacher.

In the first half of the 20-minute conference, students will display and discuss their writing and perhaps read some of their stories. They will explain why certain products were included in the portfolio and why they believe these particular pieces best demonstrate their learning efforts. The students will also show the parents and teacher some of the work they completed at the beginning of the school year and compare it to how they are performing today. During this part of the conference, it is important for parents to listen to the student's self-evaluation. Parents are encouraged to ask open-ended questions, such as:

• What did you learn the most about?
• What did you work the hardest to learn?
• What do you want to learn more about?

These questions encourage students to analyze their own learning and also help them set new learning goals for themselves. Parents should not criticize the child's work or focus on any negative aspect of any material that is presented from the portfolio. Negative comments will only inhibit learning and dampen excitement about school. During the last ten minutes of the conference, the student will be excused so that parents and teacher have an opportunity to talk about any concerns the parents may have. Be sure to complete the Preconference Questionnaire and return it prior to the conference so that the teacher may be better prepared to discuss your concerns.

October Calendar

3rd	– Visit with the eye doctor: vision testing
7th	– Visit the audiologist: hearing tests
15th	– My Favorite Smells Day: bring in your favorite smell
18th	– Taste-testing day
19th	– School pictures day–dress bright
23rd	– Touch and tell day
28th–29th	– Parent/Student/Teacher Conference
31st	– Halloween/5 senses party

Remember: Weekly notes will provide details for each event.

Story Books for October

Georgie's Halloween, by Robert Bright (Doubleday)
The Teeny-Tiny Woman, by Paul Galdone (Clarion)
The Berenstain Bears: Trick or Treat, by Stan and Jan Berenstain (Random House)
Clifford's Halloween, by Norman Bridwill (Scholastic)
ABC Halloween Witch, by Ida Dedage (Garrard)
Who Goes Out on Halloween, by Sue Alexander (Bank Street)
It's Halloween, by Jack Prelutsky (Greenwillow)

obviously more important than reciting any particular detail. In fact, quizzing children about story details will only make story time an unpleasant activity for both of you. Instead, ask open-ended, opinion questions, such as "Which was your favorite part?" or "Why do you think Max stared at the Wild Things?" Story time will also motivate your children to ask you questions! Take your time, share your views, and allow your child to hear your thought process. This activity will do more to teach them about story interpretation than 1,000 fact questions! P.S. Did you know that Sendak's relatives served as the model for the Wild Things?

FAMILY FOCUS. Because many parents have a number of questions about how their child will learn to write, it becomes essential for teachers to proactively communicate information about the normal developmental process of writing. To help parents learn about emergent writing, teachers may wish to use a more formal, direct instruction approach, such as a Your Child Learns to Write column in the monthly newsletter, like the example in Figure 11.6. We recommend that before any children's writing is sent home, the teacher educate parents about the developmental writing stages. The following is an example of the most common questions parents ask about their child's writing development. The answers provide a sample of the tone and depth of information the column should contain.

■ *When does my child really start to write?*—We live in a culture where print is used to communicate. Therefore, children begin to read and write informally long before they enter school. By the time children are able to pick up a pencil or crayon and draw or scribble, they are demonstrating their knowledge that these marks mean something, and the first step toward written communication has begun.

■ *When my child draws or scribbles, does that mean that I should begin to teach him or her how to hold the pencil and form letters correctly?*—When your child first began to sing songs, did you start teaching him to play the piano? No, of course not! But you did enjoy the songs he or she sang, and you sang along. This is exactly the approach parents should take when their child first begins to draw or scribble write. Say, "Tell me about what you wrote about." Listen to the answer and compliment the effort.

■ *How can I encourage my child's writing?*—When children watch adults write a grocery list or a letter or pay bills, they are often motivated to imitate this writing. Usually, all children need are the writing materials—paper, markers, crayons, pencils—and they will take the ideas from there. Occasionally, you could suggest that they might wish to write a letter to Grandmother or leave a note for the tooth fairy. Another perfect opportunity to encourage writing is during their dramatic play. When children play house, they can write grocery lists or leave phone messages—all you need to do is provide the writing materials and praise. A particularly exciting activity is to have your child choose a favorite stuffed animal. The stuffed animal takes a field trip to Grandmother's house or to preschool with the child. That night, parents and child may write about and illustrate a story about "The Adventures of _____ at _____." Children will write frequently if they feel their attempts to communicate are accepted and valued as meaningful.

■ *Isn't handwriting practice important for learning to read and write?*—Learning the correct written form of a letter is called *handwriting*. It is an opportunity for children to gain control of the small muscles in their fingers and hands. However, handwriting drills do not teach children how to read and write. A child who exhibits excellent penmanship will not necessarily learn to read or communicate in written form any faster than the child whose writing still resembles scribbles. Critical comments about a child's handwriting efforts can stifle the joy of communicating. When a new scribe begins to learn the "how" of writing, it is far better to praise the efforts. This will encourage the child to write more.

■ *How do I read my child's written work?*—Start by asking your child to tell you what was written. The information provided will give you context. These clues should enable you to figure out what the scribble, shapes, or letters represent. Children tend to progress through predictable developmental stages on the way to conventional spelling. This progression may proceed from scribbles, to letter strings, to single letters representing whole words or thoughts, to invented spelling, to conventional spelling. Invented spelling is using two or three letters to phonetically represent a word—this is sometimes called developmental spelling.

H fi	hpe fi	hapy fi	happy
(happy)	(happy)		(happy)

■ *Should I correct my child's invented/developmental spelling?*—Have you ever changed what you wanted to write simply because you were unsure of the spelling of a word? Research reveals that children write less and use only a limited vocabulary of known words if their spelling is criticized. However, young children of six or seven who are encouraged to use their invented spelling will often write extensive stories with complex vocabularies. Parents may help children sound out phonetic words or spell more difficult words if the child asks for assistance.

Teachers and Schools as Professional Resources

"In some schools there are still educators who say, 'If the family would just do its job, we could do our job.' And there are still families who say, 'I raised this child; now it is your turn to educate her'" (Epstein, 1995, p. 702). Most often, children who need the most help come from families that need the most support. Schools and centers that wish to make a significant difference in the lives of these children must find ways to offer support and forge successful school–family partnerships (Gardner, 1993–1994). Fortunately, most early childhood educators find that educating a child requires at least two teachers—the one at school or the center and the one at home. Following are concrete suggestions that teachers may use to help parents fulfill their role as first teacher.

Sharing Instructional Materials and Offering Guidance

Preschool teachers frequently recommend that parents read to their young children (Becker & Epstein, 1982). Unfortunately, many parents face great financial hardships and cannot provide a large number of quality reading materials in their homes. Further, parents may not know how to encourage and engage their children's interest in reading (Richgels & Wold, 1998). To help parents to fulfill their role as partners in literacy programs, it is vital for teachers to work with these families to offer easy access to both books and writing materials (Brock & Dodd, 1994) and guidance in how to use them (McGee & Richgels, 1996).

CLASSROOM LENDING LIBRARY.   One way to ensure early literacy development at home and foster the home–school connection is through a classroom lending library. A classroom lending library allows children to check out a new book each day, thus ensuring that all parents have an opportunity to read to their child frequently.

The acquisition of quality books for daily checkout is the first step in establishing a classroom lending library. Since the children will exchange their book each day, all a teacher needs to begin a library is one book per child.

Managing the classroom lending library requires that all books contain a library pocket and identification card. The teacher needs to create a classroom library checkout chart. When a child borrows a book, she simply removes the book's identification card and replaces it in her or his name pocket on the classroom checkout chart. The teacher can easily see what book each child has checked out at a glance.

The rules that accompany the classroom lending library are simple. A child may borrow one book each day. When the book is returned, the child may check out another. Teaching the children to manage the checkout routine is easy. When the children enter the classroom in the morning, they return their books to the library by removing the book's identification card from their name pocket. They place the identification card back in the book's library pocket, and they place the book back on the shelf. The children may select new books anytime throughout the day.

WRITING BRIEFCASES.   Another popular option that may be included as part of the classroom lending library is the writing briefcase. The briefcase can be an inexpensive plastic carrying case or a canvas portfolio. Inside the briefcase, the teacher may provide writing paper, colored construction paper, markers, pens and pencils, glue, tape—anything that might stimulate a child to write a story, make a greeting card, design a book cover, or create whatever they can imagine. Depending on the size of the class, teachers may have seven or eight writing briefcases—enough so that four or five children may check out the materials each day, and two or three extras so that the teacher has time to replenish the briefcase supplies frequently and conveniently. The briefcases are numbered, and each has a library pocket and identification card. The checkout procedures follow the same routine as for library books. The writing briefcase may also contain explicit suggestions that encourage parents to use writing to communicate with their children.

BOOK BAGS.   Yet another way to encourage family participation and successfully engage and guide parents' literacy interactions with their children is through book bags (Barbour, 1998–1999). Like writing briefcases, book bags may be checked out of the classroom lending library for a week at a time. Book bags contain a collection of high-quality books and offer informal, interactive activities for extending children's language and literacy acquisition. When designing the bags, teachers need to consider their children's developmental stages, interests

FIGURE 11.7

Sample Book Bag Themes

Counting Theme

Hillanbrand, W. (1997). *Counting Crocodiles.* Orlando, FL, Harcourt Brace.

Kirk, D. (1994). *Miss Spider's Tea Party.* New York: Scholastic Editions Inc.

Barbieri-McGrath, B. (1998). *Hershey's Counting Board Book.* Wellesley, MA: Corporate Board Book.

Alphabet Theme

Wilbur, R. (1997). *The Disappearing Alphabet.* New York: Scholastic.

Alexander, M. (1994). *A You're Adorable.* New York: Scholastic.

Martin, B., & Archambault, J. (1989). *Chicka, Chicka, Boom Boom.* New York: Simon & Schuster Children's Publishing.

Rhyming Books

Goldston, B. (1998). *The Beastly Feast.* New York: Scholastic.

Slate, J. (1996). *Miss Bindergarten Gets Ready for Kindergarten.* New York: Scholastic.

Wood, A. (1992). *Silly Sally.* Orlando, FL, Harcourt Brace.

Getting Dressed

Degen, B. (1996). *Jesse Bear, What Will You Wear?* New York: Simon & Schuster Children's Publishing.

London, J. (1997). *Froggy Gets Dressed.* New York: Viking Children's Press.

Regan, D. (1998). *What Will I Do if I Can't Tie My Shoe?* New York: Scholastic.

---

and experiences, and literacy levels. The book bags (nylon gym bags) typically contain three or four books and activities inspired by a specific theme (see Figure 11.7 for sample book bag themes). In addition, each bag contains two response journals (one for the child and one for the parent). Some bags contain tape recorders and the tapes that accompany the books. The tapes and tape recorders are particularly important for parents who may not be able to read English. Each bag also contains an inventory that helps parents and children keep track of and return materials assigned to each bag.

VIDEOTAPES/DVDs.   As more schools have access to video cameras, another option to consider is creating a videotape or DVD lending section for the classroom library. Videotape has the potential to become an exceptional tool for teaching parents about storybook reading skills. The teacher may wish to videotape himself or herself reading an exciting storybook. While reading a book to the children, the teacher has the opportunity to demonstrate oral fluency, enthusiasm, and the use of different voices to make the story characters come alive. In addition, the teacher can illustrate how open-ended, predictive questioning strategies can facilitate children's active involvement during story time. Likewise, using retelling prompts, the teacher can demonstrate how children discuss story events with each other and share their unique and meaningful perspectives. These informal instructive videos may significantly help parents improve and expand their own story-reading skills. Children may check out both the videotape and the storybook. The video and accompanying storybook may be stored in a large self-sealing plastic bag. The same checkout procedures as for the library books or writing briefcases may be used.

Schools as Community Resources

Because literacy is a critical component for success in all aspects of community life, schools are beginning to extend opportunities for all community members to become involved in producing literate citizens. In extending our view of literacy beyond the classroom, we also expand our views of the traditional roles of schools. In the past decade, an increasing number of schools have chosen to provide for the social, medical, and educational needs of the families in

SPECIAL FEATURE **11.2**

Family Resource Schools

The way schools care about children is reflected in the way schools care about the children's families. If educators view children simply as students, they are likely to see the family as separate from the school. That is, the family is expected to do its job and leave the education of children to the schools. If educators view students as children, they are likely to see both the family and the community as partners with the school in children's education and development (Epstein, 1995, p. 701).

The major goal of family resource schools (also called learning community schools) is to strengthen the social and economic foundations of the neighborhood community. This goal is accomplished by providing extensive support to families, both before and after school. Family resource schools offer a broad range of service, including

Student achievement and activity programs, such as

- community study hall with volunteer tutors,
- family read-alongs and family math classes,
- physical activity classes (gymnastics, dance, etc.),

- fine arts classes (arts and crafts, chorus, guitar, etc.),
- community garden.

Adult education and skill building, such as

- adult basic education,
- general equivalency diploma,
- English as a second language,
- Spanish as a second language,
- conflict management seminars,
- employment workshops.

Parent education courses, such as

- parenting education programs,
- positive discipline workshops,
- sex education workshops,
- gang prevention workshops.

Family support services, such as

- on-site case management,
- alcohol and drug prevention programs,
- before- and after-school child care,
- baby-sitting co-ops,
- food and clothing banks,
- primary health care,
- mental health services.

their community (Patton, Silva, & Myers, 1999). In Special Feature 11.2, readers will find a discussion of the major components of family resource schools.

Teacher as Community Contact

Teachers also need to think beyond the classroom and consider the many ways reading, writing, talking, and listening enhance all facets of a person's life in the home, school, church, and workplace. Teachers then must consider how they can provide opportunities for students to learn about community literacy activities.

VIP PROGRAM. The VIP, or very important person, program is effective for involving community members in classroom activities. Community members of all types—secretaries, politicians, lawyers, construction workers, computer programmers, maids, chefs, firefighters, flight attendants, store clerks, doctors, farmers, and professors—are invited to visit the classroom. When they arrive, they may read their favorite childhood story or perhaps an appropriate story that provides information about their career. After the VIP reads the story, she or he may wish to tell how reading and writing are used in the job. Children are sometimes surprised to hear how all types of jobs require literacy.

Another version of VIP is "Very Important Parents." As the name implies, this program features the children's parents. Parents may read their favorite childhood story to the class, share a favorite oral story, engage in a cooking activity using a favorite recipe, or perform another interesting activity.

BUSINESS ADOPTION PROGRAMS. In this type of community involvement program, the school or classroom is adopted by a business in the community. Businesses often provide some financial support for the purchase of books or writing briefcases. In addition, employees of the businesses may be encouraged to be VIPs or help arrange a field trip to see business literacy in action (Rasinski & Fredericks, 1991). Children viewing the work of adults may be inspired to imitate and practice many of the reading and writing activities they see performed. Teachers may capitalize on this interest by creating dramatic play centers where the adopted business is a play theme, including all the literacy props and activities the children observed.

COMMUNITY TUTORS.   Perhaps the most inclusive and dynamic method for involving adult community members in your classroom is as volunteer reading tutors. Retirees in particular enjoy the role of classroom grandparents. Classroom tutors regularly volunteer each week to cuddle with and read to a child. This consistent involvement is pleasurable for the volunteer and benefits the young children. The value of spending individual time with another caring adult is beyond calculation.

BUDDY READING PROGRAMS.   To make a significant improvement in family literacy practices, it is essential that educators begin to develop the skills of tomorrow's parents. Older students may benefit greatly by participating in a parent apprenticeship program called Buddy Reading. Unfortunately, many older children do not have strong reading skills themselves. One major strength of the Buddy Reading program is that it has the potential to simultaneously improve older students' skills while supporting young students as they learn to read.

Primary, middle, or high school teachers may arrange to have their students work with preschool children during the school day, during lunch or recess, or in an after-school program. Whatever the time arrangement, the older reading buddies need to

- learn appropriate read-aloud behaviors, such as using an expressive voice, sharing and discussing pictures and print, and facilitating comprehension;
- identify characteristics of appropriate trade books, such as predictable books with repetitive, cumulative, rhythm and rhyme, and/or chronological patterns; and
- determine the younger reading buddy's interests and how to select appropriate books of interest to the child.

Sharing your literacy program within the school and throughout the local community is a win-win proposition. Older children learn how and why it is important to read to young children, while community members learn to appreciate the work of children and teachers in the schools.

SPECIAL FEATURE 11.3

CLD = Culturally & Linguistically Diverse

Promoting Parent Involvement in Culturally and Linguistically Diverse Classrooms

Myae Han

Working with parents is one of the most important aspects of being an early childhood professional. We must acknowledge that parents are the "first teachers" of their children. Early childhood educators also agree that a strong partnership between home and school enhances children's learning, and we must strive to build partnerships that maximize children's development and learning opportunities (Bennett, 2006). Yet this is an area in which most teachers have received very little preparation, and fewer still have had the chance to work with parents of color, par-

ents of English Language Learners, and parents from low-income homes (Nieto, 2004).

Sadly, many schools view culturally and linguistically diverse (CLD) students as a liability—students who are liable to fail because they cannot speak English (Herrera & Murray, 2005). This same belief also contributes to lower expectations for parent involvement. In addition, many teachers have been led to believe that immigrant families, poor families, and minority families neither use literacy at home nor value education in general. I often hear such stereotyping comments from many preservice teachers and even some experienced teachers. For example,

"These parents don't speak English. How can they help their kids?"
"Those parents are poor and uneducated. I bet they don't read books to their kids."
"These parents are not interested in the academic success of their child."

(continued on next page)

SPECIAL FEATURE 11.3 *(continued)*

CLD parents are too often viewed as not supporting their children's school success (Darling, 1992), and their efforts often go unrecognized by school staff (Lareau, 1994). However, a growing body of research now refutes this belief. Although it is true that families vary in the ways children are involved in literacy at home, literacy nonetheless serves numerous functions in most homes, including the homes of families living below the poverty level (Chall & Snow, 1982), families in which English is not the primary language (Delgado-Gaitán, 1987), and families with low educational levels (Heath, 1983; Purcell-Gates, 1995). Many CLD parents value literacy and see it as the single most powerful hope for their children's future (Flores, Cousin, & Diaz, 1998). In addition, the first guiding principle of CEEE (Center for Equity and Excellence in Education) is that "limited English proficient students are held to the same high expectations of learning established for all students" (Herrera & Murray, 2005).

In order to build a partnership with CLD parents, it is critical to reduce the gap between the research findings and the reality–the real feelings and values of CLD families and misconceptions that preservice and in-service teachers might have of CLD parents. This feature describes ways to encourage teachers to promote CLD parent involvement at school.

UNDERSTANDING DIFFERENCES

As a member of a culture, it is easy to view the world only through the experiences you have. Your personal experiences become the "norm" against which you contrast all other experiences. However, as a teacher you must understand that differences are *not* deficits. Respecting and understanding the differences of other cultures is the most important point when working with CLD families. However, the ability to do this involves a deep reflection of your own dispositions, assumptions, and biases.

Next, it is important to go beyond stereotypes—while it may be easier to address cultural generalizations initially, it does not help you appreciate the important variability within cultural groups (Strickland, 1998). Remember, differences exist in all human society—hence it is best to look at cultural differences broadly—beyond the boundaries of countries, races, and ethnicities. Truly understanding and appreciating differences begins with each child and each family. This individualization allows you as a teacher to recognize and appropriately respond to who they are and what they need. Jennifer Bradley and Peris Kibera (2006) recommend the following suggestions (p. 39) when working with CLD families.

- Learn from families. Families are the experts of their culture. Early childhood professionals should be proactive in learning from them and integrate the family's knowledge of and goals for their child into their expertise.

- Beware of stereotyping families, and practice a nonjudgmental, unprejudiced attitude.
- Network with community organizations serving cultural/ethnic groups—these groups can help serve as potential translators or possible parent liaisons.
- Look for commonalities among children and families. Although children's development is rooted in culture, most human beings share similarities in physical, cognitive, and socioemotional development.
- Encourage the use of their native language at home. Research studies report that the use of native language does *not* hinder learning a second language. First language proficiency can be transferred in the domains of spelling, vocabulary, and word reading when learning a second language (Dressler & Kamil, 2006). Teachers' support for the use of native language at home sends parents a positive message toward their own language and culture. We cannot support bilingualism without respecting the child's first language. Raising a bilingual child requires vigilance and persistence on the part of parents and cooperation (Tabors, 1997).
- Remember that the role of school in parent involvement should be a "partner" not "dominator." Teachers should accept parents as they are and not try to fix them (Twiss, 1998). Acceptance and caring are at the heart of success in classrooms with diverse populations. Caring always involves (1) receiving the other's perspective, (2) responding appropriately to the awareness that comes from this reception, and (3) remaining committed to others and to the relationship (Beck, 1995, p. 12). Understanding cultural differences comes from the commitment to CLD children and their family. Caring is the key point to this commitment.

BUILDING FAMILY LITERACY PROGRAMS WITH CLD FAMILIES

Successful family literacy programs can lead to long-lasting, positive outcomes for the benefits of later reading success (Burns, Griffin, & Snow, 1999). Researchers say that family literacy programs, particularly those targeted toward families with low-income and diverse cultural backgrounds, need to be built on family strengths, not weaknesses (Nieto, 2002). However, many programs fail to recognize the wealth of each family's current literacy practices; instead they draw on the deficit approach (Auerbach, 1995). The following tips will help teachers develop family literacy programs that are successful with CLD families (Ordoñez-Jasis & Ortiz, 2006):

- Survey the family. Start with gathering information about each family's current literacy practices: In what language do the adult family members

SPECIAL FEATURE 11.3 *(continued)*

prefer to read? What interests does the family have? What types of reading materials do both parents enjoy? How comfortable are the parents in reading to the children? What are their goals for sharing literacy activities with their children? Such surveying provides teachers with valuable information about the perceptions and expectations of literacy held by the families so that they can build upon families' strengths.

- Teachers should reflect individually on their own personal dispositions and their assumptions about the involvement of parents from minority groups. This can influence their instructional choices. For example, when choosing books, consider families' cultures and avoid books that reflect mainstream values and lifestyles. Try to include authentic multicultural literature such as preserving tradition, celebrating the richness of culture and family life, telling one's personal story, etc.

- If possible, use the parents' primary language or a translator. The studies reveal the many positive outcomes of using families' primary languages in family literacy workshops (Delgado-Gaitán, 1990). It is recommended that teachers provide translated materials for special events and workshops in the parents' primary language. In some cases, a translator could play a role of parent liaison within schools, providing rich linguistic resources.

- Parents who cannot read or write in either their home language or in English still play a critical role in their child's literacy learning. Let the parents know the importance of oral language. Oral language is a strong precursor to early literacy development (Burns, Griffin, & Snow, 1999). Although parents may not be able to read books, they can engage in rhymes, songs, riddles, storytelling, and language play. Wordless picture books are also excellent tools to teach early literacy skills such as prediction, story sequencing, concepts of print, comprehension, etc.

CONNECTING CLD PARENTS AND SCHOOL: PRACTICAL IDEAS

There are a number of ways to involve parents at school, from minimally to maximally. We must understand that the level of involvement will vary in each family, and teachers should find appropriate levels for each family. Here are some guidance and ideas for involving CLD parents at school.

- Teachers should examine the circumstances that may prevent parent involvement at school. There might be numerous reasons why parents can not be involved at school: scheduling issues, parents' unfamiliarity with the U.S. educational system,

language barriers, their past negative experiences, etc. After considering these possible scenarios, teachers can attempt a variety of approaches to connect with parents. They should consider flexible scheduling; providing child care services during parent workshops; home visits; and using a translator.

- Send a list of read-aloud books to the homes. I often ask my daughter's preschool teacher to give a list of books in advance, because I want to read the same books at home (See page 230 for an example). It also helps our library trip to be more purposeful. Sending the list of books for read-aloud helps parents to know what the child is learning at school. Attach the letter with the list asking parents if they know other books related to the topic, other books written by same authors, or different versions of the book (e.g., translations in other languages). When I was teaching at a preschool, we read *Goldilocks and the Three Bears*, and parents from different countries brought their translated version of the book. Provide parents with a list of books on the classroom's theme; this will help parents to recognize the theme of the classroom and some famous author names. If you have extra books, send the books home with children.

- I know of one teacher who lets children take home a teddy bear for one day. The next day at school the child reports what the teddy bear did at home. Similarly, teachers can implement this idea for other literacy activities. They could send "literacy backpacks" filled with literacy materials for reading and writing such as markers, papers, storybooks, or audiotapes with a tape recorder. Teachers can explain the use of the literacy backpack during parent–teacher conferences (see pages 234–235 for more information).

- Many preschool teachers send lyrics of songs, poems, and finger plays to parents every year. Many teachers record the songs and finger plays in case parents from other countries don't know the tune. (See page 234 for more information.)

- Teachers can invite parents to participate in classroom activities. For example, one teacher I know invited a Mexican mother to make tortillas for a cooking activity and invited a Japanese mother to make a sushi roll.

- Teachers can add multicultural props in the dramatic play area. Parents can help by sending props from their cultural background. For example, I have seen many enthusiastic CLD parents bring chopsticks, woks, ponchos, sombreros, kimonos, hanboks, etc. I have included hanbok, Korean traditional cloth, in the dramatic play area; it became the favorite party dress for English-speaking children.

(continued on next page)

SPECIAL FEATURE 11.3 (continued)

In summary, teachers who view CLD children as an asset instead of a liability create a classroom rich in cultural diversity. Teachers who care about CLD children enjoy the richness of cultural diversity and seek parents as resources. Thus, strong home–school partnerships can be built on mutual interest, trust, and respect. Finally, parent involvement should be a school-wide goal. If parent involvement is a school priority, the resources can be provided for increasing home–school communication.

Summary

Families play a critical role in nurturing young children's literacy learning. Early childhood teachers must be prepared to reach out to parents to form two-way partnerships aimed at building parents' awareness of the important role they play in their children's literacy learning and providing them with strategies for nurturing their children's early reading, writing, and speaking development. Here, we return to the questions posed at the beginning of the chapter and briefly summarize the information presented.

◼ *What is known about the relationship between what parents do and children's language and literacy development?*

Research demonstrates that when parents converse a great deal with their young children, the children's vocabulary and language fluency increase. Likewise, if parents consistently engage their children in story time and storytelling, there is a greater likelihood that their children will enjoy reading and become interested in and knowledgeable about the reading process. Parents who support young children's early reading and writing attempts encourage their children to begin to read and write. In short, what parents do makes a great deal of difference in their children's literacy learning and success. The data suggest that many parents need their children's teachers' assistance in understanding the crucial role they play in helping their children become successful readers, writers, and speakers and that all parents need teachers to share strategies for nurturing their young children's early literacy learning.

◼ *In what ways might early childhood teachers communicate personally with parents?*

Communication is the key to successful parent–teacher partnerships. True two-way communication must take place between parents and teachers. Teachers can communicate personally with parents through regular phone calls and conferences. Phone calls should be used to communicate good news, not just troubling news. Regularly scheduled progress review conferences offer opportunities for parents and teachers to share information about factors influencing children's reading and writing development. Specific problem conferences are needed when difficulties arise between regularly scheduled conferences. Sharing information about the child's literacy development might occur during a home visit, another forum for personal communication. Home visits also can be used to share information with parents on how to support their children's literacy learning. While teachers can share information one on one with parents during home visits, groups of parents can learn and interact together during parent workshops.

◼ *How might teachers run a parent–teacher conference?*

Structuring the parent–teacher conference keeps the conference focused and increases the chance of both the teacher's and the parents' concerns being addressed. The teacher might begin with a positive statement and review the conference format, then ask for the parents' input, then offer input, and finally summarize points agreed on in the conference.

◼ *In what ways might teachers communicate with parents in writing?*

Teachers can send home a variety of written publications including informal weekly notes, news flashes, and monthly newsletters. News flashes might be about classroom-related events, or they might be about something special the child has done that day. Some teachers might be able to use electronic mail to communicate with parents.

■ *What resources might an early childhood teacher provide to parents and parents provide to teachers to support young children's early literacy learning?*

Teachers of young children are an important resource for parents. Through the use of classroom lending libraries, book bags, and writing briefcases, teachers can provide parents with the materials needed for home literacy activities. In addition, teacher-made videos can be sent home to show parents what they might do during an activity, like storybook reading, to help their child get the most from the activity.

Parents can be an important resource for teachers also. Teachers can recruit parents and other community adults to assist them in their efforts to offer young children the best literacy education possible. Parents and members of the community might come to the classroom to read favorite stories to the class; local businesses might adopt the school or center and offer material and people resources; senior citizens might serve as classroom volunteers, offering a lap and cuddle for one-to-one sharing of a story; and older students might be reading buddies. Bringing parental and community expertise into the classroom does much to help build powerful partnerships between home and classroom and between classroom and community. These links are critical for all children. They offer young children the opportunity to use spoken and written language to accomplish real-world learning.

LINKING KNOWLEDGE TO PRACTICE

1. With a group of colleagues, plan a workshop for parents on some aspect of children's language and literacy learning. Write a letter to invite parents to the workshop. List the supplies you will need. List the refreshments. Develop an evaluation form. Create a detailed lesson plan. Offer your workshop to a group of parents.
2. Based on a classroom experience, write a one-page weekly note for parents.
3. Work with a group of colleagues to write a monthly newsletter for your class (the one for which you are reading this book).
4. Write a Dear Teacher question-and-answer for inclusion in a preschool classroom's newsletter. Make a photocopy for everyone in your college class.
5. Visit a school or public library. Question a librarian about the check-out policy for children. If this library allows children to check out only one book per week, write a letter to convince the librarian that this is inappropriate for children.
6. With a colleague, develop a book bag around a theme for use by children's parents.

REFERENCES

Adams, M. (1990). *Beginning to read: Thinking and learning about print.* Cambridge, MA: MIT Press.

Adams, M., Foorman, B., Lundberg, I., & Beeler, T. (1998). The elusive phoneme: Why phonemic awareness is so important and how to help children develop it. *American Educator, 21* (1&2), 18–29.

Allen, R. (1976). *Language experiences in communication.* Boston: Houghton Mifflin.

Allen, V. (1991). Teaching bilingual and second language learners. In J. Flood, J. Jensen, D. Lapp, & R. Squires (Eds.), *Research in the teaching of the English language arts.* New York: Macmillan.

Allyn and Bacon. (2000). *Professionals in action: Literacy.* Boston: Author.

Altwerger, B., Diehl-Faxon, J., & Dockstader-Anderson, K. (1985). Read-aloud events as meaning construction. *Language Arts, 62,* 476–484.

Andersen, S. (1998). The trouble with testing. *Young Children, 53,* 25–29.

Anderson, R., Heibert, E., Scott, J., & Wilkinson, I. (1985). *Becoming a nation of readers: The report of the Commission on Reading.* Washington, DC: National Institute of Education.

Anderson, G., & Markle, A. (1985). Cheerios, McDonald's and Snickers: Bringing EP into the classroom. *Reading Education in Texas, 1,* 30–35.

Arizona Department of Education. (2005, April). Early Learning Standards. Retrieved August 9, 2006 from www.ade.state.az.us/earlychildhood/downloads/EarlyLearningStandards.pdf

Armbruster, B. B., Lehr, F., & Osborn, J. (2003). *A child becomes a reader: Birth through preschool.* Jessup, MD: The National Institute for Literacy.

Ashton-Warner, S. (1963). *Teacher.* New York: Simon & Schuster.

Atwell, N. (1990). *Workshop 1: By and for Teachers,* Vol. 1. Portsmouth, NH: Heinemann.

Au, K. (1993). *Literacy instruction in multicultural settings.* Fort Worth, TX: Harcourt Brace Jovanovich.

Au, K., & Jordan, C. (1981). Teaching reading to Hawaiian children: Finding a culturally appropriate solution. In H. Tureba, B. Guthire, & K. Au (Eds.), *Culture and the bilingual classroom.* Rowley, MA: Newbury House.

Au, K., & Kawakami, J. (1991). Culture and ownership: Schooling of minority students. *Childhood Education, 67,* 280–284.

Auerbach, E. (1995). Deconstructing the discourse of strengths in family literacy. *Journal of Reading Behavior, 27,* 643–661.

Avery, C. (1993). *And with a light touch: Learning about reading, writing, and teaching with first graders.* Portsmouth, NH: Heinemann.

Baghban, M. (1984). *Our daughter learns to read and write.* Newark, DE: International Reading Association.

Barbour, A. (1998–1999). Home literacy bags: Promote family involvement. *Childhood Education, 75*(2), 71–75.

Barone, D. (1998). How do we teach literacy to children who are learning English as a second language? In S. Neuman & K. Roskos (Eds.), *Children achieving: Best practices in early literacy* (pp. 56–76). Newark, DE: International Reading Association.

Barrentine, S. (1996). Engaging with reading through interactive read-alouds. *The Reading Teacher, 50,* 36–43.

Bass, G., & Bass, D. (1998). Joel's language development: The parent's perspective. Field notes and commentary.

Bateson, G. (1979). *Mind and Nature.* London: Wildwood House.

Baumann, J. F., & Kame'enui, E. J. (2003). *Vocabulary instruction: Research to practice.* Guilford: New York.

Beck, L. (1995). *Reclaiming educational administration as a caring profession.* New York: Teachers College Press.

Becker, H., & Epstein, J. (1982). Parent involvement: A study of teacher practices. *Elementary School Journal, 83,* 85–102.

Bennett, T. (2006). Future teachers forge family connections, *Young Children,* 61(1), 22–27.

Berk, L., Mann, T., & Ogan, A. (2006). Make-believe play: Wellspring for development of self-regulation. In D. Singer, R. Golinkoff, & K. Hirsh-Pasek (Eds.), *Play=learning: How play motivates and enhances children's cognitive and social–emotional growth* (pp. 74–100). Oxford, UK: Oxford University Press.

Bhavnagri, N., & Gonzalez-Mena, J. (1997). The cultural context of infant caregiving. *Childhood Education,* 74, 2–8.

Biemiller, A. (2001). Teaching vocabulary: Early, direct, and sequential. *American Educator,* (25), 24–29.

Biggar, H. (2005). NAEYC Recommendations on Screening and Assessment of Young English-Language Learners. *Young Children,* 60(6), 44–46.

Bishop, R. (Ed.). (1994). *Kaleidoscope: A multicultural booklist for grades K–8.* Urbana, IL: National Council of Teachers of English.

Bissex, G. (1980). *GNYS AT WRK: A child learns to read and write.* Cambridge, MA: Harvard University Press.

Black, J., Puckett, M., & Bell, M. (1992). *The young child: Development from prebirth through age eight.* New York: Merrill.

Bodrova, E., & Leong, C. (2007). *Tools of the Mind: The Vygotskian Approach to Early Childhood Education.* (2nd Ed.). Upper Saddle River, NJ: Prentice Hall.

Booth-Church, E. (1998). From greeting to goodbye. *Scholastic Early Childhood Today,* 13(1), 51–53.

Bosma, B. (1992). *Fairy tales, fables, legends and myths* (2nd ed.), New York: Teachers College Press.

Bowman, B. T. (2006). Standards: At the heart of educational equity. *Young Children, 61,* 42–48.

Bowman, M., & Treiman, R. (2004). Stepping stones to reading. *Theory into Practice, 43*(4), 295–303.

Brabham, E. G., & Lynch-Brown, C. (2002). Effects of teachers' reading-aloud styles on vocabulary acquisition and comprehension of students in the early elementary grades. *Journal of Education Psychology, 94*(3), 465–472.

Bradley, J., & Kibera, P. (2006). Closing the gap: Culture and the promotion of inclusion in child care. *Young Children, 61*(1), 34–39.

Bradshaw, J., & Rogers, L. (1993). *The evolution of lateral asymmetries, language, tool use, and intellect.* New York: Academic Press.

Bredekamp, S. (1989). *Developmentally appropriate practice.* Washington, DC: National Association for the Education of Young Children.

Bredekamp, S. (1999). *Developmentally appropriate practice for children birth through age 8.* Washington, DC: National Association for the Education of Young Children.

Brock, D., & Dodd, E. (1994). A family lending library: Promoting early literacy development. *Young Children, 49*(3), 16–21.

Bromley, K. (1988). *Language arts: Exploring connections.* Boston: Allyn & Bacon.

Brown, J. (1994). Parent workshops: Closing the gap between parents and teachers. *Focus on Early Childhood Newsletter, 7*(1).

Bruner, J. (1980). *Under five in Britain.* Ypsilanti, MI: High/Scope.

Bruner, J. (1983). Play, thought, and language. *Peabody Journal of Education, 60*(3), 60–69.

Burns, M. S, Griffin, P., & Snow, C. E. (Eds.). (1999). *Starting out right: A guide to promoting children's reading success.* Washington, DC: National Academy Press.

Bus, A., van Izendoorn, M., & Pellegrini, A. (1995). Joint book reading makes for success in learning to read: A meta-analysis on intergenerational transmission of literacy. *Review of Educational Research, 65,* 1–21.

Butler, A., & Turbill, J. (1984). *Towards a reading–writing classroom.* Portsmouth, NH: Heinemann.

Buzzelli, C. (1996). The moral implications of teacher-child discourse in early childhood classrooms. *Early Childhood Research Quarterly, 11,* 515–534.

Calkins, L. (1994). *The art of teaching writing.* Portsmouth, NH: Heinemann.

Cambourne, B. (1988). *The whole story: Natural learning and the acquisition of literacy in the classroom.* Auckland, New Zealand: Ashton Scholastic.

Canizares, S. (1997). Sharing stories. *Scholastic Early Childhood Today, 12,* 46–48.

Cannella, G. S. (2002). *Kidworld: Childhood studies, global perspectives, and education.* Peter Lang Publishers Inc., New York.

Cunningham, P. M., Hall, D. P., & Sigmon, C. M. (1999). *The teacher's guide to the four blocks: A multimethod, multilevel framework for grades 1–3.* Greensboro, NC: Carson-Dellosa Publishing Co.

Carey, S. (1979). The child as word learner. In M. Halle, J. Bresnan, & G. Miller (Eds.), *Linguistic theory and psychological reality.* Cambridge, MA: MIT Press.

Carlson, A. (1990). *Family questions.* New Brunswick, NJ: Transaction.

Carnine, D., Silbert, J., & Kameenui E. (2004). *Direct instruction reading.* New Jersey: Prentice Hall.

Cazden, C. (1976). Play with language and meta-linguistic awareness: One dimension of language experience. In J. Bruner, A. Jolly, & K. Sylva (Eds.), *Play: Its role in development and evolution.* New York: Basic Books.

Cazden, C. (1988). *Classroom discourse.* Portsmouth, NH: Heinemann.

Chall, J. (1996). *Learning to read: The great debate* (revised). New York: McGraw-Hill.

Chall, J., & Snow, C. (1982). *Families and literacy: The contributions of out of school experiences to children's acquisition of literacy: A final report to the National Institute of Education.* Cambridge, MA: Harvard Families and Literacy Project.

Chomsky, N. (1965). *Aspects of the theory of syntax.* Cambridge, MA: MIT Press.

Christian, K., Morrison, F., & Bryant, F. (1998). Predicting kindergarten academic skills: Interaction among child-care, maternal education, and family literacy environments. *Early Childhood Research Quarterly, 13,* 501–521.

Christie, J., Johnsen, E. P., & Peckover, R. (1988). The effects of play period duration on children's play patterns. *Journal of Research in Childhood Education, 3,* 123–131.

Christie, J., & Roskos, K. (2006). Standards, science, and the role of play in early literacy education. In D. Singer, R. Golinkoff, & K. Hirsh-Pasek (Eds.), *Play=learning: How play motivates and enhances children's cognitive and social-emotional growth* (pp. 57–73). Oxford, UK: Oxford University Press.

Christie, J., & Stone, S. (1999). Collaborative literacy activity in print-enriched play centers: Exploring the "zone" in same-age and multi-age groupings. *Journal of Literacy Research, 31,* 109–131.

Chukovsky, K. (1976). The sense of nonsense verse. In J. Bruner, A. Jolly, & K. Sylva (Eds.), *Play: Its role in development and evolution.* New York: Basic Books.

Booth-Church, E. (1999). Sharing portfolios. *Scholastic Early Childhood Today, 13,* 13.

Clark, E. (1983). Meanings and concepts. In J. Flavell & E. Markman (Eds.), *Handbook of child psychology: Vol. 3. Cognitive development* (4th ed.). New York: Wiley.

Clarke, A., & Kurtz-Costes, B. (1997). Television viewing, educational quality of the home environment, and school readiness. *Journal of Educational Research, 90,* 279–285.

Clarke, L. (1988). Invented spelling versus traditional spelling in first graders' writing: Effects on learning to spell and read. *Research in the Teaching of English, 22,* 281–309.

Clay, M. (1966). *Emergent reading behavior.* Unpublished doctoral dissertation, University of Auckland.

Clay, M. (1972). *Reading: The patterning of complex behaviour.* London: Heinemann.

Clay, M. (1975). *What did I write?* Auckland, New Zealand: Heinemann.

Clay, M. (1985). *The early detection of reading difficulties* (3rd ed.). Portsmouth, NH: Heinemann.

Clay, M. (1989). Telling stories. *Reading Today, 6*(5), 24.

Clay, M. (1991). *Becoming literate.* Portsmouth, NH: Heinemann Books.

Clements, D. H., & Sarama, J. (2003). Young children and technology: What *does* the research say? *Young Children, 58,* 34–41.

Close, R. (2004). *Television and early language development: A review of the literature.* Center on Media and Child Health. National Literacy Trust.

Cobb, C. (2003). Effective instruction begins with purposeful assessments. *The Reading Teacher, 57*(4), 386–388.

Cochran-Smith, M. (1984). *The making of a reader.* Norwood, NJ: Ablex.

Cochran-Smith, M., Kahn, J., & Paris, C. (1986, March). *Play with it; I'll help you with it; figure it out; here's what it can do for you.* Paper presented at the Literacy Research Center Speaker Series, Graduate School of Education, University of Pennsylvania.

Cohen, L. (1999). The power of portfolios. *Scholastic Early Childhood Today, 13,* 22–29.

Collin, B. (1992). *Read to me: Raising kids who love to read.* New York: Scholastic.

Collins, M. (1997). Sounds like fun. In B. Farber (Ed.), *The parents' and teachers' guide to helping young children learn* (pp. 213–218). Cutchoque, NY: Preschool Publications, Inc.

Connell, C., & Prinz, R. (2001). The impact of childcare and parent-child interactions on school readiness and social skills development for low-income African American children. *Journal of School Psychology, 40,* 177–193.

Coody, B. (1997). *Using literature with young children.* Chicago: Brown & Benchmark Publishing.

Copeland, J., & Gleason, J. (1993). *Causes of speech disorders and language delays.* Tucson, AZ: University of Arizona Speech and Language Clinic.

Corballis, M. C. (1991). *The lopsided ape: Evolution of the generative mind.* New York: Oxford University Press.

Corkum, V., & Moore, C. (1998). The origins of joint visual attention in infants. *Developmental Psychology, 24*(1), 28–38.

Cowley, F. (1997, Spring/Summer). The language explosion. *Newsweek: Your Child,* 16–18, 21–22.

Cunningham, A., & Stanovich, K. (1998). What reading does for the mind. *American Educator, 21*(1&2), 8–15.

Cuyler, M. (1991). *That's good! That's bad!* New York, NY: Henry Holt.

Darling, S. (1992). Family literacy: Parents and children learning together. *Principal, 72*(2), 10–12.

Delgado-Gaitán, C. (1987). Mexican adult literacy: New directions from immigrants. In S. R. Goldman & K. Trueba (Eds.) *Becoming literate in English as a second language.* Norwood, NJ: Ablex.

DeLoache, J. (1984). *What's this? Maternal questions in joint picture book reading with toddlers.* Paper presented at the Annual Meeting of the American Educational Research Association, New Orleans, LA.

dePaola, T. (1987). Foreword. In B. Cullinan (Ed.), *Children's literature in the reading program* (pp. v–vi). Newark, DE: International Reading Association.

Dewey, J. (1938). *Experiences and education.* New York: Collier Books.

Dickinson, D. K., McCabe, A., Anastaspoulos, L., Peisner-Feinberg, E. S., & Poe, M. D. (2003). The comprehensive language approach to early literacy: The interrelationships among vocabulary, phonological sensitivity, and print knowledge among preschool-aged children. *Journal of Educational Psychology, 95*(3), 465–481.

Dickinson, D. K., & Smith, M. W. (1994). Long-term effects of preschool teachers' book readings on low-income children's vocabulary and story comprehension. *Reading Research Quarterly, 29,* 104–122.

Dickinson, D., & Tabors, P. (2000). *Beginning Literacy with Language: Young Children Learning at Home and School.* Baltimore: Paul H. Brookes.

Dickinson, D. K., & Tabors, P. O. (Eds.) (2001). *Beginning literacy and language: Young children learning at home and in school.* Baltimore: Brookes.

Dodd, B., & Bradford, A. (2000). A comparison of three therapy methods for children with different types of developmental phonological disorder. *International Journal of Language and Communication Disorders, 35,* 189–209.

Dodge, D., & Colker, L. (1992). *The creative curriculum for early childhood education.* Washington, DC: Teaching Strategies.

Dodge, D. T., Heroman, C., Charles, J., & Maiorca, J. (2004). Beyond outcomes, how ongoing assessment supports children's learning and leads to meaningful curriculum. *Young Children, 59*(1), 20–28.

Dodici, B. J., Draper, D. C., & Peterson, C. A. (2003). Early parent-child interactions and early literacy development. *Topics in Early Childhood Special Education, 23*(3), 124–136.

Downing, J., & Oliver, P. (1973–1974). The child's concept of a word. *Reading Research Quarterly, 9,* 568–582.

Dressler, C., & Kamil, M. (2006). First and second language literacy. In D. August & T. Shannahan, *Developing literacy in second-language learners. Report of the National Literacy Panel on language-minority children and youth.* Mahwah, NJ: Lawrence Erlbaum.

Dunn, L., & Dunn, L. (1997). *Peabody Picture Vocabulary Test III.* Circle Pines, MN: American Guidance Service.

Durkin, D. (1966). *Children who read early.* New York: Teachers College Press.

Durkin, D. (1987). *Teaching young children to read* (4th ed.). Boston: Allyn and Bacon.

Dyson, A., & Genishi, C. (1983). Children's language for learning. *Language Arts, 60,* 751–757.

Early Childhood Research Institute on Measuring Growth and Development. (2000). Individual Growth and Development Indicator (IGDI).

Edelman, G. (1995, June). Cited in Swerdlow, J. Quiet miracles of the brain. *National Geographic, 187*(6), 2–41.

Ehri, L. (1991). Development of the ability to read words. In P. D. Pearson (Ed.), *Handbook of Reading Research* (Vol. II, pp. 383–417). New York: Longman.

Ehri, L. (1997). Phonemic awareness and learning to read. *Literacy Development in Young Children, 4*(2), 2–3.

Ehri, L., Nunes, S., Willows, D., Schuster, B., Yaghoub-Zadeh, Z., & Shanahan, T. (2001). Phonemic awareness instruction helps children learn to read: Evidence from the National Reading Panel's meta-analysis. *Reading Research Quarterly, 36,* 250–287.

Ehri, L., & Roberts, T. (2006). The roots of learning to read: Acquisition of letters and phonemic awareness. In S. Neuman & D. Dickinson (Eds.), *Handbook of early literacy research* (2nd ed., pp. 113–131). New York: Guilford.

Ellis, R. (1985). *Understanding second language acquisition.* New York: Oxford University Press.

Elster, C. (1998). Influences of text and pictures on shared and emergent readings. *Research in the Teaching of English, 32,* 43–63.

Enright, D. (1986). Use everything you have to teach English: Providing useful input to young second language learners. In P. Rigg & D. Enright (Eds.), *Children and ESL: Integrating perspectives.* Washington, DC: Teachers of English to Speakers of Other Languages.

Enright, D., & McCloskey, M. (1988). *Integrating English: Developing English language and literacy in the multilingual classroom.* Reading, MA: Addison-Wesley.

Enz, B. (1992). *Love, laps, and learning to read.* Paper presented at International Reading Association Southwest Regional Conference, Tucson, AZ.

Enz, B. J. (2003). The ABC's of Family Literacy. In A. DeBruin-Pareki and B. Krol-Sinclair (Eds.), *Family literacy: From theory to practice.* International Reading Association.

Enz, B. J., Kortman, S., & Honaker, C. (2002). *Trade Secret: for Primary/Elementary Teachers.* (2nd ed.). Dubuque, IA: Kendall-Hunt Publishers.

Enz, B., & Christie, J. (1997). Teacher play interaction styles: Effects on play behavior and relationships with teacher training and experience. *International Journal of Early Childhood Education, 2,* 55–69.

Enz, B., & Searfoss, L. (1995). Let the circle be unbroken: Teens as literacy teachers and learners. In L. M. Morrow (Ed.), *Family literacy: Multiple perspectives.* Reston, VA: International Reading Association.

Epstein, J. (1986). Parents' reactions to teacher practices of parent involvement. *Elementary School Journal, 86,* 277–294.

Epstein, J. (1995). School/family/community partnerships: Caring for the children we share. *Phi Delta Kappa, 76,* 701–712.

Ericson, L., & Juliebö, M. (1998). *The phonological awareness handbook for kindergarten and primary teachers.* Newark, DE: International Reading Association.

Ernst, G. (1994). "Talking circle": Conversation and negotiation in the ESL classroom. *TESOL Quarterly, 28,* 293–322.

Ezell, H. K., & Justice, L. M. (2005). *Shared storybook reading: Building young children's language & emergent literacy skills.* Baltimore: Brookes Publishing Co.

Faltis, C. (2000). *Joinfostering: Teaching and learning in multilingual classrooms* (3rd ed.). New York: Prentice Hall.

Feldgus, E., & Cardonick, I. (1999). *Kid Writing: A Systematic Approach to Phonics, Journals, and Writing Workshop.* The Wright Group/McGraw-Hill.

Fein, G., Ardila-Rey, A., & Groth, L. (2000). The narrative connection: Stories and literacy. In K. Roskos & J. Christie (Eds.), *Play and literacy in early childhood: Research from multiple perspectives.* Mahwah, NJ: Lawrence Erlbaum.

Feitelson, D., & Goldstein, Z. (1986). Patterns of book ownership and reading to young children in Israeli school-oriented and nonschool-oriented families. *The Reading Teacher, 39,* 924–930.

Fenson, L. (1984). Developmental trends for action and speech in pretend play. In I. Bretherton (Ed.), *Symbolic play: The development of social understanding.* Orlando, FL: Academic Press.

Fernandez-Fein, S., & Baker, L. (1997). Rhyme and alliteration sensitivity and relevant experiences among preschoolers from diverse backgrounds. *Journal of Literacy Research, 29,* 433–459.

Ferreiro, E., & Teberosky, A. (1982). *Literacy before schooling.* Exeter, NH: Heinemann.

Fessler, R. (1998). Room for talk: Peer support for getting into English in an ESL kindergarten. *Early Childhood Research Quarterly, 13,* 379–410.

Field, T., Woodson, R., Greenberg, R., & Cohen, D. (1982). Discrimination and imitation of facial expressions by neonates. *Science, 218,* 179–181.

Fields, M., Spangler, K., & Lee, D. (1991). *Let's begin reading right: Developmentally appropriate beginning literacy.* New York: Merrill-Macmillan.

Fillmore, L. (1976). *The second time around: Cognitive and social strategies in second language acquisition.* Unpublished doctoral dissertation, Stanford University.

Fillmore, L. (1982). Instructional language as linguistic input: Second language learning in classrooms. In L. Wilkinson (Ed.), *Communicating in the classroom.* New York: Academic Press.

Fillmore, L. (1983). The language learner as an individual: Implications of research on individual differences for the ESL teacher. In J. Handscombe and M. Clarke (Eds.), *On TESOL '82: Pacific perspectives on language learning and teaching*. Washington, DC: Teachers of English to Speakers of Other Languages.

Fillmore, L. (1991). When learning a second language means losing the first. *Early Childhood Research Quarterly, 6*(3), 323–346.

Fisher, B. (1995). Things take off: Note taking in the first grade. In P. Cordeiro (Ed.), *Endless possibilities: Generating curriculum in social studies and literacy*. Portsmouth, NH: Heinemann.

Fisher, B. (1998). *Joyful learning in kindergarten*. Portsmouth, NH: Heinemann.

Flanigan, B. (1988). Second language acquisition in the elementary schools: The negotiation of meaning by native-speaking and nonnative-speaking peers. *The Bilingual Review/La Revista Bilingue, 14*(3), 25–40.

Flaxman, E., & Inger, M. (1991). Parents and schooling in the 1990s. *ERIC Review, 1*(3), 2–5.

Flom, R., Deák, G. O., Phill, C., & Pick, A. D. (2003). Nine-month-olds' shared visual attention as a function of gesture and object location. *Infant Behavior and Development, 27,* 181–194.

Flores, B., Cousin, T., & Diaz, E. (1998). Transforming deficit myths about learning, language, and culture. In M. F. Opitz (Ed.), *Literacy instruction for culturally and linguistically diverse students*. p. 27–38. Newark, DE: International Reading Association.

Foley, D., & Enz, B. (2004). Supporting the love of reading and learning: a multi-media approach. www.onlineopinion.com.au/view.asp?article=2305

Forrest, K. (2002). Are oral-motor exercises useful in the treatment of phonological/articulatory disorders? *Seminars in Speech and Language, 23,* 15–25.

Fournier, J. Landsdowne, E., Pasteries, Z. Steen, P., & Hudelson, S. (1992). Learning with, about and from children: Life in a bilingual second grade. In C. Genishi (Ed.), *Ways of assessing children and curriculum: Voices from the classroom*. New York: Teachers College Press.

Fox, M. (1993). *Radical reflections: Passionate opinions on teaching, learning, and living*. San Diego: Harcourt Brace.

Fractor, J., Woodruff, M., Martinez, M., & Teale, W. (1993). Let's not miss opportunities to promote voluntary reading: Classroom libraries in the elementary school. *The Reading Teacher, 46,* 476–484.

Fredericks, A., & Rasinski, T. (1990). Involving the uninvolved: How to. *The Reading Teacher, 43,* 424–425.

Freeman, Y., and Freeman, D. (1994). Whole language learning and teaching for second language learners. In C. Weaver (Ed.), *Reading process and practice: From sociopsycholinguistics to whole language*. Portsmouth, NH: Heinemann.

Galda, L., Cullinan, B., & Strickland, D. (1993). *Language, literacy, and the child*. Fort Worth, TX: Harcourt Brace Jovanovich.

Gallas, K. (1992). When the children take the chair: A study of sharing in a primary classroom. *Language Arts, 69,* 172–182.

Gardner, S. (1993–1994). Training for the future: Family support and school-linked services. *Family Resource Coalition, 3*(4), 18–19.

Garvey, C. (1977). *Play*. Cambridge, MA: Harvard University Press.

Garvey, C. (1984). *Children's talk*. Cambridge, MA: Harvard University Press.

Gelfer, J. (1991). Teacher–parent partnerships: Enhancing communications. *Childhood Education, 67,* 164–167.

Geller, L. (1982). Linguistic consciousness-raising: Child's play. *Language Arts, 59,* 120–125.

Genishi, C. (1987). Acquiring oral language and communicative competence. In C. Seefeldt (Ed.), *The early childhood curriculum: A review of current research*. New York: Teachers College Press.

Genishi, C., & Dyson, A. (1984). *Language assessment in the early years*. Norwood, NJ: Ablex.

Gesell, A. (1928). *Infancy and human growth*. New York: Macmillan.

Gilbert, J. (1989). A two-week K–6 interdisciplinary unit. In H. Jacobs (Ed.), *Interdisciplinary curriculum: Design and implementation.* Arlington, VA: Association for Supervision and Curriculum Development.

Gleason, J. (1967). Do children imitate? In C. Cazden (Ed.), *Language in early childhood education.* Washington, DC: National Association for the Education of Young Children.

Goals 2000: Educate America Act (1994). H.R.1804. www.ed.gov/legislangion/GOALS2000/TheAct/Index.html.

Golinkoff, R. (1983). The preverbal negotiation of failed messages: Insights into the transition period. In R. Golinkoff (Ed.), *The transition from prelinguistic to linguistic communication.* Hillsdale, NJ: Erlbaum.

Golinkoff, R. M., & Hirsh-Pasek, K. (1999). *How babies talk: The magic and mystery of language in the first three years of life.* New York: Dutton Publishers.

González, V., Oviedo, M. D., & O'Brien de Ramirez, K. (2001). Developmental, SES, and linguistic factors affecting bilingual and monolingual children's cognitive performance. *Bilingual Research Journal* 25 (1 & 2). Electronic Journal.

Gonzalez, V., Yawkey, T., & Minaya-Rowe, L. (2006). *English-as-a-second-language (ESL) teaching and learning: Pre-K-12 classroom applications for students' academic achievement and development.* Boston: Allyn & Bacon.

Gonzalez-Mena, J. (1997). *Multicultural issues in childcare* (2nd ed.). Mountain View, CA: Mayfield Publishing Company.

Goodman, Y. (1986). Children coming to know literacy. In W. Teale & E. Sulzby (Eds.), *Emergent literacy: Writing and reading.* Norwood, NJ: Ablex.

Good start, grow smart: The Bush administration's early childhood initiative. (2002, April). Washington, DC: The White House.

Goodz, N. (1994). Interactions between parents and children in bilingual families. In F. Genesee (Ed.), *Educating second language children: The whole child, the whole curriculum, the whole community.* New York: Cambridge University Press.

Gopnik, A., Meltzoff, A., & Kuhl, P. (2001). *The scientist in the crib.* New York: Harper-Collins.

Graves, D. (1983). *Writing: Teachers and children at work.* Portsmouth, NH: Heinemann.

Graves, D., & Hansen, J. (1983). The author's chair. *Language Arts, 60,* 176–183.

Greenewald, M. J., & Kulig, R. (1995). Effects of repeated readings of alphabet books on kindergartners' letter recognition. In K. Hinchman, D. Leu, & Kinzer, C. (Eds.), *Perspectives on literacy research and practice: Forty-fourth yearbook of the National Reading Conference* (pp. 231–234). Chicago: National Reading Conference.

Griffin, E., & Morrison, F. (1997). The unique contribution of home literacy environment to differences in early literacy skills. *Early Child Development and Care* (127–128), 233–243.

Gronlund, G. (1998). Portfolios as an assessment tool: Is collecting of work enough? *Young Children, 53,* 4–10.

Gump, P. (1989). Ecological psychology and issues of play. In M. Bloch & A. Pellegrini (Eds.), *The ecological context of children's play* (pp. 35–36). Norwood, NJ: Ablex.

Hakuta, K. (1986). *Mirror of language: The debate on bilingualism.* New York: Basic Books.

Hall, N. (1987). *The emergence of literacy.* Portsmouth, NH: Heinemann.

Hall, N. (1991). Play and the emergence of literacy. In J. Christie (Ed.), *Play and early literacy development.* Albany, NY: State University of New York Press.

Hall, N. (1999). Real literacy in a school setting: Five-year-olds take on the world. *The Reading Teacher, 52,* 8–17.

Hall, N., & Duffy, R. (1987). Every child has a story to tell. *Language Arts, 64,* 523–529.

Hall, N., & Robinson, A. (1995). *Exploring writing and play in the early years.* London: David Fulton.

Halliday, M. (1975). *Learning how to mean: Explorations in the development of language.* London: Edward Arnold.

Hansen, C. (1998). *Getting the picture: Talk about story in a kindergarten classroom.* Unpublished doctoral dissertation, Arizona State University.

Harris, V. (Ed.). (1992). *Teaching multicultural literature in grades K–8.* Norwood, MA: Christopher-Gordon.

Harste, J., Woodward, V., & Burke, C. (1984). *Language stories and literacy lessons.* Portsmouth, NH: Heinemann.

Hart, B., & Risley, T. (1995). *Meaningful differences in the everyday experience of young American children.* Baltimore, MD: Paul H. Brookes Publishing Company.

Heald-Taylor, G. (1986). *Whole language strategies for ESL primary students.* Toronto: OISE Press.

Healy, J. (1997, August–September). Current brain research. *Scholastic Early Childhood Today,* 42–43.

Healy, J. M. (1994). *Your child's growing mind: A practical guide to brain development and learning from birth to adolescence.* New York: Doubleday.

Heath, S. (1982). What no bedtime story means: Narrative skills at home and school. *Language in Society, 11,* 49–76.

Heath, S. (1983). *Ways with words.* Cambridge, England: Cambridge University Press.

Hedrick, W., & Pearish, A. (1999, April). Good reading instruction is more important than who provides the instruction or where it takes place. *The Reading Teacher, 52,* 716–725.

Heibert, E. (1981). Developmental patterns and interrelationships of preschool children's print awareness. *Reading Research Quarterly, 16,* 236–260.

Heidemann, S., Chang, C.J., & Menninga, B. (2004). When teachers are learning, children are too: Teaching teachers about assessment. *Young Children, 59,* 86–92.

Helm, J. (1999). Projects! Exploring children's interests. *Scholastic Early Childhood Today, 14,* 24–31.

Henderson, A. T., & Berla, N. (1994). *A new generation of evidence: The family is critical to student achievement.* Washington, DC: National Committee for Citizens in Education. (ERIC Document No. ED 375 968)

Herrera, S., & Murray, K. (2005). *Mastering ESL and bilingual methods.* Boston, MA: Pearson.

Hetherington, E. M., & Parke, R. D. (2003). *Child psychology: A contemporary viewpoint* (5th ed.). New York: McGraw-Hill.

Hicks, D., & Mahaffeys, S. (1997). *Flannelboard classic tales.* Chicago: American Library Association.

Hirschler, J. (1994). Preschool children's help to second language learners. *Journal of Educational Issues of Language Minority Students, 14,* 227–240.

Hoffman, J., Roser, N., & Battle, J. (1993). Reading aloud in classrooms: From modal toward a "model." *The Reading Teacher, 46,* 496–503.

Holdaway, D. (1979). *The foundations of literacy.* Sydney: Ashton Scholastic.

Howard, S., Shaughnessy, A., Sanger, D., & Hux, K. (1998). Let's talk! Facilitating language in early elementary classrooms. *Young Children, 53*(3), 34–39.

Huck, C., Hepler, S., Hickman, J., & Kiefer, B. (1997). *Children's literature in the elementary school.* New York: Holt, Rinehart, & Winston.

Huck, C., Kiefer, B., Helpler, S., & Hickman, J. (2004). *Children's literature in the elementary school.* New York: The McGraw-Hill Company, Inc.

Huey, E. (1908). *The psychology and pedagogy of reading.* New York: Macmillan.

Huffman, L. C., Mehlimger, S. L., & Kerivan, A. S. (2000). Risk factors for academic and behavioral problems at the beginning of school. In *Off to a good start: Research on the risk factors for early school problems and selected federal policies affecting children's social and emotional development and their readiness for school.* Chapel Hill: University of North Carolina, FPG, Child Development Center.

Huttenlocher, J. (1991). Early vocabulary growth: Relations to language input and gender. *Developmental Psychology, 27*(2), 236–248.

Invernizzi, M., Meier, J., Swank, L. & Juel, C. (1999). *Phonological Awareness Literacy Screening Teacher's Manual* (2nd ed.). Charlottesville: University Printing Services.

IRA/NAEYC. (1998). Learning to read and write: Developmentally appropriate practices for young children. *Young Children, 53*(4), 30–46.

IRA/NCTE. (1994). *Standards for the assessment of reading and writing.* Newark, DE, and Urbana, IL: International Reading Association and National Council of Teachers of English.

Isenberg, J. P., & M. R. Jalongo. 1993. *Creative expression and play in the early childhood curriculum.* New York: Macmillan.

Jackman, H. (1997). *Early education curriculum: A child's connection to the world.* Albany, NY: Delmar Publishers.

Jacobs, H. (1989). *Interdisciplinary curriculum: Design and implementation.* Alexandria, VA: Association for Supervision and Curriculum Development.

Jacobson, L. (1998, February 11). House calls. *Education Week, 27*–29.

Jacobson, R., & Faltis, C. (Eds.). (1990). *Language distribution issues in bilingual schooling.* Clevedon, UK: Multilingual Matters.

Jalongo, M. (1995). Promoting active listening in the classroom. *Childhood Education, 72*(1), 13–18.

Johnson, J., Christie, J., & Yawkey, T. (1999). *Play and early childhood development* (2nd ed.). Glenview, IL: Scott, Foresman.

Johnston, E., & Costello, P. (2005). Principles for literacy assessment. *Reading Research Quarterly, 40*(2), 256–267

Johnston, P. (1992). *Constructive Evaluation of Literate Activity.* New York: Longman.

Jones, E., & Reynolds, G. (1992). *The play's the thing: Teachers' roles in children's play.* New York: Teachers' College Press.

Jones, J. (2004). Framing the assessment discussion. *Young Children, 59,* 14–18.

Juel C. (1999). The messenger may be wrong, but the message may be right. Journal of Research in Reading, 18, 146–153. (United Kingdom), In J. Oakhill, R. Beard, & D Vincent (Eds). Reading development and the teaching of reading: A psychological perspective (pp. 201–212). London: Blackwell.

Justice, L. M. (2002). Word exposure conditions and preschoolers' novel word learning during shared storybook reading. *Reading Psychology, 23,* 87–106.

Justice, L. M., & Ezell, H. K. (2000). Enhancing children's print and word awareness through home-based parent intervention. *American Journal of Speech-Language Pathology, 9,* 257–269.

Justice, L. M., & Pence, K. L. (2005). *Scaffolding with storybooks.* Newark, DE: International Reading Association.

Kaiser, A. P., Yoder, P. J., & Keetz, A. (1992). The efficacy of milieu teaching. In S. F. Warren & J. Reichle (Eds.), *Causes and effects in communication and language intervention* (pp. 63–84). Baltimore, MD: Paul H. Brookes.

Kalb, C., & Namuth, T. (1997, Spring/Summer). When a child's silence isn't golden. *Newsweek: Your Child,* 23.

Katz, L., & Chard, S. (1993). *Engaging children's minds: The project approach.* Norwood, NJ: Ablex Publishing Corporation.

Koppenhaver, D., Spadorcia, S., & Erickson, K. (1998). How do we provide inclusive early literacy instruction for children with disabilities. In S. Neuman & K. Roskos (Eds.), *Children achieving: Best practices in early literacy* (pp. 77–97). Newark, DE: International Reading Association.

Kotulak, R. (1997). *Inside the brain: Revolutionary discoveries of how the mind works.* Kansas City, MO: Andrews McMeel Publishing.

Krashen, S. (1982). *Principles and practices in second language acquisition.* Oxford, England: Pergamon.

Krashen, S. (1987). Encouraging free reading. In M. Douglass (Ed.), *51st Claremont Reading Conference Yearbook.* Claremont, CA: Center for Developmental Studies.

Kuhl, P. (1993). *Life language.* Seattle, WA: University of Washington.

Kuhl, P. K. (1999). The role of experience in early language development: Linguistic experience alters the perception and production of speech. In N. Fox, L. Leavitt, & J. Warhol (Eds.), *Proceedings of the 1999 Johnson & Johnson Pediatric Round Table, "The role of early experience in infant development"* (pp. 101–125). Johnson & Johnson Consumer Companies, Inc.

Kuhl, P. K., Tsao, F. M., Liu, H. M., Zhang, Y., & de Boer, B. (2001). Language/culture/mind/brain: Progress at the margins between disciplines. In A. R. Damasio (Ed.), *Unity of Knowledge: The Convergence of Natural and Human Science* (pp. 136–174). New York: The New York Academy of Sciences.

Kupetz, B., & Green, E. (1997). Sharing books with infants and toddlers: Facing the challenges. *Young Children, 52*(2), 22–27.

Labbo, L. (2005). Books and computer response activities that support literacy development. *Reading Teacher, 59,* 288–292.

Lamme, L., & Childers, N. (1983). The composing processes of three young children. *Research in the Teaching of English, 17,* 33–50.

Lapointe, A. (1986). The state of instruction in reading and writing in U.S. elementary schools. *Phi Delta Kappan, 68,* 135–138.

Lareau, A. (1994). Parent involvement in schooling: A dissenting view. In C. Fagnano & B. Werver (Eds.), *School, family and community interaction,* pp. 61–73. San Francisco: Westview.

Lass, B. (1982). Portrait of my son as an early reader. *The Reading Teacher, 36,* 20–28.

Lemish, D. (1987). Viewers in diapers: The early development of television viewing. In T. Lindlof (Ed.), *Natural audiences: Qualitative research of media uses and effects* (pp. 33–57). Norwood, NJ: Ablex.

Leseman, P., & de Jong, P. (1998). Home literacy: Opportunity, instruction, cooperation, and socio-emotional quality predicting early reading achievement. *Reading Research Quarterly, 33,* 294–318.

Lesaux, N. K., & Siegel, L. S. (2003). The development of reading in children who speak English as a second language. *Developmental Psychology, 39,* 1005–1019.

Lesaux, N. (2004). ESOL effective reading instruction. presented at the Just Read Florida conference, Florida Department of Education. Orlando, FL.

Lessow-Hurley, J. (1990). *Foundations of dual language instruction.* New York: Longman.

Levin, D., & Carlsson-Paige, N. (1994). Developmentally appropriate television: Putting children first. *Young Children, 49,* 38–44.

Lewis, R., & Doorlag, D. (1999). *Teaching special students in general education classrooms.* Columbus, OH: Prentice Hall.

Lindfors, J. (1987). *Children's language and learning* (2nd ed.). Englewood Cliffs, NJ: Prentice Hall.

Lindquist, T. (1995). *Seeing the whole through social studies.* Portsmouth, NH: Heinemann.

Lock, J. (1993). *The child's path to spoken language.* Cambridge, MA: Harvard Press.

Lomax, R., & McGee, L. (1987). Young children's concepts about print and reading: Toward a model of word reading acquisition. *Reading Research Quarterly, 22,* 237–256.

Lonigan, C., & Whitehurst, G. (1998). Relative efficacy of parent and teacher involvement in a shared-reading intervention for preschool children from low-income backgrounds. *Early Childhood Research Quarterly, 23*(2) 263–290.

Luke, A., & Kale, J. (1997). Learning through difference: Cultural practices in early childhood language socialization. In E. Gregory (Ed.), *One child, many worlds: Early learning in multicultural communities* (pp. 11–29). New York: Teachers College Press.

MacLean, P. (1978). A mind of three minds: Educating the triune brain. In J. Chall & A. Mirsky (Eds.), *Education and the brain: 77th yearbook of the National Society for the Study of Education.* Chicago: University of Chicago Press.

Mann, V. A., & Foy, J. G. (2003). Phonological awareness, speech development, and letter knowledge in preschool children. *Annals of Dyslexia, 53,* 149–173.

Manning, M., Manning, G., & Long, R. (1994). *Theme immersion: Inquiry-based curriculum in elementary and middle schools.* Portsmouth, NH: Heinemann.

Martinez, M., & Roser, N. (1985). Read it again: The value of repeated readings during story-time. *The Reading Teacher, 38,* 782–786.

Martinez, M., & Teale, W. (1987). The ins and outs of a kindergarten writing program. *The Reading Teacher, 40,* 444–451.

Martinez, M., & Teale, W. (1988). Reading in a kindergarten classroom library. *The Reading Teacher, 41,* 568–572.

Marvin, C., & Mirenda, P. (1993). Home literacy experiences of preschoolers in Head Start and special education programs. *Journal of Early Intervention, 17*(4), 351–366.

Mason, J. (1980). When do children begin to read: An exploration of four-year-old children's letter and word reading competencies. *Reading Research Quarterly, 15,* 203–227.

Masonheimer, P., Drum, P., & Ehri, L. (1984). Does environmental print identification lead children into word reading? *Journal of Reading Behavior, 16,* 257–271.

Mendes, G. (2005). Social studies in today's early childhood curricula. *Young Children, 60,* 12–19.

McGee, L., & Richgels, D. (1989). "K is Kristen's": Learning the alphabet from a child's perspective. *The Reading Teacher, 43,* 216–225.

McGee, L., & Richgels. D. (1996). *Literacy's beginnings: Supporting young readers and writers* (2nd ed.). Boston: Allyn & Bacon.

McKeown, M. G., & Beck, I. L. (2006). Encouraging young children's language interactions with stories. In D. Dickenson & S. Neuman (Eds.), Handbook of Early Literacy Research Vol. 2. New York: Guilford.

McNeal, Jr. R. B. (1999). Parental involvement as social capital: Differential effectiveness on science achievement, truancy, and dropping out. *Social Forces, 78*(1), 117–144.

McNealy, K., Mazziotta, J. C., & Dapretto, M. (2006), Cracking the language code: Neural mechanisms underlying speech parsing. *The Journal of Neuroscience, 26*(29), 7629–7639.

Meisels, S. J., & Atkins-Burnett, S. (2004). The Head Start National Reporting System: A critique. *Young Children, 59,* 64–66.

Mehan, H. (1979). *Learning lessons.* Cambridge, MA: Harvard University Press.

Menyuk, P. (1988). *Language development: Knowledge and use.* Glenview, IL: Scott, Foresman.

Miller, S. (1997). Family television viewing: How to gain control. *Childhood Education, 74*(1), 38–40.

Miller-Lachman, R. (Ed.). (1995). *Global voices, global visions: A core collection of multicultural books.* New Providence, NJ: R. R. Bowker.

Moffett, J., & Wagner, B. (1983). *Student-centered language arts and reading, K–13: A handbook for teachers* (3rd ed.). Boston: Houghton Mifflin.

Moir, A., & Jessel, D. (1991). *Brain sex: The real differences between men and women.* New York: Carol Publishing Group.

Morisset, C. (1995). Language development: Sex differences within social risk. *Developmental Psychology,* 851–865.

Morrow, L. (1982). Relationships between literature programs, library corner designs, and children's use of literature. *Journal of Educational Research, 75,* 339–344.

Morrow, L. (1983). Home and school correlates of early interest in literature. *Journal of Educational Research, 76,* 221–230.

Morrow, L. (1988). Young children's responses to one-to-one story readings in school settings. *Reading Research Quarterly, 23,* 89–107.

Morrow, L. M. (2005). *Literacy development in the early years.* New York: Pearson.

Morrow, L., & Rand, M. (1991). Preparing the classroom environment to promote literacy during play. In J. Christie (Ed.), *Play and early literacy development.* Albany, NY: State University of New York Press.

Morrow, L., & Tracey, D. (1997). Strategies used for phonics instruction in early childhood classrooms. *The Reading Teacher, 50,* 644–651.

Morrow, L., & Schickedanz, J. (2006). The relationship between sociodramatic play and literacy development. In David K. Dickinson & Susan B. Neuman (Eds.), *Handbook of Early Literacy Research.* (pp. 269–280). New York: The Guilford Press.

Morrow, L., Tracey, D., Gee-Woo, D., & Pressley, M. (1999). Characteristics of exemplary first-grade literacy instruction. *The Reading Instructor, 52,* 462–476.

Morrow, L., & Weinstein, C. (1982). Increasing children's use of literature through program and physical changes. *Elementary School Journal, 83,* 131–137.

Morrow, L., & Weinstein, C. (1986). Encouraging voluntary reading: The importance of a literature program on children's use of library centers. *Reading Research Quarterly, 21,* 330–346.

Mowery, A. (1993). *Qualifying paper on early childhood parent education programs.* Unpublished manuscript, University of Delaware, Newark, DE.

Muter, V., & Diethelm, K. (2001). The contribution of phonological skills and letter knowledge to early reading development in a multilingual program. *Language Learning, 51*(2), 187–219.

NAEYC & NAECS/SDE. (2004). Where we stand: On curriculum, assessment, and program evaluation. *Young Children, 59,* 51–54.

Namy, L., & Waxman, S. (2000). Naming and exclaiming: Infants' sensitivity to naming contexts. *Journal of Cognition and Development, 1,* 405–428.

National Reading Panel. (2000). *Teaching children to read: An evidence-based assessment of the scientific research literature on reading and its implications for reading instruction.* Washington, DC: U.S. Government Printing Office.

National Education Goals Panel. (1997). *Special early childhood report.* Washington, DC: Author.

NCLB Act of 2001. www.ed.gov/nclb/overview/intro/edpicks.jhtml?src=ln

Neuman, S. (1988). The displacement effect: Assessing the relationship between television viewing and reading performance. *Reading Research Quarterly, 23,* 414–440.

Neuman, S. (1995). *Linking literacy and play.* Newark, DE: International Reading Association.

Neuman, S. (1999). Books make a difference: A study of access to literacy. *Reading Research Quarterly, 34*(3), 286–311.

Neuman, S., & Celano, D.(2001). Access to print in low-income and middle-income communities: An ecological study of four neighborhoods. *Reading Research Quarterly, 30,* 8–26

Neuman, S. B. (2006). The knowledge gap: Implications for early education. In D. K. Dickinson & S. B. Neuman (Eds.), *Handbook of Early Literacy Research.* (Vol. 2, pp. 29–40). New York: Guilford Press.

Neuman, S., & Roskos, K. (1993). *Language and literacy learning in the early years: An integrated approach.* Fort Worth, TX: Harcourt Brace Jovanovich.

Neuman, S., & Roskos, K. (1997). Literacy knowledge in practice: Contexts of participation for young writers and readers. *Reading Research Quarterly, 32,* 10–32.

Neuman, S., & Roskos, K. (Eds.). (1998). *Children achieving: Best practices in early literacy.* Newark, DE: International Reading Association.

Neuman, S., & Roskos. K. (2005). The state of the state prekindergarten standards. *Early Childhood Research Quarterly 20,* 125–145.

Neuman, S. (2006). The knowledge gap: Implications for early education. In David K. Dickinson & Susan B. Neuman (Eds.), *Handbook of Early Literacy Research* (pp. 29–40). New York: The Guilford Press.

Nicolopoulou, A., McDowell, J., & Brockmeyer, C. (2006). Narrative play and emergent literacy: Storytelling and story-acting meet journal writing. In D. Singer, R. Golinkoff, & K. Hirsh-Pasek (Eds.), *Play=learning: How play motivates and enhances children's cognitive and social-emotional growth* (pp. 124–144). Oxford, UK: Oxford University Press.

Nieto, S. (2002). *Language, culture, and teaching: critical perspectives for a new century.* Mahwah, NJ: Erlbaum.

Nieto, S. (2004). *Affirming diversity: The sociopolitical context of multicultural education.* Boston: Pearson.

Nord, C. W., Lennon, J., Liu, B., & Chandler, K. (2000). *Home literacy activities and signs of children's emerging literacy, 1993 and 1999* [NCES Publication 2000–026]. Washington, DC: National Center for Education Statistics.

Ogle, D. (1986). KWL: A teaching model that develops active reading of expository text. *The Reading Teacher, 39,* 564–570.

O'Neill, J. (1994). Making assessment meaningful: "Rubrics" clarify expectation, yield better feedback. *ASCD Update, 36*(1), 4–5.

Ordoñez-Jasis, R., & Ortiz, R. (2006). Reading their worlds: Working with diverse families to enhance children's early literacy development. *Young Children, 61*(1), 42–48.

Orellana, M., & Hernández, A. (1999). Taking the walk: Children reading urban environmental print. *The Reading Teacher, 52,* 612–619.

Otto, B. (2006). *Language development in early childhood.* (2nd ed.). Upper Saddle River, NJ: Merrill, Prentice Hall.

Paley, V. (1981). *Wally's stories.* Cambridge, MA: Harvard University Press.

Paley, V. (1984). *Boys and girls: Superheroes in the doll corner.* Chicago: University of Chicago Press.

Paley, V. (1990). *The boy who would be a helicopter.* Cambridge, MA: Harvard University Press.

Pappas, C. (1993). Is narrative "primary"? Some insights from kindergartners' pretend readings of stories and information books. *Journal of Reading Behavior, 25,* 97–129.

Pappas, C., & Brown, E. (1987). Learning how to read by reading: Learning how to extend the functional potential of language. *Research in the Teaching of English, 21,* 160–177.

Patton, M. M., Silva, C., & Myers, S. (1999). Teachers and family literacy: Bridging theory to practice. *Journal of Teacher Education, 50*(2), 1–7.

Paulson, F. L., Paulson, P. R., & Meyer, C. A. (1991). What makes a portfolio a portfolio? *Educational Leadership, 48,* 60–63.

Peck, S. (1978). Child–child discourse in second language acquisition. In E. Hatch (Ed.), *Second language acquisition: A book of readings.* Rowley, MA: Newbury House.

Penno, J. F., Wilkinson, I. A. G., & Moore, D. W. (2002). Vocabulary acquisition from teacher explanation and repeated listening to stories: Do they overcome the Matthew effect? *Journal of Educational Psychology, 94*(1), 23–33.

Piper, T. (1993). *Language for all our children.* New York: Macmillan.

Power, B. (1998). Author! Author! *Scholastic Early Childhood Today, 12,* 30–37.

Prior, J., & Gerard, M. (2004). *Environmental print in the classroom: Meaningful connections for learning to read.* Newark, DE: International Reading Association.

Purcell-Gates, V. (1995). *Other people's words: The cycle of low literacy.* Cambridge, MA: Harvard University Press.

Raines, S., & Isbell, R. (1994). *Stories: Children's literature in early education.* Albany, NY: Delmar.

Ramachandran, V. S. (2000). Mirror neurons and imitation learning as the driving force behind "the great leap forward" in human evolution. Social Neuroscience Abstracts.

Ramey, C. T., & Ramey, S. L. (1999). Beginning school for children at risk. In *The Transition to Kindergarten.* Baltimore, MD: Paul H. Brookes Publishing Co., Inc.

Rasinski, T., & Fredericks, A. (1991). Beyond parents and into the community. *The Reading Teacher, 44,* 698–699.

Read, C. (1971). Pre-school children's knowledge of English phonology. *Harvard Educational Review, 41,* 1–34.

Reyes, M., Laliberty, E., & Orbansky, J. (1993). Emerging biliteracy and cross-cultural sensitivity in a language arts classroom. *Language Arts, 70,* 659–668.

Rhodes, L. K., & Nathenson-Mejia, S. (1992). Anecdotal records: A powerful tool for ongoing literacy assessment. *The Reading Teacher, 45,* 502–509.

Rhodes, M., Enz, B. J. & LaCount, M. (2006). Leaps and bounds: Preparing parents for kindergarten. *Young Children 61*(1), 50–51.

Rice, M., Huston, A., Truglio, R., and Wright, J. (1990) Words from *Sesame Street:* Learning vocabulary while viewing. *Development Psychology, 26,* 421–428.

Richgels, D. J. (2003). *Going to kindergarten.* Lanham, MD: The Scarecrow Press, Inc.

Richgels, D., & Wold, L. (1998). Literacy on the road: Backpacking partnerships between school and home. *The Reading Teacher, 52,* 18–29.

Robinson, L. (2003). Technology as a scaffold for emergent literacy. *Young Children, 58*(6), 42–48.

Rosenblatt, L. (1978). *The reader, the text, the poem: The transactional theory of the literary work.* Carbondale, IL: Southern Illinois University Press.

Roser, N. (1998, February). Young children as competent communicators. *Scholastic Early Childhood Today,* 45–47.

Roser, N., & Martinez, M. (1985). Roles adults play in preschoolers' response to literature. *Language Arts, 62,* 485–490.

Roskos, K. (Personal communication, October 9, 1995).

Roskos, K., & Christie, J. (Eds.). (2000). *Play and literacy in early childhood: Research from multiple perspectives.* Mahwah, NJ: Lawrence Erlbaum.

Roskos, K., & Christie, J. (2004). Examining the play–literacy interface: A critical review and future directions. In E. Zigler, D. Singer, & S. Bishop-Josef (Eds.), *Children's play: The roots of reading* (pp. 95–123). Washington, DC: Zero to Three Press.

Roskos, K., & Christie, J. (in press). Play in the context of the new preschool basics. In K. Roskos & J. Christie (Eds.), *Play and literacy in early childhood: Research from multiple perspectives* (2nd ed.). Mahwah, NJ: Lawrence Erlbaum.

Roskos, K., & Neuman, S. (1993). Descriptive observations of adults' facilitation of literacy in play. *Early Childhood Research Quarterly, 8,* 77–97.

Roskos, K., Tabor, P., & Lenhart, L. (2004). Oral language and early literacy in preschool. Reston, VA: International Reading Association.

Rowe, D. (1994). *Preschoolers as authors: Literacy learning in the social world.* Cresskill, NJ: Hampton Press.

Rubin, K., Fein, G., & Vandenberg, B. (1983). Play. In P. Mussen (Ed.), *Handbook of child psychology: Vol. 4. Socialization, personality, and social development* (4th ed.). New York: Wiley.

Rudnick, B. (1995, October). Bridging the chasm between your English and ESL students. *Teaching PreK-8,* 48–49.

Rupley, W. H., Logan, J. W., Nichols, W. D. (1999). Vocabulary instruction in a balanced reading program. *Reading-Teacher; 52*(4). 336–346.

Santos, R. M. (2004). Ensuring culturally and linguistically appropriate assessment of young children. *Young Children, 59*(1), 48–50.

Saville-Troike, M. (1988). Private speech: Evidence for second language learning strategies in the "silent period." *Journal of Child Language, 15,* 567–90.

Schickedanz, J. (1986). *Literacy development in the preschool* [sound filmstrip]. Portsmouth, NH: Heinemann.

Schickedanz, J. (1998). What is developmentally appropriate practice in early literacy? Considering the alphabet. In S. Neuman & K. Roskos (Eds.), *Children achieving: Best practices in early literacy* (pp. 20–37). Newark, DE: International Reading Association.

Scholl, M. (2005). Preschoolers study babies. *Young Children, 60,* 44.

Schon, D. (1983). *The reflective practitioner: How professionals think in action.* New York: Basic Books

Schwartz, J. (1983). Language play. In B. Busching & J. Schwartz (Eds.), *Integrating the language arts in the elementary school.* Newark, DE: International Reading Association.

Segal, M., & Adcock, D. (1986). *Your child at play: Three to five years.* New York: Newmarket Press.

Serafini, F. (2001). Three paradigms of assessment: Measurement, procedure and inquiry. *The Reading Teacher, 54,* 384–393.

Serna, I., & Hudelson, S. (1993). Emergent literacy in a whole language bilingual program. In R. Donmoyer & R. Kos (Eds.), *At-risk students: Portraits, policies and programs.* Albany, NY: SUNY Press.

Shepard, L., Kagan, S., & Wurtz, E. (Eds.). (1998). *Principles and recommendations for early childhood assessments.* Washington, DC: National Education Goals Panel, 1998.

Shepard, L., Kagan, S., & Wurtz, E. (1998). Goal 1 early childhood assessments resource group recommends. *Young Children, 53,* 52–54.

Shevell, M. I., (2005). Outcomes at school age of preschool children with developmental language impairment. *Pediatric Neurology, 32*(4), 264–69.

Shore, R. (1997). *Rethinking the brain: New insights into early development.* New York: Families and Work Institute.

Short, K. G., Schroeder, J., Kauffman, G., & Kaser, S. (2002). Thoughts from the editors. *Language Arts, 79(3),* 199.

Skinner, B. (1957). *Verbal behavior.* East Norwalk, CT: Appleton-Century-Crofts.

Smilansky, S. (1968). *The effects of sociodramatic play on disadvantaged preschool children.* New York: Wiley.

Smith, F. (1988). *Understanding reading* (4th ed.). Hillsdale, NJ: Erlbaum.

Smith, M. W., & Dickinson, D. K. (2002). Early Language and Literacy Classroom Observation Toolkit. Baltimore, MD: Brookes Publishing Co.

Smith, M., & Dickinson, D. (1994). Describing oral language opportunities and environments in Head Start and other preschool classrooms. *Early Childhood Research Quarterly, 9,* 345–366.

Snow, C., Burns, M., & Griffin, P. (1998). *Preventing reading difficulties in young children.* Washington, DC: National Academy Press.

Snow, C., Chandler, J., Lowry, H., Barnes, W., & Goodman, I. (1991). *Unfilled expectations: home and school influences on literacy.* Cambridge, Mass: Harvard University Press.

Snow, C., & Ninio, A. (1986). The contracts of literacy: What children learn from learning to read books. In W. Teale & E. Sulzby (Eds.), *Emergent literacy: Writing and reading.* Norwood, NJ: Ablex.

Sochurek, H. (1987, January). Medicine's new vision. *National Geographic, 171*(1), 2–41.

Spizman, R. (1997). *Kids on Board.* Minneapolis, MN: Fairview Press.

Sporns, O., & Tononi, G. (1994). Selectionism and the brain. *International Review of Neurobiology, 37,* 4–23.

Sprenger, M. (1999). *Learning and memory: The brain in action.* Alexandria, VA: Association for Supervision and Curriculum Development.

Stahl, S. (1992). Saying the "p" word: Nine guidelines for exemplary phonics instruction. *The Reading Teacher, 45,* 618–625.

Stahl, S., Duffy-Hester, A., & Stahl, K. (1998). Everything you wanted to know about phonics (but were afraid to ask). *Reading Research Quarterly, 33,* 338–355.

Stainback, S., & Stainback, W. (1992). *Curriculum considerations in inclusive classrooms.* Baltimore, MD: Brookes.

Stallman, A., & Pearson, P. D. (1990). Formal measures of early literacy. In L. Morrow & J. Smith (Eds.), *Assessment for instruction in early literacy.* Englewood Cliffs, NJ: Prentice Hall.

Stanovich, K. (1986). Matthew effects in reading: Some consequences of individual differences in the acquisition of literacy. *Reading Research Quarterly, 21,* 360–407.

Strickland, D. (1998). Principles of instruction. In M. F. Opitz (Ed.), *Literacy instruction for culturally and linguistically diverse students* (pp. 50–52). Newark, DE: International Reading Association.

Strickland, D., & Schickedanz, J. (2004). *Learning about print in the preschool: Working with letters, words and beginning links with phonemic awareness.* Newark, DE: International Reading Association.

Strickland, D., & Shanahan, T. (2004). Laying the groundwork for literacy. *Educational Leadership, 61*(4), 74–77.

Strong, M. (1983). Social styles and the second language acquisition of Spanish-speaking kindergarteners. *TESOL Quarterly, 17,* 241–258.

Sulzby, E. (1985a). Children's emergent reading of favorite storybooks: A developmental study. *Reading Research Quarterly, 20,* 458–481.

Sulzby, E. (1985b). Kindergartners as writers and readers. In M. Farr (Ed.), *Advances in writing research, Vol. 1: Children's early writing development.* Norwood, NJ: Ablex.

Sulzby, E. (1990). Assessment of emergent writing and children's language while writing. In L. Morrow & J. Smith (Eds.), *Assessment for instruction in early literacy.* Englewood Cliffs, NJ: Prentice Hall.

Sulzby, E., & Barnhart, J. (1990). The developing kindergartner: All of our children emerge as writers and readers. In J. McKee (Ed.), *The developing kindergarten: Programs, children, and teachers.* Ann Arbor, MI: Michigan Association for the Education of Young Children.

Sulzby, E., Barnhart, J., & Hieshima, J. (1989). Forms of writing and rereading from writing: A preliminary report. In J. Mason (Ed.), *Reading and writing connections.* Boston: Allyn and Bacon.

Sulzby, E., & Teale, W. (1991). Emergent literacy. In R. Barr, M. Kamil, P. Mosenthal, & P. D. Pearson (Eds.), *Handbook of reading research* (Vol. 2). New York: Longman.

Swain, M. (1972). *Bilingualism as a native language.* Unpublished doctoral dissertation, University of California at Irvine.

Swanborn, M., & de Glopper, K. (1999). Incidental word learning while reading: A meta-analysis. *Review of Educational Research, 69,* 261–285.

Sylwester, R. (1995). *A celebration of neurons: An educator's guide to the human brain.* Alexandria, VA: Association for Supervision and Curriculum Development.

Tabors, P. (1997). *One child, two languages.* Baltimore, MD: Paul Brookes.

Tabors, P. (1998). What early childhood educators need to know: Developing effective programs for linguistically and culturally diverse children and families. *Young Children, 53*(6), 20–26.

Tabors, R., & Snow, C. (1994). English as a second language in preschool programs. In F. Genesee (Ed.), *Educating second language children: The whole child, the whole curriculum, the whole community.* New York: Cambridge University Press.

Taylor, D. (1986). Creating family story: "Matthew! We're going to have a ride." In W. Teale & E. Sulzby (Eds.), *Emergent literacy: Writing and reading.* Norwood, NJ: Ablex.

Taylor, D., & Strickland, D. (1986). Family storybook reading. Exeter, NH: Heinemann.Teale, W. (1986). Home background and young children's literacy development. In W. Teale & E. Sulzby (Eds.), *Emergent literacy: Writing and reading.* Norwood, NJ: Ablex.

Teale, W. (1987). Emergent literacy: Reading and writing development in early childhood. In J. E. Readence and R. S. Baldwin (Eds.), *Research in literacy: Merging perspectives.* Thirty-sixth yearbook of the National Reading Conference. Rochester, NY: National Reading Conference.

Teale, W. H. (2003). Reading aloud to young children as a classroom instructional activity: Insights from research and practice. In A. van Kleeck, S. A. Stahl, & E. B. Bauer (Eds.), *On reading books to children* (pp. 114–139). Mahway, NJ: Erlbaum.

Teale, W. H., & Martinez, M. G. (1996). Reading aloud to young children: Teachers' reading styles and kindergartners' text comprehension. In C. Pontecorvo, M. Orsolini, B. Burge, & L. B. Resnick (Eds.), *Children's early text construction* (pp. 321–344). Mahwah, NJ: Erlbaum.

Teale, W., & Sulzby, E. (1986). Emergent literacy as a perspective for examining how young children become writers and readers. In W. Teale & E. Sulzby (Eds.), *Emergent literacy: Writing and reading.* Norwood, NJ: Ablex.

TESOL (1996). *Promising futures: ESL standards for prek–12 students.* Alexandria, VA: TESOL.

TESOL (1997). *ESL standards for piek––12 students.* Alexandria, VA: TESOL.

Tharp, R., & Gallimore, R. (1988). *Rousing minds to life: Teaching, learning and school in a social context.* Cambridge, England: Cambridge University Press.

Thousand, J., & Villa, R. (1990). Sharing expertise and responsibilities through teacher teams. In W. Stainback & S. Stainback (Eds.), *Support networks for inclusive schooling: Interdependent integrated education* (pp. 151–166). Baltimore, MD: Brookes.

Tincoff, R., & Jusczyk, P. W. (1999). Mama! Dada! Origins of word meaning. *Psychological Science 10*(2), 172–175.

Towell, J. (1998). Fun with vocabulary. *Reading Teacher, 51,* 356.

Trelease, J. (1989). *The new read-aloud handbook.* New York: Penguin.

Trelease, J. (2006). Why read aloud? Retrieved March 23, 2006, from www.trelease-on-reading.com/rah_chpt1_p1.html.

Treiman, R., & Kessler, B. (2003). The role of letter names in the acquisition of literacy. In R. Kail (Ed.), *Advances in Child Development and Behavior, 31*, 105–135.

Turner, E. (1994). *Emerging bilingualism and biliteracy in a primary, multi-age bilingual classroom.* Unpublished honors thesis, Arizona State University, Tempe.

Twiss, L. (1998). Acceptance and caring are at the heart of engaging classroom diversity. In M. F. Opitz (Ed.), *Literacy instruction for culturally and linguistically diverse students.* (pp. 53–58). Newark, DE: International Reading Association.

Valencia, S. (1990). A portfolio approach to classroom reading assessment: The whys, whats, and hows. *The Reading Teacher, 43,* 338–340.

van Manen, M. (1995). On the epistemology of reflective practice: Teachers and teaching. *Theory and Practice, 1,* 33–50.

Veatch, J., Sawicki, F., Elliot, G., Flake, E., & Blakey, J. (1979). *Key words to reading: The language experience approach begins.* Columbus, OH: Merrill.

Ventriglia, L. (1982). *Conversations of Miguel and Maria.* Reading, MA: Addison-Wesley.

Ventriglia, L. (1996). Empowering ESOL Teachers, Multifunctional Resource Center, Florida Department of Education, I, 93–95.

Volk, D. (1997). Continuities and discontinuities: Teaching and learning in the home and school of a Puerto Rican five year old. In E. Gregory (Ed.), *One child, many worlds: Early learning in multicultural communities.* New York: Teachers College Press.

Vouloumanos, A., & Werker, J. F. (in press). Listening to language at birth: Evidence for a bias for speech in neonates. *Developmental Science.*

Vukelich, C. (1993). Play: A context for exploring the functions, features, and meaning of writing with peers. *Language Arts, 70,* 386–392.

Vukelich, C. (1994). Effects of play interventions on young children's reading of environmental print. *Early Childhood Research Quarterly, 9,* 153–170.

Vygotsky, L. (1962). *Thought and language.* Cambridge, MA: MIT Press.

Vygotsky, L. (1978). *Mind in society: The development of psychological processes.* Cambridge, MA: Harvard University Press.

Waggoner, D. (1992, October/November). The increasing multiethnic and multilingual diversity of the U.S.: Evidence from the 1990 census. TESOL Matters, 1, 1, 5.

Wagstaff, J. (1997–1998). Building practical knowledge of letter–sound correspondences: A beginner's word wall and beyond. *The Reading Teacher, 51,* 298–304.

Walker, D., Greenwood, C., Hart, B., & Carta, J. (1994). Prediction of school outcomes based on early language production and socio-economic factors. *Child Development, 65,* 606–621.

Walker, S. L. (2004). Emergent literacy in family day care: Perceptions of three providers. *Journal of Research in Childhood Education, 19*(1), 18–31.

Washington, G. (1982). Second-language learning strategies in the elementary school classroom. In M. Hines and W. Rutherford (Eds.), *On TESOL '81.* Washington, DC: Teachers of English to Speakers of Other Languages.

Wasik, B. A., & Bond, M. A. (2001). Beyond the pages of a book: Interactive book reading and language development in preschool classrooms. *Journal of Educational Psychology, 93*(2), 243–250.

Watson, D. (1983). Bringing together reading and writing. In U. Hardt (Ed.), *Teaching reading with the other language arts.* Newark, DE: International Reading Association.

Werker, J. F., & Tees, R.C. (2005). Speech perception as a window for understanding plasticity and commitment in language systems of the brain. *Developmental Psychobiology, 46*(3), 233–251.

Weir, R. (1962). *Language in the crib.* The Hague, Netherlands: Mouton.

Weizman, Z. O., & Snow C. E. (2001). Lexical input as related to children's vocabulary acquisition: Effects of sophisticated exposure and support for meaning. *Developmental Psychology, 37*(2), 265–279.

Wells, G. (1986). *The meaning makers: Children learning language and using language to learn.* Portsmouth, NH: Heinemann.

White, B. (1985). The first three years of life. Englewood Cliffs, NJ: Prentice-Hall.

Whitehurst, R. (1992). Dialogic Reading: An Effective Way to Read to Preschoolers. Retrieved July 24, 2006 from www.readingrockets.org/articles/400.

Whitehurst, G. J., Arnold, D. H., Epstein, J. N., Angell, A. L., Smith, M., & Fiscehl, J. E. (1994). A picture of book reading intervention in day care and home for children from low-income families. *Developmental Psychology, 30*(5), 679–689.

Whitehurst, G. J., Falco, F. L., Lonigan, C. J., Fischel, J. E., DeBaryshe, B. D., Valdez-Menchaca, M. C., & Caulfield, M. (1988). Accelerating language development through picture book reading. *Developmental Psychology, 24,* 552–559.

Wien, C., & Kirby-Smith, S. (1998). Untiming the curriculum: A case study of removing clocks from the program. *Young Children, 53*(5), 8–13.

Wiggins, G. (1993). *Assessing student performance.* San Francisco: Jossey-Bass.

Wilcox, C. (1993). *Portfolios: Finding a focus.* Papers in Literacy Series. Durham, NH: The Writing Lab.

Willett, J. (1995). Becoming first graders in an L2: An ethnographic study of L2 socialization. *TESOL Quarterly, 29,* 573–603.

Winters, D. L., Saylor, C. H., & Phillips, C. Y. (2003). Full-day kindergarten: A story of successful adoption and initial implementation. *Young Children, 58,* 54–57.

Woodward, A. L. & Guajardo, J. J. (2002). Infants' understanding of the point gesture as an object-directed action. *Cognitive Development,* 17, 1061–1084.

Woodard, C. (1984). Guidelines for facilitating sociodramatic play. *Childhood Education, 60,* 172–177.

The Wright Group. (1998). *Phonemic awareness handbook.* Bothell, WA: The Wright Group.

Yaden, D., Rowe, D., & MacGillivary, L. (2000). Emergent literacy: A matter (polyphony) of perspectives. In M. Kamil, P. Mosenthal, P. D. Pearson, & R. Barr (Eds.), *Handbook of reading research* (vol. III, pp. 425–454). Mahwah, NJ: Erlbaum.

Yaden, D., Smolkin, L., & Conlon, A. (1989). Preschoolers' questions about pictures, print conventions, and story text during reading aloud at home. *Reading Research Quarterly, 24,* 188–214.

Yarosz, D. J., & Barnett, W. S. (2001). Who reads to young children?: Identifying predictors of family reading activities. *Reading Psychology, 22,* 67–81.

Yopp, H. (1992). Developing phonemic awareness in young children. *The Reading Teacher, 45,* 696–703.

Yopp, H. & Yopp, R. (2000). *Supporting phonemic awareness development in the classroom. The Reading Teacher, 54,* 130–143.

Young, T. A., & Moss, B. (2006). Nonfiction in the classroom library: A literacy necessity. *Childhood Education, 82*(4), 207–212.

SUBJECT INDEX